ANTI-BLACK LITERACY LAWS AND POLICIES

A COUNTERNARRATIVE

This groundbreaking book uncovers how anti-Black racism has informed and perpetuated anti-literacy laws, policies, and customs from the colonial period to the present day. As a counternarrative of the history of Black literacy in the United States, the book's historical lens reveals the interlocking political and social structures that have repeatedly failed to support equity in literacy for Black students. Arlette Ingram Willis walks readers through the impact of anti-Black racism's impact on literacy education by identifying and documenting the unacknowledged history of Black literacy education, one that is inextricably bound up with a history of White supremacy.

Willis analyzes, exposes, illuminates, and interrogates incontrovertible historical evidence of the social, political, and legal efforts to deny equal literacy access. The chapters cover an in-depth evolution of the role of White supremacy and the harm it causes in forestalling Black readers' progress; a critical examination of empirical research and underlying ideological assumptions that resulted in limiting literacy access; and a review of federal and state documents that restricted reading access for Black people. Willis interweaves historical vignettes throughout the text as antidotes to whitewashing the history of literacy among Black people in the United States and offers recommendations on ways forward to dismantle racist reading research and laws. By centering the narrative on the experiences of Black people in the United States, Willis shifts the conversation and provides an uncompromising focus on not only the historical impact of such laws and policies but also their connections to present-day laws and policies.

A definitive history of the instructional and legal structures that have harmed generations of Black people, this text is essential for scholars, students, and policymakers in literacy education, reading research, history of education, and social justice education.

Arlette Ingram Willis is Professor of Language and Literacy in the Department of Curriculum and Instruction at the University of Illinois Urbana-Champaign, USA.

ANTI-BLACK LITERACY LAWS AND POLICIES

Arlette Ingram Willis

Routledge
Taylor & Francis Group

NEW YORK AND LONDON

Designed cover image: © Library of Congress

First published 2023
by Routledge
605 Third Avenue, New York, NY 10158

and by Routledge
4 Park Square, Milton Park, Abingdon, Oxon, OX14 4RN

Routledge is an imprint of the Taylor & Francis Group, an informa business

© 2023 Arlette Ingram Willis

ISBN: 978-1-032-28296-1 (hbk)
ISBN: 978-1-032-27500-0 (pbk)
ISBN: 978-1-003-29618-8 (ebk)

DOI: 10.4324/9781003296188

Access the Support Materials: www.routledge.com/9781032275000

Typeset in Bembo
by SPi Technologies India Pvt Ltd (Straive)

My Grandchildren

CONTENTS

SUPPORT MATERIALS

This book includes Support Materials in the form of documents that you can view and download on your computer. You can access them by visiting the product page on our website: www.routledge.com/9781032275000. Then click on the tab that says, "Support Material," and select the files. They will begin downloading to your computer.

The files available on our website are:

Infographic of the reporting lines from NCES–NAEP

Appendices:

Appendix K APA RESOLUTION on Harnessing Psychology to Combat Racism: Adopting a Uniform Definition and Understanding

Appendix L American Psychological Association, Apology to People of Color for APA's Role in Promoting, Perpetuating, and Failing to Challenge Racism, Racial Discrimination, and Human Hierarchy in US.

Appendix M American Psychological Association, Historical Chronology. Examining Psychology's Contributions to the Belief in Racial Hierarchy and Perpetuation of Inequality for People of Color in US.

Appendix N American Psychological Association, Role of Psychology and APA in Dismantling Systemic Racism against People of Color in US.

ILLUSTRATIONS

Figures

Tables

PREFACE

This book examines the challenges and limited opportunities of access to literacy for Black people historically and contemporaneously, in the United States. I acknowledge there are non-Black ethnic and racial groups who also have suffered racial injustices; however, this book is centered on anti-Black racism and anti-Black literacy. I begin with the premise that anti-Black racism exists in US society and within the field of literacy and acknowledge that the ideology of White supremacy exists. There is an incomplete and silenced narrative of anti-Black racism and anti-Black literacy, rooted in White supremacy and nurtured within the context of the legal system that continues to echo in the present.

The importance of sharing an accurate history of racism in the United States has faced severe backlash as attempts to reproduce an imagined whitewashed history are being codified into state laws. Herein, I tell the story of how as a nation, we have profoundly misunderstood the history of literacy, particularly reading, among Black people. A history of Black literacy begins on the continent of Africa and the lives of free Black people as a counternarrative to Eurocentric histories of Black literacy in the United States. The lives of Black enslaved people existed in parallel and tandem to White enslavers, although Black people were denied equal and equitable access to literacy in English (or the language of their enslavers). Historical artifacts and documents are used to corroborate this countervailing narrative and to provide readers with a more complete and accurate understanding of centuries of anti-Black literacy. The artifacts, charts, documents, infographics, and laws reveal that indisputable records exist and must be acknowledged and shared for a more accurate understanding of anti-Black literacy. In the colonies, for example, there were customs and traditions of anti-Black literacy prohibiting Black people from learning to read and write, before there were laws. The laws codified the customs and traditions rooted in an ideology of White supremacy, seeking to "justify" anti-Black racism and anti-Black literacy. As such, this book interrogates anti-literacy laws and acknowledges they were written specifically to prohibit Black people from learning to read and write. Although collectively referenced as anti-literacy laws, more accurately they should be referenced as anti-Black literacy laws. Contemporary anti-Black literacy laws also exist yet carefully avoid any mention of race; the disparate impact of the laws fuels disproportionate and negative effects in the lives of Black people, not only as young children learning to read as the impact can be lifelong.

It is important to understand the harm and trauma foisted on Black lives, intergenerationally, as conjecture, imaginary, presumptive, or speculative characterizations of Black beliefs, cultures, intelligence, languages, and literacies are repeated within history and reading research. Too often misrepresented or maligned affordances and pleasures within Blackness and Black literacy (articles, commentaries, essays, folktales, jokes, opinions, poetry, song lyrics, websites, etc.) illustrating creativity, hope, humor, intelligence, and joy are re-presented by White commentators and researchers through a white gaze.

Traditional histories of literacy in the United States begin with discussions about access among White people and include a limited timeline of the evolution of literacy (approaches, assessments, curriculum, instruction, materials, and theories) without acknowledgment of anti-literacy actions (customs, laws, policies, statutes, and traditions) that foreclosed literacy access among Black people. The traditional positionality centers on Whiteness as well as provides an unquestioned mooring for literacy approaches, assessments, curriculum, instruction, materials, and theories. When discussions about the challenges faced by Black learners are included, there is a propensity to (a) fault a lack of research and (b) suggest reading research seeks to improve ALL students' literacy access – an equivocation meant to justify research among White students as universal. By contrast, this counternarrative is centered on the lived literacy experiences of Black people, history, scholarship, and theories within a discussion of the evolution of anti-Black literacy customs, laws, traditions, and statutes.

Anti-Black Literacy Laws and Policies exposes how the ideology of White supremacy underpins customs and traditions of anti-Black literacy and informs laws, policies, and statutes, enacted by White colonialists and politicians to codify, criminalize, legalize, and justify anti-Black literacy customs and traditions already in place. Throughout history, anodyne discourses have been used to conceal the goal of White supremacy – to maintain domination and retain power. Anti-literacy laws have evolved since their onset in the 1700s, forbidding Black people from learning to read and write to contemporary reading retention laws delimiting the quality of literacy instruction received, while holding Black students (communities, families) accountable to ensure a cheap and under-educated source of dependence and labor. In this counternarrative, I argue that anti-Black literacy laws were written specifically to prohibit Black people from becoming literate and economically independent.

Twentieth- and twenty-first-century anti-Black literacy laws claim to objectively draw on data from scientifically based and evidence-based reading research and use the data to inform reading laws, policies, and statutes. Specifically, there has been a preponderance of reading research, albeit limited among Black students, from informal reading assessments used in progress monitoring to national and state standardized reading tests used to emphasize and identify low reading performance. These actions are intentionally undertaken without acknowledgment of scientific racism underpinning reading assessments and standardized tests. Moreover, administrators, politicians, and researchers project and seek to describe Black culture, language, lives, and ways of knowing in deficit language, while simultaneously recommending similar "new" approaches, seeking funding for additional research, and supporting new laws to "help" improve the reading performance of Black students. I demystify the ideology of White supremacy framing, shaping, and informing how some people (business and corporate executives, educators, governors, parents, politicians, presidents, reading researchers, school administrators, and Supreme Court justices) have viewed/view the world and how reading/literacy has been/is conceptualized, defined, taught, and assessed.

To eliminate anti-Black literacy and to support Black literacy, ideological and moral change must occur with an investment in Black scholarship, funding research, and culturally and linguistically appropriate resources. This is a call to action: to value Black lives and Black children's literacy access, growth, and development by acknowledging that they do not need to act, be, experience, or think like their White peers to be worthy of high-quality literacy instruction and culturally and linguistically appropriate and supportive curriculum, instructions, and materials, that should be accessible to all students. Teacher education, at all levels, must include Black culture, language, literacy, and literature.

My hope is this book will help to democratize how literacy is assessed, conceptualized, defined, measured, promoted, and taught while repealing current anti-Black literacy laws and preventing future laws from being enacted.

Overview of the Book

History is ever-evolving, multilayered, and permeable, without stops and starts of chapter divisions; however, its fluidity is not easily captured as a narrative. Although this book is written in separate chapters, beliefs, concepts, customs, ideologies, and traditions are porous and flow from one constructed historical period to another. Anti-Black literacy continues to flow and erode Black lives: unabated by literacy histories seeking to purify the past, by reading research symbolically suggesting novel approaches, or by legal regulations seeking to appear equitable. Included throughout are artifacts, documents, and photos that convey bittersweet yet untold stories of the lives of Black people seeking literacy and using the power of literacy to tell our stories, our way.

Chapter 1 presents an often-overlooked narrative about the anti-literacy laws within US history and anchored within the ideology of White supremacy. I emphasize the ideological, political, and social impact of White supremacy as well as trace the evolution of weaponizing literacy and crafting anti-Black literacy laws and policies. Interwoven throughout the chapter are narratives about the lives of Black people who sought and fought for literacy rights as well as examples of their accomplishments and courageous rebuttals of mischaracterizations of Black people. Chapter 2 extends the discussion of anti-Black literacy and exposes how anti-Black racism informed psychology, reading research, and standardized reading tests. Moving chronologically through the lives of Black and White scholars, the chapter makes clear parallel efforts to construct Black students, their intellectual abilities, and their performance on standardized reading tests, more accurately. Chapter 3 links the history of anti-Black literacy, standardization of reading tests, and the politicization of reading research to multi-pronged anti-Black literacy campaigns. It examines how contemporary reading laws and policies were (are) outgrowths of the ideology of White supremacy, underpin standardized reading tests, and inform federal- and state-endorsed reading approaches and assessments. Chapter 4 examines the intersection of the ideology of White supremacy, history, and social concerns. Reading retention laws, for instance, sprang from the political backdrop of social promotion and racial inequalities. Several socio-political contexts are examined to track agencies, conditions, and events leading up to the onset of reading retention laws. Chapter 5 focuses on a corpus of extant research among Black students conducted by Black scholars and allies that is seldom included in federally funded research and "new" approaches to reading. The chapter demystifies how ever-evolving anti-Black literacy laws are created and resurrected to forestall equitable literacy access to Black students and describes how federally funded grants as well as singular approaches to reading function to extend White supremacist notions of literacy. Chapter 6 focuses on the history of anti-Black literacy in the state of Florida and serves as a case study and cautionary tale. It demonstrates the intersection of ideology, law, and politics in crafting reading laws that harm Black students. Chapter 7 extends the counternarrative of anti-Black literacy access to the present and provides updates on several key moments in history and includes ongoing efforts of anti-Black racism and anti-Black literacy in the United States. The Afterword acknowledges a seismic shift is needed to bring about foundational change in reading research and literacy equity for Black students.

INTRODUCTION

Traditional histories of literacy generally focus on reading more often than on writing. And in the United States, these histories center on the actions, experiences, languages, literacies, and lives of White people and exclude the actions, experiences, languages, literacies, and lives among People of Color. Traditional histories of literacy may reflect the ideological perspective of the author, customs or traditions in the field, or the philosophical perspective of a funding agency, wherein ideology represents "systems of representation – composed of concepts, ideas, myths, or images" (Althusser, 1970, pp. 231–236). A discernable pattern among traditional literacy histories indicates humanity is equal to Whiteness, and all other ethnicities and races are non-humans. These ideas are part of what some have called the Big Lie, and others the Original Sin of America; under either moniker, the ideas form the foundation of White supremacy. Collectively, they bear witness to the ways in which the ideology of White supremacy has helped to frame anti-Black racism and is used to influence anti-Black literacy.

Histories of literacy and reading by Graff (1979, 1991, 1995) detail the complex relationships among literacy, knowledge, privilege, and power. His research on literacy in select North American cities presents literacy as a conduit for social and cultural hegemony. He describes literacy's power to liberate as one of the great fears of the dominant class, and he has discussed the institutional, political, and social structures that have been constructed to hinder access to literacy. Graff does not provide substantive historical information about the effect of such decisions on the lives of People of Color. Likewise, Kaestle et al. (1991) present a history of White readers and reading practices in the United States. The authors state they did not seek to address differences among readers in a veiled reference to People of Color, as their focus is on (what they called) native-born and middle-class Whites. Thus, there is a very limited discussion of Black readers

DOI: 10.4324/9781003296188-1

as a comparison demographic to White readers. Shannon's (1989, 1990) early scholarship also addresses the history of reading instruction and examines the histori-cal thinking behind various instructional strategies with scant discussion about People of Color and the socio-historical contexts that barred their access to literacy. His more recent scholarship (Shannon 1992, 2007) explores the role of laws, policies, and politics in literacy education. He interrogates how reading research does, or does not, inform reading policy. He also questions who policymakers are, how reading policy is framed, the influence of agencies and organizations, and how educators are affected.

There are histories that document how literacy access and opportunity have been restricted by economic class, ethnicity, geographic locale, language, and race. The latter scholarship helps to dislodge and demystify notions of univer-sal access for people and individuals through close examinations of barriers to access, as experienced by members of marginalized communities. R. C. Morris (1976) examines a decade of the Freedmen Bureau's efforts to provide edu-cational access and opportunity throughout the South to Black people. J. D. Anderson's (1988) history of education among Black people living in the South between 1860 and 1935, presents a comprehensive history of Black education, and less of a history of reading. He admits that Black people held literacy in high regard and fought against customs, traditions, and racial animus to obtain literacy. He argues, "the denial of opportunities for schooling has translated into the denial of access to literacy" (J. D. Anderson, 1988, pp. 35–36). Another example is found in Prendergast's (2003) adoption of a critical race theoretical lens in a selective review of educational practices, laws, and literacy research. Her text is limited in its historical breadth as it is centered primarily in the twentieth century and Supreme Court cases and does not directly address reading instruc-tion or local and state laws. She draws on the critical race scholarship of Cheryl Harris (1993), seeking to extend the notion of Whiteness as property to literacy: "I use a concept of property in its broader definition, as quality, trait, or attribute. Recognizing that literacy has been often regarded as a white trait, something that whites possess naturally, rather than as a white privilege" (p. 8). She ponders the lengths taken to keep literacy White, observing literacy "has been sustained primarily as a response to perceived threats to White property interests, White privilege, the maintenance of White identity, or the conception of America as a White nation" (p. 7). She posits literacy practices often mask racism in society and education; thus, it is unreasonable to expect equal outcomes. Givens (2021) crafts a historical narrative centering on the life and scholarship of Carter G. Woodson, by weaving thoughtful discussions about the role of literacy in the lives of Black people. He details how Black people struggled to access literacy in opposition to anti-literacy laws, Jim/Jane Crow laws, White resistance, and White supremacy. He draws on the notion of fugitivity, as a grounded reality of Black people's lives in the United States, when "acquiring knowledge was a criminal act" (p. 27). He suggests that in the Black community literacy often has been understood as communal, something shared, an intergenerational practice, and a resource (see also Royer, 1994; T. Perry, 2003). Givens (2021) also observes it was not uncommon for Black people to share their literacy with others, reading text aloud while all were free to offer an interpretation. He articulates how "antiliteracy laws and the intellectual surveillance that accompanied them … enforced the idea that blacks are outside the social contract of American society – inconceivable as fully human, citizen, or student" (p. 28). His narrative conveys the value placed on education and literacy by Black people as significant tactics for fighting against institutional and structural racism.

There is no definitive or official history of literacy in the United States; there have been hundreds of books written as if there is a single source of information. The history of literacy in the United States is seldom conveyed with accuracy, given there is little-to-no conscious effort to include the reading histories of Black people, except for attempts to portray Black people as illiterate by biology, choice, intellect, and values. Too often such versions are concocted from a White-centric, point of view:

> History, as nearly no one seems to know, is not merely something to be read. And it does not refer merely, or even principally, to the past. … On the contrary, the great force of history comes from the fact that we carry it within us, are unconsciously controlled by it in many ways, and history is literally present in all that we do.
>
> *(Baldwin, 1965, p. 47)*

Noted historian Timothy Snyder (2021) discusses a series of global historical events that preceded what he calls memory laws. He defines *memory laws* as "government actions designed to guide public interpretation of the past … by asserting a mandatory view of historical events, by forbidding the discussion of historical facts or interpretations or by providing vague guidelines that lead to self-censorship" (para 10). There appears to be a push for *memory laws* within the teaching of US history and the history of literacy. Contemporary attempts to establish memory laws are not sanctioned by the federal government, albeit state and local governments are proceeding with memory laws, which gives the appearance they are government-approved and endorsed to promote a best-of-all-worlds version of White supremacy. C. M. Blow (2021) observes that it is important who crafts the whitewashed, imagined, US, historical narrative taught in schools:

> the ability and authority to create narrative – or to challenge or change it – is an awesome power. … Stories have the power to profoundly move people, to create societal frameworks. … It is the story and the ideal that create the American story and the American identity. … The American narrative that we have built is mostly about the valor, brilliance and determination of white people. Largely absent from it is all the pain, oppression

and death that are woven into that story. Absent is the enslavement, the massacres and lynchings. Absent are the broken treaties, the internment camps and racial exclusion laws. Absent are the black codes, Jim Crow and mass incarceration. … But many Americans, like the sanitized version of their history … altering that narrative, correcting it, filling it out with the uncomfortable bits, with the truth, is an affront to the very ideal of America as they have come to conceive it.

(para 10–17)

Endemic in traditional historical narratives, Black literacy is either absent or misrepresented; the lives and literacies of Black people are undervalued and only mentioned in comparison to White people. This framing is a replication of seeing Black people as non-human, centering histories within the lives of White people, and failing to acknowledge Black people's beliefs, cultures, experiences, ingenuity, languages, research, and values. It is on these foundations of traditional US history/memory that the history of literacy, specifically reading (approaches, assessment, curriculum, instruction, and measurement), is based and positioned as the purview of White people – who alone define and determine merit. Thus, reading has been codified, legalized, and politicized – as well as weaponized, to help White people retain authority, control, dominance, and power.

This book presents a counternarrative of the history of literacy in the United States, which unearths the intent of the ideology of White supremacy to conceptualize, frame, and shape literacy. This book examines attempts to forestall literacy for Black people deliberately undertaken by White people. It emerged from a disbelief in the dominance and supremacy of Whiteness and presents a counternarrative of the actions, beliefs, and experiences Black people undertook to acquire literacy, while acknowledging that a single text cannot provide a comprehensive account of every action.

A Path Forward

In a 2020 webinar, "History Is Now: What Is America's Story," the Secretary of the Smithsonians, Lonnie G. Bunch, III, and documentarian Ken Burns describe how American history has been portrayed. They focused on who tells the story and from what perspectives, while conceding the history of the United States is a complex story, filled with events and ideas we should celebrate and shortcomings and weaknesses that should be acknowledged. Public schools in the United States teach a constructed history of the Revolution and the making of the American flag, designed to instill admiration, devotion, loyalty, and reverence for the "founders of the nation" and those who aided the cause. However, depictions of the founding fathers as enslavers, fathers who sold their enslaved mixed-race children, and as men who benefited from the unpaid labor of enslaved Black people, do not appear among these history lessons: "history loses its value and incentive and example; if it paints perfect men and noble nations, but it does not tell the truth" (Du Bois, 1966, p. 722). Bunch and Burns expressed concern about narratives that drive American history as created, manufactured, and promoted to serve White people in power, support White supremacy, and convey a White savior mentality. Burns likened the narratives to historical memory: "the stories we tell ourselves" (Bunch & Burns, 2020) as if it is a balm to soothe the wounds inflicted upon one another. Considering anti-Black literacy, the chapters in this book portend

> the economic history of this country is among other things, the study of generations and generations of free labor used to make the country grow. The legal history of this country is very heavily weighted with the courts, particularly the Supreme Court's, relation to Black people, and the legislation designed specifically, deliberately, to keep them oppressed.
>
> *(Morrison, 1975, p. 6)*

This counternarrative challenges how the complexity of the history of literacy in the United States has been streamlined into a palatable, sanitized, romanticized, and whitewashed myth created to soothe White people's consciousness.

In the United States, anti-literacy is rooted in an ideology of White supremacy, the belief and idea that White people are human, dominant, and superior to all other humans. People who hold this view believe Black people are not human, are unintelligent, and must be dominated. These anti-Black beliefs and ideas existed for centuries so much so they are understood (by those who hold them) to be commonsensical and all other beliefs aberrations. It is this anti-Black racism that informs customs and traditions of prohibiting Black people from learning to read and write. When anti-literacy laws were established, they specifically forbade literacy among Black people; hence, I renamed them anti-Black literacy laws – because they were enacted to prevent Black people from learning to read or write and to punish people who taught Black people to read and write. The narrative surrounding anti-literacy laws implies they were abolished and no longer exist. This counternarrative posits that the deeply held beliefs about White superiority underpin contemporary anti-Black literacy laws, evolving and manifesting in contemporary reading laws and policies.

Anti-Black Literacy Laws and Policies takes an uncompromising focus on how race and racism have influenced access to literacy and by extension the disparate impact the lack of literacy access has had on the lives of Black people. I examine and interrogate why and how anti-Black racism and anti-Black literacy have been weaponized in support of White supremacy. I use several terms – race and racism in the common/colloquial sense, without providing definitions because definitions are not solutions when discussing race and racism. When such queries are posed – to provide a definition of race and racism – what is really being asked is to prove racism exists, as Toni Morrison (1975) remarks: "the very serious function of racism, is distraction. It keeps you from doing your work.

It keeps you explaining, over and over again, your reason for being... None of that is necessary. There will always be one more thing" (n.p.). I write from experience, knowing that in the United States racism exists, that anti-Black racism exists, and that anti-Black literacy exists. Another term used throughout this book is *anti-literacy*; there is no official definition of anti-literacy although taken literally means to oppose literacy. The term was used in the 1700s to identify a series of laws enacted under the Slave Codes to prohibit Black people from learning to read and write. Anti-Black literacy customs, laws, policies, and statutes were specifically written to prohibit Black enslaved people from learning literacy; it is important not to erase the people for whom the laws were enacted. Snyder (2021) reminds us, "early memory laws were generally designed to protect the truth about victim groups" (p. 10). Finally, I use the term *counternarrative* to convey the text can "splinter widely accepted truths about people, cultures, and institutions as well as the value of those institutions and the knowledge produced by and within those cultural institutions" (Mutua, 2008, p. 133). This counternarrative by presenting more accurate and detailed information, "counters unquestioned narratives or 'official stories' that are sometimes backed by 'scientific' evidence or unquestioned conventional wisdom—that state 'truths' about people, situations, or places" (p. 133).

Myriad traditional histories of literacy (reading) have been written about education, generally and specifically about reading or writing. These histories portray the evolution of reading in the United States from a Eurocentric and Western point of view with scant recognition of People of Color as literacy learners. They replicate sanitized traditional versions of US history and do not present an accurate history that celebrates achievements, acknowledges failures, recognizes human rights abuses, and thus sustains entrenched racial inequities. The history of literacy also suffers from a myopic, oversimplified, and romanticized version of the complicated nature of the evolution of literacy in the United States. Missing, whether because of historical amnesia or denial, are descriptions of anti-Black racism and anti-Black literacy by refusing to "grapple [*sic*] with a history of White supremacy" (Crenshaw quoted in McLaughlin, 2021, n.p.), as the consequences of actions in the past continue to influence consequences within the lives of people today. The history of anti-Black racism, anti-Black literacy, and educational inequality experienced by Black people in the United States continues to unfold, not as a singular event or moment in time, but as a continuous evolution and remaking.

A review of US anti-Black literacy customs, laws, policies, and statutes also helps unmask the blinding legacy of systemic anti-Black racism and anti-Black literacy within the history of literacy, prohibiting equal and equitable access to literacy. It is imperative we understand *why* anti-Black racism and anti-Black literacy campaigns were established, codified, and legalized against Black people. As much as I wanted the text to move forward and begin to deconstruct contemporary versions of anti-Black literacy, I was always drawn back to chattel

Black enslavement to better understand Black life under enslavement as foundational to understanding anti-Black racism and literacy. Recognizing how White supremacy functioned then is imperative to understanding how it functions now: anti-Black racism and anti-Black literacy are part of the nation's legacy of systemic racism lying at the core of reading access. The failure to acknowledge – or learn – about why Black people were enslaved and forbidden from learning to read and write redound within the nation's constant desire to replicate the past and frame the present.

This counternarrative is centered on the experiences of Black people in the United States, with a focus on anti-Black literacy customs, laws, policies, and statutes crafted and designed to deny equitable access to reading. My examination of primary source documents reveals the root causes of anti-Black literacy are embedded within White supremacy's notions of White commonsense beliefs, local customs, and federal and state laws. I move beyond what happened to why events happened to reveal the interplay between how White supremacy informed anti-Black literacy and how their relationship is embedded in federal and state laws. Importantly, I examine the ethos of the ideology of White supremacy and interrogate it as a seemingly invisible web of influence in anti-Black literacy laws. In short, I simultaneously and unashamedly draw connections to how White supremacy was used in the past, evolves, and how it is currently used to inform and frame literacy laws, policies, and statutes (the ideology of White supremacy and the history of White racism are not the foci of this book; they are undeniable forces within all facets of life in the United States and help to expose how anti-Black racism is interwoven within anti-Black literacy legislation).

This history reflects how and why the languages, literacies, and lives of Black people have been denigrated, erased, and ignored, by expanding a US history of literacy, with a focus on reading among Black people. The history of Black literacy is complicated and multilayered, as anti-Black literacy rests at the nexus of anti-Black racism and White supremacy, as it exposes how the ideology of White supremacy is a ubiquitous construct infecting the way of life in the United States. Black literacy history includes the anti-Black literacy campaigns that began in the 1600s after enslaved Africans were brought to the United States; although an untold number of African people were literate, they were not literate in the language of their capturers and enslavers. Anti-Black literacy customs and traditions preceded anti-Black literacy laws that were established to prohibit Black enslaved people from learning to read and write as well as from teaching literacy to other enslaved Black people. White colonizers and enslavers made concerted efforts to frame Black enslaved people as less than human and incapable of conscious thought and literacy. These actions, beliefs, and events prompt several questions addressed in this book: How can a history of literacy be conveyed and shy away from the truth? How has an ideology of White supremacy evolved and subverted Black literacy development and growth? How does unraveling anti-Black racism expose anti-Black literacy in the United States? What might a history of literacy look like when starting the narrative from the positionality of Black people? In what ways do singular reading approaches, multitiered reading assessments, and reading retention laws reflect the continuation of anti-Black literacy? Racially, which students benefit from reading reform legislation and which students do not?

Historical vignettes are interwoven throughout the text to establish and represent the humanity of Black people and to serve as antidotes to the whitewashing of the history of literacy among Black people in the United States. The vignettes bring to light the beliefs, choices, and experiences of Black people and reveal how our humanity is attacked, denied, ignored, minimized, questioned, subjugated, and trivialized. The vignettes reflect a well-rounded understanding of literacy as desired and an ever-present concern

> We want our children educated. … And when we call for education we mean real education. … We want our children trained as intelligent human beings should be, and we will fight for all time against any proposal to educate black boys and girls simply as servants and underlings, or simply for the use of other people. They have a right to know, to think, to aspire.
>
> *(Du Bois, 1905, para 9–10)*

The vignettes also convey how Black people expressed themselves through art, beauty, community, family, laughter, joy, song, and religion. Moreover, the vignettes serve to expose anti-Black racism and injustices endured by Black people, often in their own words. Poetry is also used as a leitmotif, capturing the lives of Black people much like West African griots: Through poems, some of which were put to music, the voices of Black people communicated and expressed cautions, dreams, fears, hope, joy, sorrow, tears, and victories through oral and written literature. The context of historical events of anti-Black racial violence is highlighted to convey anti-Black racism and how it was experienced, understood, and shared among Black people.

This book challenges educational, ethical, historical, moral, and political narratives that fail to acknowledge the actions, cultures, experiences, languages, and literacies of Black people. Herein, Black people are fellow humans, worthy of equal and equitable literacy access and instruction. Black people have consistently fought for literacy along with struggling for freedom, human rights, and racial justice. The key to preserving an accurate history of Black literacy is to provide one.

We cannot ignore the past, nor sit on the sidelines and remain strategically silent in the present; we must work to address and eradicate anti-Black racism in literacy.

Portions of Chapter 2 have appeared in:

Willis, A. I. (2008). *Reading comprehension research and testing in the United States: Undercurrents of race, class, and power in the struggle for meaning.* Lawrence Erlbaum.

Willis, A. I. (2002). Literacy at Calhoun colored school, 1892–1943. *Reading Research Quarterly, 37*(1), 8–44.

Portions of Chapters 2, 3 and 4 have appeared in:

Willis, A. I. (2019a). Race, response to intervention, and reading research. *Journal of Literacy Research, 50*(4), 1–26.

Willis, A. I. (2019b). Response to intervention: An illusion of equity. *Language Arts, 97*(2), 83–96.

Willis, A. I. (2018). Re-positioning race in English language arts research. In D. Lapp & D. Fisher (Eds.), *Handbook of research on teaching the English language arts research* (4th ed., pp. 30–56). Routledge.

1

A BRIEF HISTORY

Anti-Black Racism and Anti-Black Literacy in Federal and State Laws

The history of anti-Black racism, anti-Black literacy, and educational inequality as experienced by people of African descent in the United States begins this chapter. Woodson (1933) observed: "if a race has no history, if it has no worthwhile tradition, it becomes a negligible factor in the thought of the world, and it stands in danger of being exterminated" (p. 87). The history linking anti-Black racism and anti-literacy laws in the United States provided context for understanding why and how anti-Black literacy laws were codified, justified, and legalized. For hundreds of years, White people created acts, codes, laws, policies, statutes, and structures to deny, limit, and prevent Black peoples' access to literacy. On the one hand, laws were established that criminalized Black people from acquiring and teaching literacy, attempts to teach and learn literacy, and forbade Black and White children from attending the same school and being taught literacy by the same teacher. And the separate-but-equal doctrine shielded inequities by creating unequal educational institutions for Black and White students. On the other hand, Black people learned to read, and they built, furnished, and financed their own schools, although some were dependent on federal and philanthropic funding (J. D. Anderson, 1988). There were two undeniable outcomes: White supremacists prohibited Black people from learning to read and write to control their thoughts and retain a free source of labor during enslavement and a free or cheap source of labor thereafter, and Black people resisted customs, laws, statutes, and traditions to declare their humanity, intellect, and resistance to White supremacy. Black people learned to read and write as literacy as a form of power and resistance. A review of multiple federal documents and laws (Declaration of Independence, Supreme Court cases, and the US Constitution); state constitutions and laws; as well as local customs, laws, policies, and statutes – the

DOI: 10.4324/9781003296188-2

ever-present unresolved issue of the enslavement of Black people – remains, along with efforts to prohibit their access to literacy.

The never-ending efforts to delimit Black people's access to literacy was one of many forms of oppression used to control Black people. Fueled by an ideology of White supremacy and anti-Black racism, the late 1800s was a time of anti-Black literacy customs, laws, and statutes; Black enslavement, Jim/Jane Crow laws, segregation, and race-based inequalities were ignored or whitewashed to imply ongoing progress. Drawing on negative and stereotypical images of Black people popularized in the customs, laws, and media, this period became one of Black victimization: portrayals of Black people's reading ability were presented as evidence of biological inferiority and low intelligence. White people claimed dominion over literacy by controlling, defining, and limiting who was permitted access and under what conditions. Legal and societal efforts to forestall access to literacy were undertaken with intentionality: "it was not done by well-meaning people muddling into something which they didn't understand. It was a deliberate policy hammered into place" (Baldwin, 1963, p. 2). The concerns of Black parents for their children's education did not abate; they continued to seek legal redress as in the cases of Sarah Roberts in the 1800s, Linda Brown in 1954, and Ruby Bridges in 1960. The Black girls had parents who wanted them to attend elementary schools closer to their homes. Their efforts were followed by White people changing school districts, parents removing their children from schools to attend suburban schools, and building alternative schools (Christian, church-affiliated, charter, elite public, etc.). White power elites chaffed at Black people who articulated, challenged, questioned, and responded to White supremacist assumptions, customs, laws, traditions, and statutes.

Given the history of literacy, anti-Black literacy laws continued to unfold long after the initial laws were seemingly abolished, moves the narrative forward. The role of White supremacy – not as a singular event or moment in time but a continuous evolution and remaking – represents a tapestry of local beliefs and customs about White racial superiority and was foundational to many legal federal, state, and local racist laws and policies established in support. In this chapter, the seeming "placelessness" of Black people within the history of reading has been revised by extending and complicating the history of anti-literacy for Black people in the United States. A goal of this chapter is to expose the assumptions and relationships governing literacy in the United States. The geographical references and locations of place were important to acknowledge as literacy has never been a singularly Western commodity nor do the concepts about literacy belong only to the West or the global North (the discussion of which is beyond this chapter).

An examination of legal federal and state primary source documents as well as federal, state, and local customs, policies, and statutes exposes how anti-Black racism was/is threaded through legislation that affected access to literacy for Black people. The review of customs, laws, policies, and statutes helped to unmask the blinding legacy of systemic racism in literacy access. For over four hundred years, White supremacist ideological positioning and legal efforts, coupled with social customs and traditions, prohibited equal and equitable access to literacy for Black people in the United States.

A Conscious and Legal Effort to Deny Literacy to People of African Descent

Black historians (B. Bell, 1987; Franklin & Moss, 1994) drew on knowledge of literacy among the people of Africa and provided an alternative narrative to explain the literacy habits of African people. Importantly, they conceived of literacy in much broader terms than reading and writing by including communication, entertainment, orality, and traditions. B. Bell (1987) provided an extended understanding of literacy to include orality:

> various forms of verbal art were used by Africans to transmit knowledge, value, and attitudes from one generation to another, enforce conformity to social norms, validate social institutions and religious rituals, and provide psychological release from the restrictions of society.
>
> *(p. 16)*

Franklin and Moss (1994) also acknowledged the

> literary activities of Africans with their everyday lives. Oral literature, made up of tales, proverbs, epics, histories and laws, served as an educational device, a source of amusement, and a guide for the administration of government and the conduct of religious ceremony.
>
> *(p. 25)*

People of African descent, primarily from the vast area of West and Central Africa, were brought to the "new world" on the shores of North America. There was not a single language of communication among the African people as "enslaved black people came from regions and ethnic groups throughout Africa. Though they came empty-handed, they carried with them memories of loved ones and communities, moral values, intellectual insight, artistic talents and cultural practices, religious beliefs and skills" (Elliot & Hughes, 2019, n. p.). Black people possessed critical consciousness; that is, they "read" their environment, from landing on the shores of the Americas to the armed resistance against the inhumanity imposed by White enslavers. Through their resistance, they created a new life, a mélange of cultures, ethnicities, languages, literacies, and religions.

There were an unknown number of literate African people captured or kidnapped, enslaved, and transported during the transatlantic slave trade throughout the Americas. Diouf (2019) estimates that over one million literate African

Muslims were able to read and write in Arabic before they arrived in the Americas. Biographies about literate African Muslim men from powerful and royal families were produced by White people: Prince Ayuba Suleiman Diallo (aka Job Ben Solomon), and Abdul Rahman (Abd-Al Rahman, Ibrahima abd-Al Rahman). Omar ibn Said (1770–1863), by contrast, was the only enslaved African person to write an autobiography while enslaved. Scholars (Alryyes, 2011; Diouf, 2019; Jameson, 1925), among others, observe there was an extensive legalized educational system throughout the Sengambia region of West Africa where Omar ibn Said spent over two decades studying at the university level, before he was captured, enslaved, and transported to Charleston, South Carolina (please see Omar ibn Said photo, Figure 1.1). After years of chattel enslavement, he escaped from his harsh enslaver and walked 200 miles to North Carolina, before he was recaptured and incarcerated. While imprisoned, he wrote in Arabic on the walls, before being "purchased" by John Owen, the governor of the state. Omar ibn Said's autobiography included quotations from the Qur'an, apologies as he had forgotten his first language as well as literateness (Alryyes & Said, 2011, p. 61).

FIGURE 1.1   Omar ibn Said, portrait ca. 1850, in Randolph Linsly Simpson African-American collection.

Credit: Wikimedia Commons

When brought to the "new world," African people were forced to learn the cultures, languages, and values of their oppressors; had to suppress their home languages as well as their literate abilities; and faced dispossession of their languages, personhood, and ways of life. Other African men wrote their autobiographies such as Olaudah Equiano (Gustavus Vassa), or dictated their autobiography. Venture Smith (1729–1805), for instance, was born in Guinea, Africa, and dictated his autobiography in 1798 to "Elisha Niles, a Connecticut schoolmaster" (para 2). He detailed his life prior to bondage and enslavement as well as described how he purchased his freedom and the freedom of his wife, children, and other enslaved Black people.

Historians Bly (2011) and Monaghan (2005) proffered that some White Christians were more likely to teach Black people to read than to write, as some believed teaching Black people to write would disprove their theory that Black people were unable to think and reason. Moreover, Black people who were able to write would appear more human (Willis, Thompson-McMillon, & Smith, 2022). In 1740, South Carolina passed a law forbidding teaching literacy to enslaved people:

> Whereas, the having slaves taught to write, or suffering them to be employed in writing, may be attended with great inconveniences; Be it enacted, that all and every person and persons whatsoever, who shall hereafter teach or cause any slave or slaves to be taught to write, or shall use or employ any slave as a scribe, in any manner of writing whatsoever, hereafter taught to write, every such person or persons shall, for every such offense, forfeit the sum of one hundred pounds, current money.
>
> *Simkin, 2014, n.p.*

No one living today truly understands the depth of depravity foisted upon one human by another during Black chattel enslavement. We know there were untold human rights abuses as William Wells Brown (1814–1884), a formerly enslaved mixed-race man observed, "slavery has never been represented, slavery never can be represented" (quoted in J. Johnson, 1999, p. 10). Samuel Wood wrote, printed, and disseminated a broadside *Injured Humanity; Being a Representation of What the Unhappy Children of Africa Endure from Those Who Call Themselves Christians* (1805), meant to demystify and shock people through his text and pictures. He shared graphic examples of Black enslavement in the West Indies: affixing mouthpieces, beating, branding, kidnapping, starving, whipping, and separating families.

Zora Neal Hurston, best known as a novelist, was also a trained anthropologist whose research provided counternarratives to inaccurate academic discourses about Black people. Her scholarship included in-depth interviews, extensive field work, and nuanced understandings of the cultures, languages, and ways of Black people. Hurston (1927) published an article in the *Journal of Negro History*, in which she conveyed the cultural and domestic life in an African village, as shared with her by a formerly enslaved Black man, whose name was changed to Cudjo (Kujjo) Lewis. He recalled, in heart-rending detail, how he was captured and held in Dahomey (Benin), Africa, after a massacre by a rival tribe. The captured people walked from their village to the port, imprisoned before being sold White slavers, the transport on the *Clotilde*, and experiences once on the US soil where he was enslaved. Hurston's more in-depth portrayal of Mr. Oluale Kossola (his given name) was completed in 1931 amid some controversy, and it was published posthumously in 2018 as *Barracoon: The Story of the Last "Black Cargo."* Hurston's book includes transcriptions of her recorded interviews with Oluale Kossola, the name they both preferred. Importantly, she retained Kossola's language, West African Pidgin English, and refused to alter it as doing so would be an erasure of an integral part of his life. Kossola, for instance, described his experience of learning of his emancipation:

> I doan forgit. It April 12, 1865. De Yankee soldiers dey come down to de boat and eatee de mulberries off de trees close to de boat, you unnerstand me. Den dey see us on de boat and dey say "Y'all can't stay dere no mo'. You free, you doan b'long to nobody no mo'." Oh, Lor'! I so glad. We astee de soldiers where we goin'? Dey say dey doan know. Dey told us to go where we feel lak goin', we ain' no mo' slave.
>
> *(pp. 62–63)*

The Black people in Africatown, Alabama, are descendants of Africans brought to the United States, including Kossola. They held on to the memories of their forebears, who were the human cargo on the last slave ship, the *Clotilda*, in 1860 (currently, the ship is being resurrected using federal and state funds). The ship illegally transported 110 African people — who were sold into enslavement once the ship reached the United States. Black people, who lived in Africatown, Alabama, shared oral histories passed down through generations of their Black enslaved forbears.

Slave Codes

Gates (2011) noted African people came to the landmass known as the United States as early at 1513, in present-day Florida. Enslaved Africans, kidnapped from their homelands and carried across the Atlantic aboard ships, were also brought by Spanish expeditions in present-day South Carolina in 1525 and 1565. In the United States, people of African descent were considered property, or chattel, and thus confined to a system of oppression that had no end. Chattel slavery centered on enslaving African people, as White settler-colonizers invoked "*partus sequitur ventrem*" or '*that is which brought forth follows the womb*,' defining slavery as a heritable condition from the mother" (Parker, 2020, para 1). In 1662, a Virginia law stated:

Whereas some doubts have arisen whether children got by any Englishman upon a Negro woman should be slave or free, *be it therefore enacted and declared by this present Grand Assembly*, that all children born in this country shall be held bond or free only according to the condition of the mother …

(n.p., emphasis in the original)

In this way, the lives of Black people were firmly severed from racial equality as a racial line had been codified to deny any person with Black blood equal status under the law. As Patrick Wolfe (2007) explained:

Black people's enslavement produced an inclusive taxonomy that automatically enslaved the offspring of a slave and any other parent. In the wake of slavery, this taxonomy became fully racialized in the "one-drop rule," whereby any amount of African ancestry, no matter how remote, and regardless of phenotypical appearance, makes a person Black.

(quoted in Tuck & Yang, 2012, p. 12)

Similar laws were enacted in other colonies,

declaring that children assume the same status as their mother meant that white male slave owners' rape and sexual exploitation of Black enslaved women was as much an economic model as it was a tactic of psychological and physical torture.

(Greenidge, 2021, para 6)

The progeny faced a life of enslavement and an uncertain future as they could be nurtured, taken from their mothers and given away, or sold into enslavement. As laws were enacted to bar the importation of African people, enslaved Black people were bred and bartered across colonies and, later, state lines.

Parker (2020) observed, "one of the legal strategies that Euro-American enslavers devised to control the time, energy, and mobility of enslaved people of African descent were slave codes. Enslavers began to codify these restrictions into laws in the 17th century" (para 1). The Virginia Slave Codes of 1705, the basis for Virginia slave laws, listed dozens of prohibitions for enslaved people that included "an enslaved person carry a pass that authorized travel away from the plantation. Enslaved people could not own guns, *could not learn to read or sing*, beat drums, or gather in groups without their enslaver's permission" (Parker, 2020, para 1, emphasis added). Singing was discouraged as it permitted enslaved Black people to communicate their fears and grief:

They would compose and sing as they went along, consulting neither time nor tune. The thought that came up, came out – if not in the word, in the sound – and as frequently in the one as in the other… They told a tale of woe which was then altogether beyond my feeble comprehension; they were tones loud, long, and deep; they breathed the prayer and complaint of souls boiling over with the bitterest anguish. Every tone was a testimony against slavery, and a prayer to God for deliverance from chains.

(Douglass, 1845, p. 14, cited in Greenidge, 2021)

Enslaved Black people sang to soothe their souls as they toiled in harsh conditions as well as to provide directions to other Black people seeking freedom on the underground railroad. Slave codes prohibited Black people from having access to, acquiring, and teaching literacy, as "literacy constituted one of the terrains on which slaves and slave owners waged a perpetual struggle for control" (H. A. Williams, 2005, p. 13). Chattel slavery dehumanized Black people and had the "negative effect of divesting Africans of a substantial portion of their own culture" (Barksdale & Kinnamon, 1972, p. 2). For Black people, learning to read and write was an act not only of defiance and resistance but also of liberation and survival. Colonies adopted slave codes, although they varied and were constantly revised to justify and legalize White supremacy as well as in response to Black slave uprisings or revolts.

Federal Laws: Citizenship and Equality

Historians have debated the intentions of the US founding fathers' discourse in the Declaration of Independence and the US Constitution regarding the institution of chattel slavery because the word "slave" was not mentioned in either document. In a draft of the Declaration of Independence, Thomas Jefferson (1774) included a statement implicating King George as the impetus for slavery in the colonies:

He has waged cruel war against human nature itself, violating its most sacred rights of life & liberty in the persons of a distant people who never offended him, captivating & carrying them into slavery in another hemisphere or to incur miserable death in their transportation thither.

(para 27)

For unknown reasons, the statement was deleted in the final version. To be clear, Jefferson did not free the hundreds of enslaved Black people he owned, including his own children. Likewise, many of the signers of the Declaration of Independence (Charles Carroll, Samuel Chase, Benjamin Franklin, Button Gwinnett, John Hancock, Patrick Henry, Thomas Jefferson, Richard H. Lee, James Madison, Charles C. Pinckney, Benjamin Rush, Edward Rutledge, and George Washington) were enslavers, including three presidents. These men were aware of the oppressive living conditions of enslaved people. It was assumed, they enjoyed the economic gain from enslavement and desired the support of Southern politicians; thus, they had no intention of ending slavery.

The Declaration of Independence

In 1775, John Murray, the Earl of Dunmore and Virginia's governor, voiced concerns about the prospects of revolution by the colonies and threatened to free enslaved people as well as burn Williamsburg, to quell colonists' attempts to defy the British rule. He published a proclamation read throughout the colonies:

> I do hereby farther declare all *indented servants, Negroes,* or others (appertaining to rebels) *free,* that are able and willing to bear arms, they *joining his Majesty's troops,* as soon as may be, for the more speedily reducing this colony to a proper sense of their duty, to his Majesty's crown and dignity.
>
> *(p. 1, italics in the original)*

Upon learning about a release from chattel enslavement, hundreds of enslaved Black men joined the British Army's Royal Ethiopian Regiment (Gilder Lehrman, 2021).

Anti-Black racism fueled pervasive ideas about Black people as inferior to White people and in need of oversight by White people. Historians (Allen, 1983; Bogin, 1983; Morse, 1919; Quarles, 1961; Sailant, 2002; Woodson, 1937a) provided insight into Lemuel Haynes's (1776) text "Liberty Further Extended: Or Free Thoughts on the Illegality of Slave-keeping." Haynes, the son of a man of African descent and a former White indentured servant, described the hypocrisy of chattel slavery:

> We hold these truths to be self-Evident, that all men are created Equal, that they are Endowed By their Creator with Ceartain unalienable rights, that among these are Life, Liberty, and the pursuit of happyness.

Haynes's pamphlet reminded the world of the humanity of people of African descent as he called for equality between Black and White people (the exact date of the document is unclear; given the language used, it is likely written before the Declaration of Independence) (see Bogin, 1983). Later, the Declaration of Independence (1776) also stated, "all men are created equal, that they are endowed by their Creator with certain unalienable Rights."

Another Black author, Benjamin Banneker (1793–1806), born to free Black parents, was taught to read by his White grandmother, a Quaker, Mary Bannaky. In his *Almanacs,* he called for racial equity, and in 1791, he published a letter he had written to Thomas Jefferson, then Secretary of State. He implored Jefferson and his counterparts to acknowledge that the absurdity of "the almost general prejudice and prepossession" of Black people was "so prevalent in the world against those of my complexion" (n.p.). He demanded the authors of the Declaration of Independence uphold its claim "that all men are created equal" (n.p.) and submitted that White people must "wean yourselves from those narrow prejudices which you have imbibed with respect" to people of African descent. Unfortunately, his lofty words were unheeded as the Congressional Fugitive Slave Law of 1793 empowered local governments to apprehend runaway enslaved Black people and return them to their enslaver as well as to capture and enslave free Black people.

David Walker (1829) also challenged the text of the Declaration of Independence in his broadside, *Appeal to the Colored Citizens of the World* (McHenry, 1996), that "illustrated the ability of Black people to articulate their thoughts with clarity and exposed their equal status as fellow humans" (Willis, 2022, n.p.). His document also was written as a critique of equality described in the Declaration of Independence (McHenry, 1996). Walker made several strong assertions, including White people were mistaken to call themselves Christian as they supported slavery and Black people were the true Americans as they built the country with their unpaid labor.

Black enslaved people refused to be thought of as the property of another person, or chattel, and believed the promises outlined in the Declaration of Independence extended to them as people living in the United States. Among the many human rights abuses (emotional, physical, psychological, and sexual) used during the enslavement of Black people, family separation was especially feared. Faced with an uncertain future and inspired by the ideas of the Declaration of Independence (used for impetus), William Craft (1860/1969), and his wife, Ellen, developed a plan of escape from enslavement in Georgia (p. iii). They ingeniously escaped when Ellen pretended to be a young White man traveling with an enslaved Black man, William. Ellen's disguise included bandages and a sling to avoid suspicion as neither could read or write. Once they reached Philadelphia, with the help of abolitionists, they were taught to read and write. The Crafts learned quickly, although they lived under constant fear of being caught and returned to Georgia. Eventually, they moved to England, then returned to the United States and opened a school for Black people (see Woodson, 1937b and Woo, 2023).

As part of the 1850 Compromise, the law extended the 1793 Fugitive Slave Law to include the federal government in the capture and enslavement of Black people. The Fugitive Slave Law of 1850, Section 5, referenced the Constitution as extending authority to commissioners to permit "any one or more suitable persons, from time to time, to execute all such warrants and other process as may be issued by them in the lawful performance of their respective duties" (para 5). The commissioners were encouraged to request "all good citizens are hereby commanded to aid and assist in the prompt and efficient execution of this law, whenever their services may be required ..." (para 6) to help secure runaway Black enslaved people or face penalties.

Claims of equality were not extended to the hundreds of thousands of enslaved Black people, as Frederick Douglass (1852), a formerly enslaved Black man, remarked: "the rich inheritance of justice, liberty, prosperity and independence, bequeathed by your fathers, is shared by you, not by me" (p. 4). He decried the hypocrisy of national celebrations and observed, "America is false to the past, false to the present, and solemnly binds herself to be false to the future … slavery – the great sin and shame of America!" (p. 5). Douglass acknowledged the ongoing anti-Black racism caused White people to declare – Black people were not human:

> the manhood of the slave is conceded. It is admitted in the fact that Southern statute books are covered with enactments forbidding, under severe fines and penalties, the teaching of the slave to read or to write … it is enough to affirm the equal manhood of the Negro race. Is it not astonishing that, while we are ploughing, planting, and reaping, using all kinds of mechanical tools, erecting houses, constructing bridges, building ships, working in metals of brass, iron, copper, silver and gold; that, while we are reading, writing and ciphering, acting as clerks, merchants and secretaries, having among us lawyers, doctors, ministers, poets, authors, editors, orators and teachers; …
>
> *(p. 5)*

Further, he observed the hypocrisy surrounding celebrations of the Declaration of Independence and revised the US notions of exceptionalism:

> What, to the American slave, is your 4th of July? I answer; a day that reveals to him, more than all other days in the year, the gross injustice and cruelty to which he is the constant victim. To him, your celebration is a sham; your boasted liberty, an unholy license; your national greatness, swelling vanity; your sounds of rejoicing are empty and heartless; your denunciation of tyrants, brass fronted impudence; your shouts of liberty and equality, hollow mockery; your prayers and hymns, your sermons and thanksgivings, with all your religious parade and solemnity, are, to Him, mere bombast, fraud, deception, impiety, and hypocrisy – a thin veil to cover up crimes which would disgrace a nation of savages. There is not a nation on the earth guilty of practices more shocking and bloody than are the people of the United States, at this very hour.
>
> *(p. 6)*

As a new nation and a federal government emerged, White supremacy influenced the laws for all citizens, who were only White people, and embedded these ideas within the Declaration of Independence (1776), US Constitution (1787), as well as H. R. 40, Naturalization Bill (1790), a series of slave trade acts (1794, 1800, 1803, 1807, 1808), and the 1857 *Dred Scott v. Sandford* (60 US 393).

The US Constitution and Naturalization Bill

These documents sought to rest economic and political power in the hands of White men, conceal the enslavement of Black people within federal laws, as well as codify and legalize White supremacy while simultaneously justifying the enslavement of Black people. The founding fathers were not fumbling toward some evolutionary course to end chattel slavery; they made conscious choices to retain chattel slavery and secure the wealth of White men at the cost of the lives of enslaved Black people. Under the US Constitution (1788), Black people were considered people, albeit only three-fifths of a (White) person, as noted in Article *1* §§ *2–9*-:

> Representatives and direct Taxes shall be apportioned among the several States which may be included within this Union, according to their respective Numbers, which shall be determined by adding to the whole Number of free Persons, including those bound to Service for a Term of Years, and excluding Indians not taxed, three fifths of all other Persons.

Further, Article 1, Section 9, Clause 1, was a provision in the Constitution that addressed slavery. The word "slave" was not used but implied as African people were imported for the purpose of enslavement:

> The Migration or Importation of such Persons as any of the States now existing shall think proper to admit, shall not be prohibited by the Congress prior to the Year one thousand eight hundred and eight, but a Tax or duty may be imposed on such Importation, not exceeding ten dollars for each Person.
>
> *(n.p.)*

Thus, protecting the slave trade for 20 years in a concession to Southerners, "where slavery was pivotal to the economy, and states where the abolition of slavery had been accomplished or was contemplated" (Lloyd & Martinez, 2021, para 1). Perea (2016) also noted Article I, Section 2, discounted the personhood of Black enslaved persons in support of greater Southern state representation. P. Williams (1987) summarized the era by noting Black people "were, by constitutional mandated, outlawed from the hopeful, loving expectations that being treated as a whole, rather than three-fifths of human being can bring" (p. 138).

The US Congress also created and established H. R. 40, Naturalization Bill, on March 4, 1790, outlining naturalization procedures and limiting

> access to US citizenship to white immigrants—in effect, to people from Western Europe—who had resided in the US at least two years and their children under 21 years of age. It also granted citizenship to children born abroad to US citizens.
>
> *(Records of the US Senate, National Archives and Records Administration)*

Under this law, only White people could claim citizenship, reinforcing the ideology of White supremacy and setting a precedent for all future laws requiring citizenship status. Importantly, the clause permitted states to continue importing "persons" (knowingly Black people) until the expiration of the Clause in 1808 (although in 1790, President George Washington forbade the importation of slaves to the United States). Subsequent acts (1800, 1803, and 1807) increasingly prohibited US citizens from importing (Black) people to the United States for the purpose of enslavement, with accompanying fines, but did not address the trading of enslaved Black people living in the United States. Together, these federal laws provided "a shield behind which to avoid responsibility for the human repercussions of both governmental and public harmful private activity" (P. Williams, 1987, p. 134). White men of wealth continued to transport enslaved Black people from Africa to the United States, as "human cargo," as 500 enslaved Africans were loaded on to the *Wanderer* in 1858.

The federal government's practice was followed by states like Missouri, the 24th state in the Union, that passed several laws to restrict the lives of enslaved Black people (please see Appendix A, page 273). This law made clear the intent to deny the humanity of Black people and to prohibit Black enslaved people from learning literacy.

Dred Scott v. Sandford

Dred Scott, an enslaved Black man who had been owned by a series of White men and their wives, requested release from his servitude but was denied freedom. He and his wife filed lawsuits in Missouri seeking their freedom; however, his White enslaver argued that enslaved people were not citizens and had no rights under the US Constitution (please see Figure 1.2).

In *Dred Scott v. Sandford* (1857), one of the hundreds of cases filed in Missouri by Black people seeking freedom from enslavement, the majority decision was written by the Honorable Roger B. Taney, who provided an explanation of the foundational beliefs of White supremacy regarding Black people and White citizens:

> In the opinion of the court, the legislation and histories of the times, and the language used in the Declaration of Independence, show, that neither the class of persons who had been imported as slaves, nor their descendants, whether they had become free or not, were then acknowledged as a part of the people, nor intended to be included in the general words used in that memorable instrument … [Or] when the Constitution was framed and adopted … [Negroes] had for more than a century before been regarded as beings of an inferior order, and altogether unfit to associate with the White race, either in social or political relations; and so far inferior, that they had no rights which the White man was bound to respect …
>
> (Scott v. Sandford, 1857, p. 407)

FIGURE 1.2 Dred Scott Family Photos: Eliza and Lizzie, children of Dred Scott. Below: Dred Scott and his wife, Harriet.

Credit: Wikimedia Commons

Blacksher and Guinier (2014) observed, "White supremacy, as defined by Dred Scott, was becoming the theme that white Americans would rally around to reunite citizens of the North and South" (p. 57). Taney's argument revealed how the ideology of White supremacy was commonly understood as an accepted belief. The ruling in the case, however, attempted to legalize and federalize White supremacy under the US Supreme Court (please see Appendix B, Dred Scott Case, in Support Materials www.routledge.com/9781032275000).

Slavery was an issue not only in states but also in US territories. While some White settler-colonizers did not agree with slavery, many did not want to be in a state that included Black people. In what is now Oregon, the 1843 Organic Laws addressed both concerns: banned slavery and limited the number of Black people in the territory. In the following year, 1844, a more clearly worded Black Exclusion Law continued the ban on slavery but also required Black people to leave the territory within three years. Additional exclusion laws were passed (1847, 1849), prohibiting Black people from entering or living in the territory. When statehood was granted in 1857, Oregon added Section 35 to its Bill of Rights:

> No free negro or mulatto not residing in this state at the time of the adoption of this constitution, shall come, reside or be within this state or hold any real estate, or make any contracts, or maintain any suit therein; and the legislative assembly shall provide by penal laws for the removal by public officers of all such negroes and mulattoes, and for their effectual exclusion from the state, and for the punishment of persons who shall bring them into the state, or employ or harbor them.
>
> *(Section 35, Bill of Rights of the State of Oregon)*

The Civil War ended all such Exclusion Laws, yet the indignity of enslavement for Black people continued, as did efforts to retain White supremacy as Bryan Stevenson observed:

> the true evil of American slavery was the narrative we created to justify it. They made up this ideology of white supremacy that cannot be reconciled with our Constitution, that cannot be reconciled with a commitment to fair and just treatment of all peoples. They made it up so they could feel comfortable while enslaving other people … [S]lavery didn't end in 1865, it just evolved.
>
> *(quoted in Chotiner, 2020, n.p.)*

Anti-Black Literacy Laws

Black children in Boston, Massachusetts, had access to literacy and attended public schools with White children. They faced racial harassment and "physical and emotional discrimination that led to the creation in 1798 of the Smith School, a private school for Blacks" (Browne-Marshall, 2013, p. 20). Sarah Paul

(1809–1841) was born to free Black parents, the Reverend Thomas Paul and Catherine Waterhouse Paul, a teacher. Like her parents, she valued education and taught at two neighborhood primary schools, Boston Primary School No. 6 and Abiel Smith School. She was a stalwart supporter of the anti-slavery movement and made a special effort to inform her students about Black chattel enslavement and the abolitionist movement (Blain, 2022; the National Park Service, 2022).

Later, in 1850, a lawsuit was brought against the City of Boston's School Committee by printer Benjamin F. Roberts on behalf of his five-year-old daughter, Sarah. In the *Roberts v. Boston* (1850) case, the plaintiffs argued she should be permitted to attend the White school near their home. Chief Justice, Lemuel Shaw, however, ruled in favor of the Boston School Committee, by suggesting how people perceive racial differences are "not created by law, and probably cannot be changed by law" (Massachusetts Historical Society, 1848, n.p.). The case, however, was used as a legal precedent to justify unequal access to education for Black students (Browne-Marshall, 2013).

In most of the country, slave codes included anti-literacy customs, laws, and traditions that set a pattern for denying literacy access to Black people. White enslavers were aware of the liberating effect of literacy and severely limited access and opportunity to acquire literacy. Goodell quoted an unnamed legislator from 1832 who summarized the prevailing reasoning to establish these laws:

> It was well reported in the abolitionist press: "We have, as for as possible, closed every avenue by which light might enter their [the slaves'] minds. If we could extinguish the capacity to see the light, our work would be completed; they would then be on a level with the beasts of the field, and we should be safe! Denying education to an entire race was indeed an attempt to reduce its members to 'a level with the beasts of the field.'"
>
> *(quoted in Monaghan, 1998, p. 323)*

As Black people endured the horrors and mistreatment of chattel slavery, they were "characterized as less-than-human, intellectually and morally inferior to White people, and without independent actions or thoughts" (Willis, 2022, n.p.). Nonetheless, Black people learned to read and write: "literacy *was* more than a symbol of freedom; it was freedom. It affirmed their humanity, their personhood. To be able to read and right was … a mighty weapon in the slave's struggle for freedom" (T. Perry, 2003, p. 13, emphasis in the original). Douglass (1845) recalled how Mr. Auld scolded his wife once he learned she was teaching Douglass to read, "a nigger should know nothing but to obey his master — to do as he is told to do. Learning would spoil the best nigger in the world" (p. 47). Douglass recalled,

> If you teach that nigger (speaking of myself) how to read, there would be no keeping him. It would forever unfit him to be a slave. He would at once become unmanageable, and of no value to his master. As to himself,

it could do him no good, but a great deal of harm. It would make him discontented and unhappy.

(p. 47)

David Walker's (1829) *Appeal to the Colored Citizens of the World* was among the reasons given for a rush of anti-literacy laws (McHenry, 1996). Several states passed laws specifically prohibiting the teaching of reading; others prohibited the teaching of writing. Moreover, earlier anti-literacy laws were revised to prohibit the teaching of literacy to enslaved Black people.

Enslaved Black people brought a unique understanding to literacy acquisition: "while learning to read was an individual achievement, it was fundamentally a communal act ... literacy was something to share" (T. Perry, 2003, p. 14). Learning to read and write became a collective effort among Black people, and when one person learned to read and write, no matter how minimally, it was shared with others. Black people who were literate read to others as well as taught one another to read and write. Francis E. W. Harper (1825–1911), a poet, captured the desire to learn to read in her poem:

> ...
> Our masters always tried to hide
> Book learning from our eyes;
> Knowledge did'nt agree with slavery—
> 'Twould make us all too wise.
> But some of us would try to steal
> A little from the book.
> And put the words together,
> And learn by hook or crook.
> *(F. E. W. Harper, 1893)*

Harper was born to free Black parents in Philadelphia, and she became an abolitionist, activist, author, lecturer, and poet. She poignantly captured the inhumanity of enslavement in her poem "Slave Auction," describing defenseless Black people (men, women, and children), couples, and families who, again, were mercilessly torn apart. After enduring the lingering trauma of the transatlantic voyage – forcibly removed from their cultures, families, and way of life – people constantly fought to reunite with their families, searching for and posting ads in local newspapers, seeking to reunite with their family members.

In a unique tactic, Hannah and Mary Townsend, Quaker sisters and members of the Philadelphia Female Anti-Slavery Society, wrote and published the *Anti-slavery Alphabet* in 1846. The book was displayed as part of a fair to raise funding for the abolitionist cause. Sledge (2008) recorded it as one of two published books during the antebellum period and proffered the abolitionist's alphabet "was a clever strategy ... to convert the next generation of citizens and potential activists at a very young age and connecting to reading" (p. 69). She observed the books were written in the abolitionist style focusing on the "horrors of slavery and the abuses of slaveholders" (p. 73). Abolitionist literature was written for an audience of White people, not for Black enslaved people, the primary audience of this book was young impressionable White children although the adult readers were also likely to be informed. Sledge (2008) acknowledged the irony in young White children learning to read about the horrors of enslavement, while Black enslaved people about whom they read were prohibited from learning to read and write. She also recognized that Black people envisaged literacy as a source of physical and psychological freedom (please see Figure 1.3).

Anti-literacy laws were enacted in Alabama (1831, 1832), Georgia (1770, 1829, 1833), North Carolina (1818, 1830, 1835), South Carolina (1740), and Virginia (1819, 1832) (see Table 1.1). Anti-literacy laws were enacted for several reasons: to portray enslaved Black people as unhuman, retain chattel slavery and increase White people's economic wealth, retain power in the hands of White people, and curtail violent revolt. On April 12, 1860, Senator Jefferson Davis

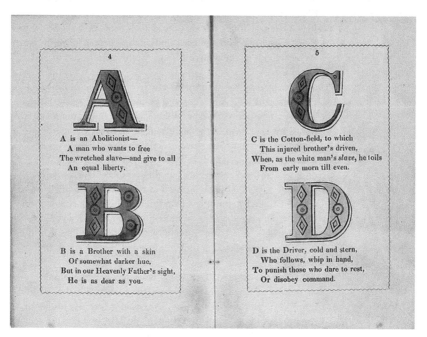

FIGURE 1.3 The Anti-Slavery Alphabet.

Credit: Wikimedia Commons

TABLE 1.1 Anti-Black Literacy Laws and Statutes

Colonies/States	Legislation
South Carolina (1740)	Whereas, the having slaves taught to write, or suffering them to be employed in writing, may be attended with great inconveniences; Be it enacted, that all and every person and persons whatsoever, who shall hereafter teach or cause any slave or slaves to be taught to write, or shall use or employ any slave as a scribe, in any manner of writing whatsoever, hereafter taught to write, every such person or persons shall, for every such offense, forfeit the sum of one hundred pounds, current money.
Georgia Literacy Law (1770, 1829, 1833)	Sec. 11. And be it further enacted, That if any slave, negro, or free person of colour, or any white person, shall teach any other slave, negro, or free person of colour, to read or write either written or printed characters, the said free person of colour or slave shall be punished by fine and whipping, or fine or whipping at the discretion of the court; and if a white person so offending, he, she, or they shall be punished with fine, not exceeding five hundred dollars, and imprisonment in the common jail at the discretion of the court before whom said offender is tried.
North Carolina (1818, 1830, 1831, 1835)	AN ACT TO PREVENT ALL PERSONS FROM TEACHING SLAVES TO READ OR WRITE, THE USE OF FIGURES EXCEPTED Whereas the teaching of slaves to read and write, has a tendency to excite dis-satisfaction in their minds, and to produce insurrection and rebellion, to the manifest injury of the citizens of this State: Therefore, I. Be it enacted by the General Assembly of the State of North Carolina, and it is hereby enacted by the authority of the same, That any free person, who shall hereafter teach, or attempt to teach, any slave within the State to read or write, the use of figures excepted, or shall give or sell to such slave or slaves any books or pamphlets, shall be liable to indictment in any court of record in this State having jurisdiction thereof, and upon conviction, shall, at the discretion of the court, if a white man or woman, be fined not less than one hundred dollars, nor more than two hundred dollars, or imprisoned; and if a free person of color, shall be fined, imprisoned, or whipped, at the discretion of the court, not exceeding thirty nine lashes, nor less than twenty lashes. II. Be it further enacted, That if any slave shall hereafter teach, or attempt to teach, any other slave to read or write, the use of figures excepted, he or she may be carried before any justice of the peace, and on conviction thereof, shall be sentenced to receive thirty nine lashes on his or her bare back. III. Be it further enacted, That the judges of the Superior Courts and the justices of the County Courts shall give this act in charge to the grand juries of their respective counties.

(Continued)

TABLE 1.1 (Continued)

Colonies / States	Legislation
Virginia (1819, 1832)	"That all meetings or assemblages of slaves, or free negroes or mulattoes mixing and associating with such slaves at any meeting-house or houses, &c., in the night; or at any schools or schools for teaching them reading or writing, either in the day or night, under whatsoever pretext, shall be deemed and considered an unlawful assembly; and any justice of a county, &c., wherein such assemblage shall be, either from his own knowledge or the information of others, of such unlawful assemblage, &c., may issue his warrant, directed to any sworn officer or officers, authorizing him or them to enter the house or houses where such unlawful assemblages, &c., may be, for the purpose of apprehending or dispersing such slaves, and to inflict corporal punishment on the offender or offenders, at the discretion of any justice of the peace, not exceeding twenty lashes."
Missouri Literacy Law (1819, 1847)	Be it enacted by the General Assembly of the State of Missouri, as follows: 1. No person shall keep or teach any school for the instruction of negroes or mulattoes, in reading or writing, in this State.
Alabama (1821, 1831, 1832, 1833)	"[S31] Any person who shall attempt to teach any free person of color, or slave, to spell, read or write, shall upon conviction thereof by indictment, be fined in a sum of not less than two hundred fifty dollars, nor more than five hundred dollars."

argued, in part, "this Government was not founded by negroes nor for negroes … but by white men and for white men" (p. 1682), before voting against tax dollars to support public education.

Despite state laws and local customs, several slave narratives provided autobiographical details of enslaved people being taught to read and write by abolitionists, a benevolent White person, or free or enslaved Black people. As more Black people learned to read and write and as they taught other Black people, literacy among Black people spread and was shared with those who were illiterate so the Black community could thrive.

The Civil War was a turning point in the US history for Black people. President Lincoln, who in debates with Stephen A. Douglas expressed White supremacist ideas, met frequently with Frederick Douglass. As Lincoln began to question his assumptions about Black people and slavery, he abandoned plans to deport Black people to Haiti and Liberia. Douglass (1864) was unrelenting in his pursuit of racial justice, as he observed (much like Haynes, 1776) the Declaration of Independence was not extended to Black people and (much like D. Walker, 1829) the US Constitution was broken. He declared the Civil War was "an Abolition war" (para 13). Speaking after the war, in his second inaugural address, Lincoln (1865) observed:

Ye, if God wills that it continue until all the wealth piled by the bonds-man's two hundred and fifty years of unrequited toil shall be sunk, and until every drop of blood drawn by the lash shall be paid by another drawn with the sword, as was said three thousand years ago, so still it must be said, "The judgments of the Lord are true and righteous altogether."

(para 5)

Following the Civil War, the education of Black people was debated in Congress and federal support of Black education was extended to Black people living in Washington, DC.

The state of Missouri, in 1865, passed an emancipation resolution freeing all enslaved Black people in the state. Sheals (2018) described the history of the Neosho Colored School (1872–1891) founded in Neosho, Missouri, after the state required all students be educated. Now a historic landmark, the school was attended (1876–1878) by George Washington Carver (1864–1943), before pursuing additional education. Once literate, Black people often taught other enslaved people to read and write, some of whom wrote slave narratives about their experiences, although some slave narratives were orally dictated and others were written by White imposters. Typically, slave narratives (a) had to be authenticated by Whites and (b) were tempered as to not offend Whites, while appealing to abolition. Harriet Jacobs (1813–1897) narrative, *Incidents in the Life of a Slave Girl: Written by Herself* (1861),

replicates a pattern within slave narratives meant to endear the reader to (a) the plight of the enslaved Black women, (b) a description of the horrors of slavery, (c) temperate descriptions of sexual abuse, (d) pacification of White guilt and sensibilities, (e) a strong pronouncement of Christian beliefs, and (f) the importance and value of literacy.

(Willis et al., 2022, p. 25)

Being literate allowed Black enslaved people to challenge the hypocrisy of US laws denying Black people citizenship status and equal rights.

Federal Laws: Redefining Citizenship, Equality, and Literacy Rights

After the Civil War (1861–1865), Civil Rights Laws (1866, 1875) were adopted but not without controversy. President Andrew Johnson in March of 1866 vetoed a draft of the Civil Rights Law, arguing it would:

establish for the security of the colored race safeguards which go indefi-nitely beyond any that the General Government has ever provided for the white race. In fact, the distinction of race and color is by the bill made to operate in favor of the colored against the white race. They interfere with the municipal legislation of the States; with relations existing exclusively between a State and its citizens, or between inhabitants of the same State; an absorption and assumption of power by the General Government which, if acquiesced in, must sap and destroy our federative system of limited power, and break down the barriers which preserve the rights of the States.

(n.p.)

His statement supported White supremacy recognizing that the needs of Black people, post-Civil War should not extend beyond the needs of White people. The Civil Rights Act (1866) sought equality, i.e., equal rights under the law, 42 U.S.C. §1981, to protect formerly enslaved Black people from economic and legal exclusions. A revised version was passed in April of 1866 when Johnson disregarded hundred years of Black chattel enslavement and sought to please White Southern politicians, by including the needs of White people in the law. The decision created a legal precedent, whereby the federal government envisaged support of Black equality as an affront to White superiority; thus, any provision for the needs of Black people also had to include accommodations for White people, whereby White people received a preponderance of available funds, goods, land, and services.

The Civil War recognized the abhorrent and inhumane chattel slavery foisted upon Black people, and the Civil War amendments (13, 14, 15) – to some degree – were a legal response to denounce and criminalize chattel enslavement. Following the Civil War, despite the promise of equality, land, and voting rights, Black people were not given 40 acres and a mule, endured the never-ending sharecropping system that often cheated Black people out of their land and wages, and were denied the right to vote. The original Homestead Act (1862), signed into law by President Lincoln, granted land to US citizens (White people) and immigrants to the United States who had been naturalized. Later, the Civil War Amendments granted citizenship status to Black people, who were then eligible to purchase land under the Homestead Act. Anti-Black racism, however, barred land acquisition for Black people yet simultaneously served as a windfall for White people and immigrants who freely amassed millions of acres of US land as they displaced Native Americans. The enforcement of the Act was marred by anti-Black racism, and a second Homestead Act (1866) conveyed free land for homesteaders in the Southern United States. The land giveaway displaced Native Americans and was largely consumed by millions of White US citizens and immigrants and a few thousand Black people (please see Appendix C, Civil War Amendments, page 277).

The Civil War Amendments (Thirteenth, Fourteenth, and Fifteenth) provided opportunities for the federal government to create a nation where all citizens had equal rights under the law, but such was not the case. The Thirteenth Amendment abolished slavery, although in many states, servitude continued to exist in different forms. In part, because of an "exception clause:" "Neither slavery nor involuntary servitude, except as a punishment for crime whereof the party shall have been duly convicted, shall exist within the United States, or any place subject to their jurisdiction" (n.p.). The Fourteenth Amendment defined equal rights, due process, and citizenship, along with greater access to schooling/literacy for Black people. And the Fifteenth Amendment extended voting rights to Black men who previously had been denied the right to vote. The 1875 Civil Rights Act stated that all men were created equal before the law and had equal access to public places and facilities such as restaurants and public transportation; however, it was ruled unconstitutional and overturned by the US Supreme Court in 1883. Some states and locales did not accept or enforce the constitutional amendments and Civil Rights Laws, thereby creating an ever-revolving set of new laws.

Black Literacy Rights Arise

During Reconstruction, several agencies worked at the federal and state levels to extend literacy access: the American Missionary Association (AMA) and the Bureau of Refugees, Freedmen, and Abandoned Lands (Freedmen's Bureau). The latter was established by Congress under the Freedmen's Bureau Acts (1865–1866) and was initially designed to address the needs of newly freed Black people. The agencies shared a focus on literacy, "to meet their [Black people's] economic, educational, political, and social obligations and construct a barrier to further exploitation" (Cabral, 2006, p. 13). A revised act on July 25, 1868 (15 Stat. 193), included chapter 22, Section 12, and directed the "seizure of land for educational buildings and the education of formerly enslaved people and "the education of their citizens without distinction of color" (p. 176). This latter portion of the statement, "citizens without distinction of color," was added after earlier versions had been vetoed by President Johnson because they did not benefit White people. The replacement of racialized language with ambiguous language was meant to convey an intended meaning, one that was necessary to describe and set a precedent whereby – despite the oppression of formerly enslaved Black people for centuries – all rights they were previously denied were now available only if they included the care and education of White people (as other racial groups were not considered citizens). Section 13 directed the Commissioner "to co-operate with private benevolent associations in aid of freedmen, &c.; to provide buildings and furnish teachers and protection" (p. 176). President Andrew Johnson signed these Acts and was unapologetic in his desire to appease Southern Whites, as he did not want to appear solely focused on the needs of Black people. His intentional decision-making codified a federal government pattern to provide redress for Black people, only if White people also were accommodated first and foremost, irrespective of whether provisions manifested for Black people.

Among the Freedmen's Bureau teachers was Charlotte (Forten) Grimke, a poet and published author. She taught at St. Helena Island in South Carolina, in the late 1800s, and published excerpts of her journal in the *Atlantic* in 1861. Of paramount importance to her was sharing the accomplishments of Black people: "I told them about Toussaint, thinking it well they should know what one of their own color had done for his race. They listened attentively, and seemed to understand" (Forten, 1861, para 15). Alvord, a Freedmen's Bureau superintendent in 1866, appeared to confirm her observations when he wrote about the zeal among Black people to learn, especially to learn to read:

1. They have the natural thirst for knowledge common to all men.
2. They have seen power and influence among white people, always coupled with *learning* – it is the sign of elevation to which they now aspire.
3. Its mysteries, hitherto hidden from them in written literature, excite them to the special study of books.
4. Their freedom has given wonderful stimulus to *all efforts*, indicating a vitality which augurs well for their whole future condition and character.

(quoted in Quarles, 1969, p. 124)

Acquiring literacy led to increased knowledge, and Black people believed literacy was "the most significant weapon to ward off deliberate, calculated, and dehumanizing confrontations with the White power structure and members of the local White community who attempted to take advantage of the Blacks' lack of basic literacy skills" (Cabral, 2006, p. 14). Dalton (1991) also noted how anti-Black literacy was entangled within Black people's enslavement and debates about extending literacy evolved from questions about whether Black people could become literate to whether it was advisable that Black people obtain literacy to whether literacy acquisition was a *"necessity"* for Blacks and *"urgency"* for Black people to acquire literacy (p. 546). Black schools were routinely burned to intimidate and terrorize Black people as well as to destroy access to education. Literacy was weaponized to deny Black people's humanity, to thwart recording inhumanity under enslavement, and to deny citizenship and voting rights.

The life of William Edward Burghardt Du Bois (1868–1963), born to Alfred Du Bois and Mary Burghardt Du Bois in Great Barrington, Massachusetts, traced his genological roots to Haiti and West Africa, provides an example of the power of literacy. In his small town, all students, Black and White, attended the same local public school from which he graduated and where he was valedictorian of his class. Following his secondary education and the death of his mother, local White people financially supported his education at Fisk University. After graduation with a BS, he was later admitted to Harvard as a junior, where he excelled and graduated *cum laude* in 1890. He became the first Black person to earn a doctorate in 1895, and his dissertation, *The Suppression of the African Slave-Trade to the United States of America, 1638–1870*, was an exemplary text.

Du Bois's (1996) *Souls of Black Folk* (originally published in 1903) presented an analysis of the Civil War years, Civil War amendments, and legislation as well as a discussion of the ideologies informing politics and actions of White people, from a Black perspective. His essay, Of the Dawn of the Nation, articulated, "an account of that government of men called the Freedmen's Bureau, one of the most singular and interesting of the attempts made by a great nation to grapple with vast problems of race and social condition" (Du Bois, 1996, p. 7). Although he also acknowledged that after the Civil War

> former slaves were intimidated, beaten, raped, and butchered by angry and revengeful men … almost every law and method ingenuity could devise was employed by the legislatures to reduce the Negroes to serfdom, to make them the slaves of the State, if not of individual owners.
>
> *(p. 15)*

Du Bois's essay provided a discussion of the contexts and events surrounding the founding and failure of the Freedom's Bureau, from the position of a Black person. He admitted the unrealistic expectations placed on a single bureaucratic agency to address the needs of thousands of Black people who, after two centuries of being held under enslavement, were suddenly freed. He observed,

> the greatest success of the Freedmen's Bureau lay in the planting of the free school among Negroes, and the idea of free elementary education among all classes in the South. It not only called the school mistresses through the benevolent agencies and built them schoolhouses.
>
> *(Du Bois, 1996, p. 14)*

He also acknowledged that their freedom required a change in the dominant notions of White superiority, an economic shift away from a free source of labor, a societal acceptance of Black people as human who could not be treated as property, and a political necessity of finding a way to uphold the legal rights of Black people.

Despite the passage of Civil Rights Laws and Civil War Amendments, formerly enslaved Black people did not enjoy all the freedoms and liberties of the nation. In 1870, a Civil Rights Act was introduced to Congress, granting unrestricted access to accommodations, permission to serve on juries, and adjudication of violations of the law in federal court, irrespective of the ethnicity and race of people. The Act was stalled as members of Congress fiercely debated portions of the bill and the parameters between federal and state courts; thus, with some changes, a bill was passed on March 1, 1875:

> That all persons within the jurisdiction of the United States shall be entitled to the full and equal enjoyment of the accommodations, advantages, facilities, and privileges of inns, public conveyances on land or water, theaters, and other places of public amusement; subject only to the conditions and limitations established by law, and applicable alike to citizens of every race and color, regardless of any previous condition of servitude. ...
>
> ... that any person denied access to these facilities on account of race would be entitled to monetary restitution under a federal court of law.

The changes to the original Act included retaining school segregation and a state's right to determine the composition of jury members. In 1893, the US Supreme Court ruled the Act as unconstitutional. These changes foreshadowed the Black Codes, laws created to deny Black people full rights under the Constitution (Finkelman, 2011). Black Codes reconstituted the ideology of White supremacy reinstated customs and traditions among White people who believed they should have the power to control the lives of Black people, legally, morally, politically, and socially. Individual states wrote new state constitutions; for instance, the Florida Constitution (1885) criminalized White and Black students from attending the same school. It was revised in 1895 and extended crimes to include Black and White students from being taught in the same classroom and by the same teacher.

White Resentment and Retrenchment

Among the most ardent supporters of the racial segregation and the oversight of education for White children were the United Daughters of the Confederacy and the Preservation of Confederate Culture. Founded in 1894, the membership grew to over 100,000 White women from across the nation in support of a multi-prong approach to uphold White supremacy and the Confederacy. One of their most enduring efforts was their quest to portray the history of the Civil War by (a) discounting all other histories, (b) valorizing and memorializing White Confederate generals and White Southern culture, (c) ignoring anti-Black racism and minimizing the centuries for which Black people endured chattel enslavement, and (d) indoctrinating school children through curricula and textbooks to believe their version of the history of the Civil War. Although the physical war had ended, another was being advanced by Southerners, known as the Lost Cause narrative, as a war for the hearts, minds, and memories, that romanticized the Confederacy, plantation life, and chattel enslavement. Mildred L. Rutherford (1851–1928) was born in Athens, Georgia, to a political, privileged, and Southern White family who were Confederates and enslavers and held an unwavering belief in White supremacy. Her life exemplified a woman's role during the Confederacy and the Lost Cause, as she founded a local United Daughters of the Confederacy (UDC) chapter, where she was the chapter's historian. Later, she served as the UDC historian for Georgia and the national organization, where she championed the "Lost Cause" (an attempt to rewrite and valorize the Civil War by Southern White people). The UDC took their mission to classrooms, curriculum decisions of school boards, and their plight to state legislatures to control the narrative about the Confederacy.

Rutherford was a former classroom teacher and lecturer who wrote articles, books, pamphlets, and textbooks and sought to rewrite history from the perspective of White Southerners as maligned and misunderstood heroes. She presented her thoughts extensively through lectures and presentations, sharing her belief that the cause of the Civil War was not slavery, "but a different and direct opposite view as to the danger of the government of the United States" (quoted in Case 2002, p. 16). Her interpretation of Civil War history was presented at colleges, libraries, schools and universities, and institutions were encouraged to adopt her guidelines for book selections found in *A Measuring Rod to Test Textbooks, and Reference Books* (Rutherford, 1920):

> The Committee charged, as it is, with the dissemination of the truths of Confederate history, earnestly and fully and officially, approve all that is herein so truthfully written as to that eventful period.
>
> The Committee respectfully urges all authorities charged with the selection of text-books for colleges, schools and all scholastic institutions to measure all books offered for adoption by this "Measuring Rod" and adopt none which do not accord full justice to the South. ... And all library authorities in the Southern States are requested to mark all books in their collections which do not come up to the same measure, on the title page there of, "Unjust to the South." This Committee further asks all scholastic and library authorities, in all parts of the country, in justice and fairness to their fellow citizens of the South, to yield to the above request.
>
> *(paras 1 and 2)*

Her beliefs are strikingly like contemporary arguments about the government as she claimed the illegitimacy of the government's documents and voting rights that followed; Rutherford wanted to "justify the extensive segregation and disenfranchisement laws passed by southern state legislators and the 1890s and early 1900s in direct violation in the 14th and 15th Amendments … also the plantation system and slavery" (Case, 2002, p. 610). All school children read and were indoctrinated into a mythical version of US history, in which the lives of White Southern insurrectionists were romanticized.

The US Supreme Court Upholds Anti-Black Racism

Among the most significant events of the period was the *Plessy v. Ferguson* (1898) case, occurring less than 50 years after the *Scott v. Sanford* case. The case began with the Louisiana Separate Car Act (1890), which required Black people to sit in separate cars from White people. Homer Plessy believed he was legally permitted to sit in the White section because he claimed he was 7/8s White. In a landmark Supreme Court decision, the Court ruled – despite the Civil Rights Act of 1875, racial segregation was constitutionally legal, under the "separate but equal" doctrine. Justice Brown argued, "a statute which implies merely a legal distinction between the white and colored races has no tendency to destroy the legal equality of the two races, or reestablish a state of involuntary servitude" (p. 543). He added, the Fourteenth Amendment was not written "to enforce the absolute equality of the two races before the law," because the amendment "could not have been intended to abolish distinction based upon color, or to enforce social, as distinguished from political, equality, or a commingling of the two races upon terms unsatisfactory to either" (p. 544). The majority drew from the Roberts case and ruled:

> [The] establishment of separate schools for white and colored children … has been [deemed] a valid exercise of the legislative power even by courts of States where the political rights of the colored race have been longest and most earnestly enforced.
>
> *(p. 544)*

Justice John Harlan (1896) lodged the lone dissent:

> The white race deems itself to be the dominant race in this country. And so it [is], in prestige, in achievements, in education, in wealth, and in power. So, I doubt not, it will continue to be for all time, if it remains true to its great heritage, and holds fast to the principles of constitutional liberty. But in view of the constitution, in the eye of the law, there is in this country no superior, dominant, ruling class of citizens… In respect of civil rights, all citizens are equal before the law. The humblest is the peer of the most powerful…The arbitrary separation of citizens on the

basis of race, while they are on a public highway, is a badge of servitude wholly inconsistent with the civil freedom and the equality before the law established by the Constitution. It cannot be justified upon any legal grounds.

(p. 559)

Importantly, he declared, "our Constitution is color-blind," and states should not be permitted to "regulate the enjoyment of citizens' civil rights solely on the basis of race" (p. 559). The case, nonetheless established legal racial segregation as codified and racial inequality as it privileged White people and extended extra-judicial actions against Black people. Gates (2011) succinctly summarized the lasting effects of the *Plessy* case that legalized racial segregation:

> The court cases and acts of legislation that enshrine Jim Crow as the law the land did not unfold in a vacuum. The larger context for them was the ideology of white supremacy, the set of beliefs and attitudes about the nature of black people that arose to justify their unprecedented economic exploitation and the transatlantic slave trade. Following the Civil War, this ideology evolved in order to maintain the country's racial hierarchy in the face of emancipation and black citizenship. ... white power was reinforced in this era by the nation's cultural, economic, educational, legal and violently extralegal systems, including lynching. Among its roots and branches were the ... convict-lease system, disenfranchisement, and the choking off of access to capital and property ownership. In many ways, this ideology still roams freely in our country today.
>
> *(p. 37)*

Throughout US history, federal legislation was intentionally written to obfuscate the guilty, by avoiding the use of the word "slave" to shield their complicity, although drafts of the Declaration of Independence and the Constitution mentioned the enslavement of people of African descent. As Judge Taney in the Dred Scott case admitted, people then, as now, were aware of White supremacy as they knowingly crafted documents where it would be assumed by implication.

Education for Black People

Education for Black people had always been a source of concern for White people whose preference (Slave Codes and Black Codes) was not to educate Black people. The schools constructed after the Civil War for Black students were limited and not equal to the schools for White students. Although Black people paid taxes for local schools, the funds were used in support of schools for White students (J. D. Anderson, 1988). Several schools constructed for Black students were set aflame by White people, schools were rebuilt or new schools were erected. In some areas of the country, Black people who were able to attend school attended unequally funded and ill-equipped segregated schools that were "a particular target of white terror groups" (Young, 2019, para 1). Schools for Black students were perceived as a threat to the White community; even though schools were racially segregated, "burning the black schoolhouse caused no loss for white children. Since the school had often been built through considerable sacrifice by the black community, its loss was extremely painful" (Young, 2019, para 1). The practice of burning Black schools was a violent and economically costly way to prevent the spread of education and literacy. Beyond burning schools, Black churches and entire communities were destroyed by fearful White people. The 1898 Wilmington Race Riot, for example, was not a riot. It was a strategically planned insurrection and massacre by disaffected former Confederate soldiers and White businessmen against elected Black city officials. The exact number of Black people who were killed by White murders is unknown; other Black people fled for fear as White people bombed Black churches and burned the Black community. Then, insurrectionists gained political control of the city and crafted laws that suppressed the voting rights of Black men. Their efforts are recognized, sadly, as the only successful coup d'état in the United States.

The doctrine of "separate but equal" was upheld for 50 years at the expense of Black people who believed in the promise of equal protection, due process, and the rights of citizenship under the Constitution. Considering the ruling individual states seized upon the opportunity to revise their constitutions, for instance, the 1901 Virginia Constitution codified anti-Black racism as well as voting rights, as articulated by State Chairman, J. Taylor Ellyson:

> The best men in this Commonwealth have been selected as the representatives of their people in the Convention. They will not fail to be responsive to the wishes of their constituents, for every Democrat in that convention, knows that the convention would never have been held but for the desire of the white people of this Commonwealth to have enacted such a constitutional provision as would take away from the negro the right to vote, and at the same time preserve to the white men of the Commonwealth their right of suffrage.
>
> *(Ellyson, Goode, & Montague, 1901, pp. 32–33)*

The Virginia Constitution also legalized poll taxes (*Article II*), required literacy tests for voting (*Section 19. 4*), and mandated separate schools for Black and White students (*Section 140*). Of importance is the wording of *Section 19.4*, the literacy test was given to determine if a:

person [was] able to read any section of this Constitution submitted to him by the officers of registration and to give a reasonable explanation of the same; or, if unable to read, such section, able to understand and give a reasonable explanation thereof when read to him by the officers.

Under Jim/Jane Crow (1870–1950), Black people remained economically, politically, and socially oppressed because of racially discriminatory education laws and disenfranchisement.

Anti-Black Racial Violence and Black Resistance

Anti-Black racism underpinned White anger, crimes, and violence against Black people as businesses, churches, homes, and schools were destroyed by vigilante White mobs. Among the most horrific were in Detroit, Michigan (1863), the burning of Black businesses and homes; the massacre of Black people at a picnic in Clinton, Mississippi (1875); the massacre of an untold number of Black people in Wilmington, North Carolina (1898); the killing of hundreds of Black children, men, and women in East St. Louis, Missouri (1917), after which thousands of Black people left the area; and the race massacre of "Black Wall Street" in Tulsa, Oklahoma (1919), with a left an immeasurable loss of Black lives and livelihoods. For example, there was the horrific use of bombs dropped by airplanes, the burning of the Greenwood (Black) district, and the indiscriminate murders of Black people as captured by attorney B. C. Franklin (in a recently transcribed 10-page essay housed in the National Museum of African American History and Culture, (2022). Nearly each of these events allegedly began with a story about a Black man assaulting, hurting, molesting, or raping a White female, "causing" White men to protect their women, selves, and livelihoods by killing Black people. Most often, lynchings and massacres were whitewashed in the White press as race riots; however, the Black press described mobs of White people killing Black people as murderers. And, reported the lack of justice, as seldom were White people prosecuted, and when they were, they were found not guilty by all-White juries.

Throughout this era, Black people continued their fight for equality and freedom, publishing articles to correct misrepresented descriptions of lynchings in Black-owned newspapers. Ida B. Wells-Barnett (1862–1931), born enslaved, later a teacher and a journalist, for instance, wrote extensively about the lynching of Black people in the United States. She worked for a newspaper in Memphis, TN, before starting her own newspaper, *The Free Speech*; however, it was burned by White people (McNamara, 2020, para 7). Wells-Barnett was a fearless author, civil rights activist, investigative journalist, lecturer, and suffragist, who exemplifies such heroism. She was an outspoken critic of anti-Black racism whose lifework included exposing the hypocrisy at the core of American's vision of itself. How could the so-called land of the free be somewhere that saw the lynchings of countless Black people? How could a country that called itself a world leader be so far behind others in the treatment of women?

(Duster, 2021, p. 2)

She fought against Jim/Jane Crow laws and racial segregation as she traveled throughout the country lecturing and publishing numerous influential articles, exposing thousands of lynchings of Black people throughout the United States, and noting mobs of White people were not held accountable. Wells-Barnett also lobbied Congress for an anti-lynching federal law but was unsuccessful in her attempt. She was one of the co-founders of the National Association for the Advancement of Colored People (NAACP) and posthumously was awarded a Pulitzer Prize Special Citation in 2020, for her investigative journalism and activism (Duster, 2021).

Lynchings of Black people were public events advertised by White people and people were invited to attend, as well illustrated by postcards, photographs, and reported in newspapers. Alternatively, Black people and White allies resisted lynchings as in a poem by Lewis Allen, aka Abel Meeropol (1937), a Jewish school teacher from the Bronx who depicted lynched Black people as Southern trees bearing 'bitter fruit' (later called strange fruit). He wrote and composed the musical version sang by Billie Holiday in 1939.

Brothers James Weldon Johnson (1871–1938) and John Rosamond Johnson (1873–1954), born in Virginia to free Black parents, James and Helen Dillet Johnson, also put a poem to music. They attended the Edwin McMasters Stanton School, a free public school for Black students in Jacksonville, FL. Their mother was their first teacher at the school, and later James was named the school's principal. He wrote a poem to commemorate Abraham Lincoln's birthday in 1900 and, working with his brother, John, the poem, *Lift Every Voice and Sing*, was set to music to be sung by the elementary school children at Stanton. The popularity of the song spread, and it was soon referenced as the Negro National anthem.

Lift every voice and sing
Till earth and heaven ring
Ring with the harmonies of Liberty
Let our rejoicing rise
High as the listening skies
Let it resound loud as the rolling sea
Sing a song full of the faith that the dark past has taught us
Sing a song full of the hope that the present has brought us
Facing the rising sun of our new day begun
Let us march on till victory is won
Stony the road we trod

Bitter the chastening rod
Felt in the days when hope unborn had died
Yet with a steady beat
Have not our weary feet
Come to the place for which our fathers sighed?
We have come over a way that with tears has been watered
We have come, treading our path through the blood of the slaughtered
Out from the gloomy past
Till now we stand at last
Where the white gleam of our bright star is cast
God of our weary years
God of our silent tears
Thou who has brought us thus far on the way
Thou who has by Thy might Led us into the light
Keep us forever in the path, we pray
Lest our feet stray from the places, our God, where we met Thee
Lest, our hearts drunk with the wine of the world, we forget Thee
Shadowed beneath Thy hand
May we forever stand
True to our God
True to our native land
Our native land

Imani Perry's (2018) history of the song referred to the poem/song as "our common thread" (p. xiii), a "procession toward liberation" (p. 19), and a "collective resilience as well as devotion" (p. 20). James W. Johnson called it a "hymn for Negro people" (p. 20, quoted in I. Perry), as many Black people were linked in their remembrances of singing the song, in times past, present, and times yet to come. I. Perry also observed, the song allows "the singer to see herself or himself as emerging. Magnificently through struggle. It nurtures an identity rooted in community. … It was and is the song of a people, *my* people" (p. xiv, italics in the original). Further, she noted the song reflects the lives of Black people throughout the diaspora.

Three decades later, Carter G. Woodson, a fearless advocate for Black people, fought for freedom through education, lectures, and writing. Among his publications was the *Negro History Bulletin* (1937b), in which he shared news within the Black community, accomplishments, educational changes, and historical facts about the contributions Black people made in the United States. For example, he described Lemuel Haynes's popularity among White Christians in New England and the daring escape from enslavement of William and Ellen Craft. The anti-Black literacy efforts of the past failed to stop Black people from creating literature (novels, poems, and short stories) to express their daily lives, joys, and sorrows; genres of music (Black folk, blues, country, jazz, and swing) to soothe their souls; as well as reported incidents of anti-Black racism in articles, essays, histories, and newspapers to ensure an accurate record of Black accomplishments and experiences and miscarriages of justice. These written documents importantly provided a more accurate and positive portrayal of the lives of Black people as accomplished, courageous, creative, hardworking, human, generous, intelligent, loved, and valued.

Brown v. Board of Education of Topeka, Kansas (1954, 1955)

After 50 years of overt anti-Black racism under Jim/Jane Crow laws of legal racial segregation, a new era appeared to unfold in the landmark case of *Brown v. Board of Education of Topeka, Kansas (1954, 1955)*. The Brown family was part of a class-action lawsuit brought by aggrieved parents on behalf of their Black children who were forced to attend segregated schools. Much like the Roberts case, the parents of Linda Brown, a first grader, joined a class-action suit challenging the law requiring their daughter to walk a considerable distance from her home to attend a Black school. The psychological trauma inflicted on Black children who attended segregated schools appeared to be a key component of the Brown case (Browne-Marshall, 2013). The plaintiffs sought relief of segregated schooling based on their interpretation of the Fourteenth Amendment, arguing there are extreme differences in educational opportunities and physical facilities between Black and White schools (Supp. 797—Dist. Court, D. Kansas, 1951). The US Supreme Court unanimously passed *Brown*, ruling a violation of the equal protection clause of the Fourteenth Amendment. The Court claimed, education:

> … is a principal instrument and awakening the child to cultural values, preparing him for later professional training, and in helping him adjust normally. It is doubtful that any child may reasonably be expected to succeed in life if he is denied that opportunity of an education. Such an opportunity of an education. Such an opportunity, where the state has undertaken to provide it, is it right which must be made available for all on equal terms.
>
> *(Brown I, 1954, page 493)*

The US Supreme Court's ruling of a violation of the equal protection clause thus dismantled the doctrine of "separate but equal." Chief Justice Warren declared, "In the field of public education, the doctrine of 'separate but equal' has no place. Separate facilities are inherently unequal" (*Brown v. Board of Education I*, 1954, p. 495). The implementation of *Brown* hinged not only on federal law but also on the willingness of state and local officials to enforce the law, which was not immediately forthcoming. *Brown II* (*Brown v. Board of Education II* 349 US 294, 1955) was argued before the Court because the notion of "all deliberate speed" was an imprecise demand. At state and local levels, school districts did not rush to comply with the law, trying various ways to subvert the federal order by removing White students from public schools or moving to all-White suburbs to avoid integration; "compliance is arbitrary; … The extent to which technical legalism obfuscates and undermines the human motivations that generated our justice system is the real extent to which we as human beings are disenfranchised" (P. Williams, 1987, p. 133). Drawing on White supremacy and admonitions of "states' rights," the process to end racial discrimination in public education was undermined. Several Southern states defied the Supreme Court's ruling and refused to integrate schools. In *Cooper v. Aaron* (1958), for instance, the state of Alabama held that the Supreme Court's ruling violated the Constitution, as states were the arbiter of education. The case was dismissed: states cannot nullify or supersede federal law.

Anti-Black Racism, Voter Suppression Laws, and Literacy

For over 50 years, federal, state, and local laws upheld Jim/Jane Crow actions decimated the voting rights of Black people. The right to vote, however, remained suppressed, and literacy was weaponized as a key issue. Among the multiple tactics used to suppress Black voters were literacy tests, requiring Black people (many were illiterate due to centuries of White supremacy, anti-Black racism, and anti-literacy laws) to read text in order to vote.

Citizenship Schools

There were people, much like the abolitionist of the nineteenth century, who fought for equal rights, in this case, Black voting rights, for Black people. Septima Poinsette Clark (1898–1987), born in Charleston, SC, during the oppressive Black Codes that disenfranchised Black people, sought to assure Black people could exercise their voting rights. As a teacher and civil rights advocate, she worked with Myles Horton of Highlander Folk School and in Citizenship Schools created to teach Black adults to read and pass the state literacy tests to vote. Bernice Robinson, Septima's cousin, was hired to avoid suspicion as she was not a teacher, although she taught Black people to pass the "literacy test" required to register to vote in South Carolina. Septima and Bernice believed teaching literacy

> should not try to isolate people's learning of reading, writing, and critical thinking from the community in which they reside; the historical roots from which they follow; the language they use in defining their existence; and the politics and economics that shape and reshape their critical thinking/reflections of themselves and others.
>
> *(Peavy, 1993, p. 213)*

Black Voter Suppression

Southern politicians supported a state's right to use literacy tests as a requirement for voting; in an attempt to add a literacy requirement for federal elections, without adding a new amendment to the US Constitution, by creating S. 2750. Although states were forbidden from "requiring literacy, education, intelligence, or understanding qualifications above the level represented by a sixth-grade education" (Van Alstyne, 1963, p. 805), it was argued that the proposed legislation would extend and improve Black people's voting rights (section 2(b)):

> No person … may subject any other person to the deprivation of the right to vote in any Federal election … "Deprivation of the right to vote" shall include but shall not be limited to (1) the application to any person of standards or procedures more stringent than are applied to others similarly situated and (2) the denial to any person otherwise qualified by law of the right to vote on account of his performance in any examination, whether for literacy or otherwise, if such other person has not been adjudged incompetent and has completed the sixth primary grade of any public school or accredited school in any State …
>
> *(pp. 808–809)*

The focus of the bill was on federal voting and appeared to question the type of literacy "testing" required for voting, although people could be denied the right to vote based on the presumed level of literacy acquired by the sixth grade. The 20 states in support of the Senate Bill 2750 crafted a straw man argument, suggesting then-current laws forbidding local registers to administer literacy tests on more Black people than White people would be strengthened as only people without a sixth-grade education could be required to take a test. The proposed bill does not acknowledge that in supportive states, the percentage of Black people who had not acquired a sixth-grade education exceeded that of White people. The proposed bill would identify more Black people as ineligible to vote, although it did not rely on the register's opinion to determine the "veracity of responses was decided by the register's discretion" (Willis et al., 2022, p. 36).

The proposed bill continued Jim/Jane Crow voter suppression tactics; registers could determine functional literacy and whether some were able to "interpret complicated sections of state constitutions, to determine their age exactly in terms of years, months, and days, or to demonstrate good citizenship" (Van Alstyne, 1963, p. 821). In 1965, the Voting Rights Act was ratified, extending voting rights to all US citizens along with a set of restrictions outlined in Sections 4 and 5 and revised in 1970, 1975, and 1982 (sections were stricken in 2013, and in 2022, there remains a push to make voting rights a federal law).

Freedom Schools

The Citizenship Schools for adult literacy served as a prelude to the Freedom Schools organized by a variety of Black community, political, and student groups to improve the quality of education received by Black students in the rural South. The Freedom Schools consisted of "a network of over 40 schools served two thousand Black students in Mississippi from July–August 1964" (Willis et al., 2022, p. 38), where improving the literacy skills of students was a major component. Literacy instruction, led by Black and White teachers focused on "basic grammar, improved their reading comprehension, and used writing for expression and protest" (Willis, 2022, np). The pedagogical approach they developed was based on accepting each student as a fellow human who should be treated with dignity:

> Teachers sought to build students' self-esteem, linked cultural understandings to the curriculum, and encouraged students to use their voice to protest racial injustice. The Citizenship and Freedom Schools were grassroots efforts as well as political extensions to provide and ensure Black people had access to literacy.
>
> *(Willis, 2022, n.p.)*

The complex history of anti-Black racism and anti-Black literacy was supported and defended by US laws. It is ignored through historical amnesia or cultural erasure as it whitewashes and presents anti-Black literacy actions, customs, laws, slavery, statutes, and other race-based inequalities as minor inconveniences.

The Civil Rights Act (1964) effectively struck down Jim/Jane Crow laws and legally ensured human and civil rights were extended to all US citizens (Sec. 601; 78 Stat. 252; 42 U.S.C. 2000d). The Act was part of a multi-pronged federal socioeconomic plan implemented by President Lyndon B. Johnson. His strategy sought to link political and social reform efforts to civil rights legislation and enforcement as well as to educational reform and funding. Under this plan, the 1965 Elementary and Secondary Education Act (ESEA) was designed to work in concert with the Civil Rights Act to address racial and social inequality: "Congress would not have taken this step [passing ESEA] had Title VI [of the Civil Rights Act] not established the principle that schools receiving federal assistance must meet uniform national standards for desegregation" (US v. Jefferson Co. Bd. Of Ed., 372, E. 836, 5th Cir. 1966, cited in Frankenberg & Taylor, 2015). ESEA made possible financial support to address economic, racial, and social discrimination and created political avenues for educational access and opportunity, specifically for Black students, students living in poverty, and students with disabilities (ESEA, Sec. 201).

TABLE 1.2 Chronology of Race-based Education Legal Cases and Legislation Policies Focused on Reading Access

Legal Cases/Legislation	Legal Issues/Purpose	Findings	Rationale	Effect on Literacy
Roberts v. City of Boston (1849)	A school district denied a Black child access to a primary school because of her race, so the child's father sued the school district for illegally excluding the Black child.	The Massachusetts Supreme Court held the lawsuit could not stand against the City of Boston School District.	In the absence of special legislation, the school committee could regulate the school system including separating the races. While maintaining separate schools perpetuates the distinction of class, these prejudices are not created by law and cannot be changed by law.	Legally permitted the continued segregation of education between Black and white students, and the unequal access to literacy
Dred Scott v. Sanford (1857)	A slave living in the free state of Illinois wanted to become a citizen in that state and be entitled to all the rights, privileges, and immunities, guaranteed by the US Constitution.	The US Supreme Court held that Mr. Scott was not a US citizen, and his residence in Illinois did not change his slave status.	Blacks were property, inferior, to 3/5 of a person, so they were not accorded the rights and privileges that the US Constitution extended to naturalized citizens.	Identified and codified Black people as less than human, non-citizens, and ineligible for the rights of citizens
13th Amendment of US Constitution (1865)	The legality of slavery.	Abolished and forbade slavery.	To promote human rights.	Legally all Black people were granted citizenship, and all the rights therein.

(Continued)

Table 1.2 (Continued)

Legal Cases/Legislation	Legal Issues/Purpose	Findings	Rationale	Effect on Literacy
14th Amendment of US Constitution (1868)	Amendment required equal civil rights for all US citizens, specifically Black freedmen (former slaves).	Formally and legally provided equal protection, privileges, and rights to all Black freedmen like that of White men.	To alleviate the racism and discrimination against the newly freed slaves and support special relief and programs for blacks.	Restated the legally Black people should receive equal protection, privileges, rights.
Civil Rights Act of 1866	To provide equal rights and benefits for all citizens of every race and color, including Blacks being considered citizens and provided them with schooling, land, and housing.	The President vetoed the original bill because it provided too much to Blacks over Whites. Congress enacted part of the bill and considered all Blacks, including former slaves, to be US citizens entitled to equal rights	To alleviate the racism and discrimination against the newly freed slaves.	Legally extended the right to schooling, hence literacy access, to all citizens, including Black people.
Plessy v. Ferguson (1896)	A railroad company denied Mr. Plessy, a man of mixed race, seating in the railway car for Whites in violation of the equal protection clause of the 14th Amendment.	The US Supreme Court held that the policy and practice of separate-but-equal was constitutional and appropriate, so Mr. Plessy was properly seated in the railway car for Blacks instead of Whites. The doctrine of separate-but-equal was born.	Mr. Plessy's mixed race of 1/8 African blood and 7/8 Caucasian made him a Colored man, so Plessy was not entitled to the privileged reputation or the property right of White men. Thus, he had to sit in the railway car for Blacks.	Re-instated white supremacy into laws characterized Black people as inferior to white people. Separate and segregated education justify as 'equal'.

Brown, et al. v. Board of Education of Topeka, et al. (1954)	Whether racially segregated public schools are unequal in violation of the equal protection of the laws under the 14th Amendment.	The US Supreme Court held that in the field of public education the doctrine of separate-but-equal has no place; separate educational facilities are inherently unequal.	The segregation of White and Black children in public schools has a detrimental effect upon the Black child, and a sense of inferiority affects the motivation of a child to learn.	Legally ended racially segregated education.
Civil Rights Act of 1964	To eradicate discrimination and segregation against Blacks and other subjugated minorities as well as to eliminate economic and social oppression against minority groups.	Generally, the Act prohibits an employer or organization from discriminating against individuals because of their race, color, religion, sex, or national origin. Also, provides legal remedies for those discriminated against.	To provide equal opportunities in employment, education, housing, etc., for all US citizens.	Reinstated Black people's civil rights including the right to an equal education

Adapted from Dorsey, D. T. (2008). An examination of the legal debate regarding race-based education policies from 1849 to 1964. *The Negro Educational Review, 50*(1-2), 7-26. (Appendix, pp. 23 – 26).

2

AN OVERVIEW OF THE HISTORY OF READING RESEARCH, 1800–1999

For hundreds of years, White people created acts, codes, laws, policies, statutes, and structures to deny, limit, and prevent Black peoples' access to literacy. The history linking anti-Black racism and anti-literacy law in the United States provided context for understanding why and how anti-Black literacy laws were codified, justified, and legalized: "American history is longer, larger, more various, more beautiful, and more terrible than anything anyone has ever said about it" (Baldwin, 1963, p. 5). Anti-Black racism in the US was rampant during the antebellum period as White people, while oppressing Black people, expressed their prevailing thinking about Black people's humanity and intellect. Black people experienced emotional, physical, and psychological trauma at the hands of White people, who greatly feared the spread of literacy would lead to rebellions and the loss of free labor and income. Their fears led them to prohibit Black people from learning to read, possessing paper and writing instruments, anti-literacy laws, and burning schools to delimit the spread of literacy. After the Civil War, access to literacy increased in Black communities as schools were built and education spread. However, oppression also continued through a host of Jim/Jane Crow campaigns, policies, and schemes (double taxation, land theft, mass incarceration, voter suppression) implemented to retard Black literacy access. Anti-Black racism fueled efforts to limit literacy and retain power and control knowledge.

The racial inequities of the nineteenth century continued as Du Bois (1996) mused: "the problem of the twentieth century is the problem of the color line" (p. 7). The enslavement of Black people during the antebellum period was replaced with other forms of enslavement of Black people and the advent of Jim/Jane Crow and anti-Black racism written into state constitutions and laws, as well as practiced within local customs, policies, and statutes. The never-ending efforts to delimit Black people's access to literacy was one of the many forms of

DOI: 10.4324/9781003296188-3

oppression. Traditional histories of literacy often ignored the period with a sense of historical amnesia and failing to acknowledge anti-Black literacy and race-based and segregated educational policies.

Negative and stereotypical images of Black people popularized in the customs, laws, and the media intensified Black victimization by more aggressively using "science," as educational psychology provided portrayals of Black people's reading ability and alleged racially inherited low intelligence. White supremacist ideology informed research and claimed dominion over literacy by controlling, defining, and limiting who was permitted access and under what conditions. Legal and societal efforts to forestall access to literacy were undertaken with intentionality; nonetheless, the concerns of Black parents for their children's education did not abate as they continued to seek legal redress, as in the cases discussed in Chapter 1.

This chapter extends the history of anti-Black literacy's evolution through a review of the history and uses of standardized reading assessments, another instrument of White supremacy. Chapter 1 exposed the assumptions on which an ideology of White supremacy informed daily life in the colonies and later states, including the establishment of anti-Black literacy customs, laws, policies, and statutes. In addition, it demystified the alarming and continuous efforts undertaken by White people to retain power at local, state, and federal levels. And it included the efforts made at the judicial and executive levels of the federal government; that is, President Thomas Jefferson, an enslaver, defended the enslavement of Black people, by using "science" as a means of "proving" racial superiority of White people (Sensoy & DiAngelo, 2017). He was not alone in his efforts as the role of "science" in proving racial superiority grew exponentially in the twentieth century, especially among educational researchers and those studying literacy. Educational psychologists, informed by an ideology of White supremacy, conceived, developed, and promoted standardized testing in general and standardized reading tests specifically, as evidence of White racial superiority. There were numerous responses of Black academics, community folk, and researchers to Black students' performance on standardized reading assessments, as part of an ongoing resistance to anti-Black racism and anti-Black literacy that are examined in this chapter. In addition, the chapter demystifies the role of federal and quasi-federal agencies that worked in concert with the federal government to forestall reading access and improvement for Black students.

Anti-Black Racism and Reading Research, 1880–1914

The ideology of White supremacy was a prevailing worldview among White politicians as well as academics and researchers. Popular theories about evolution were promoted in England by Charles Darwin's (1859) study: *The Origin of the Species: The Preservation of Favored Races in the Struggle for Life.* The subtitle, often not cited, suggested that humankind would evolve to preserve White people

(Willis, 2008). The roots of educational testing in the United States can be traced back to Francis Galton, a cousin of Darwin's, who in 1883, after a series of published studies on heredity and inheritance, coined the word eugenics. He defined *eugenics* as "the study of the agencies under social control that seek to improve or impair the racial qualities of future generations either physically or mentally" (n.p.). His belief in positivism and the divine nature of Nordic Europeans suggested that this ethnic and racial group represented the apex of intellect. He also suggested Africans were the least intellectual. His ideas inform *scientific racism*, the "deliberate attempt to justify and protect a system that allows exploitation … to reap economic and political rewards" (Thompson, quoted in Paludi & Haley, 2014, p. 1697). The notions of eugenics and scientific racism also existed in Germany, although at the time simply called "science," and included US converts who studied in Europe. Among the early researchers were scholars who also studied reading and supported these beliefs.

Standard Reading Testing, Reading, and World War I

Among the early US citizens to embrace the new "science" was James McKeen Cattell (1860–1944). He was a privileged White male graduate student and an early pioneer of reading research who studied in Germany with Wundt and who conducted a series of reaction-time experiments, including one to calculate the time it took for a person to recognize alphabetic letters. Philosophically, Cattell's (1890, 1896) work was more aligned with Galton's interest in individual differences and proving differences among racial groups, believing Whites were intellectually superior to all other races. Cattell set out to prove those differences through psychological experiments.

With considerable influence from his farther, Cattell secured a faculty position at the University of Pennsylvania, where he quickly acquired a full professorship. He conducted a series of psychological tests and coined the phrase "mental tests" (Cattell, 1890, p. 373). Later, he accepted a position at Columbia and continued his quests: the recognition of psychology as a science and proof of the intellectual and moral superiority of White males, specifically "great men," or scientists. Educational psychologists who followed Cattell also have compared well-educated White males to all other groups including but not limited to people of African, Asian, Native American, and Southeastern European descent; females of all ethnicities and races; and people living in poverty with limited access to, or opportunity for, a quality education. Research by Cattell and many of his students and devotees found people who were demographically most like the experimentalist scored higher than people who were demographically least like them (see Willis, 2007).

The practice of testing reading ability was not a novel pedagogical practice when Cattell conducted his study. For example, the Boston School Committee (1845–1846) created a printed survey to determine reading achievement among

Boston school children (Caldwell & Courtis, 1924). The survey consisted of a range of subjects drawn from school textbooks, and reading was tested by written responses to passages and definitions of select vocabulary. The results compared achievement among schools and noted that Smith School, a school serving mostly African American and West Indian students, was the lowest-performing school. The School Committee interpreted the results as the school administrators' lack of faith in the abilities of the students (Caldwell & Courtis, 1924).

Theories about reading held by White educational psychologists (Huey, Judd, Courtis, Thorndike, and Gray) framed the field and helped to cast a shadow over the reading performance – as measured on standardized reading tests – of Black readers (most of whom had limited opportunities for quality education). In addition, George R. Stetson (1833–1923), a White supremacist, worked with the reading researcher Edmund Burke Huey (1870–1913) on several experiments. Stetson (1897) wrote extensively about the lives and literacy of Black students and conducted a series of memory tests comparing Black and White students. He found Black children outperformed White children on most tests, although he also noted their "lack" of language (Standard English) and limited vocabularies. Huey (1908) also relied on racist pseudoscientific notions of intelligence and inheritance in his landmark text *The Psychology and Pedagogy of Reading*. He crafted a historical overview of reading and scientific literature and informed reading research, featuring reading and writing since 4000 BC, within the biological and social Darwinist thought of his time. His evolutionary description of reading and writing centered on the superior nature of the Anglo-Saxon culture and their literacy. He believed there were genetic and racial differences in students' ability to read, whereby literacy methods and tests privileged the dominant culture.

Another prominent figure in the field was Charles Judd (1913), a member of the Committee of Standards of the National Council on Education, who expressed "standardized tests could prove a means whereby the individual teacher could obtain objective evidence of what a pupil can accomplish" (p. 2). He also served as the editor of the *Elementary School Teacher* (renamed the *Elementary School Journal*) and promoted the use of standardized tests to improve school and teacher efficiency. Courtis (1914) suggested standardized measures were able:

> (a) to secure information that will enable school authorities to formulate in objective terms the ends to be attained in any educational process; (b) to measure the efficiency of methods designed to produce desired results; (c) to determine the factors and laws which condition learning and teaching; (d) to furnish data that will enable comparison of school with school, and teacher with teacher for purposes of supervisory control to be made upon scientific, impersonal, and *objective* data.
>
> *(p. 375, italics in the original)*

The arguments made by Courtis, and supported by Judd, were aligned with the prevailing thinking in support of the veracity of standardized test use to structure instruction, and their use continued through the early part of the century. Courtis was not alone in his quest to anchor standardized testing to meritocracy:

> Day by day, however, the school is attempting to make certain well-defined changes in the minds and habits of the children in its care. The character in the amount of these changes is not determined by chance, but in accordance with laws, which, in their operation, are as consistent as those determined… Until these laws are known, scientific control of the efficiency of the educational process will be impossible.
>
> *(p. 374)*

A protégé of Cattell's and a prominent supporter of eugenics and the inheritability of intelligence, Edward L. Thorndike was called the father of educational psychology. He in/famously stated: "Whatever exists at all exists in some amount … as that of physicist or chemist or physiologist engaged in quantitative thinking… the nature of educational measurement is the same as that of all scientific measurements" (Thorndike, 1918, pp. 16–17). He sought to create tests (reading comprehension, spelling, vocabulary, and word recognition) that were scaled for increasing difficulty to assess students' knowledge of literacy.

Thorndike also strongly supported his graduate student William S. Gray, whose dissertation contained the same preference for reading research among (what he referenced as) "native American" schoolchildren, identified as English dominant, middle to upper middle class, and White. He compared their performance with students he identified as foreign-born with limited English and students who were low class and lived in the "Negro" neighborhoods. Gray (1917) reported on a 1914 reading study in which he, along with a group of researchers, tested students' reading in several cities as they sought to standardize a test. In the study, many of the students spoke home languages other than English. He recalled teachers from Cleveland, Ohio

> made recommendations regarding the measurement of reading comprehension, suggesting that students be given a few extra seconds at the onset of testing to familiarize themselves with the subject matter before beginning the tests … many teachers felt that relying on questions as a method of determining comprehension was too narrow as a means of assessment. They proposed other methods be used in combination with standardized tests to determine a student silent reading comprehension ability.
>
> *(p. 129)*

Gray created oral reading comprehension tests that mimicked those created by Thorndike, by gradually increasing difficulty among the passages. His central focus was on developing and promoting oral reading comprehension tests of scaled oral reading passages:

> George Washington was in every sense of the word, a wise, good, and great man. But his temper was naturally irritable and high toned. Through reflection and resolution, he had obtained a firmed and habitual ascendancy over it. If, however, it broke loose its bounds, he was most tremendous in his wrath.
>
> He was six feet tall, and his body was well-proportioned. His complexion inclined to the florish; his eyes were blue and remarkably far apart. A profusion of hair covered his forehead. He was scrumptiously neat in his appearance, and, although he eventually left his tent at an early hour, he was well dressed.
>
> *(Gray, 1917, Standardized oral reading passages, p. 67)*

The passages served a dual purpose, allegedly to standardize oral reading and valorize White males considered heroes. The passages clarified how researchers conceptualized White supremacy and infused their acculturation and assimilation beliefs within standardized reading tests. Their reading assessments and reading research studies reflected their ideological and philosophical beliefs, a romanticized view of history, and the sanctity of Whiteness.

Other likeminded reading researchers used scientific racism to conduct early literacy studies, normalizing White culture and language as reflective of "native born" White Americans, to the exclusion of all other ethnic/linguistic/racial groups. Not all students required to take these reading assessments were White, although all were assessed on the same standards of Whiteness in "an ever-changing European-American Protestant standard [that] is the unachievable goal placed on people of color and poor Whites... placing people of color beneath Whites in all aspects of life" (Browne-Marshall, 2013, p. 5). Narratives were crafted to discuss the reading performance of Black students on standardized tests as inferior to White students and providing the false impression of White intellectual superiority.

Carolyn Roberts, a historian of medicine and science at Yale University, articulated the disconnect between standardization and reality this way: "it's easier, ... to believe these are innate biological differences than to address the structural racism that caused them" (quoted in Smith & Spodak, 2021, n.p.) Standardized tests helped to provide and concretize conclusive evidence "proving" White intellectual superiority. Although historians and reading researchers knew Black people were legally barred from learning to read for hundreds of years, they claimed the ability to read influences criminality. The mythical linkages were created to distract attention away from literacy and material inequities among schools and to victimize Black students by pointing to the linkages between low literacy rates and criminal behavior. Graff (1995) exposed myths linking reading to criminality and reading as a solution to equalize economic and social discrepancies:

> ethnicity, class, sex, and the suspected crime, rather than illiteracy alone, determined conviction, as those with fewest resources were most often convicted. Systematic patterns of punishment, apparently, might relate to factors other than guilt.
>
> *(p. 201)*

It was more likely, as M. Alexander's (2012) book, *The New Jim Crow*, revealed, the "tight network system of laws, policies, customs, and institutions that operate collectively to ensure the subordinate status of a group defined largely by race" (p. 13). Race, became the failsafe response to historical and systemic anti-Black racism.

Responses by Black Scholars

Generally, Black communities shared unwavering support for education; however, there was no singular or monolithic response to the ongoing anti-Black racism in education and anti-Black literacy campaigns. W. B. Johnson (1991) noted during Reconstruction that Black people often preferred schools established by other Black people as they were "distrustful of whites, while whites were disdainful of black teachers and dismayed at the popularity of black-controlled schools among black families who preferred them to the white-managed counterparts, even when the latter were free and the former charged tuition" (p. 90). In the new century, White mobs continued to burn Black churches, homes, and schools to deter Black people from seeking an education and literacy. Black people's beliefs and perspectives included people who internalized anti-Black racist assumptions, people who worked to prove that White assumptions were in error, and other people who resisted anti-Black assumptions and mischaracterizations. Besides, there were Black people who believed and invested in the dignity, humanity, intelligence, and worthiness of Black people.

The history of US reading instructions and materials (Shannon, 1989, 1990; N. B. Smith, 1986, among others) revealed relatively little about the reading instruction and materials in Black schools. Black teachers included people who had attended colleges and universities for teacher training as well as teachers who did not have any formal training. Among the thousands of Black schools established throughout the South after the Civil War to educate Black people was Calhoun Colored School (CCS). The school's curriculum followed the Hampton–Tuskegee model to convince Black people to remain in the South and be complacent and law-abiding, while working for White people. The founders and most teaching faculty were White Northerners, who created a curriculum in which it took 12 years to complete an eight-grade education. In terms of literacy, they used materials conceived and written by White American authors.

Teachers at CCS emphasized (a) oral reading; (b) elocution; (c) rote memory; (d) appreciation for literature; and (e) connecting home, school, and community life to schoolwork. An untold number of Black teachers taught Black students to be proud of the accomplishments of Black people.

When Georgia Washington got tired of the restrictive curriculum and vision for the lives for Black people promoted at CCS, she accepted the invitation from the Black community to establish a school in Mount Meigs, Alabama. Black teachers who opened their own schools used whatever materials they had – often the discarded and dated materials given to them from White schools, along with Black literature and newspapers, if they could be located. Although the tax dollars of Black families supported public schools, the tax income was used to support White schools and not extended to Black schools (J. D. Anderson, 1988). Most importantly, Black teachers supported access to literacy as a pathway to freedom: they believed in the humanity, intellect, and creativity of their students. And they cared deeply for their students' success in and out of the classroom and sought to prepare them for life beyond their humble beginnings (Willis et al., 2022).

World War I and Standardized Testing

Among Cattell's many students was Lewis Terman, a fellow eugenicist who worked with a team of White men to create the Stanford–Binet IQ test (Gould, 1996). He believed White people were intellectually superior to other races and characterized People of Color as mentally deficient:

> [It] is very, very common among Spanish-Indian and Mexican families of the Southwest and also among negroes. That dullness seems racial, or at least inherent in the family stocks from which they come… from a eugenic point of view they constitute a grave problem because of their unusually prolific breeding.
>
> *(Terman, 1916, pp. 91–92)*

He also remarked that no amount of teaching or training would eradicate racial intellectual differences and identified these students as a "problem."

Terman worked alongside educational psychologists, members of eugenics organizations (Bingham, Goodard, Yerkes, and Wissler), as well as in concert with the federal government during World War I to develop tests for Army recruits. Their stated goal was to locate men for officer training; however, the tests they created were largely, but not exclusively, like Thorndike's literacy tests of "verbal skills." Black men (and other non-Anglo Saxons) did not perform as well as their White peers on the Army tests. Their poor performance was celebrated as scientific "proof" of the intellectual superiority of White people based on objective and scientific measures:

it was men like Thorndike, Terman and Goddard, supported by corporate wealth, who successfully persuaded teacher, administrators and lay school boards to classify and standardize the school's curriculum with a differentiated track system based on ability and values of the corporate liberal society.

(Karier, 1972, p. 166)

The apparent success of Army tests at sorting individuals and groups according to a putative innate intelligence inspired many psychologists to push forward their research and testing agendas into education (Samuelson, 1977). Several educational psychologists involved in the creation of the Army intelligence tests, including Carl C. Brigham, Lewis Terman, Edward L. Thorndike, Guy Whipple, and Robert Yerkes, were particularly influential and helped extend the use of standardized achievement testing to the schools. Their efforts were aided by a grant from the General Education Board of the Rockefeller Foundation and support of the American Medical Association (Willis, 2008, p. 157). By 1920, tests were administered to 400,000 school children in the United States (Terman, 1920) and the results of national testing were interpreted as an indicator of the intellectual functioning of school children. Terman also suggested reforms were needed, consisting of tracking students into classes based on test scores.

There was a great deal of support of Terman's ideas among White power elites who wanted to control not only K–12 testing but also college admissions. They created a narrative based on notions of individualism and meritocracy to promote the use of standardized college admissions tests. Additionally, Brigham (1923) published *A Study of American Intelligence* in which he declared:

> The decline of American intelligence will be more rapid than the decline of the intelligence of European national groups, *owing to the presence here of the negro.* These are the plain, if somewhat ugly, facts that our study shows. The deterioration of American intelligence is not inevitable, however, if public action can be aroused to prevent it. There is no reason why *legal steps should not be taken which would insure continuously progressive upward evolution.*
>
> *(p. 210, emphasis added)*

His statement acknowledged an anti-Black racist attitude and support of codifying opportunities for White economic and educational advancement. Later, his influence informed the college admissions testing. In 1900 the College Entrance Examination Board, later the College Board, was established as a nonprofit organization. It considered ways to enhance the enrollment of the country's most intelligent students. The group quickly moved to produce standardized admissions to be used by member institutions. Member institutions consisted of many prestigious universities seeking to ensure the most intelligent students were admitted. Originally, the entrance exams consisted of tests in nine areas of study, including German, Greek, and Latin. After World War I, when there was an emphasis on intelligence testing, Brigham, a eugenicist, served as the chair of psychological testing. By 1926, the College Board created a new standardized admission test, the Scholastic Aptitude Test (SAT), later renamed the Scholastic Achievement Test. Two decades later, a splinter group was established to score the tests, the Educational Testing Service. After considerable criticism of classism and racism, a competitor, the American College Testing (ACT), was established at the University of Iowa, led by E. F. Lindquist. Both tests have evolved overtime and extended or revised their tests in response to political and social concerns. Thus began a relationship and institutional structure where colleges and universities worked in concert with organizations, promoting and requiring standardized metrics for college admissions. Although not stated among the organizations' goals, their reliance on scientific racism framed their tests and perpetuated the role of White supremacy in crafting a racist legacy of admissions.

Early Childhood Reading

Given the numerous concerns about reading ability, parents, politicians, teachers, and researchers wanted to know when the optimal time was to begin reading instruction, especially the best time to begin reading instruction. Mabel Morphett and Carleton Washburne's publication of a 10-year longitudinal study focused on reading in first grade conveyed the effects of the *Winnetka Plan*, a test crafted by the superintendent of schools in Winnetka, Illinois, an upper-middle-class, White, English-dominant suburb of Chicago. Morphett and Washburne's (1931) published description of the plan had long-reaching effects. They used the Detroit First-Grade Intelligence Tests and Stanford–Binet test that were administered to all children seeking to determine general intelligence and how closely students were tied to reading progress. Next, the students were taught to read by the Winnetka technique, before being assessed on the *Gray Oral Reading Check Test*. Their results indicated that for successful reading, students should be taught to read at age six. The *Winnetka Plan* also called for diagnostic tests, self-pacing, and workbooks. The authors' findings became the benchmark for beginning reading instruction nationwide and concretized White, middle-to-upper class, suburban students as representative of US school children. The results of this study were used to support early reading initiatives across the nation and to suggest all school-aged children should begin reading during first grade.

To be clear, the results of standardized testing were not limited to the US Army or schooling. Moten (1999), for instance, examined how Virginia politicians used eugenics (scientific racism) to "rationalize withholding rights from certain racial or ethnic groups" (p. 7). He noted these beliefs undergird the history of racial integrity laws in the state, including the 1924 Racial Integrity Act.

The laws were based on the fear of despoiling the purity of White people with so-called inferior Negro blood and extended to mixed-raced students' admittance to White schools. Extending anti-Black racism as legalized and codified racial segregation known under Jim/Jane Crow laws, the laws and extra-judicial actions permitted unequal access in all areas of life: education, employment, entertainment, health care, and transportation.

Black Researchers Respond

The Black community as well as scholars had waged a long, unheeded response to White racial intellectual superiority. In the late 1890s, Black scholars argued intelligence test score differences between Blacks and Whites reflected differences in social and economic conditions. African American scholars argued the poor test performance of Black people and other Americans of other ethnic groups was due to cultural, economic, historical, linguistic, and social, differences as well as educational access and opportunities (see Willis, 2008).

Du Bois (1903/1996) had long argued the accomplishments of Black men were overlooked, "throughout history, the powers of single black men flash here and there like falling stars, and die sometimes before the world has rightly headed their brightness" (p. 4). Since his years as an undergraduate at Fisk, Du Bois had studied Black life, and during his brief tenure at the University of Penn, he completed a year-long study, *The Philadelphia Negro*, presenting Black life in Philadelphia, Pennsylvania. His detailed sociological narrative consisted of empirical and statistical information in which he "posited environmental, oppression and personal attributes as central causes for the status of Philadelphia blacks" (Harris & Willis, 2016, p. 215). His text also proffered an alternative understanding of Black life "rather than blame black solely for their condition, Du Bois argued for behaviors that would lead to uplift -- moral, educational, economic, cultural and political" (p. 216).

Beginning in 1923, Du Bois, the publisher of the *Crisis*, and Charles Johnson, the publisher of *Opportunity*, published numerous research articles about racial differences and intelligence testing. Johnson (1923) challenged the Army tests results, noting that the tests given to Black recruits, according to the Army's report, were centered on practical needs. He also found cultural bias in several of the test questions, requiring all test-takers to know about White Hollywood actresses, types of automobiles, brands of tobacco and coffee, and terms used in bowling and golf; in other words, many of the questions normalized White middle-class beliefs, knowledge, lifestyles, and values. Early in the testing hysteria, H. A. Miller (1923) argued, "the vocabulary of science has been appropriated and its methods prostituted to prove what men want to prove ... [and] the most fruitful medium for this method has been intelligence testing" (p. 229). Long (1923, 1925) also rejected the interpretations of the Army intelligence tests as reflective of environment and not "native intelligence" between racial groups: "we need to question very seriously the test applied to groups having quite different experiences and the incentives from those on whom the tests have been standardized" (p. 138). Bond (1924) added that the Army test results reflected the following: "the groups which they compared had a common background of experience, while a careful analysis of the fact would have shown that variation among social class will explain the phenomena, they have ascribed to inherent intelligence" (p. 202). Bond (1927) reported on the results of intelligence testing conducted among Black students in Chicago and noted they outperformed White students.

Another outlet for Black scholarship on intelligence was the *Journal of Negro Education* (1932+). Jenkins (1936a) took a special interest in Black children who scored well on the Stanford–Binet, who he believed it did not represent "the two brightest Negro children in America" (p. 159), a remark commonly made by White researchers. His case study consisted of 14 Black students with IQs of 160 and higher, and his results claimed more than two Black students with high IQs, although he questioned the results as none of the students lived in the South. In a second study, conducted among students from seven Chicago Public Schools, he reasoned other researchers did not locate these students because "most of the studies concerned with mental tests performance of Negro children have been conducted in localities which proved meager opportunities for educational and cultural development" (Jenkins, 1936b, pp. 189–190). Finally, Price (1934) reviewed research based on Stanford–Benet, National Intelligence Tests, Otis Primary and Advance Examinations, and the Terman Group Tests of Mental Ability. He concluded from an analysis of studies focused on intelligence and race:

> The test used have been standardized upon northern whites, largely, who's calling, has been different in amount and kind from the great bulk of Negroes, who, of course, are in the South. And, on the other hand, the sampling has neither been random or representative, for the groups compared have either (or both) been too small and or they have been unlike in socio-economic status, school training, and cultural background.
>
> *(p. 452)*

He recognized institutionalized racism embedded within US society affected economics and school enrollment, factors that also affected student performance. Black scholars also were vocal opponents of scientific racism, the Eurocentric ideas embedded in education, and the failed promise of equal justice in the United States. Woodson (1933) drew a connection between the horrors of lynching and education for Black students: "there would be no lynching if it did not start in the schoolroom" (p. 4). He, along with other Black scholars, advocated for the teaching of Black history in schools. Revered as the father of Black history, Woodson established Negro History Week in 1926 as an addition to the curriculum used in Black schools:

> every individual of the social order should be given an unlimited opportunity to make the most of himself. Such opportunity, too, should not be determined from without by forces it to direct the proscribed element and in a way to redound solely to the good of others but should be determined by the make-up of the Negro himself and by what his environment requires of him.
>
> ... Only by careful study of the Negro himself in the life which he is forced to lead can we arrive at the proper procedure in this crisis... it is merely a matter of exercising common sense in approaching in people through their environment in order to deal with conditions as they are rather than as you would like to see them or imagine that they are. There are there may be a difference in method of attack to the principal remains the same.
>
> *(pp. ix–xii)*

A kindred spirit, Du Bois was an editor, historian, novelist, political and social activist, and sociologist whose scholarship provided counternarrative challenging histories written by White academics. In 1940, Du Bois observed psychological testing-supported racist theories and refuted the reasoning given for low performance on the tests by Black people:

> I see absolutely no proof that the average ability of the White man's brain to think clearly is any greater than that of the yellow man or of the black man. If we take even that doubtful but widely heralded test, the frequency of individual creative genius (when a real racial test should be their frequency of ordinary common sense) – if we take the Genius as the savior of mankind, it is only possible for the white race to prove its own incontestable superiority by appointing both judge injury and summoning its own witness.
>
> *(p. 141)*

Research by Black scholars disrupted the misinformed narratives repeated and perpetuated by White politicians and researchers and rebutted the racist interpretation of Army testing. They argued psychologists ignored contextual factors (cultural differences and economic circumstances of slavery, history of educational denial, and the social caste system) of non-White Americans. Moreover, the intelligence and reading tests they conducted among Black students resulted in very different views of achievement and intelligence.

White academics, politicians, researchers, and test makers dismissed challenges to their ideological assumptions, the content of the test/test items, the administration of the test, and the published – and often sensationalized – interpretations of test results. The results of the Army tests were challenged by numerous scholars (Gould, 1981; Lippman, 1922; Montagu, 1945; Rury, 1988; Sokal, 1978; Spring, 1972; Travers, 1983) who struggled with the idea that psychological tests measured innate intellect, a normal curve of intellectual functioning existed, Blacks were intellectually inferior to Whites, and people who live in poverty were intellectually inferior to those who do not. The zeal that accompanied the use of intelligence tests in education was predicated on the "belief of the psychologists that they were scientifically measuring essentially native ability rather than the results of school training" (Samuelson, 1977, p. 279). The continued influence of psychological testing on schooling, especially intelligence, cannot be overemphasized. The concept of an innate intelligence and natural distribution of intellect among humans, as indicated by the normal curve, has achieved a level of "common sense," among educators and psychometricians, and has served as a foundation for the field of educational psychology and assessment more generally.

The proliferation of "intelligence tests [that] were created as an accurate and efficient sorting mechanisms that reinforce dominant values and contribute to social stability by justifying inequality of outcomes as a natural and objective process" (Richardson & Johanningermeier, 1998, p. 711). Educational assessment and tests are promoted to suggest they are a fair, equitable, unbiased, and culturally neutral measures of innate intellectual ability based on a natural (i.e., normal) distribution of intelligence. The concept of a normal curve was underpinned by values, beliefs, and assumptions about relations of power forming the bedrock of traditional education, research, assessment, and practice (Karier, 1986; Langemann, 2000; Popkewitz, 1994). In terms of reading, Graff (1995) observed:

> the purpose of literacy, in the past as in the present, was to integrate society and to foster progress by binding men and women in its web and instilling in them the guidelines for correct behavior. The importance of print and the concomitant ability to read and write were grasped by those most interested in social order.
>
> *(pp. 39–40)*

It was unclear from his observation if the purpose of literacy was extended to all people, but the notion of "social order" implied a way to sustain White dominance. The history of literacy in the United States always has been complex and interwoven with White supremacist ideological assumptions, fear, politics, power, social class, and religion. Reading researchers built upon their assumptions in the conception and construction of standardized reading assessments. Many of the early reading researchers were eugenicists who helped to construct the Army tests as well as scholastic and college admissions tests. They did not waiver in their promotion of the false narrative: reading research was scientific and sought to equalize reading outcomes.

The Boy Next Door

By the mid-century, the nation was not convinced about the most effective way to teach reading proposed by reading experts and preferred Rudolf Flesch's (1955/1968) self-published book *Why Johnny Can't Read*. His text appeared to awaken the nation out of hazy notions about beginning reading instruction. We do not know who Johnny was, other than allegedly a child who lived next door to Flesch, but given the nation's discriminatory housing patterns, we can be assured Johnny was probably not a person of color, or living in poverty. In short, Johnny – unless otherwise explicitly stated – was a White, male, English-dominant reader and imbued with beliefs, values, and worldviews neatly aligned with school literacy expectations (Heath, 1983).

The evolution of reading research and instruction was rooted in the field of psychology as well as reflective of the economic, political, and racial histories in the United States. The fear of addressing race and racism head-on continued an intellectual dishonesty, supporting the continuance of systematic racism and the weaponization of reading as White and anti-Black.

The American Psychological Association (APA) in 2021, noted since the 1950s, the organization, aware of ethnic and racial concerns, sought to "address" these concerns with a focus on testing standards and acknowledged:

> From the 1950s on, psychologists received money from the Pioneer Fund, created in the 1930s to promote racial homogeneity, "repatriation" of Black Americans to Africa, and segregation. Money was funneled to White Citizens Councils for "massive resistance" to the *Brown* decision, and later funded nearly all major scientific racist projects (Tucker, 2002). From the 1960s on, psychologists gave explicit assistance to and participated in racial extremist, White nationalist.
>
> *(para 58)*

Importantly, the (APA) also acknowledged that a former president, Henry E. Garrett, shared his opinions in a segregation case, *Davis v. County School Board*, prior to the more-well-known case of *Brown v. Board of Education*. They noted that Garrett "argued that segregation would not harm Black or White students if school facilities were equal. This idea was later echoed by the three judges who ruled in favor of continued segregation" (APA, 2021, para 62).

A Shift in Educational Equality

In 1947, the US Supreme court ruled in a case of racial segregation, *Mendez v. Westminster*, in favor of the plaintiffs. They stated that students of Mexican descent had a right to an equal education, and "all other groups" are protected under the Fourteenth Amendment. Judge McCormick wrote:

[t]he equal protection of the laws pertaining to the public school system … is not provided by furnishing in separate schools …. A paramount requisite in the American system of public education is social equality. It must be open to all children by unified school association regardless of lineage.

(n.p., quoted in Strum, 2010)

In the landmark case of *Brown v. Board of Education of Topeka, Kansas* (1954, 1955), the Court made another important finding in support of minoritized students. The Brown case was part of a class-action lawsuit brought on behalf of Black students who were forced to attend segregated schools. The lawyers for the plaintiffs drew from research; they argued there was an emotional and psychological toll on Black children living in a society dominated by Whiteness, which had been documented as early as the 1940s by the famous "doll test" administered by Drs. Kenneth and Mamie Clark.

FIGURE 2.1   The Clark Doll Test

The Doll Test

The Clarks conducted a study among young Southern Black children to understand their perceptions of race. Using four dolls, although "the Clarks had to paint a white baby doll brown for the tests, since African American dolls were not yet manufactured" (Blakemore, 2022, para 12), they asked: "which doll is nice, which doll is mean, which doll is good, which doll is bad, which doll is pretty, which doll is ugly, which doll would they like to play with, which doll is White, which doll is Black, and which doll looks like you." Most Black children attributed positive characteristics to the White doll (nice, good, pretty, and one they wanted to play with) and negative characteristics to the Black doll (bad, mean, ugly, and not one they wanted to play with). When asked which doll looked like them, some children refused to answer the question and others ran out of the room in tears (NAACP Legal Defense and Educational Fund, Inc., 2022, para 5). The findings of the Clark's study concluded Black children were negatively affected by racism in society and had internalized racism, which affected their emotional and psychological self-image. They concluded, "racism was an inherently American institution, and that school segregation inhibited the development of white children, too" (NAACP Legal Defense and Educational Fund, Inc., 2022, para 7). Dr. Kenneth Clark commented during the *Briggs v. Elliot* case (1951), "my opinion is that a fundamental effect of segregation is basic confusion in the individuals and their concepts about themselves conflicting in their self-images" (quoted in Blakemore, 2022, para 12). The research is often referenced as a catalyst for the unanimous decision in the US Supreme court's decision in *Brown v. the Board of Education*. The study by the Clarks was pivotal as they were able to show psychological trauma was inflicted on Black children who attended segregated schools. Their testimony appeared to be a key component of the *Brown* cases (Browne-Marshall, 2013). While many Black people sought integration of public schools, some leaders like Martin Luther King, Jr., did not, arguing, "white people view black people as inferior…People with such a low view of the black race cannot be given free rein and put in charge of the intellectual care and development of our boys and girls" (quoted in Kendi, 2019, p. 173). King, Jr. (1963) also invoked the thinking expressed by Black men since the late 1770s, who understood that the promises of founding fathers were not extended to Black people. At the state and local levels, "the implementation of *Brown* hinged not only on federal law but on the willingness of state and local officials to enforce the law" (Willis, 2019a, p. 4). As the APA (2021) chronicled, "The International Association for the Advancement of Ethnology and Eugenics … promoted race science, lobbied to overturn the *Brown* decision, and fought to preserve segregation. The Board and editors include noted academics and neo-Nazi activists" (para 66).

Historically, academics claimed Black students were intellectually inferior when assessed on reading tests, and federally funded studies accepted and concretized these ideas, linking them to geography, poverty, transiency, and parental education, while ignoring centuries of economic oppression. Yet, the lack of literacy education of birth parents, particularly mothers, to the educational attainment of their children from the twentieth century remains part of explanations when research fails to "solve" educational problems. Deficit beliefs and thinking found footing on:

> the notion that youth of color lack the language, the culture, the family support, the academic skills, even the moral character to succeed or excel. But the true deficiency lies ... on deeply problematic ideological assumptions rather than solid empirical evidence about the nature in the experience of social inequality.
>
> *(Bucholtz, Casillas, & Lee, 2017, pp. 43–44)*

Despite the resistance of some White people to address anti-Black racism, President Johnson signed the Civil Rights Act (1964), effectively striking down Jim/Jane Crow laws and issued human and civil rights for all US citizens. Gadsden (1994) argued the 1964 Civil Rights Act was pivotal and helped address changes in literacy access for Black people, as historically Black communities, families, and individuals have valued education and literacy. Citing the results of numerous studies conducted by Black scholars since the mid-twentieth century, they provided culturally informed descriptions of Black children, communities, families, and students in stark contrast to the deficit depictions provided by many White scholars. Importantly, in 1965, President Johnson also signed the Elementary and Secondary Education Act (ESEA), which "emphasizes equal access to education, sets high standards for academic performance, and demands a rigorous level of accountability from schools and districts" (www.k12.wa.us/esea/).

The Elementary and Secondary Education Act: A Focus on Reading

The Elementary and Secondary Education Act ESEA (1965) was passed more than a decade after the *Brown* ruling. White resistance to the ruling was demonstrated by a significant number of local schools refusing to desegregate or create obscure desegregation plans. Among the many Southern school districts to enact such plans was the proposed "grade-a-year" program (Erickson, 2012), in Nashville, TN, a 12-year plan to desegregate schools. Likeminded plans were a way to appear in compliance with the law but took advantage of the notion of the "all deliberate speed" mandate (Willis, 2019a, p. 4). Kidder and Rosner (2002) make the case for recognizing the impact of standardized testing as acknowledged in *Griggs v. Duke Power Co*, when the Supreme Court ruled that Title VII of the 1964 Civil Rights Act extended to acts of unintentional discrimination: Griggs was the case of first impression in which the Court established a framework for assessing 'disparate impact' discrimination, criticizing the unwarranted reliance on standardized tests that operate as 'built in headwinds' against minority groups" (p. 133).

The Federal Government's Role in Education Expands

The passage of the 1964 Civil Rights Act and ESEA in 1965 helped to usher in the politicization of literacy in education that continues. Congress authorized early childhood experts to investigate early student learning to prepare children for kindergarten and first grade. The Early Training Program at Vanderbilt University was selected as it was in place and included a program for parents and families. The participants in the program were Black poor children whose parents had limited education. Using experimental methods, researchers declared participants exhibited mental retardation (Zigler & Styfco, 2010), although involvement in the program improved their level of intelligence. Their findings supported eugenicist and White supremacy narratives of Black intellectual inferiority (Kennedy, Van de Riet, and White, 1963; A. Woodson, 2017). The misidentification of Black intelligence also continued the colonialist tropes of racializing Black lives (culture, families, language, lives, and students) as well extended anti-Black literacy efforts. Some psychologists rejected the support of early childhood education, arguing "compensatory education programs make no difference for people of color ..." (APA, 2021, para 75).

Congress moved forward with President Johnson's 'War on Poverty,' and charged reading experts to help them understand how to improve early reading among first graders by identifying the best way to teach reading as well as the effects of early reading success on academic progress. At the First Grade Reading Studies preconference in 1964, reading researchers expressed interest in examining the intersection of reading and the socioeconomic status within communities and among diverse students and their experiences. They appeared aware of, and concerned about, addressing the effects of class, gender, race, and early childhood experiences, on beginning reading instruction. Bond and Dykstra (1967) reported reading experts solicited studies that applied experimental research methods to the study of beginning reading programs: 76 research proposals were submitted, 27 were funded, and 15 were used in a cross-study analysis (Chall, 1967). Research studies not used were studies among Black students living in urban areas, students who were Spanish-dominant and learning English, and students who were low income. Following the prevailing thinking among reading researchers, "the idealized student in the final report was English dominant, middle-to-upper class, with above normal abilities, and White" (Willis, 2019a, p. 6). In reading research, the decisions to limit research methods and student demographics reflected earlier research studies and forecasted generations of federally funded reading research that ignored Black student readers.

Black Scholars Respond

Black students were (and continue to be) disproportionately labeled as mildly retarded. In a provocative speech that was later published, Lloyd M. Dunn

(1968), then the outgoing president of the Council for Exceptional Children, critiqued the overrepresentation of students in special education as "low status backgrounds—including Afro Americans, American Indians, Mexicans, and Puerto Ricans; those from nonstandard English speaking, broken, disorganized, and inadequate homes; and children from non-middle-class environments" (quoted in Willis, 2019a, p. 7). In concert with Dunn's speech, the National Association for the Advancement of Colored People (NAACP) drew attention to the Office of Civil Rights (1968) *Elementary and Secondary Schools Civil Rights Survey* (2004) on school desegregation because among their findings was the disproportionate percentage of Black students placed in special education classes, thus re-segregating Black students within schools. The following year, "the NAACP also published their findings about how federal funds, under ESEA/ Title I, were used, pointing to the lack of compliance with the law, mismanagement of funds, and failure to address noncompliance" (Willis, 2019a, p. 6). As well, in 1969, the APA made a bold claim in the publication *Standards for Educational and Psychological Tests and Manuals*: "the guidelines for test use, centered primarily on test validity. However, concerns regarding discriminatory use of tests that nonetheless met these validity guidelines continued to be voiced ..." (APA, 2021, para 70). Arthur Jensen (1969) also reignited racist claims about the inheritability of intelligence and in subsequent publications (1972, 1973) continued to argue people of color were intellectually inferior to White people. Research produced by Black scholars and findings of the NAACP survey challenged the dominant narrative about Black student learners and the willingness of Congress to correct centuries of educational inequality.

The National Education Association commissioned a historical review of US education revealed underlying assumptions about US education. Heffernan's (1969) chapter, for instance, recounted a best-of-all-worlds view of US education with a generous explanation of the needs of the new nation for White schoolchildren to obtain an education and scant information about the education of students in other ethnic or racial groups. She also presented remarks by Bloom in 1964, regarding the importance of early childhood education and early reading:

> We may conclude from our results on general achievement and vocabulary development that by age 9 (grade 3) at least 50% of the general achievement pattern at age 18 (grade 12) has been developed whereas at least 75% of the pattern has been developed by age 13 (grade 7) ...
>
> *(Heffernan, 1969, p. 129)*

From this perspective, Bloom, an educational psychologist, appeared to confirm folk wisdom about reading and students by the end of third grade: first you learn to read, then you read to learn.

Special Education and Black Students

The concept of racial intellectual differences began centuries before the history of special education, although there was overlap in the notion that biological differences were evolutionary, and that Black people were less intellectually evolved than White people. In the United States, these ideas were expanded and used to justify chattel slavery and the denial of literacy access among Black people with claims they were intellectually and morally inferior to White people. The history of special education sought equitable educational rights of people with disabilities, although Black people were often identified as mentally retarded. Federal laws reflected notions of inferior Black intellectual and moral character as noted in Chapter 1. By the mid-twentieth century, the federal government passed legislation to address the educational needs of students with disabilities within *ESEA* (1965), along with funding for programs. In addition, Congress approved the Children with Specific Learning Disabilities Act (1969), which outlined guidelines for specific learning disabilities identification.

Defining Specific Learning Disabilities

Special education was an under-defined area of educational concern in the late 1960s before a series of federal special education laws evolved. In 1969, the Specific Learning Disabilities Act (SLDA) was enacted and required educational support services for all children with learning disabilities and later was embedded within the Education of the Handicapped Act (EHA), P. L. 91–230 (Willis, 2019b, p. 86). SLDA outlined the following characteristics:

> A disorder in one or more of the basic psychological processes involved in understanding or in using language, spoken or written, that may manifest itself in an imperfect ability to listen, think, speak, read, write, spell, or do mathematical calculations, including conditions such as perceptual disabilities, brain injury, minimal brain dysfunction, dyslexia, and developmental aphasia.
> *(34 C.F.R. 300.8)*

A diagnosis of SLD included communication abilities linked to early reading: language, literacy, speaking, and thinking. The law also included exclusions from SLD diagnosis: "learning problems that are primarily the result of visual, hearing, or motor disabilities, of mental retardation, of emotional disturbance, or of environmental, cultural, or economic disadvantage" (34 C.F.R. 300.8). Notably, ethnicity and race were not explicitly described but commonly understood as represented in notions of "environmental, cultural, or economic disadvantage." Importantly, the listed exclusions, as a proxy for ethnicity and race, most often were cited as the reason for low reading achievement among Black students.

A revision of special education law, the Education of the Handicapped Act (1970) added educational programs and additional funding to existing laws.

The changes were prompted in part because of the racial disproportionality among students identified with disabilities, for example, Black students were identified as mentally retarded more often than other racial groups, especially White students. Another version of the act was passed, the Education for All Handicapped Children Act of (1975), to ensure students identified would have the least restrictive educational environment, appropriate educational services, specific educational plans and goals, monitoring of student performance on standardized tests, and extending special education services to students from the age of 3 to 21. The amendments were aligned with nationwide efforts to address the percentage of students dropping out of school and improving high school graduation rates (please see Appendix D, "Definition of Individualized Education Program," page 279).

A Federal Agency, Reading Research, and Black Resistance

Several federally funded agencies were established by Congress and charged with the task of improving beginning reading and addressing reading difficulties, among which was the National Assessment of Educational Progress (NAEP).

National Assessment of Educational Progress (NAEP)

NAEP was established in 1964, with grants from the Carnegie and Ford Foundations (Bourque, 2009), and federal support was commissioned in 1968. A brief history of NAEP by L. V. Jones (1996) emphasized connections among the government agency and wealthy Carnegie and Ford foundations and observed that the initial goals of forerunners to NAEP "were to report what the nation's citizens know and can do and then to monitor changes overtime using objective-referenced assessment" (p. 15). By contrast, Mary L. Bourque (2009), a former assistant director of psychometrics at the National Assessment Governing Board (NAGB), explained the evolution of NAEP, noting it needed leadership and was "developed carefully to protect the rights of states ... precluded using NAEP as a lever for policy changes in American education" (p. 1). Leadership for NAEP came after Secretary of Education, William Bennet, appointed the NAGB to oversee NAEP, later authorized in 1968 by Congress (P L. 100–297). Bourque (2009) acknowledged the NAGB was established to address policy and set student performance standards: "identify appropriate achievement goals for each age and grade in each subject area to be tested (Section. 3403, (6)(A))" (quoted, p. 4). The NAGB identified three achievement levels – basic, proficient, and advanced – with accompanying brief descriptions, although the descriptions have changed over time.

Jones (1996) listed 15 features of the early program, including a focus on reading as one of the subject areas, age ranges of students to be tested, multiple-choice formatting of the instruments, and correlation between learning objectives and test questions, among others. Importantly, he noted standardized test exercises relied on statistical criteria; however, with new assessments, "every exercise would be perceived by lay critics [as] related to an agreed upon objective" (p. 16). The new assessments born out of NAEP were contractedly housed under the Educational Testing Services (ETS). The first national assessments occurred in 1969 and included criteria for exercises.

Over the next two decades, NAEP assessments evolved as they moved from national trials to state assessments and were used more inclusively among public and nonpublic schools. Katzmann and Rosen (1970) acknowledged there was controversy during the evolution of NAEP and the agency was criticized for:

1. measuring questionable educational outcomes with questionable techniques;
2. classifying student subpopulations on largely irrelevant dimensions and or insufficient detail; and
3. neglecting to collect information on school characteristics, which would identify policy performance relationships.

(p. 584)

Despite these criticisms, NAEP reports have been produced regularly since 1971, presenting students' scores in various subjects, including reading, disaggregated by race, gender, and social economic class, based on a presumably representative sample of US school children. Historically, NAEP oversampled economically poor students of color living in urban areas while comparing them to economically middle- to upper-middle class White students living in suburban areas. The data replicated and reproduced similar results and was a process undertaken by states. NAEP data on subject matter achievement, which has been published in the form of *National Report Cards* for over four decades, are frequently referenced in policy discussions and used as a template by states to create standardized reading assessments. *NAEP Reading Report Cards* provided results, disaggregated by gender, race, and social class, and revealed that reading results for Black, Latinx, and Native American/Indigenous students are below Asian, Asian Pacific Islanders, and White students. Educational researchers and political stakeholders consistently pointed to the trustworthiness and veracity of the experimental/scientific methods and ignored how the processes support White superiority. The discourse used by reading research included: 1) unquestioned support of the ideology informing NICHD research and methods; 2) belief in the veracity of scientific data/facts regarding reading achievement as measured by reading tests; 3) a lack of acknowledgment and concern about the socio-historical factors and racially discriminatory practices that influence educational access; 4) consistent reference to the amount of funding received and the lack of results, without a viable solution; and 5) extension of funding concerns beyond reading (including teacher education and public health). Explanations of differences are filled with discussions seeking to validate the researchers' theory or methodology devoid of concern for the students' well-being, who are often blamed/victimized for their performance on standardized tests. Koretz and Diebert (1996) acknowledged: "achievement levels have been the focus of intense controversy. Researchers have criticized the process by which the levels were set, the appropriateness of the levels themselves, and the validity of their interpretation" (p. 53). They argued the language used to discuss NAEP achievement levels, for example, basic, proficient, and advanced, and performance needs to be more accurately described and interpreted for the politicians and the public by the media. Au (2013) also remarked, "by 1994, 43 states implemented state-wide assessments for K-5, and by the year 2000 every US state but Iowa administered a state mandated test" (p. 10). Undeterred by the protests of Black scholars, educational psychologists, in general, and those in ELA research, specifically, proceeded to popularize their ideological position and to promote educational research (approaches, methodologies, methods, and results) as acultural, yet universal, that is, professing cognition is race-neutral and their research color-blind. Leonardo (2012) remarked that this research is where the "dominant race's particularity is disguised as universal" (p. 439).

Seeking Justice for Black Students

T. L. Smith's (1972) investigation of educational opportunities for "Native Blacks" and "foreign Whites," from 1880 to 1950, provided an alternative perspective about educational attainment in the United States. He argued the wide gap between the school performance between children of formerly enslaved Black people and children of immigrants was deeply rooted in their racial attitudes and prejudices, hampering the education of both groups more than their desire to obtain an education. He found the differences in performance centered on "the sharply divergent set of rewards which racially prejudice urban societies provided to those who stayed in school" (p. 335). His claims were in stark opposition to the scientific racism supporting the inheritability of intelligence perspective.

Black psychologists also argued standardized intelligence tests, normed on White students, consequently found White children's intelligence superior. They raised oppositional voices just as their predecessors in the 1930s had done. Turning the tables, Boone and Adesso (1974) reported the results of a *Black Intelligence Test* where Black cultural references predominated. The test was administered to White and Black students, and, not surprisingly, the Black students outperformed the White students. The authors of the test declared it validated concerns of cultural bias in standardized testing. Boozer (1978) detailed the concerns of the Association of Black psychologists who opposed the use of standardized testing:

> current standardized tests should not be used to test Black children because they have been used in labeling Black people as uneducable. Placing Black children in 'special classes' in schools, perpetuating inferior education for Blacks, assigning Black children to educational tracts, denying Black students higher educational opportunities, restricting positive growth and development of Black people, and destroying the delicate self-image of many students.
>
> *(p. 415)*

Black psychologists' concerns, insights, research, and voices were dismissed and ignored. Moreover, research conducted by Black scholars remained sidelined as research conducted by White scholars predominated the extant literature and were highlighted in federal reviews. Palmer and Hafner (1979), for example, provided a brief overview of several reading studies, describing negative and stereotypical reasons why Black students lack reading progress. The authors summarized the findings of the studies and pointed to ill-conceived assumptions researchers made about Black language acquisition and use and its effect on beginning reading. Their summary acknowledged schools used Standard English as a metric for language and often discouraged Black language. They also reviewed two studies overlooked in the discussion of Black student reading acquisition, noting students were equally capable of learning to read when the materials were culturally informed and engaging and Standard English was not required.

Although Black organizations, parents, scholars, and researchers had long protested the scientific racism used to inform standardized achievement tests and the meritocratic use of the tests in education, their demands for justice were often unheeded. Several Black parents used existing laws in the San Francisco Federal District Court *Larry P. v. Riles* (1979) case. Their case rested on the Fourteenth Amendment, the violation of the equal protection clause, as they challenged the use of IQ tests to measure intelligence and place Black students in special education classes. The plaintiffs specifically claimed six Black students were discriminated against because IQ tests were used to place them in special education classes. They successfully argued that IQ tests were culturally biased and inequitable. Leon Kamin, an expert witness, articulated this point:

> The very fact that the tests must depend upon particular information that a child has acquired in his past means that they are bound to be culturally biased. In different social classes in our society, in different ethnic groups in our society, in different racial groups in our society, the experiences which a child has vary. Now, the tests, for the most part, have been designed by White middle-class psychologists who are familiar with White middle-class environment, White middle-class culture and understand what it is that one learns and acquired in that environment... Obviously, the children from other backgrounds will not have had the same access to, and the same experience with, the bits of knowledge tested on these tests as the modal white middle class child.
>
> *(quoted in Gordon & Rudert, 1979, p. 180)*

Judge Peckman ruled that "IQ tests were found to discriminate against Black children" (Coddington & Fairchild, 2012, p. 11) and should not be used, "or their substantial equivalent" (p. 11). Although he did not define equivalents, he wrote, "tests administered to minority children must have been validated for use with that population ... IQ tests have been found wanting in their utility for special education placements" (p. 11). The ruling was challenged in subsequent cases, but upheld. The onslaught of high-stakes standardized testing in education consumed the nation in the last two decades of the century.

African American Language Court Cases

Concerns by Black parents and caregivers had long existed and gained national attention during the height of national debates about Black language. Although Johnson and Simons's (1972) article was ignored, they presented three suggestions to better educate Black students: knowledge of Black culture, knowledge of Black dialect/language, and teaching approaches to engage Black students. They suggested, "teachers are both ill-prepared and perhaps unwilling to move in directions which could make the difference between the success and failure of their black students" (p. 288). They further claimed, "there is no excuse for allowing a teacher's ignorance of his students' culture and language to stand in the way of a child learning to read" (p. 290). Moreover, they argued that to improve Black student reading performance, teachers needed more information about Black dialect. The idea created backlash across the nation, as educators, journalists, political pundits, researchers, and teachers debated whether Black dialect was a language. There was considerable discussion, but few media outlets contacted or interviewed linguists. A tangible concerned was whether the African American language was recognized as a language, if so schools would be eligible to receive Title IV funding.

The complex, intersecting, political, and social roles of language, reading, standardized testing, and special education placement were called into account in the 1979 federal case, *Martin Luther King Junior Elementary School Children et al. v. Ann Arbor School District (MLK v. Ann Arbor)*, or the Ann Arbor decision. The plaintiffs were 11, economically poor, Black students who had attended Martin Luther King Junior Elementary School and experienced reading difficulties. The case hinged on the Fourteenth Amendment's equal protection clause, whereby it was argued whether the plaintiffs' language was a barrier to an adequate education where they were able to participate, the school board's processes to assure the students were receiving an adequate education, and the students were disproportionately placed in special education classes. Their case was about language and literacy rights of students who speak African American Language (AAL) and who were experiencing difficulties learning to read.

> The allegation was that the defendants had failed to properly educate the children, who were thus in danger of becoming functionally illiterate. Specifically, plaintiffs charged that school officials had improperly placed the children in learning disability and speech pathology classes;

that they had suspended, disciplined, and repeatedly retained the children at grade level without taking into account their social, economic, and cultural differences; and that they had failed to overcome language barriers, preventing the children from learning standard English and learning to read.

(Smitherman, 1981, p. 41)

The school district, like others in the past, had labeled some students handicapped or learning disabled and implied they were mentally retarded. The parents, particularly the mothers, disagreed with the mischaracterizations of their children. Advocates for the students created a more culturally and linguistically appropriate reading program for the students, but it was rejected by the school district (Smitherman, 1981). The Honorable Judge Joiner further narrowly limited the case to address

1703(f), which reads in part: "No state shall deny equal educational opportunity to an individual on account of his or her race, color, sex, or national origin, by…the failure to overcome language barriers that impede equal participation by its students in its instructional programs."

(quoted in Smitherman, 1981, pp. 41–42)

As Smitherman (1981), the plaintiff's expert witness and consultant, recalled:

the precedent established by the King decision represents the first test of the applicability of 1703(f), the language provision of the 1974 Equal Educational Opportunity Act, to Black English speakers. The case suggests new possibilities for educational and social policies in our struggle to save the children and develop future leadership.

(pp. 41–42)

After a four-week trial, the judge ruled in favor of the plaintiffs, finding the school district had violated the students' rights. Smitherman wrote:

the school district had failed to recognize the existence and legitimacy of the children's language, Black English. This failure of the teachers to recognize the language as legitimate and the corresponding negative attitudes toward the children's language led to negative expectations of the children which turned into self-fulfilling prophecies. One critical consequence was that the children were not being taught to read.

(p. 42)

Although the school district filed a motion to dismiss the case, arguing in part that AAL was not a language and 1703(f) was limited to foreign languages, not AAL, the motion was denied. Insightfully, Smitherman (1981) acknowledged that the use of standardized tests, normed among middle-class, Standard English dominant, White students represented an "institutional policy detrimental to the educational success of Black English-speaking children ... are obviously linguistically and culturally biased against poor black children" (p. 47). The school staff was given directives to better inform their teaching of Black students.

Dreeben (1987) agreed, adding beyond administrators and teachers who exhibited racist attitudes toward Black students, that school districts and schools enforced policies and teaching practices harmful to Black students (p. 28). His study conducted in three Chicago public school districts among first-grade classrooms suggested differences between high-quality reading instruction (ability grouping, challenging materials, and increasing instructional time and pacing) experienced by Black and White students. He claimed: "The remedies that equalize the learning of black and white children are not race specific; they have to do with the ordinary activities and policies of school districts, schools, and classrooms" (p. 35). He concluded two ideas increased instructional time and engaging reading material were paramount for improved early reading performance.

Decades later, the importance of African American language re-emerged in the Oakland, CA, school district when parents demanded improved quality of education and diminished placement of Black students in special education and suspensions. In 1996, the Oakland school board decided to pass the Ebonics resolution, acknowledging Ebonics as a legitimate language. The Oakland School Board's decision to recognize Black English/Ebonics as a language and the fount of cultural knowledge for speakers was also understood as a pathway to standard English and a way to receive federal bilingual education funding. Banks and Banks (2019) summarized the events:

> the parents of a group of African-American children alleged that the school was not enabling their children to succeed and a variety of ways, including preventing them from learning standard English. The judge ruled that the school had not helped it's teachers and personnel to respond to the linguistic needs of its African-American children. As a result of the ruling, black English has also been given legal standing in some districts, such as in Oakland, California.
>
> *(p. 181)*

There was considerable media coverage and backlash as the facts informing the Oakland School Board's decision were minimalized, ridiculed, and second-guessed in the media. Findings suggested otherwise as "the school had not helped its teacher and personnel to respond to the linguistic needs of its African American children" (Varghese, 2017, p. 195). The linguistic challenges brought on behalf of Black students in Ann Arbor, MI, and Oakland, CA, were "as much about educating black children as about Black English" (Smitherman, 1998, p. 163). The cases did not result in equitable education, although the Ann Arbor case did establish that a "linguistic precedent" occurred given "for the first time, it was written into law, … that AAL was a legitimate form of speech" (Smitherman & Baugh, 2002, p. 10). In a retrospective critical discourse and policy analysis of the *MLK v. Ann Arbor* case, Peele-Eady and Foster (2018) acknowledged a minor change in public school personnel's attitude and knowledge of AAL exits: "having legal access to educational opportunity does not guarantee educational equality in practice to African American learners" (p. 654). Despite seminal research by sociolinguists who acknowledged Black English/Ebonics was a language with rule-governed features, Black students' performance on reading assessments, especially oral assessments, continued to reflect racialized misunderstandings about AAL that identified them as having reading difficulty and a pathway for some students into special education.

In another important case, this one reaching to the US Supreme Court in *Plyler v. Doe* (1982), the class-action lawsuit was filed on behalf of undocumented children of Mexican descent who alleged they were treated inequitably. The judges agreed with the plaintiffs, citing the equal protection clause of the Fourteenth Amendment and acknowledging the importance of a person's psychological well-being. Moreover, they highlighted the importance of literacy. As Justice Brennan wrote in his opinion:

> illiteracy is an enduring disability. The inability to read and write will handicap the individual deprived of a basic education each and every day of their lives. The inestimable toll of that deprivation on the social, economic, intellectual, and psychological well-being of the individual, and the obstacle it poses to individual achievement, make it most difficult to reconcile the cost or the principle of a status-based denial of basic education with the framework of equality embodied in the Equal Protection Clause.
>
> *(n.p.)*

A Nation at Risk, Goals 2000, and America 2000

The publication of *A Nation at Risk: The Imperative for Education Reform* (1983) began with the following opening statement:

> *All, regardless of race or class or economic status, are entitled to a fair chance and to the tools for developing their individual powers of mind and spirit to the utmost. This promise means that all children, by virtue of their own efforts, calmly, guided, can hope to attain the mature and informed judgment needed to secure gainful employment, and to manage their own lives, thereby serving not only their own interests but also the progress of society itself.*
>
> *(Gardner, 1983, p. 1, italics in the original)*

The text described who was included in the term "all" as defined by race and socioeconomic status. The authors (several former governors, university presidents, school administers, and others) suggested individuals were responsible for their own learning, irrespective of the legacy of slavery, social inequity, and racism. They also implied a lackluster educational system placed national security at risk and forecasted a dismal future for education in the United States:

> Our nation is at risk. Our once unchallenged preeminence in commerce, industry, science, and technological innovation is being overtaken by competitors throughout the world...the educational foundations of our society are presently being eroded by rising tide of mediocracy that threatens our very nature as a nation and as a people... we have dismantled essential support systems which helped to make these gains possible. We have in effect been committing an act of unthinking, unilateral education disarmament.
>
> *(p. 112)*

After its publication, US Secretary of Education T. H. Bell created a wall chart ranking states, "by their educational attainments, ... ACT and SAT scores—even though they measured only the progress of college-bound students and varied considerably among the states in the percentage of students who took those examinations" (Vinovskis, 1999, p. 13). The wall chart served as a stark display of the academic achievement differences among students across states and was unwelcomed by the Council of Chief State Officers. In 1986, the 'public shaming' resulted in eight Southern states adopting versions of NAEP testing for their state achievement tests (Vinovskis, 1999, p. 14). Under new US Secretary of Education, W. Bennett, a 22-member "NAEP study group headed by Tennessee Gov. Lamar Alexander ... chair of the National Governors' Association and H. Thomas James (former president of the Spencer Foundation)" (p. 14) was established. In concert with the *Nation at Risk*, they maintained achievement test scores between the United States and other nations, adult literacy rates, and high-stakes test results of US school and college students placed the nation at risk (pp. 115–116). Their recommendations included greater state oversight of educational standards and assessments, and suggestions to improve academic achievement, including a focus on reading comprehension. The report also promoted the passage of legislation, permitting the use of trial-level assessments by states, but did not permit state-by-state comparisons. Vinovskis (1999) summarized the intersection of education and social contexts of the period, noting that many original goals to boost educational standards were unmet (desegregating schools, improving early childhood education, and raising academic performance of students living in poverty and racialized minorities). Fueled by the questionable use of data and negative discourse of the publication of the text, concerns were raised about American competitiveness and economic crises (Vinovskis, 1999).

America 2000

In the fall of 1989, President George H. W. Bush in collaboration with Governor Bill Clinton convened an Education Summit in Charlottesville, VA, to reform education. The meeting was attended by several members of Congress, 49 of 50 governors, and the US Secretary of Education and his special assistant. They crafted six goals to reform education, which were shared with the nation.

President Bush first announced the six goals in his State of the Union speech. They differed slightly in wording and content from the ones finally released by the National Governors' Association (NGA) in February 1989 and accepted by the Bush administration. The six goals originally put forth by President Bush were:

- By the year 2000, every child must start school ready to learn.
- The United States must increase the high school graduation rate to no less than 90 percent.
- And we are going to make sure our schools' diplomas mean something. In critical subjects – at the 4th, 8th, and 12th grades – we must assess our students' performance.
- By the year 2000, US students must be first in the world in math and science achievement.
- Every American adult must be a skilled, literate worker and citizen.
- Every school must offer the kind of disciplined environment that makes it possible for our kids to learn. And every school in America must be drug-free.

(footnote, p. 44)

In 1994, an oversight committee, the National Education Goals Panel, added three goals, designed to set academic standards for public school (K–12) education, based on standardized test results:

1. To demonstrate the President's interest in and commitment to education as a central national priority.
2. To engage the nation's governors in a substantive discussion of the nature of the challenge we face, of alternative ways of improving our educational performance, and of those ideas for reform that seem to have the greatest promise.
3. To set the stage for a series of education proposals and national goals to be unveiled in early 1990 possibly as part of the State of the Union Address. (Vinovskis, 1999, p. 39)

Several ideas about education, among politically diverse participants, coalesced around a few common themes: students being ready to read by first grade, improving the high school dropout rate, and reducing achievement disparities among students from different economic and racial groups. The agreed-upon goals were:

- The readiness of children to start school;
- The performance of students on international achievement tests, especially in math and science;
- The reduction of the dropout rate and the improvement of academic performance, especially among at-risk students;
- The functional literacy of adult Americans;
- The level of training necessary to guarantee a competitive workforce;
- The supply of qualified teachers and up-to-date technology; and
- The establishment of safe, disciplined, and drug-free schools.

(Vinovskis, 1999, p. 40)

Goals 2000

A second set of educational goals were published as a nine-year national strategy to improve education. The strategy included support for national achievement testing in some subjects, e.g., reading, would be screened to eliminate bias (America 2000, April 1991, p. 32). In 1994, under the Clinton administration, additional goals were added, and the name was changed to *Goals 2000: Educate America Act.* The new goals included a focus on early learning readiness and reducing the dropout rate, along with creating an educated citizenry.

A parallel and related set of actions had occurred and included increased federal support of special education in the Individuals with Disabilities Education Act (1990), followed by a series of refinements through reauthorizations.

Federalizing Reading Reform

Since the authorization of ESEA, cyclically Congress made evermore refined requests to explore the intersection of student demographics and socioeconomic status to improve educational opportunities. A particular interest was to understand the impact of early reading programs on student academic success. Among the requests was a federally supported review of literature completed by Adams (1990) focused on early reading. Her review presented both a description of reading development and instructional approaches needed to improve reading. Among her findings was the need for phonemic awareness and systematic phonics instruction for all, especially children who were developmentally behind and children living in poverty.

Republican US Senators Thad Cochran and Arlen Spector pushed forward an agenda to address the alleged "growing national education crisis," in pursuit of a solution to early reading difficulties. Mississippi Senator Cochran, a son of educators, introduced federal legislation to improve the reading performance and outcomes of school children following the release of the NAEP, *Reading Report Cards* (National Center for Education Statistics, 1992, 1994). The reports portrayed students in Mississippi among the lowest ranked in reading achievement. Specifically, 88% of students in grade 4 scored at the basic level, of which 63% were

White students and 25% were Black students (Bryant, 1998). The percentage of White students in Mississippi assessed at the basic level exceeded the percentage of White students assessed at the basic level nationally. Senator Cochran partially acknowledged Mississippi's history of civil rights abuses, although he failed to present data or facts explaining Mississippi's history of anti-Black educational and racial discrimination (https://millercenter.org/the-presidency/interviews-with-the-administration/thad-cochran-senator-mississippi). His testimony provided a summary of educational abuse focused on the *Gong Lum v. Rice* (1927) case as an example of racial discrimination in the history of Mississippi's public education:

> A child of Chinese blood, born in and a citizen of the United States, is not denied the equal protection of the law by being classed by the state among the colored races who are assigned to public schools separate from those provided for the whites when equal facilities for education are afforded to both classes. P. 275 US 85.
>
> *(https://supreme.justia.com/cases/federal/us/275/78/case.html)*

As a result, without accurately or completely acknowledging the history of racial discrimination and servitude under Jim/Jane Crow laws, or racial discrimination in employment and housing, or the dire social contexts under which all minoritized people lived in Mississippi, the senator positioned reading as a national crisis. Cochran also criticized reading research as filled with confusing results, failing schools, underprepared teachers, and weak education programs in higher education, although he did not present any evidence for these critiques. He insisted, "rigorous scientific research [is needed] to understand not only the causes but the consequences of reading problems and related cognitive difficulties" (143 Cong Rec H 4072). In addition, he insisted that "rigorous scientific research [is needed] to understand not only the causes but the consequences of reading problems and related cognitive difficulties" (105 Cong. Rec S5978 (1997)/Senate Report 105-58, p. 5). He did not define rigorous research, but it was understood to mean experimental research.

On April 16, 1997, Senator Cochran reminded his colleagues of "the administration's proposal that every child in America should be able to read well and independently *by the end of third grade*" (143 Cong. Rec. 86. 1997, emphasis added). He mentioned the amount of funding received by the National Institute of Child Health and Human Development (NICHD): "NICHD has spent over $100 million to follow about 2,500 young children in rigorous scientific research to understand not only the causes but the consequences of reading problems and related cognitive difficulties" (105 Cong. Rec S5978 (1997)/Senate Report 105-58, p. 5). He continued, highlighting that "the NICHD findings underscore the need to do a better job of teacher training. Researchers found fewer than 10 percent of teachers actually know how to teach reading to children who don't learn reading automatically" (105 Cong. Rec S5978 (1997)/Senate Report 105-58, p. 5). Senator Spector added his support to NICHD's efforts, commenting he was "impressed with the important accomplishments reported from the NICHD research program on reading development and disability and is eager to have this information brought to the attention of educators, policy makers, and parents" (105 Cong. Rec S5978 (1997). He noted the work of NICHD had focused on "multidisciplinary research programs to study genetics, brain pathology, developmental process and phonetic acquisition" (*NRPR*, 2000, p. 2). Shortly thereafter, Senator Cochran (June 19, 1997) introduced the Successful Reading Research and Instruction Act (s. 939), arguing to improve early reading instruction:

> Research shows fewer *than one child in eight who is failing to read by the end of first grade ever catches up to grade level* … This indicates that we need to start solving the problem of poor readers at the beginning, instead of working backward.
>
> *(p. 213, emphasis added)*

Dr. Alexander, a supporter of the bill, testified before Congress by extending reading into mental health:

> I think that it is important to point out that our intensive research efforts in reading development and disorders is motivated to a great extent by our seeing difficulties learning to read as not only an educational problem, but also a major public health issue. Simply put, if a youngster does not learn to read, he or she will simply not likely be able to make it in life. Our longitudinal studies that study children from age five through their high school years have shown us *how tender these kids are with respect to their own response to reading failure.* By the end of the first grade, we begin to notice *substantial decreases in the children's self-esteem, self-concept, and motivation to learn to read if they have not been able to master reading skills and keep up with their age-mate*s. As we follow them through elementary and middle school *these problems compound*, and in many cases very bright youngsters are deprived of the wonders of literature, history, science, and mathematics because they cannot read the grade-level textbooks. By high school, these children's potential for entering college has decreased to almost nil, with few choices available to them with respect to occupational and vocational opportunities.
>
> *(143 Cong. Rec. 86, 1997, p. S6002, emphasis added)*

Importantly, he provided a cautionary tale about the possible mental health issues for students who are retained because of reading performance. Senate bill 939, "The Successful Reading Research and Instruction Act," was proposed in part to address reading achievement by grade 3 (Congressional Record, June 1997).

The State of Mississippi's auditor, Bryant (1998), produced a new report, A Review of the Reading Program of the Mississippi Department of Education, without recalling the history of educational and racial discrimination, differences among school funding resources, or the demographic composition of each school (ability, ethnicity/race, gender, languages, social economic status). The impetus for the Mississippi Report, in part was the reading results on the Iowa Test of Basic Skills and NAEP report cards (1992 and 1994), detailed by school district in the appendices. The Mississippi Report offered a sanitized discourse and data that suggested the state of Mississippi was meeting its stated goals for reading in public schools.

The Reading Excellence Act

Congress continued to pass legislation for "the nation's children" with a focus on reading. Drawing on 1994 NAEP reading achievement data, they remarked: "44 percent of school children are reading below a basic level of achievement" (p. 2). Then, they linked data from the National Adult Literacy Survey of "over 40 million adults were at the lowest literacy level" (p. 2), to emphasize the importance of reading and push forward the Reading Excellent Act (1998).

Reading researchers either ignored or minimized racial differences among subjects, preferring to focus on cognitive, cultural, economic, or psychological explanations for reading problems.

The Reading Excellence Act (1998) was established following the dismal NAEP results of fourth-grade readers and after multiple federal programs to improve reading, for example, Even Start and Reading Is Fundamental, did not appear to make adequate progress. The purpose of the bill was to

> improve the reading and literacy skills of children and families by improving in-service instructional practices for teachers who teach reading, to stimulate the development of more high-quality family literacy programs, to support extended learning-term opportunities for children, to ensure that children can read well and independently not later than third grade, and for other purposes, having considered the same, reports favorably thereon with an amendment (in the nature of a substitute) and recommends that the bill (as amended) do pass.

> *(p. 1)*

The Act also focused on teacher training and professional development. Grants were awarded to states that oversaw the distribution of funds to local school agencies as well as local libraries. With a focus on training reading teachers, the Reading Excellence Act stated, "we must have teachers who are appropriately trained to teach reading to both children and adults. ... By emphasizing the importance of professional development for reading, those programs that currently attempt to address literacy issues will be greatly enhanced" (p. 3). Congress listed several federally funded programs designed to improve reading achievement, student access to books, and the teaching of reading. No singular program made a significant difference in the reading performance between Black and

White students. The funding for the Reading Excellence Act was distributed to states to work with local educational agencies

> providing technical assistance to schools and local educational agencies; conducting an assessment pertaining to the State's needs for reading and literacy professional development, including an assessment adequate and age-appropriate reading and library materials; coordinating reading and literacy programs; and conducting evaluations of local educational agency literacy activities. Each grant that is awarded will be for three years in duration.
>
> *(p. 6)*

As the program was underway, additional federal funding was extended by the National Academy of Sciences to empanel reading experts to review research on preventing reading problems among young children (Snow, Burns, & Griffin, 1998).

Expert Reading Panel

The expert panel, chaired by Adams, included several scholars of color who were charged to review research centered on "the effectiveness of interventions for young children who are at risk of having problems learning to read" (Snow, Burns, & Griffin, 1998, p. 18). The panel produced a text, *Preventing Reading Difficulties in Young Children*, that acknowledged difficulties were "inextricably embedded in educational, social, historical, cultural, and biological realities" (p. 33). They explained:

> children from poor families, children of African American and Hispanic descent, and children attending urban schools are at much greater risk of poor reading outcomes than are middle-class, European-American, and suburban children. Studying these demographic disparities can help us identify groups that should be targeted for special prevention efforts.
>
> *(pp. 27–28)*

The discourse embraced language coded for racial neutrality: at-risk, cultural factors/culturally diverse, disadvantaged, ethnic groups, environmental differences, high-risk, language-minority, low-income, minority, minority-dialects, nonstandard varieties of English, the poor/poverty, rural, socioeconomic status, Spanish-speaking, and urban. All students of color were collectively given the ambiguous term "minority/minorities" as in opposition to the majority group, Whites. Students from ethnic/racial groups were compared to Whites, who are presented as a monolithic group.

In 1998, a panel established by Dr. Alexander, consisting of reading experts, community members, medical doctors, parents, and teachers, was introduced as the National Reading Panel (NRP). Drawing on procedures and processes from NICHD and the Department of Education and chaired by Donald N. Langenberg, a physicist, the panel was charged to

> examine critically the research literature with respect to the basic processes by which children learn to read, and the instructional approaches used in the United States to teach children to learn to read … and evaluate research on teaching of reading to children, identify proven methodologies, and suggest ways for dissemination of this information to teachers, parents, universities, and others.
>
> *(quoted in the National Reading Panel Report, 2000, pp. 1–2)*

His ideas aligned with those of Senator Cochran and Dr. Alexander, as they narrowly defined what they considered to be legitimate methods of reading research: "we cannot separate truth from conjecture, or distinguish what really works from what might work without scientifically rigorous, experimental, or quasi-experimental research of the kind on which this Panel focused its work" (*National Reading Panel Report*, 2000, p. 2). Key terms, science or scientifically based, were repeated and extended to reassure stakeholders the changes were based on science. Au (2016) differently summarized the zest for support of high-stakes testing campaigns during this period. He noted that during the twentieth and twenty-first centuries,

> arguments for using high-stakes testing for racial equality all assume that our standardized tests provide accurate measurements of teaching and learning. This presumption does not hold true. Test scores correlate most strongly with family income, neighborhood, educational levels of parents, and access to resources — all factors that are measures of wealth that exist outside of schools.
>
> *(p. 2)*

Meyer, Park, Bevan-Brown, and Savage (2015) observed and identified educational issues confronted by students who are culturally and linguistically diverse as well as students who also receive special education services and acknowledged that "low-income boys who are African American or Native American are those most likely to be diagnosed as having disabilities such as mental retardation and emotional disturbances, and they are least likely to be labeled as gifted or talented" (p. 237). The muted discourse about race/racism within the federal government's actions and its proxy agencies tangential to reading demonstrated a lack of support for improving reading among Black students. Much like President Andrew Johnson's strategizing, efforts to improve reading performance on standardized reading tests among Black students were usurped by an unyielding focus on the needs of White students: the never-ending desire to "prove" White intellectual superiority, by emphasizing the number and percentage of Black students receiving special education services. In terms of reading, this meant proving and advertising that White students consistently outperformed all other racial demographic groups (often Asians and Asian Pacific Islanders performed higher than White students). Although the tests were fraught with racist overtones, they were part of the master narrative and were "constructed so that responsibility for their own subordination falls on the subordinated people" (Love, 2004, p. 229). Results from standardized reading tests appeared as unquestionable "facts" in reading reform.

Concerns surrounding reading among students with disabilities morphed legally, as recognized and sanctioned disabilities to reflect fluid definitions of reading disabilities under the umbrella term specific learning disabilities, the category with the largest percentage of Black students. The use of metrics established by research among able, English-dominated, middle- to upper-middle class, White students created a "legal" force field for the mis/over/use of standardized reading testing. Black students continued to be three times as likely to be labeled mentally retarded, two times as likely to be labeled emotionally disturbed, and one and a half times as likely to be labeled learning disabled compared to their white peers (p. 3). Given that Black students in particular did not perform well on standardized reading tests, the strategic vulnerability of many Black readers was promoted, rhetorically, as a benevolent, albeit a false, choice to improve reading outcomes. Research by Annamma, Connor, and Ferri (2013) found that

> African American students continue to be three times as likely to be labeled mentally retarded, two times as likely to be labeled as emotionally disturbed, and one and a half times as likely to be labeled as learning disabled, compared to their white peers.
>
> *(p. 3)*

Au (2021) acknowledged low scores on standardized tests historically have been used "to track Black students into vocational education or for White teachers to simply explain away any difficulties they might be having with non-White students in their classrooms" (p. 102). He also noted standardized tests "*are not effective at improving achievement, and they still produce unequal, discriminatory outcomes*" (p. 105, italics in the original). His observations echoed the history exposed in this chapter: the science underpinning standardized testing was framed by the ideology of White supremacy and bolstered by the ideas of the eugenics movement among educational psychologists who also created early standardized reading tests. Their efforts were supported and popularized among corporate and philanthropic interests with ties to the federal government, connections to elite universities, and the testing industry. Their collective ideological bent synced with White Americans who desired to normalize White supremacy and used science as the "fool-proof" venue to establish and maintain intellectual dominance and racial inequality. Moreover, they used their status to influence the federal government, establish ties to universities and academic scholarship, as well as create federal government structures and federal government-adjacent agencies to promulgate their ideas within the public.

3

THE POLITICIZATION OF READING AND READING RESEARCH, 2000–2022

During the first two decades of the twenty-first century, the ideology of White supremacy remained anchored in the notion "scientific methods;" racist assumptions; and notions of individualism, merit, and standardization. Federal support of reading research agendas continued to promote twentieth-century scientific racism, with a twenty-first-century version, as the "gold standard" of experimental and quasi-experimental reading research. Reading assessments expected a dominant response aligning beliefs and cultural and linguistic knowledge, not an independent thinker, reader, or writer. Reading comprehension assessments also continued to draw on deficit perspectives and produced deficit responses about the performance of students of color. Politicians and educators (district administrators and classroom teachers) seldom acknowledged publicly; students were categorized by class, ethnicity, geography (zip code), language, and race. The personhood of individual students was represented administratively in stereotypically unchallenged discourse patterns and was reflective of local, state, and national "conservative" media rhetoric. The harmful and negative impact on the lives and academic progress of students was incalculable. Across the two centuries, however, the efficacy of novel approaches did not significantly change the reading performance of Black students on standardized reading assessments, nor substantively improve literacy.

When George W. Bush was a candidate for governor of Texas in 1994, part of his platform centered on reforming education in the state. Among his education reform ideas was to eliminate social promotion and increase graduation rates, drawing upon the "Texas Miracle" in the Houston public schools. The superintendent of Houston schools, Dr. R. Paige (1994–2001), and the high school principal of Sharpstown Senior High, shared how their reform efforts resulted in a zero-dropout rate. Governor G. W. Bush (1995–2000) signed his

DOI: 10.4324/9781003296188-4

first bill into law: Senate Bill 1 consisting of several reform features: establishing charter schools, statewide school district accountability through assessments, and revising the duties of the State Commission of Education to report directly to the governor much like his brother, Jeb Bush did as governor of Florida.

Stanford (2013) reported that the Texas Miracle requiring all students to take state achievement tests was pitched to appear as an equalizer: "the state could direct resources where they would do the most good, and eventually African-American and Hispanic kids would catch up to the white kids. It was a great theory, and initially the scores rose" (n.p.). It was not long before the Texas Miracle collapsed as data did not accurately reflect state test scores; many students were untested or dropped out before the tenth grade. Stanford revealed a connection between Sandy Kress, George W. Bush's education advisor as governor of Texas, and later a lawyer-lobbyist for the Pearson testing company. The same company created the State of Texas Assessments of Academic Readiness (STARR) and with contracted to develop state-level tests, garnering millions of dollars for Pearson. Finally, Stanford's review of the tests created by Pearson exposed a weakness: their tests measured test-taking ability more than academic achievement (n.p.). Sharpstown High School assistant principal, Robert Kimball, disputed the facts about the number of high school dropouts. He became a whistleblower when educators refused to address his concerns and turned to the media (Capellaro, 2004). An official state audit of the Houston high school dropouts found 3,000 unaccounted dropouts; thus, the reported results were fraudulent and were undiscounted (Loyola, 2016). In an interview, when asked about the intersection of academic achievement and race, Dr. Kimball responded:

> Institutional racism is the main factor in causing the achievement gap. Educators should be taught in colleges and in schools how to recognize racism and develop policies that result in an excellent education for all students, regardless of color or ethnicity.
>
> *(Capellaro, 2004, p. 18)*

Drawing on the fraudulent data, however, presidential candidate Bush had declared education was a national crisis and sought to

> draw a clear link between the nation's future economic health and the quality of its schools, … [he] asserted that the nation faced a reading crisis that had contributed to crime and caused American students to fall behind their peers in other industrialized nations.
>
> *(Dao, 2000, para 2)*

He sought to convince politicians and the public he could resolve differences in the academic achievement gap between students of color and their White peers. To do so, he drew heavily upon the results of the National Reading Panel (NRP).

In the interim, the National Research Council (NRC, 2001) not so coincidentally provided guidelines for education research (Towne, Shavelson, & Feuer, 2001), privileged experimental and quasi-experimental research, and an unvoiced but White-centric view of culture, education, research, science, and the world. The Committee on Scientific Principles for Education Research within NRC developed federal guidelines for scientific education research (NRC, 2002). With respect to reading research, repeated ideas mentioned by previous studies included:

> scientifically researched and evidence-based reading instructional strategies that improve reading performance for all students, including explicit, systematic, and sequential approaches to teaching phonemic awareness, phonics, vocabulary, fluency, and text comprehension and multisensory intervention strategies.
>
> *(para 4)*

This chapter examines the first two decades of the twenty-first century, and the laws affecting reading (assessment, instruction, policies, and research) as well places them in the historical and political context. In addition, ESEA reauthorizations, No Child Left Behind Act (NCLB, 2001), and Every Student Succeeds Act (ESSA) are reviewed as a continuation of an anti-Black literacy campaign. Finally, there is an investigation of multiple extra-political agencies working in support of federal laws and policies to frame reading – and reading laws and policies – as acultural, neutral, apolitical, and universal to understand how they institutionally and structurally help to maintain anti-Black literacy under cover of the federal, state, and local laws and policies.

The National Reading Panel

The United States Department of Education (USDOE) and NICHD released *The National Reading Panel Report* (*NRPR*), freely distributed the report and ancillary materials to schools nationally, and subsequently created federally funded research opportunities. Findings by the *NRPR* mirrored the psychological processes and reading deficits described in other federally sponsored reports. Of particular interest is the Alphabetics subgroup report, a meta-analysis of original experimental and quasi-experimental studies to determine the basic skills needed for reading, that is, early reading or alphabetics (phonemic awareness and phonics) as a necessary for early readers to acquire. A close review of studies conducted in the United States revealed a range of student abilities (at-risk, LD, normal, and struggling), *a disproportionate focus on students identified as LD* (emphasis added), and the exclusion of students who are not English-dominant; very few studies included Asian American and Asian Pacific Islanders, *Black*, Latinx, and

Native American students (Willis, 2008, emphasis added). To be clear, race was a variable in original studies and described to varying degrees as the original studies had heavily investigated reading among students labeled as learning disabled (Willis, 2008; Willis & Williams, 2001) and unambiguously applied deficit and negative characterizations of students of color, their communities, their families, and their schools. Gersten, Darch, and Gleason (1988), for example, characterized the families of students in their study as "approximately 65% of the families   had female heads of households over 70% of the students families were receiving welfare" (p. 231) without supplying any supporting data. The choice of discourse aligned with stereotypical images used to categorize Black student readers' families and social class. In another study, Foorman, Francis, Fletcher, Schatschneider, and Mehta (1998) suggested reading failures existed "in urban settings, there are entire schools in which reading failure is the norm, in part because of lack of home preparation in understanding the alphabetic principle … and also because of inadequate instruction in the classroom" (p. 38). They also implied students' community, economic class, and home life were linked to reading failure along with absent fathers, living in an urban setting, lack of home pre-literacy training, and poor-quality instruction in schools; such narratives "typically frame these disparate outcomes as products of a racialized culture of poverty created within the home and the hood" and "within the students themselves versus society's recognitions of them" (Rosa, 2019, pp. 9, 11). The studies did not position the failure of Black and Brown readers to ideological, theoretical, or methodological issues in reading research or assessments, instructions, interventions, or referral procedures, thus leaving reading research blameless and unchallenged. Only a limited number of studies included SOC, and only one in which the subjects are predominately Black students (Gersten et al., 1988); the most identifiable students are demographically represented as English-dominant, middle-class, learning disabled, and White (Willis & Williams, 2001). In addition, Spanish-dominant students were not included in the original studies, replicating the omission of Spanish-dominant speakers in reading research used decades earlier in the federally supported *First Grade Reading Studies* (Bond & Dykstra, 1964). Importantly, there was a disproportionate number of studies focused on the early reading achievement of students with learning disabilities. Not surprisingly, the findings of the Alphabetics subgroup report paralleled those identified for early reading in a previous study funded by the federal government. Yatvin (2000) added a minority view to the report, suggesting some members of the NRP wanted a more thorough review, "an exhaustive and objective analysis of correlational, descriptive, and qualitative studies relevant to reading development and reading instruction" (*Report of the NRP*, 2000, p. 24). In another publication, she revealed the report was "unbalanced, and, to some extent, irrelevant" (Yatvin, 2000, p. 3) and claimed the contributors knew the shortcomings of the report and were poised to propose reading reform policy at federal, state, and local levels (p. 3).

The first chapter of the *NRP*, Alphabetics, was a meta-analysis of selective experimental and quasi-experimental research of early reading. The chapter's recommendations on reading instruction identified five components believed imperative for early readers, the same five components identified in the 1994 SLD summit and *PRD* (1998):

> Phonemic awareness: The knowledge that spoken words are made up of individual sounds, or phonemes.
> Phonics: The relationship between phonemes and printed letters.
> Fluency: Being able to read quickly, accurately, and with understanding, aloud and to oneself.
> Vocabulary development: Knowledge of what words mean and how they sound, across a variety of topics.
> Reading comprehension: An active process of understanding written text using a variety of comprehension skills and strategies. Reading comprehension closely interlinked with all of the four other skills. For example, a sufficient vocabulary is a prerequisite to comprehension, and comprehension skills can help students expand and retain new words in their vocabulary.
>
> *(p. 4)*

The studies reviewed in the Alphabetics section, the section most often referenced on early reading and reading achievement, did not include significant numbers of Black students or Spanish-dominant students, and students from these ethnic and racial groups were not identified among middle- to upper-middle-class students.

Among the free materials distributed to attendees at professional conferences, sent to school districts and schools, was a video appearing to concretize unquestioned assumptions about Black and Brown male children and links to intelligence, reading, and race. In a snippet from the video, there are pictured Black and Brown, young male children, in a city, under a viaduct, who appear to be comfortably talking and hanging out in front of trash bins while a subway car travels in the background. Along with this scene, the narrator declared: "When children fail to learn to read this downward spiraling continues until children avoid reading and develop a sense of failure that affects all other aspects of their lives" (n.p.). The voice-over was not supported by the studies reviewed or the data presented in the NRP, given the relatively limited numbers of Black and Brown male students in the report on Alphabetics. Thus, the call for an overhaul of beginning reading instruction relied heavily on racist tropes and mistruths as well as White supremacy. The video, paid for and distributed by the federal government, victimized young Black and Brown male children by using deficit-laden language racist tropes and profiled young Black and Brown male children, as if they are "problems-in-waiting." Most disarmingly, the errors in the video and content were unaddressed by academics, administrators, citizens, politicians, and most reading researchers. Given the NRP's position as a catalyst for the passage of the NCLB (2001), the media featured support of NCLB offered by many Black and Brown activists and journalists, although the error made by the producers of the video reflected a mischaracterization of Black and Brown male readers and the reading research reviewed. The results of NRP, especially the Alphabetics subsection on beginning reading instruction, were promoted as the panacea for struggling readers: who were failing to read in the first grade, but clearly this could not be true, given the large numbers of missing subjects and unaccounted aggregate subgroups. Promotionally, Black and Brown students were pictured and described as the most likely to benefit from increased use of phonemic awareness and phonics in early reading programs (although they were not part of the original studies).

No Child Left Behind Act

Drawing comparisons to *Brown v. Board of Education* (1954) and the Civil Rights Act (1964), Bush's message is captured in a speech before the NAACP (2000), as he characterized educational equity and fairness: "reading [as] the new civil right" (as cited in Stanford, 2013). He campaigned on a "reading crisis," identified as the need to improve the reading outcomes for Black students, other students of color, low-income students, and students with disabilities and identified early reading achievement as a lynchpin to academic success. These pronouncements were not happenstance but calculated political maneuvers to sway politicians and the public. President Bush drew on data reported by the NRP (2000) to address what he defined as a "reading crisis." As the president, George W. Bush named Dr. R. Paige US Secretary of Education to help replicate the "Texas Miracle" for the nation. Bush (2002b) also revised and broadened his platform, stating, "education is the greatest civil right issue of our time," as he extended educational equity to address students with disabilities. To assure support by the Black community, several prominent Black people received payments of $250,000 (e.g., Dorothy Haight and Armstrong Williams) for their advertised and vocal support of the NCLB.

On March 22, 2001, the NCLB Act was introduced to address the educational and reading crises as well as a possible replication of the Texas Miracle. It was heralded as a way "to close the achievement gap with accountability, flexibility, and choice, so that no child is left behind (n.p., https://www.govtrack.us/congress/bills/107/hr1/text/ih). The bill was signed into law on January 8, 2002. Title 1 included funding sources dictated by the federal government to shape educational policy and to offer support of federal dollars for privatized education in the form of vouchers and charter school funding.

> The advocacy of voucher systems – which would in effect, commodify public education by making it more portable, … [NCLB] legislation at the federal level represents pressure for measuring performance, seen by some as a preliminary step towards commercialization.
>
> *(https://definitions.uslegal.com/c/charter-school/)*

A closer look at the notion of privatization revealed former President George H. W. Bush supported similar legislation: workarounds to racial equity and integration with the rise in "White flight" redrawn school district borders, increase in the number of all-White suburban schools, and voucher programs for elite schools. Under NCLB, extended privatization included charter schools to close the achievement gap (in terms of academic performance on standardized achievement tests) between SOC and White students. The bill was promoted as a way to address racial inequality in education. On January 19, 2002, President G. W. Bush articulated:

> Americans can proudly say that we have overcome the institutionalized bigotry that Dr. King fought. Now our challenge is to make sure that every child has a fair chance to succeed in life. That is why education is the greatest civil rights issue of our time.
>
> *(Applied Center for Research, 2003, p. 5)*

Under President G. W. Bush's leadership, Congress reauthorized ESEA, as the NCLB (2001) sought to promote equality and equity through a narrowing of the achievement gap among aggregate racial groups, with a focus on the achievement gap between Black and minority readers and their White peers (USLegal. com). Reading was recognized as pivotal to the effectiveness of NCLB, and the law sought to **ensure every student learned to read by grade 3**.

The discourse of White supremacy framed NCLB as a reasonable response to the current education/reading crisis. Other features of the law, much like the revised educational reforms in Texas, tied accountability of schools to the use of scientific/evidenced-based approaches and measures based on students' performance on standardized assessments. A subtle but important framing occurred, as previously identified scientific/scientifically based research took on the mantle of evidenced research, meaning multiple studies (replications of White supremacist ideology, methods, and theories) yielded similar results as evidence. The use of the term "evidence" was to allay two concerns: (1) reassuring the stakeholders research was "scientific," drawing on ideological, methodological, and theoretical schools of thought and (2) verifying the research guiding instruction had been tested.

Title I, "Improving the Academic Achievement of the Disadvantaged" (USDOE Title I, 2019), was written to "ensure that all children have a fair, equal, and significant opportunity to obtain a high-quality education and reach, at a minimum, proficiency on challenging State academic achievement standards and state academic assessments" (NCLB, Sec. 1001 Statement of Purpose). In this way, all funding for Title I was "tied to student test scores" (Au, 2013, p. 10). NCLB also "requires schools to implement research-based reading programs" and to use "effective instructional materials, programs, learning systems, and strategies that have been proven to prevent or remediate reading failure" (https://www.wrightslaw.com/nclb/rreading.grade3.htm). Finally, school districts were required to assure adequate yearly progress was made by students living in poverty, students from major racial and ethnic groups, students with disabilities, and students with limited English proficiency.

The NCLB (2001) appeared to present lawmakers and the public with lofty egalitarian goals of improving education in general and reading education, particularly. Among the stated purposes of the law was "to ensure that every student can read at grade level or above … [by] the end of grade 3" (n.p.). The law also required schools to use research-based reading programs and "prepare teachers, including special ed teachers … so teachers have the tools to effectively help their students learn to read" (n.p.). The requirements were supported by the National Research Council (2002) also issuing a rationale and principles for scientific education: (1) pose significant questions that can be investigated empirically, (2) link research to relevant theory, (3) use methods that permit direct investigation of the question, provide a coherent and explicit chain of reasoning, replicate and generalize across studies, and disclose research to encourage professional scrutiny and critique (pp. 2–10). The use of quantitative methods, primarily experimental and quasi-experimental research, was heralded as the "gold standard," while simultaneously supporting hegemonic, ideological, and theoretical likemindedness among supporters. Like prior reading reform efforts, NCLB did not address the socio-historical contexts of some students and the intergenerational legacy of anti-Black literacy.

Research studies conducted by NAEP and NRP (2000) were important resources to frame reading initiatives. NAEP data (1992–2015) included reading assessment scores for students in grade 4 (please see Table 3.1).

The importance of literacy to this law was demonstrated by the multiple extensions under Title I (*Federal Early Reading First Initiative, Part B, Subpart 1*; *Federal Reading First Initiative, Part B, Subpart 2*; *William Goodling Even Start Family Literacy Programs, Part B, Subpart 3*; *Improving Literacy Through School Libraries, Part B, Subpart 4*). In addition, there were extensions under Title IV, *Part B, 21st Century Community Learning Centers; and Title V, Part B, Subpart 5, Reading Is Fundamental Inexpensive Book Distribution* as well as *The No Child Left Behind Summer Reading Program* and *The Partnership for Reading Program*. NCLB required states and school districts to select or develop "effective instructional materials, programs, learning systems, and strategies that have been proven to prevent or

TABLE 3.1 NAEP 1992–2015, Fourth Grade Reading

		Sex			Race/ethnicity									
		Average Reading Scale Score			Average Reading Scale Score			Asian/Pacific Islander						
Grade and Year	All Students	Male	Female	Gap between Female and Male Score	White	Black	Hispanic	Total	Asian[1]	Pacific Islander[1]	American Indian/Alaska Native	Two or More Races[1]	Gap between White and Black Score	Gap between White and Hispanic Score
1	2	3	4	5	6	7	8	9	10	11	12	13	14	15
Grade 4														
1992[2]	217 (0.9)	213 (1.2)	221 (1.0)	8 (1.6)	224 (1.2)	192 (1.7)	197 (2.6)	216 (2.9)	— (†)	— (†)	‡ (†)	— (†)	32 (2.1)	27 (2.9)
1994[2]	214 (1.0)	209 (1.3)	220 (1.1)	10 (1.7)	224 (1.3)	185 (1.8)	188 (3.4)	220 (3.8)	— (†)	— (†)	211 (6.6)	— (†)	38 (2.2)	35 (3.6)
1998	215 (1.1)	212 (1.3)	217 (1.3)	5 (1.8)	225 (1.0)	193 (1.9)	193 (3.2)	215 (5.6)	— (†)	— (†)	‡ (†)	— (†)	32 (2.2)	32 (3.3)
2000	213 (1.3)	208 (1.3)	219 (1.4)	11 (1.9)	224 (1.1)	190 (1.8)	190 (2.9)	225 (5.2)	— (†)	— (†)	214 (6.0)	— (†)	34 (2.1)	35 (3.1)
2002	219 (0.4)	215 (0.4)	222 (0.5)	6 (0.7)	229 (0.3)	199 (0.5)	201 (1.3)	224 (1.6)	— (†)	— (†)	207 (2.0)	— (†)	30 (0.6)	28 (1.4)
2003	218 (0.3)	215 (0.3)	222 (0.3)	7 (0.5)	229 (0.2)	198 (0.4)	200 (0.6)	226 (1.2)	— (†)	— (†)	202 (1.4)	— (†)	31 (0.5)	28 (0.6)
2005	219 (0.2)	216 (0.2)	222 (0.3)	6 (0.4)	229 (0.2)	200 (0.3)	203 (0.5)	229 (0.7)	— (†)	— (†)	204 (1.3)	— (†)	29 (0.4)	26 (0.5)
2007	221 (0.3)	218 (0.3)	224 (0.3)	7 (0.4)	231 (0.2)	203 (0.4)	205 (0.5)	232 (1.0)	— (†)	— (†)	203 (1.2)	— (†)	27 (0.5)	26 (0.6)
2009	221 (0.3)	218 (0.3)	224 (0.3)	7 (0.4)	230 (0.3)	205 (0.5)	205 (0.5)	235 (1.0)	— (†)	— (†)	204 (1.3)	— (†)	26 (0.6)	25 (0.6)
2011	221 (0.3)	218 (0.3)	225 (0.3)	7 (0.5)	231 (0.2)	205 (0.5)	206 (0.5)	235 (1.2)	236 (1.3)	216 (1.9)	202 (1.3)	227 (1.2)	25 (0.5)	24 (0.6)
2013	222 (0.3)	219 (0.3)	225 (0.3)	7 (0.5)	232 (0.3)	206 (0.5)	207 (0.5)	235 (1.1)	237 (1.1)	212 (2.5)	205 (1.3)	227 (1.0)	26 (0.6)	25 (0.6)
2015	223 (0.4)	219 (0.4)	226 (0.4)	7 (0.6)	232 (0.3)	206 (0.5)	208 (0.8)	239 (1.4)	241 (1.6)	215 (2.9)	205 (1.5)	227 (1.2)	26 (0.6)	24 (0.9)

NOTE: Scale ranges from 0 to 500. Includes public, private, Bureau of Indian Education, and Department of Defense Education Activity schools. For 1998 and later years, includes students tested with accommodations (2 to 14 percent of all students, depending on grade level and year); excludes only those students with disabilities and English language learners who were unable to be tested even with accommodations (2 to 6 percent of all students). Data on race/ethnicity are based on school reports. Race categories exclude persons of Hispanic ethnicity. Standard errors appear in parentheses.

— Not available.

†Not applicable.

‡Reporting standards not met. Either there are too few cases for a reliable estimate or the coefficient of variation (CV) is 50 percent or greater.

1 Prior to 2011, separate data for Asian students, Pacific Islander students, and students of Two or more races were not collected.

2 Accommodations were not permitted for this assessment.

SOURCE: US Department of Education, National Center for Education Statistics, National Assessment of Educational Progress (NAEP), 1992, 1994, 1998, 2000, 2002, 2003, 2005, 2007, 2009, 2011, 2013, 2015, 2017, and 2019 Reading Assessments, retrieved October 30, 2019, from the Main NAEP Data Explorer (https://

remediate reading failure" (*NRPR*). The Bush administration earmarked "$5 billion investment to ensure that every child in America can read well by the end of third grade" (USDOE, The Facts) and "federal funds are sent directly to states, then on to local educational agencies, thus, state and local agencies determine use" (quoted in Willis, 2019b, p. 92).

McQuillan (1998) succinctly noted, politically, there appeared reoccurring literacy crises in the United States, with varying points of origin. Historically, the use of standardized testing became a sacrosanct accountability feature:

> A narrow focus on the achievement gap predictably leads to policies grounded in high-stakes testing, which in turn leads to narrow thinking about groups of students, their teachers, and their schools. While these assessments attempt to determine where students are, they ignore how they may have gotten there and what alternative pathways might be available for future students … accountability, however, is rarely extended to those making these demands. Policy makers are not required to provide supports necessary for equitable learning opportunities, nor are they held accountable for the consequences of these tests.
>
> *(Welner and Carter, 2013, p. 3)*

Educators, politicians, reading researchers, and stakeholders embedded the ideological assumptions of the past within assessments, laws, and policies while simultaneously electing to ignore a constant crisis, the low literacy performance of Black readers, particularly males, on standardized reading tests.

Discourse addressing ethnic and racial differences, for instance, used deficit descriptors to characterize literacy learners as "at-risk" or "struggling readers" were understood to describe students identified as in need of literacy support (who may fail to learn to read or who may experience continual reading difficulties). Deficit language also was used to compare students' performance on standardized reading tests as well as conflate economic status (of their parent/childcare providers/communities/families) with test performance. Students identified as Black, Latinx, and Native American/Indigenous often lived in communities/homes with limited income, attended under-resourced schools, and were learners whose first language was not English or standard English. Other catchphrases were dog whistles to administrators, literacy/reading coaches, specialists, and teachers as well as federal funding and research agendas, from corporate and philanthropic groups to policy makers and reading researchers, seeking to close the reading achievement gap and to benevolently "help" students of color to prevent reading failure/long-time reading difficulties and tax burdens for the general (positioned as primarily White) public.

The illusion was made possible under the unvoiced assumption that reading assessments were conceived, constructed, tested, and representative of reading among all US students. To be clear, funding agencies needed poor readers to "struggle," as they promoted approaches, procedures, programs, research, and theories, likely improving performance on standardized reading tests. There was a constant urgent refrain in reading research and federal laws that more needed to be done. Readers identified as at-risk and "struggling" were a source of income for government agencies, state and local school boards, and researchers (disability, literacy, and reading).

Reading assessments expected a dominant (beliefs, cultural, linguistic, knowledge) response but not an independent thinker, reader, or writer. Reading comprehension tests assumed there were some things some students may not know, also known as background knowledge, or the knowledge White people think should be known. Reading comprehension test passages or literature predominately were written by White people, including examples alleging to be representative of cultural, ethnic, linguistic, and racially specific texts.

A Link in the Chain: Response to Intervention

President Bush (2002a) also authorized Executive Order 13227, to review extant reading literature for children with disabilities. The President's Commission on Excellence in Special Education emerged as a key document connecting reading and special education research. The panel was directed to consider "the education of all children, regardless of background or disability, must always be a national priority … [and] among those at greatest risk of being left behind are children with disabilities" (Bush, 2002a). The commission's report, *A New Era: Revitalizing Special Education for Children and Their Families* (President's Commission on Excellence in Special Education, 2002), presented three general recommendations: focus on results, not on process; embrace a model of prevention, not a model of failure; and consider children with disabilities as general education children first. The report noted a singular approach, Response to Intervention, was able to address reading needs of all students and to reduce the percentage of students of color referred to special education placement. RTI was endorsed as the preferred approach for reading intervention, as a reasonable alternative to IQ–achievement discrepancy models and to screen for special education.

A Caveat: Reading First. US Secretary of Education Paige, on August 7, 2002, cited the work of the NRP in support of President Bush's reading reform initiative, Reading First:

> The program's focus on scientific evidence, including the essential elements of proven reading instruction, constitutes a recipe for success. Now we can ensure that all children will be given the tools and instruction they need to read well by the end of the third grade.
>
> *(quoted in www.nrrf.org/old/pr_doe_states_8-7-02.html)*

A focus on Reading First serves as an example of how reading reform was envisaged. As part of NCLB, Reading First was designed for:

> raising the caliber and quality of classroom instruction; Basing instruction on scientific research proven to work in the teaching of reading; Providing professional training for educators in reading instruction; and Supplying substantial resources to support the unprecedented initiative.
>
> *(www.nrrf.org/old/pr_doc_states_8-7-02.html)*

As designated by Congress, and in accord with the findings of multiple federally funded reviews of early reading research, Reading First programs were to reflect scientifically based research and exhibit "proven methods" of teaching reading and the five key components of reading outlined by the federal reports: phonemic awareness, phonics, vocabulary, comprehension, and fluency (https://education.uslegal.com/no-child-left-behind-act-of-2001/provisions-of-no-child-left-behind/title-i-and-reading-first/).

The National Council of Teachers of English (2002) voted on a resolution not to support Reading First. Their argument centered on the narrow review of extant literature on reading research used: "the National Reading Panel report is incomplete, narrowly focused, and flawed. The research examined does not represent the full range of scientifically valid research methodology" (n.p., www.ncte.org/positions/statements/readingfirst). The organization's resolution includes a "call upon Congress to commission knowledgeable, independent professionals to critique the currently promoted research base for the Reading First Initiative, specifically the National Reading Panel report" (n.p., www.ncte.org/positions/statements/readingfirst). NCTE also requested a five-year review of Reading First. The latter resolution came sooner than anticipated, as controversy about the way Reading First conducted business. In a qualitative meta-analysis, Au (2007) reviewed 49 qualitative studies to determine the impact of high-stakes testing on curriculum. Among the findings of high-stakes testing were "narrowing of curricular content to those subjects included in the tests, resulting in the increased fragmentation of knowledge forms into bits and pieces learned for the sake of the tests themselves" (p. 264) and "high-stakes testing represents the tightening of the loose coupling between policymakers' intentions and the institutional environments created by their policies" (p. 264).

The US Department of Education's (2008d) Inspector General's Final Report noted that "increased instructional time was positively correlated with improved reading skills, the phonemic awareness, phonics, vocabulary, fluency, and comprehension); however, there was no impact on reading comprehension as measured by the SAT 10" (p. xvii). Importantly, there were allegations of ethics violations among Reading First administrators,

Developed an application package that obscured the requirements of the statute;

Took action with respect to the expert review panel process that was contrary to the balanced panel composition envisioned by Congress;

Intervened to release an assessment review document without the permission of the entity that contracted for its development;

Intervened to influence a State's selection of reading programs; and

Intervened to influence reading programs being used by local educational agencies (LEAs) after the application process was completed. These actions demonstrate that the program officials failed to maintain a control environment that exemplifies management integrity and accountability.

(US Inspector General's Final Report, p. 2)

The administrators of the Reading First initiative were undone by mismanagement and the appearance of conflicts of interest. Once again, there was an outcry about billions of dollars allocated to improve reading performance, failing to improve the reading performance of Black and Brown students. Gamse, Jacob, Horst, Boulay, and Unlu (2008) filed a more positive final report executive summary about the measurable progress made among sites with Reading First grants.

It is important to mention using the improved reading achievement of Black and Brown children who attended under-resourced schools and drawing on normalized stereotypes of Black and Brown learners as well as poor-quality teaching – billions of dollars were spent on Reading First, only to be later withdrawn due to conflicts of interest, graft, and mismanagement among multiple stakeholders. Two ideas stick out: (a) "the canary in the mind" – we will try this idea out on Black children, while knowing the research was not conducted among Black children but assuming it will work as it worked for special needs White children (as if the two groups were somehow synonymous) and (b) follow the money – as in multiple other federal government ventures – as pointed out by Chairman Miller – funding was earmarked to help the most vulnerable but was siphoned off by the powerful for themselves, without anyone being held criminally/legally responsible. In the twenty-first century, it appears some politicians and reading researchers knowingly used racially identifiable images, coded language, and rhetoric to promote federal reading reform with little accountability for failed programs.

During testimony before the Congressional Subcommittee on Education Reform, Carnine (2003) articulated connections between LD and early reading problems and emphasized the need to improve general and special education's quality of instruction with "scientifically based" interventions. In his testimony, he framed reading intervention as a multistep approach, like those undertaken in medicine and social work. He proffered general education needed improvement and the best way to do so was through scientifically based education, along with a multi-staged intervention program. He explained RTI was focused on early intervention, students were identified quickly, and referrals for special education placement were reduced. Carnine also claimed prevention of early reading problems would lead to a reduction of racial disproportionality in special education. The congressional testimony of Carnine (2003) and the reauthorization of the Individuals with Disabilities Education Act (2004) as IDEIA redefined and enumerated criteria for a student's individual education plans to include measurable outcomes and research-based approaches (300.320–300.324). Students' reading achievement was recognized as pivotal to the effectiveness of NCLB and the national focus on reading resulted in significant increases in federal research funding. Underpinning the push for increased testing and support of scientific/evidence-based results in the ideology of White supremacy recast as a reasonable response to the literacy crisis.

The reauthorization of US Department of Education (2006), included RTI funding under Title I, Title III, and Coordinated Early Intervening Services (CEIS), of which RTI was the favored component (US Department of Education Assistance to States, 2006). The new guidelines authorized local school districts to use RTI to support reading and behavior, general education, and early reading interventions for students with SLD and to serve as a remedy for racial disproportionality in special education. States were required to "have policies and procedures in place to prevent the inappropriate overidentification or disproportionate representation by race or ethnicity of students with disabilities" (34 C.F.R. 300.173; 20 U.S.C. 1412(a)(24)). Under Part B, states were required to "collect and examine data to determine whether significant disproportionality on the basis of race and ethnicity is occurring in the state, or its school districts, with respect to the identification, placement, and discipline of students with disabilities" (US Office of Special Education and Rehabilitative Services, 2016, p. 5). States were required to "monitor local education agencies using quantifiable indicators of disproportionate representation of racial and ethnic groups in special education" (34 C.F.R. 300.600(d)(3); 20 U.S.C. 1416(a)(3)(C)). In addition, states had a separate obligation to annually report significant race and ethnicity disproportionality under 20 U.S.C. 1418(d) and 34 C.F.R. 300.64. Notions of "flexibility" permitted states to use the IQ-discrepancy achievement metric, create racial categories, and determine what constituted significant race and ethnicity disproportionality (USDOE, 2008b). The flexibility options weakened chances for equality, obfuscated attempts to track and monitor compliance, and made noncompliance difficult to prove.

The content area of reading was one of many covered under the reauthorization of IDEIA (2004) that failed to address culture, ethnicity, language, and race adequately and appropriately. Numerous studies suggested the lack of improvement under RTI for students of color was not because the approach was flawed but a lack of teacher fidelity in implementing the approach. These researchers ignored the ideological assumptions about culture, ethnicity, language, and race undergirding the approach, instruction, and reading assessments. Meyer et al. (2015)

observed IDEIA had an "emphasis on early intervention of at-risk CLD students in order to prevent inappropriate referrals to special education by requiring evidence of culturally responsive teaching and learning in the mainstream" (p. 237). Some members of Congress expressed reservations about RTI as a universal remedy and questioned the merits of "scientific evidence," limited data, a focus on reading, subjectivity in determining SLD, and the effectiveness of RTI among SOC and students who are not native English speakers. Supporters of RTI, however, pointed to the breadth of available research on its effectiveness while admitting more research was needed for the identified groups. Their rebuttal gave policy makers and researchers, often the same people (D. Fuchs & Fuchs, 2006), more time to address these concerns. In addition, mutual relationships and lack of dissension concretized RTI within educational, political, and institutional arenas.

After more than a decade of RTI implementation, there was a noticeable increase in the number of students of color identified as having SLD. The racial/ethnic groups most likely to be enrolled in SLD programs were American Indian/Alaskan Natives (6.8%) and African Americans (5.8%). In 2017, the National Center for Learning Disabilities acknowledged referrals of SLD were more common among students of color, students learning English, and students who lived in poverty during the 2015–2016 school year (Horowitz, Rawe, & Whittaker, 2017, p. 2). The report indicated one in five students has "learning and attention issues" (p. 1), "39% of students are identified as [having an] SLD" (p. 2), and "bias plays a key role in over- and underrepresentation" (p. 2). The authors did not present any plans to ameliorate ethnic, linguistic, racial bias or representation.

Researchers (Artiles, 2013; Artiles, Kozleski, Trent, Osher, & Ortiz, 2010; O'Connor & Fernandez, 2006) critiqued the consistent pattern of racial disproportionality in special education. Though scholars emphasize different aspects, they cohere around the inability to accurately track racial disproportionality and the failure to address students' cultural/ethnic, socioeconomic, linguistic, and racial differences. Shifrer, Mueller, and Callahan (2011) suggested special education's unease with racial disproportionality recognizes

> (1) students may be referred to special education in response to issues other than a learning disability, (2) the identification process may be inconsistent and/or inaccurate, (3) the disproportionately under-identified may not receive needed services.
>
> *(p. 247)*

Under NCLB, the use of a narrow approach to beginning reading instruction, the use of standardized reading assessments, and the implementation of RTI were unable to improve the reading performance of Black students.

Willis (2015) observed after more than a decade of implementation of the notion of Alphabetics, accompanied by increases in the charterization and privatization of education as noted in the 2009 and 2013 reports by the Center for Research on Education Outcomes (CREDO), NAEP reading scores of school children in general, and, especially, students of color, had not increased substantially (*NCES Reading Report Card*, 2014). The use of experimental and quasi-experimental studies was promoted as more valid and "scientific" than other methods of education research, while critiques of such work and alternatives were dismissed and ignored. Data produced by NAEP reading assessments, *National Reading Report Cards*, were used to influence states', school districts', and schools' responses to low student reading achievement. States also received financial incentives to distribute to districts implementing reading strategies identified by the NRP. The financial incentives were welcomed by shrinking available state and local funding sources, unvoiced assumptions of dominant hegemony, and the politicized discourse about supporting "failing" public education. Moreover, teachers were required to use scientifically based reading programs and conduct reading assessments; many used interventions promoted within the RTI approach. Among the first assessments of academic progress was a universal screening tool with multiple screening measures of student performance: naming letters, phonemic awareness, reading comprehension, reading letters/words, and vocabulary (Jenkins & O'Connor, 2002). Multiple measures seemed efficient, but Cramer (2015) argued there was a dearth of students of color in intervention studies of universal screenings, reading assessments, and process-monitoring measures. The Center for Response to Intervention (2018) revealed that among 49 states the generalizability of Measures of Academic Progress (MAP) at the first-grade level was a stronger indicator of progress for White students than for students of color.

A federal government initiative, *Race to the Top* (2009), and an ESEA reauthorization, Every Student Succeeds Act (ESSA) (2015), continued to tie education reform to improved standardized test performance, although the reading proficiency goal for third graders was not met under NCLB. In concert with these ESEA reauthorizations, multiple state laws passed third-grade reading laws and policies as well as punished students for reading on grade level by the end of third grade, while disregarding the roles of school districts, schools, or classroom teachers in student failure. This reauthorization:

Advances equity by upholding critical protections for America's disadvantaged and high-need students.

Requires – for the first time – that all students in America be taught to high academic standards that will prepare them to succeed in college and careers.

Ensures that vital information is provided to educators, families, students, and communities through annual statewide assessments that measure students' progress toward those high standards.

Helps to support and grow local innovations – including evidence-based and place-based interventions developed by local leaders and educators – consistent with our Investing in Innovation and Promise Neighborhoods.

Sustains and expands this administration's historic investments in increasing access to high-quality preschool.

Maintains an expectation that there will be accountability and action to effect positive change in our lowest-performing schools, where groups of students are not making progress and where graduation rates are low over extended periods of time. (https://www.ed.gov/essa)

ESSA endorsed the NCLB's use of student academic achievement as measured by standardized assessments for state and local accountability. The reauthorization of NCLB, as Every Child Succeeds Act, was crafted to exempt some students with disabilities from required standardized testing. Thus, the acts sought to address equity, which they appeared to do for students with disabilities, however, less so racial disproportionality among students with disabilities. The latter was left unaccomplished, and in 2020, a federal judge required immediate action and accountability to address racial disproportionality in special education reporting. Despite the multiple amendments to special education laws, in 2022 Black students remained racially disproportionately overrepresented, and performance on standardized tests had not significantly improved, nor had the rate of high school completion.

Since the early 1990s, there has been federal support to improve the reading performance of Black and Brown students on high-stakes tests; government-funded reading research often claimed the latest approach was a panacea addressing both racial disproportionality and closure of the achievement gap, but little substantive data emerged to support such claims. The failure of NCLB and subsequent ESEA authorization of ESSA (2009, 2015), to improve the literacy educational performance of Black students, indicated legal remedies for racial injustice are undermined by White supremacy. Au (2013) noted how the Obama administration's Race to the Top initiative and ESSA exacerbated the use of and dependency on high-stakes standardized tests results. These missteps led to a doubling down of efforts to exalt the five (or six) pillars, discussions about a Science of Reading (SoR), evolution of RTI to MTSS, and "reading wars." The so-called power five pillars of reading celebrated in reading research since the early 1990s could not guarantee all children were learning to read.

By contrast, there was ample evidence to suggest reading approaches have done just the opposite: expanded racial disproportionality and widened the achievement gap. It was unrealistic to assume addressing reading performance differences between Black and White students rested on research conducted among predominately White students. The failure of the standardized reading assessments, the five pillars of literacy, RTI as special education's singular approach to improve literacy and reduce racial disproportionality, and ESEA reauthorizations to improve the literacy performance of Black students, continued the legacy of anti-Black literacy education. The politicization of education and anti-Black literacy access were not new, nor was the use of reading research in support of White supremacist notions. In the late twentieth century, however, novel reforms emerged from federal-agency support groups – among interlocking federal agencies and the educational testing industry – were determined to argue for standardization as the only solution to improve students' literacy performance, despite the lackluster historical record as a failed remedy to improve Black literacy.

Disentangling the Web of Intersecting Federal Agencies and Programs

Educational researchers, political stakeholders, and scholars, in the early years of the twenty-first century, consistently ignored the history of anti-literacy laws and literacy research among Black readers. Many reading researchers found themselves saddled with a renewed interest in, and demand for, renewed twentieth-century positivism and a legacy of White supremacy as well as a large push from outside the field by politicians and other stakeholders. Politicization of education existed within a web of intersecting federal agencies under the National Center for Education Statistics (NCES) and the Institute of Education Science (IES), agencies legally responsible for NAEP, mandated the following:

- collect and analyze educational information and statistics in a manner that meets the highest methodological standards. Statistics must be timely, objective, neutral, and unbiased. The US Office of Management and Budget provides guidance on responsibilities and statistical practices to which several federal statistical agencies, particularly NCES, must adhere (OMB Statistical Policy Directive No. 1);
- maintain data credibility through its assessment design, collection, analysis, release, and dissemination procedures;
- administer NAEP reading and mathematics assessments for grades 4 and 8 every other year in all states;
- test these subjects on a nationally representative basis for grade 12 either as often as it has in the past or every 4 years;
- test additional assessment subjects – such as writing, science, history, geography, civics, and arts – on a varying 3- to 8-year cycle. NCES also conducts long-term trend assessments of academic achievement at ages 9, 13, and 17 in reading and mathematics;
- set standards for student data collection and random sampling processes;
- secure personally identifiable information (PII) about students, their academic achievement, and their families. Information with respect to individual schools also must remain confidential;

- publish NAEP results for selected student characteristics, including race/ ethnicity, eligibility for the National School Lunch Program (which serves as an indicator of socioeconomic status), and school location.
- These data are published in official reports and data tools, enabling users to perform their own analyses; and
- uphold the prohibition of using NAEP items and data to rank, compare, or otherwise evaluate individual students or teachers or to provide rewards or sanctions for individual students, teachers, schools, or local educational agencies. Furthermore, NAEP cannot be used to establish, require, or influence the standards, assessments, curriculum, or instructional practices of states or local educational agencies.

(para 3) https://nces.ed.gov/nationsreportcard/about/ organization_governance.aspx)

Recall in the Education Sciences Reform Act, P.L. 107-279 of 2002, the governing statute of NAEP, "stipulates that NCES develops and administers NAEP and reports NAEP results" (para 2). The law established "the National Assessment Governing Board is given responsibility for setting the assessment schedule, developing the frameworks that provide the blueprint for the content and design of the assessment, and setting achievement levels" (para 2). The National Assessment Governing Board (NAGB, 2022) remained "an independent body appointed by the Secretary of Education" (para 1) and helped to set the NAEP policy (https:// nces.ed.gov/nationsreportcard/about/organization_governance.aspx). The duties included helping to "coordinate NAEP duties and activities":

selection of assessment subjects for administration;

development of student achievement levels;

development of assessment objectives and specifications that reflect current professional standards;

assessment reviews that involve active participation of teachers, curriculum specialists, local school administrators, parents, and the public;

design of assessment methodology to ensure that assessment items are valid and reliable;

measurement of student academic achievement in grades 4, 8, and 12;

development of guidelines for reporting and disseminating results;

development of standards and procedures for regional and national comparisons;

acting to improve the form, content, use, and reporting of results of any assessment and planning and execution of the initial public release event of NAEP reports. (para 4; https://nces.ed.gov/nationsreportcard/about/ organization_governance.aspx)

To be clear, NAEP was a "congressionally mandated program" (NCES, para 1) and cyclically assessed school children's subject matter knowledge including reading to produce the *Nation's Reading Report Card* (please see Infographic of the Reporting Lines, from NCES-NAEP in Support Materials at www. routledge.com/9781032275000). Each report provided a data-rich document about students' reading performance from an alleged national representative sample, although the composition of the student population has shifted or been redefined overtime. Data, disaggregated by gender, race, and social class, was used by Congress, states, and local school districts in support of reading programs (please see Table 3.2).

Petrilli (2019) provided an update on student achievement drawing on data from decades of NAEP results. He argued in large part students' academic achievement has improved overtime, noting vast improvements since the 1990s and specifically addresses the intersection of race and NAEP test performance. He remarked, "at the fourth and eighth grade levels, progress in student achievement went well beyond reading and math, especially for low-performing students and students of color, at least until 2007 or so" (p. 9). Petrilli also attributed improvement to a range of factors: (1) decrease in crime, poverty, and teen pregnancy rates and (2) effective measures of NCLB, improved social economic status of SOC, more school funding, and focused teacher training in reading instruction. The most recent NAEP (2019) data, however, revealed a stunning lack of reading proficiency among all twelfth-grade students, most especially Black students since the reauthorizations of ESEA: *Race to the Top* (2009) and Every Child Succeeds Act (2015). The failure of these reauthorizations to improve the literacy performance of Black students can be traced to a history of legal barriers to literacy access; legal remedies for racial and educational inequities are undermined by an ideology of White supremacy, extending regress to Black students only if accompanied by likeminded remedies for White students; national and state laws and policies centered on a narrow definition of literacy and White-centered standardized reading assessments, and a faux educational system built upon the notion of meritocracy. Kidder and Rosner (2002) illustrated how the testing industry functions to manipulate test performance of Black students:

> Compare two 1998 SAT verbal [section] sentence-completion items with similar themes: *The item correctly answered by more Blacks than Whites was discarded by ETS, whereas the item that has a higher disparate impact against Blacks became part of the actual SAT. On one of the items, which was of medium difficulty, 62% of Whites and 38% of African-Americans answered correctly, resulting in a large impact of 24. … On this second item, 8% more African Americans than Whites answered correctly and 9% more women than men answered correctly. … This item was omitted form the actual SAT.*
>
> (pp. 152–153, emphasis added)

TABLE 3.2 NAEP Summary for Reading Assessment by Race, 1992–2019

Year	White	Black	Latinx	Asian Pacific Islander	Asian/ Hawaiian/Other Pacific Islanders	Native Hawaiian/ Other Pacific Islanders	American Indian/ Alaska Native	Two or more races
1992	218	185	203	***			***	
1994	217	181	192	***			***	
1998	219/217	188/186	198/198	***			***	
2002	236	196	207	228			***	
2013	236	212	225	248 (Asian)	244	***	***	232
2015	235	213	224	250 (Asian)	249	***	***	226
2017	239	212	225	250 (Asian)	249	***	***	230
2019	233	211	221	249 (Asian)	249	***	***	222

Accommodations were acknowledged for NAEP in 1998 and 2002, but have since not been reported on the same reading score charts. The 2002 NAEP Report Card for reading, reported averages for years 1992, 1994, 1998, 2002. The 2009, 2011 NAEP Report Card, displays national reading scores by race but not state-by-state. The 2013 NAEP Report Card, separate Asian students from Native Hawaiian/Other Pacific Islanders, and added students who identify with two or more races. https://nces.ed.gov/programs/digest/d21/tables/dt21_221.10.asp

How often this practiced occurred is unknown for all standardized assessments, including reading assessments like those used in NAEP and state reading tests.

Other agencies with federal government support included the Council of Chief State School Officers (CCSSO) and the National Governors Association (NGA), had significant influence over US education. The history of NAEP, embedded within a history of the NCES, was overseen by the very powerful and politically appointed CCSSO. The office's mission statement claimed:

> We are committed to ensuring that all students participating in our public education system – regardless of background – graduate prepared for college, careers, and life.
>
> The Council of Chief State School Officers (CCSSO) is a nonpartisan, nationwide, nonprofit organization of public officials who head departments of elementary and secondary education in the states, the District of Columbia, the Department of Defense Education Activity, the Bureau of Indian Education and the five US extra-state jurisdictions.
>
> As an organization, we are committed to ensuring that all students participating in our public education system – regardless of background – graduate prepared for college, careers, and life. To realize this, we bring together dedicated leaders and exceptional ideas to achieve measurable progress for every student.
>
> *(https://ccsso.org/about)*

L. V. Jones (1996) commented on how the changing nature of NAEP assessment instruments and outcomes helped to spur the establishment of the NAGB as an agency acting "relatively independent both of any federal agency and of NAEP contractors and to assume responsibility for the policy guidance of NAEP" (p. 17). P. Wood (2015) revealed these organizations:

> Are private, non-governmental bodies dash in effect, education trade organizations. The National Governors Association, despite its name, isn't just a group of sitting governors. It includes many ex-governors and current or former gubernatorial staff members. The deliberations of NGA and the CCSSO are not open to the public, and the work that these bodies did to develop … remains for the most part unavailable to outsiders. Neither body, being private, is subject to the Freedom of Information requests. The standards themselves are copyrighted by the NGA and the CCSSO.
>
> *(p. 17)*

Phelps (2018) also expressed concern: "despite what their names might suggest, they are not government entities, even though most of their members are elected or appointed state government officials" (p. 1). The CCSSO website stated:

CCSSO provides leadership, advocacy, and technical assistance on major educational issues. The Council seeks member consensus on major educational issues and expresses their views to civic and professional organizations, federal agencies, Congress, and the public.

(https://ccsso.org/)

Members of the NGA Best Practices group, under the CCSSO, encouraged the adoption of the Common Core State Standards (CCSS), which 48 states, the District of Columbia, and several territories initially adopted but later abandoned:

federal law prohibits the federal government from creating national standards, so the Common Core efforts were framed within the National Governors Association, the Council of Chief State officers, and a private consulting firm, Achieve. Funding from private … more than $160 million from the Gates Foundation, which entered into partnership with profit-making publishers to produce full K-12 curriculum materials. These publishers also produce the broadest portion of the market of standardized tests for students in early childhood grades, all the way through college teacher licensure programs.

(Nieto & Bode, 2017, p. 259)

From the onset, academics viewed the CCSSO with concern and literacy researchers voiced objections to the approach recommended for teaching reading and literature as well as assessment instruments. Under CCSSO, for instance, the reading of a required text drew comparisons to new criticism: a view of reading-dependent assumptions about the intent of the author, which is problematic when most of the authors in the suggested text are White people (Inoue, 2015). Critiques of curricular materials, particularly reading and literature, were excused because of their canonical status and universal messages. Inoue (2015) argued, "assessments and guides for assessments promote a particular ideal text … formed by a dominant white discourse seen in the rubric as they way readers judge it" (p. 42). Phelps (2018) confirmed only selective data for each working body is made public and the bulk of the millions of dollars received by the CCSSO are from grants. CCSSO has received funding from:

Sandler Foundation, Pearson Charitable Foundation, National Education Association, Knowledgeworks Foundation, Educational Testing Service, College Entrance Examination Board, Birth To Five Policy Alliance, and American Institutes For Research in The Behavioral Sciences.

(p. 11)

He exposed the organizational information about each agency in comparison to the American Psychological Association:

> the cast of nominal members and leaders changes frequently, with every election turnover, or resignation and replacement, while salaried staff tend to remain in place for longer durations;
> all but a few of the nominal members and leaders live and work outside of Washington, some of them thousands of miles away, and travel to Washington only occasionally; and permanent staff live in the Washington, DC area.
>
> *(p. 7)*

Phelps also questioned the veracity of the processes used in the membership composition of the board of each agency, the use of vocabulary meant to convey trust in the test instruments' ability to measure student learning, and "the various techniques of altering definitions, manipulating data, cherry-picking references, hiring only sympathetic evaluators, etc., [which] continue apace with ample funding" (p. 19). Peterson (1995) also observed,

> [Institutions] have often provided subordinate groups with a means to power: they create organized consent among their members by means of specific cultural, social, and intellectual activities; they work to promote the welfare of the population as a whole over that of specific individuals or groups; they encourage the powerful planning of resistance strategies; they make public and thus more effective hitherto privately held sentiments.
>
> *(p. 11)*

The ill-fated CCSSO requirements of the Common Core State Standards for the English language arts with an appeal to ideas popular in the 1930s did not include an accurate or authentic view of reading by emphasizing close reading, text complexity, and greater focus on informational texts and literacies (NGA Center for Best Practices, 2021). The standards did not exhibit thoughtful responses to the ethnic and racial diversity of students in grades K–12 and provided a limit number of texts written by People of Color. Unfortunately, standardized reading test creators, politicians, and researchers have doubled down on their positions as they retrenched from addressing racial inequities. Efforts by the federal government, however, supported the use of CCSSO with ties to *Race to the Top* funding and ESSA-related grants.

The role of these proxy organizations as agents of White supremacy helps to perpetuate systemic racism undercover of the federal government. Yet, they are supported by the federal government and fund research in support of the ideology of White supremacy. Historically and contemporaneously, the federal government and their proxy agencies have consciously ignored and undermined Black intelligence and failed to acknowledge the intellect of Black children. An example of the ongoing search for proof of White male superiority was found in the notion of individual grit.

Duckworth, Peterson, Matthews, and Kelly (2007) defined *grit* as "perseverance and passion for long-term goals. Grit entails working strenuously toward challenges, maintaining effort and interest ... despite failure, adversity, and plateaus in progress" (pp. 1087–1088). The authors' claimed grit is a personality trait needed for success; not surprisingly they referenced the scientific racist research of Galton, Cattell, Terman, and Thorndike. These researchers, much like their predecessors, identified demographic differences (age, gender, and race/ethnicity) as well as personality traits among scientists, although the scientists included in their studies were predominately US White males. Duckworth et al. failed to acknowledge the scientific racism and gendered issues undergird concepts of individual differences and the inheritability of intelligence. Moreover, they did not acknowledge historic, institutional, and structural inequities constrained minoritized learners' access and opportunities or the intersection of inequities with varied contemporary educational, political, and social contexts. The researchers also did not expressly mention gender, social class, or race, yet their findings and conclusions were heralded most often for minoritized learners. Their results supported the scientific racism of the twentieth century and helped to maintain the tradition of normalizing the favored, idealized, and valued individual/subject in educational research as middle- to upper-class, English-dominant, White, and male (Willis, 2007). The US government (2015) adopted grit as a valued individual characteristic, suggesting failure to acquire or express grit was an individual failure. They funded research on grit, which was articulated as helpful, if not needful, especially for minoritized and economically poor students:

> Academic mindsets. These are how students frame themselves as learners, their learning environment, and their relationships to the learning environment. Mindsets include beliefs, attitudes, dispositions, values, and ways of perceiving oneself.
>
> Effortful control. Students are constantly faced with tasks that are important for long-term goals but that in the short term may not feel desirable or intrinsically motivating.
>
> Successful students marshal willpower and regulate their attention in the face of distractions.
>
> Strategies and tactics. Students are also more likely to persevere when they can draw on specific strategies and tactics to deal with challenges and setbacks. They need actionable skills for taking responsibility and initiative, and for being productive under conditions of uncertainty – for example, defining tasks, planning, monitoring, and dealing with specific obstacles.
>
> *(Culatta, 2022, para 4–6)*

Sophisticated psychometrics were unable to eradicate the racist ideology and assumptions supporting "grit," among minoritized youth. Grit was positioned as a new silver bullet and continued a tradition of circumventing a focus on the assets Black students possess and bring to literacy. There was a false impression NCLB and grit somehow helped Black students, while simultaneously focusing on Black students as problems in need of fixing. The rhetoric depended on a White supremacist throughline perpetuating anti-Black racism and anti-Black literacy laws interwoven within institutional structures.

Nexus of Disability, Racial Discrimination, and Reading 2016–2021

Several court cases emerged in the last few years seeking to address the ongoing battle for high-quality and equitable literacy instruction for Black students. For decades, critiques and reviews of literacy laws and practices as expressed within NCLB, IDIEA, and RTI found a pattern of racial disproportionality among Black and Native American students. Despite the 1969 SLD definition and law, as well as NCLB requirement to track student racial demographics, school districts and states dodged addressing and accounting for racial disproportionality.

Federal Demand: Account for Racial Disproportionality

Under NCLB, although states were required to report and monitor racial disproportionality, the law "authorizes each state for defining major racial and ethnic subgroups itself" (NCLB, 20 USCS § 6301). States also were allowed to determine what constitutes significant disproportionality. New federal government guidelines (USDOE, 2008c) were enacted requiring racial and ethnic data be identified using seven ethnic/racial groups. However, without standard definitions and methodologies, noncompliance was difficult to determine and proving significant racial disproportionality was undermined. The ambiguity of discourse was reminiscent of the notion of "all deliberate speed" used in *Brown v. Board*, recommending but not mandating change and permitting states do self-govern.

In the waning months of the Obama administration, three steps were taken to address racial disproportionality. First, Secretary of Education, John King (2016), reminded states of their legal responsibilities and the department's Office for Civil Rights produced a fact sheet to illustrate pervasive racial disproportionality in special education (please see Appendix E, page 282). Second, Assistant Secretary of Education, Catherine Lhamon (2016), explained the subtleties of disproportionality, noting especially "(1) over-identification of students of color as having disabilities; (2) under-identification of students of color who do not have disabilities; and (3) unlawful delays in evaluating students of color for disability and their need for special education services" (p. 2). She also restated how every misidentification is a violation of Title VI and Section 504 and may "harm students' civil rights to equal educational opportunity" (Lhamon, 2016, p. 3). Third, the Obama administration legislated a policy, effective July 1, 2018, to standardize the methodology used to "identify and address the factors contributing to the significant disproportionality, which may include … economic, cultural, or linguistic barriers to appropriate identification or placement in particular educational settings" (Assistance to States for the Education of Children with Disabilities, 2016). Under the Trump administration, the USDOE resolved to "postpone by two years the date for States to comply with the 'Equity in IDEA' or 'significant disproportionality' regulations, from July 1, 2018, to July 1, 2020" (Assistance to States for the Education of Children with Disabilities, 2018). They cited concerns over the proposed standard methodology, lack of evidence of discrimination, and need for additional research. The Council of Parent Attorneys and Advocates filed a lawsuit against then Secretary of Education, Betsy DeVos, and the USDOE for failure to uphold IDEA/IDEIA regarding racial disproportionality (National Center for Youth Law, 2018). On March 8, 2019, a federal judge ruled the Department of Education illegally delayed the Obama-era mandate and ordered the mandate "take effect immediately" (E. L. Green, 2019, para). Amid the federal court cases, multiple state-level cases also litigated anti-Black literacy cases of racial discrimination.

Anti-Black Literacy State-Level Court Cases

Historic trends of anti-Black literacy customs, laws, policies, and statutes re-emerged in defense of minoritized students' right to culturally and linguistically effective, high-quality, reading instruction. Among the high-profile state cases were those conducted in Michigan and California, respectively.

Gary B. v. Snyder

A new challenge to equitable educational access and opportunity for Black students existed in *Gary B. v. Snyder* (2016), as it revisited historic patterns of educational and racial injustice (aka *Gary B. v. Whitmer*). The plaintiffs' lawyers argued Black students who attended one of five identified Detroit public schools were not receiving an equal and equitable education compared with their White peers. They emphasized the plaintiffs had not received adequate reading instruction to propel them to a meaningful life or future. The lawyers cited several alleged violations of the Fourteenth Amendment: due process and equal protection clause, state-created danger, discrimination based on race in violation of Title VI of the Civil Rights Act of 1964, 42, U.S.C., and 34 C.F.R. 1000.3((b)(2), and declaratory relief (*Gary B. v. Snyder*, 2016). Their case hinged, in part, on whether literacy was a fundamental right (*Gary B. v. Snyder*, 2016). Intriguingly, their request for relief echoed dominant narrative assumptions and recommended the implementation of RTI (*Gary B. v. Snyder*, 2016), although the use of RTI or the current iteration was unlikely to remedy the literacy concerns of the plaintiffs.

In 2018, the case was dismissed, as US District Judge Stephen Murphy opined: "literacy – and the opportunity to obtain it – is of incalculable importance" but not necessarily a fundamental right. The plaintiffs appealed to the Sixth Circuit Court, and two of the three judges wrote:

> The recognition of a fundamental right is no small matter. This is particularly true when the right in question is something that the state must affirmatively provide. But just as this Court should not supplant the state's policy judgments with its own. ... Access to literacy is such a right. ... And education – at least in the minimum form discussed here – is essential to nearly every interaction between a citizen and her government. Education has long been viewed as a great equalizer, giving all children a chance to meet or outperform society's expectations, even when faced with substantial disparities in wealth and with past and ongoing racial inequality.

Their opinion suggested literacy is a Constitutional right. Judge Eric Clay put it this way: where "a group of children is relegated to a school system that does not provide even a plausible chance to attain literacy, we hold that the Constitution provides them with a remedy." Several amicus briefs were filed; for example, PEN America (2018) argued "the right to education, and therefore to literacy, is ... recognized in the 1948 Universal Declaration of Human Rights, the International Covenant on Civil and Political Rights, and the International Covenant on Economic, Social and Cultural Rights" (p. 10). Another amicus brief (Brief for Detroit Literacy, as Amicus Curiae, *Gary B. v. Snyder*, 2018) was filed by the National Council of Teachers of English, the International Literacy Association, Dean Moje (of the University of Michigan, College of Education), and an impressive list of reading researchers. The Sixth District Court of Appeals *Gary B. v. Whitmer*, 2020, overturned the idea that reading was a constitutional right. Shortly thereafter, a settlement was reached between the state of Michigan (Gov. Gretchen Whitmer) and the plaintiffs, granting $94.4 million to the Detroit Public Schools to improve reading programs, to create the Detroit Literacy Equity Task Force and the Detroit Educational Policy Committee to improve cultural competence and literacy instruction for students in the Detroit Public Schools, and to provide financial compensation for the plaintiffs.

Ella T. v. State of California

In California, the *Ella* case sought to determine, in part, whether reading was a right for all students. The onset of reading retention laws was traced to 1998, California's Assembly Bills 1626 and 1636, and this case revealed California was among the first states to be sued over failure to provide adequate reading instruction. Following a 2012 report, *Striving Readers Comprehensive Literacy Plan*, the plaintiffs filed a case to assure literacy equity in California, *Ella T. v. State of California* (2017). They sought literacy access for students under the California state constitution, most especially students identified as underserved:

> The California Constitution guarantees every child a basic education … correctly recognized a "critical need to address the literacy development of California children…" particularly dire in California's underserved populations, specifically English learners, students with disabilities, socioeconomically disadvantaged students, and African American and Hispanic students. … The State acknowledged a "sense of urgency in implementing a state literacy plan."
>
> *(p. 1)*

Counsel for the plaintiffs argued although the state of California acknowledged the need for improving literacy access and instruction to improve literacy performance and had implemented literacy plan, the performance of underserved students as indicated on the California Assessment of Student Performance and Progress remained low. In the *Ella T. v. State of California* case, students in three different elementary schools won literacy for all California students based on the Fourteenth Amendment. The plaintiffs' lawyers argued California was doing a poor job of teaching students to read, and the performance of economically poor students on literacy assessments was a violation of the California constitutional mandate, to provide equal access to education. The State of California sided with the plaintiffs' ruling (attorneys for the student plaintiffs: https://www.mofo.com/special-content/ca-literacy/). The case against the state of California was a victory for students of color and students living in poverty who had not received high-quality literacy instruction but were asked to endure state assessments and, when they performed poorly, were retained. An award of $53 million was allocated to provide resources to the state's 75 lowest-performing elementary schools.

As a nation, the history of legal processes used by federal, state, and local government to obfuscate the potential for Black literacy access and educational equality, in general, and specifically in reading (assessment, concepts, curriculum, definitions, materials, instruction as well as measurement, processes, and procedures) continued to evolve. Each new tactic redoubled efforts to "prove" White intellectual supremacy by creating additional barriers to educational advancement for Black students.

4

LIKE LAMBS TO THE SLAUGHTER

Grade Retention Research, Reading Retention
Research, and State Reading Retention Laws

Earlier chapters provided historical, political, and social contexts to understand how the intersection of anti-Black racism, White supremacy, and institutional racism influenced and framed anti-Black literacy laws, reading assessments, and reading research. The efforts included customs, laws, traditions, and statutes to prohibit Black people from learning to read. Next, scientific racism embedded within standardized reading assessments and tests was used to bolster claims of White intellectual superiority and meritocracy. The testing complex in the United States influenced by eugenicists and educational psychologists evolved to include standardized testing at all educational levels, including post-secondary admissions. Achievement, aptitude, and intelligence test requirements continued in pursuit of the unrelenting need to prove White racial intellectual superiority. Educational, institutional, political, and structural alliances were used to inform state laws and policies that served as gatekeepers and sorters of admission. Several federal government divisions and adjacent agencies, corporations, and nonprofits combined to inform and support federal and state anti-Black laws and policies.

Reading as a school subject was used as a political football and response to social promotion customs in education. Schools often promoted students who were considerably older than expected for the grade level in which they were placed. Accompanying the concern and use of social promotion was the reading level of the students who were over-age and who withdrew before graduating from high school. These educational and social concerns informed national educational policies, grade retention laws and policies, and political careers. The state laws and policies of grade retention laws aimed to retain students who did not read on grade level by the end of third grade, based on a false equivalency: Not reading on grade level by the end of third grade and

DOI: 10.4324/9781003296188-5

graduating from high school, were equivalent to becoming a productive citizen. Agreeably, there were students who failed to read on grade level by the end of third grade, did not graduate from high school, and were not productive citizens. There also were students who read on grade level by the end of grade 3, graduated from high school, and were not productive citizens. The schooling between grade 3 and 12, along with requirements for high school graduation, involved myriad factors that forestall graduation.

This chapter provides historical context for the nexus of reading research and special education, as well as examines educational research that informed grade retention studies, although they varied widely and addressed a host of issues (assessment, comparison groups, data collection, and methods of analysis). The variety of studies made it difficult to locate a definitive or singular conclusion about grade 3 reading performance. Reliable and consistent findings revealed the ineffectiveness of third-grade reading retention to improve reading performance on standardized tests, high school graduation rates, and productive citizenship. Other findings exposed a pattern of economic and racial disproportionality among students who were retained and abject failure of politicians and reading researchers to acknowledge the extant research and findings about grade retention. Finally, a review of current state grade 3 reading retention laws and demographic data about the students most effected by the laws are interrogated.

Reading, Response to Intervention, and NCLB

The Summit on Learning Disabilities: A National Responsibility, 1994, marked a watershed moment in the evolution of RTI. The two-day event, held by advocates and allies of special education and the federal government and sponsored by the National Center for Learning Disabilities (NCLD) in Washington, DC, included political attendees working to move a special education agenda forward. In attendance were then-first lady Hilary Clinton; Duane Alexander, the director of NICHD; Richard Riley, US Secretary of Education; Donna Shalala, US Secretary of Health and Human Services; Janet Reno, US Attorney General; and other politicians, physicians, and education researchers. A contemporaneous report by Ellis and Cramer (1995) presented claims linking LD and reading:

> Research indicates that 70–80% of students identified as LD have their primary deficits in basic language and reading skills, very specifically manifested in deficits in phonological awareness. Studies show that 74% of students who are unsuccessful readers in the third grade are still unsuccessful readers in the ninth grade.
>
> *(p. 8)*

The report did not reference specific studies, although it suggested a connection among language competencies, noting "a variety of disorders in the domains of listening, speaking, basic reading skills, reading comprehension" (pp. xxvii–xxviii). It indicated problems in early reading, especially among students identified as LD. The goals of the summit included encouraging the federal government to invest in improving support services for LD, bringing national attention to LD, and seeking consensus among stakeholders to chart a pathway for support of LD funding (S. C. Cramer & Ellis, 1996). The declarations also were used to garner political support for addressing problems in early reading as potentially lifelong; researchers drew heavily from two studies and suggested that if LD is unaddressed, people with LD create grave societal costs: illiteracy, incarceration, substance abuse, and unwed motherhood.

In a subsequent book published by Brooks Publishing, a frequent publisher of federally funded research, Lyon's (1996) chapter presented a selective review of literature for LD in math, oral language, and reading; debated a shared definition of LD; dismissed the discrepancy model; and repeated the racial tropes about Black and White reading achievement. Lyon acknowledged LD definitions "cannot be attributed to cultural factors (including race and ethnicity), [as] limited information exists how race, ethnicity, and cultural background might influence school learning" (p. 10). Lyon's work drew heavily from neurobiological research by Wood, Fenton, Flowers, and Naylor (1991), whose findings offered a window into how dominant assumptions undergird research as they examined "parental marital status, parental education, parental status as welfare recipient, social economic status, the number of books in the home, and occupational status" (p. 10). Lyon shared Wood's impression that African American dialect also may be a contributing factor in "sound-symbol" reading approaches (p. 11). Lyon surmised, "some aspects of race and culture can influence the development of reading abilities" (p. 11). He also declared, without evidence, "bias or disadvantage is not reflected in referral patterns" (p. 11). Lyon's statement aligned with Stanovich and Siegel's (1994) perspective of intervention failures highlighting culture, economic class, ethnicity, environment, language, and race as possible factors for low achievement. The researchers implied these factors were potential predictors of reading difficulties, impressions conflicting with the federal 1969 SLDA definition.

Lyon proposed several ideas aligned with the purpose of the summit: early interventions, collaboration among stakeholders, teacher development, acknowledgment of potential biases in referral patterns, and increased funding. General education instructions also found support from Representative Owens, then-first lady Clinton, and US Secretary of Education Riley. They argued for more whole-classroom instruction to include students with LD and less segregation of minoritized students (S. C. Cramer, 1996). Their ideas were initially sidelined but resurfaced as key features in multitiered interventions to thwart segregation claims.

Lyon's comments about race and the inaccuracies of IQ testing, on one hand, admitted the IQ–achievement discrepancy approach produced "invalid diagnostic markers for LD in basic reading" (p. 24) and acknowledged the tests were poor indicators of early reading difficulties among Black students. On the other hand, he dismissed the equal protection clause of the Fourteenth Amendment and the findings of *Larry P. v. Riles* (1979 & 1986). In the latter, the plaintiffs argued there was bias in testing procedures and the placement of SOC in special education: "labeling and placement decisions reflected stereotypic beliefs about White intellectual superiority" and "the widespread use of 'scientifically' objective measures to gauge intellectual ability" (Ferri & Connor, 2005, p. 94). Lyon (1996) argued for replacing the longstanding use of the IQ–achievement discrepancy approach for SLD placement, especially, but not singularly, among SOC. The alternative approach simply replaced the use of IQ tests, as it drew from the same ideological beliefs in White supremacy (intellectual superiority and the use of "scientifically" objective measures). Legally, the alternative approach also permitted the disproportionate identification of SOC for special education and did not provide equal educational opportunities.

To illustrate the need for early reading intervention among SOC, students whose first language is not English, and students living in poverty, as well as drawing on the dominant narrative, D. Fuchs, Fuchs, Mathes, and Simmons (1997) crafted a hypothetical sketch – which allegedly reflected an actual urban school environment:

> Now picture this: 34 children in an urban third-grade classroom, one-third of whom live in poverty. Six live with grandparents, and three are in foster care. Five come from homes in which a language other than English is spoken; two children do not speak English at all. Seven, six, five, three, two, and one are African American, Hispanic American, Korean, Russian, Haitian, and Chinese, respectively. Six are new to the school, and four will relocate to a different school next year. Only five of the 34 students are at or above grade level in reading; 10 are two or more grade levels below. There is a five-grade spread in reading achievement. In addition, three students have been certified as learning disabled. One is severely mentally retarded, and another is deaf. According to the Department of Health and Human Services, the child with mental retardation and two other students in the class have been physically or sexually abused.
>
> *(p. 176)*

The sketch exposed an uninformed and impoverished characterization of urban classrooms, families, immigrants, schools, and students; it also clarified researchers were racially conscious while dismissing the research about inequalities in the field. MacMillan and Reschly (1988); MacMillan, Siperstein, and Gresham (1996); and Reschly (1997) examined the over-representation of SOC in special education and concluded a host of intervening factors influenced placements. Likewise, politicians were aware of perceptions of racial bias and disproportionality linked to special education, as evident in the 1997 reauthorization of IDEA.

The law required states to collect and report race/ethnicity data to document and address racial disproportionality (34 C.F.R. 300.755). It also provided outlines of specific requirements to better track racial disproportionality: reporting data by race, analyzing disproportionality data from states and schools, and revising policies, procedures, and practices when significant disproportionality is found (please see Table 4.1).

TABLE 4.1 Historical Timeline

Date	Education Reform, Special Education, Reading, and Response to Intervention
1962	Public Law 87-838 establishes the National Institute of Child Health and Human Development (NICHD).
1965	ESEA - purpose
	Cooke Report – key foci
	Head Start – class, poverty, race - pathology
1966	Bureau for the Education of the Handicapped (BEH) under Title VI of the ESEA
1968	Russell Dunne – overrepresentation of racial minorities
1969	Children with Specific Learning Disabilities Act (LD Act)
	act became part of Education of the Handicapped Act (EHA), P. L. 91-230. The law described SLD characteristics: a disorder in one or more of the basic psychological processes involved in understanding or in using language, spoken or written, that may manifest itself in an imperfect ability to listen, think, speak, read, write, spell, or do mathematical calculations, including conditions such as perceptual disabilities, brain injury, minimal brain dysfunction, dyslexia, and developmental aphasia. (34 C.F.R. 300.8)
	First Grade Reading Studies, Final Report – remove class, lang., & class; prefer White students
1970	Education of the Handicapped Act
1973	Rehabilitative Act, Section 504, provides that any recipient of federal financial assistance, must end discrimination in the offering of its services to persons with disabilities
1975	Education for all Handicapped Children Act (renamed The Individuals with Disabilities Education Act)
1977	Carrie and Pete Rozelle establish the Foundation for Children with Learning Disabilities
1979	National Research Council Report
1982	National Research Council Report, Placing children in special education: A strategy for equity.
1987	National Summit on Learning Disabilities
1989	National Center for Learning Disabilities (formerly Foundation for Children with Learning Disabilities)
	Learning Disabilities Research Centers (LDRC) Consortium established
1990	The Americans with Disabilities Act
1994	Learning Disability Summit

(Continued)

TABLE 4.1 (Continued)

Date	Education Reform, Special Education, Reading, and Response to Intervention
1995	Learning Disabilities: A National Responsibility. Report of the Summit on Learning Disabilities.
1997	IDEA Amendments, P. L. 105-17
1998	Preventing reading difficulties in young children.
2000a	NICHD: the National Reading Panel Report
2001	No Child Left Behind Act, Pub. L. Mo.107-110, 115 Stat. 1425(2002). Title I, Title III
	President's Commission on Excellence in Special Education
	LD Initiative Summit, sponsored by the US Office of Special Education Programs
2002	National Research Council Report – Minority students in special and gifted education, Committee on Minority Representation in Special Education use of the discrepancy model for use with SLD, racial disproportionality in special education referrals
2003	House Report. 108-77 – IMPROVING EDUCATION RESULTS FOR CHILDREN WITH DISABILITIES ACT
	Implementing RTI using Title 1, Title III, and CEIS funds: Key issues for decision-makers
2004	IDEA reauthorization, Publ. No., 08-446, 118., Part B
	Individuals With Disabilities Education Improvement Act of 2004 (IDEIA)
	RTI – specifically + SLD + behavior
	Reading First and other named Programs under reauthorization 2004
2005	IDEA reauthorization (addition), No Child Left Behind: Expanding the Promise, Guide to President Bush's FY 2006 Education Agenda
	Office of Special Education and Rehabilitative Services, Memorandum.
2007	NICHD renamed Eunice Kennedy Shriver National Institute of Child Health and Human Development
2008	Knudsen Memorandum. Coordinated Early Intervening Services (CEIS) Guidance
2009	Race to the Top
2011	United States Department Education's Office of Special Education and Rehabilitative Services - Memo
2012	The LD Hubs, currently held at Baylor College of Medicine, Florida State University, and Vanderbilt University. LD Hubs seek to address "the causes, symptoms, and treatments of learning disabilities that impact reading, writing, and mathematics.
2015	Evaluation of response to intervention practices for elementary school reading
2016	US Office of Special Education and Rehabilitative Services Report, Racial and ethnic disparities in special education

(Continued)

TABLE 4.1 (Continued)

Date	Education Reform, Special Education, Reading, and Response to Intervention
2019	In December of 2016, the Obama administration created a set of regulations to more accurately track racial disproportionality in special education … which is a broader call to action than a specific regulation for SLD. The regulations were scheduled to go into effect on July 1, 2018. However, implementation was delayed, as the Trump administration granted a two-year delay until July 1, 2020. Immediately, court cases ensued, and a judge ruled in October 2018, that the delay was illegal based on procedural errors. The USDOE appealed the ruling, however, on March 7, 2019, a second federal judge also RULED in favor of the Obama administration's regulations - demanding the regulations begin immediately. As of today – the regulations have NOT been implemented, as additional appeals by the USDOE are being considered. Many students thus identified – are NOT receiving an equal education as required under the Fourteenth Amendment, clearly this is an educational and social justice issue that is unaddressed.

Dates and brief description of selective events, laws, and policies of racial disproportionality in special education for students identified with specific learning disabilities (SLD), beginning in the mid-1960s.

Linkages between student communication abilities and characteristics and diagnosis of SLD were described in SLDA (1996) and included a list of exclusions but did not include race, albeit culture was often used as a proxy. The focus on reading achievement and development in the sketch is alleged to have identified which students might benefit from reading support: students who are disabled, English language learners, minoritized, and poor. It also signaled reading progress by third grade was a benchmark that aligned with a proposal under consideration by Congress, whereby "*every child* in America should be able to read well and independently by the end of third grade" (143 Cong. Rec. 86, 1997, emphasis added). The authors implied if early reading interventions had occurred, students' reading failures would have been prevented. L. S. Fuchs and Fuchs (1998) acknowledged legislation challenged the over-representation of SOC in special education due to the use of IQ discrepancy measures and offered an alternative approach for early reading intervention. They mentioned the ineffectiveness of IQ–achievement discrepancy measures; racial disproportionality among students who are American Indian, Black, and Latinx; and increasing costs of funding special education. Repeating claims that IQ–achievement discrepancy models should be abandoned, and replaced with their alternative approach: a four-staged multitiered approach (RTI) along with teacher judgment. In this model, students received effective general education, small-group instruction, and individualized tutoring before referral for special education placement. The researchers claimed their approach was aligned with federal law and presented a likelihood of reducing the over-representation of SOC in special education: "Equity is achieved when, before placement, evidence verifies that special education is actually a valuable service because it enhances the learning of the individual" (p. 216). Later, they summarized RTI as "a research-based multitiered system of preventive intervention to prevent LD for students who are otherwise 'instructional casualties'" (L. S. Fuchs & Fuchs, 2007, p. 15). They did not guarantee their model and suggested additional research was needed.

Alternative research conducted by the Civil Rights Project at Harvard University and the NCES and shared via Public Broadcasting Service (PBS) (2004) revealed patterns of racial disproportionality in special education placements. It also calibrated the use of "mentally retarded" labeling of Black students as related to educational opportunity, race, and tracking. Among the findings were repeated dominant narratives of White supremacy and Black intellectual inferiority:

> Black children constitute 33% of those labeled "mentally retarded." Black children are nearly three times more likely than Whites to be labeled "mentally retarded." States with a history of legal school segregation account for the highest overrepresentation of African Americans labeled "mentally retarded." In wealthier districts, Black children, especially Black boys, are more likely to be labeled "mentally retarded." Studies of disproportionate placement indicate unconscious racial bias on the part of school authorities.
>
> *(PBS, 2004)*

A 2005 amendment to IDEIA outlined steps to remedy racial disproportionality by addressing cultural differences, the involvement of families, and students whose first language is not English. Several USDOE (2005a, 2005b, 2008a, 2008b, 2011) memorandums were issued to states reiterating the legal requirements for accurate reporting of racial disproportionality in special education – yet racial disproportionality persisted.

RTI was portrayed as the solution to educational inequality by preventing reading difficulties and diminishing racial disproportionality in special education, herein SLD. The logic centered on a multitiered approach to reading intervention and prevention: avoiding the wait-to-fail syndrome, closing the reading achievement gap, and preventing reading failure and long-time reading difficulties. Under RTI, Tier I, all students would receive 'high-quality general education,' instruction and 'universal' screening. Tier II presented small-group instruction focused on the needs of the learners. Tier III expanded the equity theme by offering individualized instruction but otherwise mimicked Tier II. RTI as an approach identified students who do not reach benchmarks and referred them for SLD screening and additional support in special education, or Tier IV. RTI appeared to offer a scientific, research-based intervention for reading including processes, procedures, and documentation to track equal educational access but did not address racial disproportionality. Supporters argued the multiple steps helped to document compliance and "determine if significant disproportionality based on race and ethnicity is occurring at the State or local level with respect to disability, placement in particular settings" (34 C.F.R. 300.646(a); 20 U.S.C. 1418(d)(l)). States were afforded flexibility to determine SLD placements and permitted consideration of "a child's response to scientific, research-based intervention as part of the SLD determination process" (USDOE, 2007, p. 1). D. Fuchs et al. (2007) explained RTI was legally sanctioned as "a method of disability identification" (p. 58), and personnel were "expected to reduce the likelihood that untaught or poorly taught nondisabled students are misidentified as disabled" (p. 58). RTI appealed to educators, politicians, and the public because it provided federal funding to all students (beyond the previously identified groups), was a multi-stage process based on research, and thus appeared more equitable.

Under RTI, initially, all students received "universal," high-quality, literacy instruction in Tier I and implied the approach offered equitable instruction to all students. The moniker universal was a misnomer, though, as assessments reflected dominant systems of knowing. Tier II, centered on small-group instructions, offered additional skill support and included progress monitoring. This step implied greater equity as students' individual needs were being more directly addressed. The processes, however, were unregulated, and interventionists (teachers or staff) implemented informal reading assessments. Although, the assessments were hailed as "scientifically based" and "nationally normed," but they were drawn from the same ideological assumptions as the discredited IQ–achievement discrepancy model. In addition, interventionists were allowed to make decisions (evaluations and judgments) regarding students' language dialects and variations (although the legal description of SLD prohibits consideration of cognitive, cultural, and linguistic factors). Tier III offered individual tutoring and assessments that were progress monitored but equally wanting. Tier IV moved students into special education.

Numerous scholars observed special education's unease with racial disproportionality. Kratochwill, Clements, and Kalymon (2007) pointed out "considerable ambiguity exists in the exact definitions of what is evidence-based within the RTI model with a full range of opinions about how the intervention is developed, implemented, and evaluated" (p. 26). Hosp and Madyun (2007) suggested that when guidelines are followed, "it can be inferred that each individual's needs are being met, no matter what race, ethnicity, socioeconomic status, gender, native language, or any other factor" (p. 173). Other scholars voiced concerns about the use of RTI and its link to racial disproportionality in special education. Skiba et al. (2008) asserted, "It cannot be assumed that interventions that have been shown to work on average in improving educational outcomes will also be effective for groups that have been traditionally marginalized" (p. 281). Castro-Villarreal, Villarreal, and Sullivan (2016) observed an "unintended outcome of RTI is subjectivity and variability in decisions about who should be eligible for special education" (p. 15). NCLD also revealed during the 2015–2016 school year, SLD identification among SOC, students learning English, and students who live in poverty remained constant and disproportionate (Horowitz, Rawe, & Whittaker, 2017).

Among reading researchers, a consistent narrative pointed to RTI as an approach to prevent reading failures. However, missing was any discussion of the role RTI has played in the placement of SOC in SLD and sustaining racial disproportionality. Over the last two decades, RTI research evaluations, reflections, reports, and reviews failed to acknowledge the link between reading difficulties and special education eligibility as well as the role of IDEA funding in support of special education (Gersten & Dimino, 2006). There was a dearth of RTI research among SOC (Lindo, 2006), and few studies focused on SOC and universal screenings, reading assessments, and process monitoring (L. Cramer, 2015). Evaluations and reports centered on student group size; paraprofessionals (educators/tutors); reading (informal assessments, instructional scripts, materials, and reading strategies); student and teacher schedules; and teachers' skills (fidelity, knowledge, training). Reviews consistently pointed to teacher fidelity as the major culprit in the ineffectiveness of RTI to improve reading achievement among students, along with factors related to culture, economic status, and environment (in violation of SLDA 1969). Despite widespread implementation of RTI, NAEP (National Center for Education Statistics, 2015) data revealed reading achievement gaps persisted between SOC and their White peers. Reading research eschewed discussions of RTI as a pathway of SLD and as a remedy for racial disproportionality, and has remained silent about its role in sustaining both. Meyer, Park, Bevan-Brown, and Savage (2015) revealed "large scale investigations of the interrelationships between race and poverty as factors influencing educational outcomes have consistently found that ethnicity has contributed independently to placements in special education, over and above the impact of social economic status" (p. 237). They acknowledged a repeated pattern used by reading assessment researchers "to magnify existing racial disparity" (Skiba et al., 2008, p. 273). Ethnicity/race and socioeconomic status were conflated and discussed as a singular category: poverty – labeled low-income or under-resourced.

Wag the Dog: Grade Retention Research, Laws, and Policies

Historically, a consistent drumbeat in education was a looming crisis as reflected in ongoing debates about the need for an educated citizenry, for whom, and who would pay for education. Most debates, however, were better summarized as a wag-the-dog crisis scenario used to distract attention away from the actual crisis by creating an alternative one. Concerns about grade retention reflected shifts in the national view of education goals: the overcrowding in schools of the 1800s, for example, promoted a review by state and local administrators to begin tracking grade retention and promotion: the use of intelligence and standardized achievement tests to evaluate student learning and in support of White supremacy and meritocracy. Grade retention was known by different monikers, as Xia and Kirby (2009) explained:

> Grade retention, also known as "nonpromotion," "being retained," "flunking," "repeating a grade," and "being held back," is the practice of keeping students at the same grade level for an additional year, usually because of poor academic performance or emotional immaturity. The rationale behind retention is that it gives low-achieving students an extra year to catch up to the grade-level standard. ... Critics of grade retention contend that it fails to benefit children academically in the long run, hurts children's self-esteem, leads to behavioral problems often associated with being over-age for grade, has a correlative relationship with dropping out of school, and incurs significant financial costs of having children repeat a grade.
>
> *(p. 1)*

With increased calls for accountability in education, there was an increase in the number of students who were retained, as occurred with the desire to end social promotion and the increased demand for greater student performance, as judged by performance on standardized achievement tests. Reschly and Christenson (2013) provided a more nuanced description:

> Grade retention refers to the practice of having students repeat a year of schooling in which they did not meet certain educational, or in some cases, social (maturational) standards, whereas social promotion is the practice of advancing students to the next grade with their same-age peers despite not having met these standards. At times, educational practice has been dominated by one or the other. However, even within this broader national context, local communities and states have often developed their own set of norms or policies surrounding grade retention and promotion.
>
> *(p. 319)*

The definitions and practices were created based on a false choice: social promotion or grade retention as the only possible options. The binary options were made without consideration of the social and structural barriers that created unequal and inequitable learning environments.

In the last half of the twentieth century, politicians raised these issues: the cost of public education, for whom, and the use of public tax dollars to fund private education. Embedded within these debates in the 1980s was a discussion and legislation to address the practice of social promotion, loosely defined as promoting students from one grade to the next, whether they learned enough to be promoted. After the publication of *A Nation at Risk* along with its siren call to address the failing public school educational system and fears of falling economically behind other nations, standardized assessments were encouraged to determine and document student academic achievement. An underlying assumption held standardized assessments provided accurate, cultural free, and unbiased assessments of academic achievement, irrespective of the quality of instruction students received. The implication was clear: stricter promotion policies would encourage students to avoid being retained.

Publicly, to address social promotion, concerned educators and politicians argued for an alternative practice: grade retention. The idea was endorsed as a "common sense" approach as more time in one grade to learn information would help students throughout their scholastic pursuits. At the turn of this century, the reauthorization of ESEA/NCLB also helped to encourage the use of standardized testing to "prove" academic improvement:

> High-stakes, standardized testing has become ubiquitous in the United States, where, since the passing of the No Child Left Behind Act (United States Congress, 2002), all US states were mandated to test public school students in grades 3-8, and once in high school, be tested in reading and math, with future provisions for students to also be tested in science.
>
> *(Au, 2013, p. 7)*

Several syntheses of grade retention literature have been conducted since the 1980s, based on varying questions, data, methods, and recommendations, most have a common finding.

Grade Retention Research

A brief chronological overview of grade retention research revealed a disconnect between research and practice. Shepard and Smith (1989) observed that historically there is an over-riding belief in the efficacy of grade retention held by administrators, educators, politicians, the public, and teachers. The seemingly commonsense notion of more time in a grade level was needed to acquire knowledge and skills will be beneficial, does not hold:

> retention in grade has no benefits for either school achievement or personal adjustment; retention is strongly related to later dropping out; two years in kindergarten, even when one year is labeled a "transition program," fails to enhance achievement does or solve the problem of inadequate school readiness; and from the students' perspective, retention is conflict-laden and hurtful.
>
> *(pp. 215–216)*

They observed "what began as an attempt to enforce standards at the exit from public education was translated downward into 'promotional gates' at the earlier grade levels" (p. 3). The authors specifically tied the notions of academic accountability and the use of testing to President Clinton's call for abolishing social promotion. Jacob, Stone, and Roderick, M. (2004) understood the historical moment differently as they argued in 1996 when the Chicago Public Schools instituted a new program:

> on an ambitious accountability agenda by coupling a new school-level accountability program with high-stakes testing for students. Under this new initiative to end social promotion, the city's lowest-performing third, sixth, and eighth graders would repeat a grade at least once if they did not meet minimum reading and math test-score cutoffs on the Iowa Tests of Basic Skills (ITBS), and in subsequent years, additional metrics of student performance ... low-performing schools were placed on academic probation, receiving significant intervention and pressure to improve.
>
> *(p. 1)*

Roderick's (1994) longitudinal study found little support for the notion that more time in grade supports public school student graduation. Her results indicated, "of one cohort of public-school youths, nearly 80% of students who repeated a grade dropped out of school compared to only 27% of those who were never retained" (p. 730). Her review of literature confirmed previous reviews that "almost unanimously concludes that retention is not as effective as promotion in improving student performance" (p. 732). Roderick observed, "one of the most consistent findings in research on school dropout is that high school students who drop out are more likely than graduates to be overage for grade or to have repeated grades previous to high school" (p. 733). She concluded, "students who experienced early grade retentions dropped out at higher rates, even when differences in the grades and attendance of retained and promoted youths as late as middle school" (p. 749). Roderick's conclusions supported other research about the lack of sustained positive gains of early grade retention and the deleterious effects of early grade retention. Likewise, Grissom and Shepard (1998) noted retention, not reading ability, increases high school dropout rates.

Marsh, Gershwin, Kirby, and Xia (2009) declared, "the converging evidence indicates that grade retention alone is not an effective intervention strategy for improving academic and longer-term life outcomes" (p. 23). Demographics of retained students appeared to cluster around the following: behavior (disciplinary actions), content (math and reading), gender (males), low economic income, race (predominately minorities), parental education levels, and special education placement. Research revealed – irrespective of how grade retention was parsed – the negative effects have historically, and currently, exceeded perceived benefits. Drawing on extant literature, particularly the retention studies by Jimerson, Anderson, and Whipple (2002), Xia and Kirby (2009), and Huddleston (2014) also presented ample evidence about the lack of academic improvement, associated with grade retention. They noted several possible negative effects of retention: emotional, psychological, and social harm to students. A review of research by Jimerson, Ferguson, Whipple, Anderson, and Dalton (2002), for instance, found students retained during elementary school are at an increased risk for dropping out of high school. Findings from these studies indicate that retained students are between two and 11 times more likely to drop out during high school than non-retained students and that grade retention increases the risk of dropping out between 20 and 50% (cited in Jimerson and Kaufman, p. 626).

Jimerson and Kaufman (2003) provided a review of hundreds of studies of research on grade retention conducted over a century and argued "research does not demonstrate academic advantages for retained students relative to comparison groups of low-achieving, promoted students" (p. 624). They noted, as have others, some studies reveal gains in academic achievement; however, the gains are short term and not sustained. Reschly and Christiansen (2013) claimed "*the experience of grade retention is one of the most powerful predictors of high school dropout*" (p. 319, emphasis added). Research conducted by Warren, Hoffman, and Andrew (2014) confirm between 1995 and 2021, "retention rates are highest in Grades 1 or 9 or that they are highest among boys, racial/ethnic minorities, those living in the South, or less advantaged children" (p. 400). Other syntheses (Xia & Kirby, 2009; Winters & Greene, 2012) acknowledged academic gains often are short lived. Irrespective of how and why students are retained, many dropped out of school and their life prospects were not improved.

The most thorough review of 91 grade retention studies, a synthesis, was conducted by Xia and Kirby (2009), in which they concluded:

- Relative to students who are promoted, retained students are more likely to be male, minority, younger than their peers, of low socioeconomic status, and living in poor households and single-parent families. They are also more likely to have poorer academic performance prior to retention; significantly lower social skills and poorer emotional adjustment; more problem behaviors, such as inattention and absenteeism; more school transfers; poorer health; and disabilities. Parents of retained students are more likely to have lower IQ scores and lower levels of cognitive functioning, lower educational levels, lower occupational levels, less commitment to parenting responsibilities for their children's education, lower expectations of their children's educational attainment, and less involvement in school.

- In general, retention does not appear to benefit students academically. In most of the studies included here, we find negative relationships between retention and subsequent academic achievement. On the other hand, a few studies have found academic improvement in the immediate years after retention. Even so, these gains are often short lived and tend to fade over time. Findings from the few studies using rigorous methods to adjust for selection bias have been mixed as well – with some showing short-term gains and others reporting gains that disappeared over time.

- Retained students have a significantly increased risk of eventually dropping out of school.
- Compared with their peers, retained students also appear less likely to pursue postsecondary education and more likely to have poorer employment outcomes in terms of earnings (although only a few studies have looked at this outcome).
- Findings on social, emotional, attitudinal, and behavioral outcomes among the retained students compared with their promoted peers appear mixed, with some studies reporting positive outcomes and others finding insignificant or even negative results.

(pp. x–xi)

Their analyses were consistent with other systematic grade retention reviews: grade retention does not benefit students: especially Black males in early elementary school, living in poverty, and with some behavioral, disciplinary, emotional, and social issues. Xia and Kirby (2009) proffered, "the research shows that retention alone is ineffective in raising student achievement. Studies that reported positive or mixed findings focused on short-term effects, used same-grade comparisons, or evaluated retention policies that included additional, supportive components" (p. 19). They summarized that their review found "overall grade retention is associated with an increased risk of dropping out of school" (p. 26) and concluded:

Past research has consistently shown that retained students are at significantly increased risk of dropping out of school. ... Overall, the literature indicates mixed findings on attitudinal, socioemotional, and behavioral outcomes among the retained students.

(p. 29)

Huddleston (2014) provided a synthesis of grade retention studies using a fresh perspective through careful analyses of research centered on teacher-based retention and research centered on high-stakes assessments/testing for promotion. He clarified differences between meta-analyses and reviews of literature as well as among methodological approaches within studies. He also observed differences in the quality of research studies on grade retention by graduate-level papers and peer-reviewed research studies conducted by agencies, corporations, government, and institutes. All differences were important when seeking to understand what at the surface may appear to be conflicting evidence and findings. Huddleston identified four distinctive categories of results: positive, negative, unintended, and under-determined. His review confirmed the findings of numerous studies of grade retention using high-stakes testing: "there is little evidence suggesting that these policies have actually resulted in academic achievement gains" (p. 7). He noted among the negative and unintended consequences, curriculum influences played a role by altering instructional time to address testing and teaching to the test, especially among schools whose student population was minoritized and in low-income communities. Importantly, his analysis also revealed that "studies suggest that the positive gains in aggregate scores in districts and states produced through high-stakes testing policies occur most often in White, middle-class schools" (p. 8). He surmised grade retention studies informed by teacher-based recommendations, "even in the cases where these students do receive an academic boost from repeating a grade, ... fade over time. The children eventually fall behind and are at a much higher risk of dropping out of school" (p. 11). Finally, he acknowledged numerous professional organizations challenged the grade retention policies, issued strong statements in support of suspending the practice, and questioned the ethical practice of retention as "retaining students without providing different instruction places the blame for low academic achievement solely on the student and offers little hope for improvement" (p. 23). All these studies found Black and Latinx students and students who live in poverty were most often retained, especially males. NCES (2019) noted a slight improvement in the percentage of elementary and secondary students retained in 2000–2016. (Please see Figure 4.1).

In sum, grade retention studies revealed that being retained increased the likelihood a student will not complete high school (Allensworth, 2005; Huddleston, 2014; Jimerson, 2001a, 2001b; Marsh, Gershwin, Kirby, & Xia (2009); Xia & Kirby, 2009). Scholars often parsed the studies, debating age/grades, community/families, student demographics, methods used (literature review, meta-analysis,

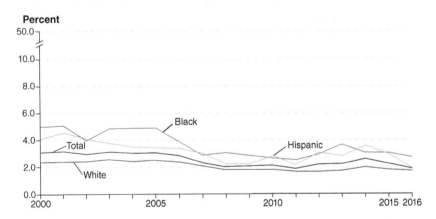

FIGURE 4.1 NCES Summary of Grade Retention by Race. Percentage of elementary and secondary school students retained in grade, by race/ethnicity: 2000–2016.

Source: https://nces.ed.gov/programs/raceindicators/indicator rda.asp.

and syntheses), and the questions guiding the study. Consistently, the studies found grade retention did not improve academic progress and was a predictor of failing to complete high school.

Grade Retention as an Intervention

Silberglitt, Appleton, Burns, and Jimerson (2006) declared: "grade retention is an intervention that has received increasing scrutiny as policies, practices, and results of research diverge" (p. 255), yet it has remained a popular practice and received legislative support in the form of state laws. In 2011, the National Association of School Psychologists issued a position paper on grade retention and social promotion in which they decried the practice. They noted the history of the practice and inconsistent results from research studies on grade retention and concluded that "the majority of studies conducted over the past four decades on the effectiveness of grade retention fail to support its efficacy in remediating academic deficits ... there is no evidence of long-term benefits for students" (p. 1). The report suggested alternatives to both grade retention and social promotion:

- Multitiered problem-solving models to provide early and intensive evidence-based instruction and intervention to meet the needs of all students across academic, behavioral, and social–emotional domains
- Equitable opportunities to learn for students from diverse backgrounds
- Universal screening for academic, behavioral, and social–emotional difficulties
- Frequent progress monitoring and evaluation of interventions.

(pp. 1–2)

The position paper claimed "grade retention is a costly intervention with questionable benefits to students because, for students who attended school regularly, having them repeat the same grade with the same instruction will yield no improvement for the student" (p. 2). Although the statement was written over a decade ago, states ignored the warnings and created laws and policies in support of the practice especially related to reading retention by the end of third grade.

Squires (2015) published a *FastFact* review of literature for the Center on Enhancing Early Learning Outcomes, summarizing data from several studies. His review included a broad range of studies, from teacher-based and test-based retention, as multiple methods are used in data analyses of grade retention. He concluded:

> meta-analyses of teacher-based retention provide more comprehensive analysis than individual studies; generally concluding there is little compelling justification for the claim that there are benefits of retention. The bulk of evidence suggests that children who are retained learn less than they would have had they instead been promoted.

(p. 5)

He described grade retention findings on academic performance (short and long term) as well as the effects on students' social/emotional/behavioral lives. Demographically, this review of literature on grade retention among young children revealed the same findings about grade retention: "students who are African-American, Latino-American, eligible for special education, or low-income are more likely to fail standardized tests and consequently be retained" (p. 7).

The Intercultural Development Research Association (2019) also suggested, "policymakers look to retention as a method of trying to increase student achievement by squarely placing the blame on the student and hoping that the fear of consequences, being held back, will scare them into compliance and satisfactory achievement" (p. 3). Given the brief historical overview of research on history grade retention and its deleterious effects on students who are retained, why and how was reading selected as the barometer for grade retention?

Reading Assessment and Grade Retention

Lloyd (1974) conducted a study about the relationship between sixth-grade achievement and high school completion. He identified five "dimensions" that appeared to work independently yet affected dropout rates: "achievement, socio-economic status, family characteristics, non-promotion, and absenteeism" (p. 1194). Building on this same data, but using third grade as a point of comparison, Lloyd (1978) considered the relationship between third-grade achievement and high school completion. He offered justifications for the selection of third grade as the end of the primary grades and as a time when it was hoped students had obtained basic reading skills. He surmised that four of the five variables he identified in the sixth-grade study were affirmed in the third-grade study, although he added an independent variable: ability as indicated by students' IQ. When he compared the findings from the sixth- and third-grade studies, he noted the third-grade study had several high predictors: absenteeism, global IQ, non-promotion and retention, socioeconomic status and family characteristics, and reading. Lloyd's (1978) studies were the touchstone documents used for third-grade reading achievement and the metric for reading retention laws.

There were few consistent findings of linkages in reading and grade retention studies when compared to graduation rates. Roderick and Nagaoka (2005) conducted a study among Chicago Public Schools students two years after they were retained in third and sixth grades (1997–2000) and where schools were required to use standardized reading test scores for retention. Their study found reading achievement did not improve among the students who were retained, and many students were placed in special education. A longitudinal study of Texas elementary grade students who were retained due to low reading achievement indicated students were better positioned for academic success than socially promoted peers; however, graduation rates were not established (Lorence & Dworkin, 2006). The authors suggested, "making students repeat a grade, when supplemented with additional educational assistance, can benefit academically challenged children" (p. 999). In a follow-up study, Lorence (2014) appeared to confirm the findings. Hughes, Chen, Thoemmes, and Kwok (2010) provided a more nuanced look at high-stakes testing data from Texas and acknowledged differences in research study outcomes are affected by the definition of terms, question/s asked, and methods used:

> Our study used statewide criterion referenced tests based on statewide curriculum standards for third grade students. Our results suggest, but cannot prove, that students who are retained in first grade are more likely to pass these tests than they would have been if they had been promoted to second grade. If the purpose of retention is to be a one-time adjustment in the student's academic pathway, these results suggest that retention served its intended purpose.
>
> *(pp. 179–180)*

Another longitudinal study conducted in Texas by Hughes, West, Kim, and Bauer (2018) found grade retention was the most significant factor influencing high school completion and negative effects are keenly experienced by Black students.

Some studies revealed students initially appeared to improve their reading achievement after being retained in third grade (Alexander, Entwisle, & Dauber, 1994), while other studies reported improved reading achievement scores were short lived or non-existent (Greene & Winters, 2009; Hong & Yu, 2007; Silberglitt, Appleton, Burns, & Jimerson, 2006). Neal and Schanzenbach (2010) found reading achievement gains among students who were on grade level and those who were slightly below grade level, but not for students at the lowest performance levels. Other studies suggested gains were affected by the application of policies (Greene & Winters, 2009), and some studies reported early grade retention does not appear to affect high school completion (Greene & Winters, 2009; Robinson-Cimpian, 2015). Unquestionably, grade retention research provided an impetus *not* to retain students, "the confluence of research results fails to demonstrate academic achievement advantages for retained students relative to comparison, groups of low achieving promoted peers" (Jimerson, 2001b, p. 50). Irrespective of these findings, many states established third-grade reading policies and some enacted third-grade retention laws.

Third-Grade Reading Retention State Laws

Jimerson, Anderson, and Whipple (2002) warned early grade retention was "one of the most powerful predictors of later school withdrawal" (p. 452). As reviewed above, grade retention research consistently declared: (1) grade retention was not a viable intervention, (2) early grade retention was an indicator of failure to complete high school, and (3) demographically, grade retention policies disproportionately affected students who were Black, Latinx, and low income. State policies focused on grade retention were often linked to the desire to abolish social promotion yet hinged on students' reading performance. For example, in 1984, Texas adopted a state curriculum and prohibited social promotion, Texas Education Code [TEC] §21.721, *Grade Requirement for Advancement or Course Credit*, 1986 (Grade-Level Retention), before requiring statewide testing in 1990. Since then, several state laws have been repealed, revised, and established to (a) prohibit retention below first grade; (b) retain students not reading on grade level in grades 3, 5, and 8; and (c) provide intensive educational support to students not promoted.

The "roots and routes" (Hall, 1980) to contemporary grade 3 reading retention laws and policies are embedded in the history of education and politics. President Clinton's strategies presented in *Goals 2000* conveyed a clear message from the federal government by encouraging states to address student achievement and reduce dropout rates. Reading was a key subject matter of concern, as states had placed reading performance in the crosshairs for promotion. Jimerson (2001b) acknowledged California's response to President Clinton's 1998 call, abolished social promotion, and was the first state to create promotion and retention standards (p. 48). California passed legislation in the State Assembly Bills 1626 and 1628 (1998a, 1998b). Bill 1626 states

> This bill would, in addition to the policies adopted pursuant to those provisions, require the governing board of each school district and each county board of education to approve a policy regarding the promotion and retention of pupils between specified grades, and would require that policy to provide for the identification of pupils who should be retained or who are at risk of being retained in their current grade level on the basis of specified factors.

This bill would require the Superintendent of Public Instruction to recommend, and the State Board of Education to adopt, levels of pupil performance for the achievement tests administered under the STAR Program in reading, English language arts, and mathematics for each grade level, and would require that those performance levels identify and establish the level of performance that is deemed to be the minimum level required for satisfactory performance in the next grade. (p. 91)

School districts were permitted to set their own standards if they were following state minimal requirements on achievement tests. At the elementary level, promotion and retention standards began between second and third grades and proceeded through grade 12. Importantly, reading was a key factor in consideration of promotion or retention:

The policy shall base the identification of pupils pursuant to subdivision (b) at the grade levels identified pursuant to paragraph (1) and (2) of subdivision (a) primarily on the basis of the pupil's level of proficiency in reading. The policy shall base the identification of pupils pursuant to subdivision (b) at the grade levels identified pursuant to paragraphs (3) through (5) of subdivision (a) on the basis of the pupil's level of proficiency in reading, English language arts, and mathematics.

(p. 91, please see Appendix F, California Assembly Bill No. 1626, page 286)

California's state law was the first to clearly indicate the need to read on grade level by the end of third grade. Jimerson and Kaufman (2003) observed, "in 1999, US Department of Education published a guide encouraging state and federal educators to take responsibility for ending social promotion, while at the same time limit limiting reliance on retention as the preferred alternative" (p. 623). The push for additional states to adopt grade 3 reading retention laws included corporate and quasi-federal support. Several debates about grade retention research ensued and included when grade retention should occur (in support of retention in early grades K through 3) to whether grade retention affected later quality of life. Supporters argued more negative effects occurred if students were retained after the third grade. The bulk of empirical research on which these arguments were made drew from Lloyd (1978), NAEP data (1992–2007), and a hodgepodge of federally and philanthropically funded research, but not from the hundreds of empirical studies that established grade retention increased high school dropout rates, irrespective of grade, and there were negative outcomes for students who were retained (Jimerson 2001a). Recent published briefs and studies anchor their support by selectively citing research studies on grade 3 reading retention.

Not all literacy organizations agreed with these practices; for example, the Literacy Research Association (2012) produced a policy brief on grade retention policies and acknowledged that "retention policies and initiatives are not consistent with the research literature, which overall does not support any long-term academic benefits for retention, but does suggest that there are negative social ramifications of such policies" (p. 2). They identified four possible reasons for the staying power of the practice:

> disdain by policymakers for the practice of social promotion, conventional expectations about time and progress in reading favor our propensity to honor efficiency, appeal of grade retention is supported by the current climate of test-driven school accountability and elementary school teachers and other stakeholders frequently cite anecdotal improvements in the performance of students in the months following the decision to retain ....

(pp. 4–5)

The policy brief called for "states to suspend the use of policies mandating test-based grade retention until further research is conducted to examine the efficacy and ramifications of such policies" (Dennis, Kroeger, O'Byrne, Meyer, Kletzein, & Huddleston, 2012). A study by Barrett-Tatum, Ashworth, and Scales (2019) reviewed grade retention, added confirmatory findings, and revealed several states, "Arizona, Indiana, Oklahoma, and Ohio, created third grade test-based retention gateway policies modeled after Florida between 2010 and 2012" (p. 1). And Reff (2018) observed:

> policy prescriptions that insist on fidelity to instructional models around "Scientifically Based Reading Instruction" (SBRI) and Response to Intervention (RtI) as the key to reading proficiency fail to acknowledge the limited success of these prescriptions … using compliance mechanisms that include the withholding of funding pending annual submissions of school and district literacy plans, school reading programs are tightly coupled to the policy.
>
> *(p. 18)*

By contrast, The Council of Chief State School Officers (2019) published a report, *Third Grade Reading Laws: Implementation and Impact* a detailed review of reading by grade 3 laws selectively reviewed extant literature on grade retention. The report displayed selective grade retention studies and concluded "retention policies that include third grade but do not specifically mention third grade or literacy as third grade reading policies" (p. 29, endnote iii). Although the report claimed not to be an advocate for third-grade retention, the laws and policies of each state were a central focus. Ignoring nearly a century of grade retention research. The report overlooked grade retention studies that provided alternative perspectives about how and why grade retention occurred. The study also ignored the preponderance of grade retention research, recognizing the strongest indicator of high school dropouts was retention, *not reading*. Yet, the report pinpointed select areas of reading concern as reflected in federally funded reading reports and in the 1994 LD Summit.

The CCSSO report also suggested state policies varied, but "the goal of these policies is to improve reading outcomes by bringing attention and resources to early literacy, and by recommending or requiring some combination of prevention, intervention, and/or retention" (p. 3). The approaches to third-grade reading retention laws by state were identified under four categories: states without reading laws, states with laws and set retention requirements, states with laws that delegate authority to school districts, and states with comprehensive third-grade reading laws (pp. 7–9). States using NAEP data, Indiana, Mississippi, Nevada, and Tennessee, were examined, and recommendations for state legislators and leaders seeking to create a state law included the following: the science of reading and child development is clear, passing a law is only the beginning, consider the theory of action from the state to the classroom, change must happen across multiple fronts, communication is key, build connections and coherence, and commit over the long term and evaluate from the beginning (pp. 22–23). The Council of Chief State School Officers (2019) recognized the science of reading (SoR) as necessary – a pretext for future decisions supporting SoR in contrast to other reading approaches – and positioning SoR as a way to retain anti-Black literacy laws. Beyond the federal government's many proxy agencies working in support of reading by grade 3 retention laws, there also were corporate interest providing support.

Recently, Della Vecchia (2020) has provided a brief history of grade and reading retention laws, noting grade retention is the strongest indicator of failure to complete high school, and reading retention does not improve reading standardized test performance. He explained grade retention disproportionately affected students who are poor, attend under-resourced schools, and were Black and Latinx:

> Rather than lawmakers viewing low reading scores as an outcome of attending under-resourced schools, these low reading scores are instead identified as the cause of students failing to graduate high school. As a consequence, rather than being provided with the resources they have been denied, students and families are threatened with mandatory retention.
>
> *(p. 10)*

He recalled an oft-cited reference to a study by Yamamoto and Byrnes (1987): "sixth-grade students rated retention as being more stressful than any event other than losing a parent or going blind" (p. 120). He also noted the study was replicated by Anderson, Jimerson, and Whipple (2005) and students who "rated grade retention as *the single most stressful life event*" (p. 11, italics in the original). DellaVecchia concluded, "if the majority of young people share these feelings, then retention is indeed a drastic method for improving reading outcomes" (p. 11). Finally, Peguero, Varela, Marchbanks, Blake, and Eason (2021) observed there are ethnic/racial disparities in grade retention and disciplinary practices among schools in rural, suburban, and urban settings. They acknowledged SOC continue to be at heightened risk for grade retention and school punishment, regardless of whether their school is in an urban, rural, or suburban community and regardless of the disciplinary practices of any particular school" (p. 250). They concluded schools need to review policies and practices for grade retention, interventions, and school discipline.

No one really knows the cumulative effect of microaggressions in the lives of young Black students learning to read, although a recent study has shared the stress of retention on the psychological body. Some Black students may experience historical trauma when anti-Black racism's historical facts are misrepresented. They also may internalize constant communicative (language, speech, and reading) corrections as indicators of their intellectual ability. The unending search for reading deficits or areas of weakness, and ongoing assessments also may heighten a sense of failure. Low performance on standardized reading tests and being retained, as well being bullied, were likely to cause stress and trauma as well as have a disparate impact on the lives of Black students. It is difficult to overstate the potential harm and impact of state-sponsored anti-Black literacy laws and policies on the lives of Black communities, families, and students. Grade and reading retention studies that attempted to describe the immeasurable effects of failing grade 3 – beyond students' graduation rates – noted the emotional and psychological burden was borne by Black students, without recommending repealing the laws.

Non-governmental-Affiliated Agencies' Influence: Read by Grade Retention

Throughout the history of education, proxy and non-governmental agencies as well as interested stakeholders have participated in shaping educational laws and policies.

Education Commission of the States

The Education Commission of the States (ECS) provided a history of the organization in their publication *The Compact of Education*, which claimed "does not have authority, nor will it be expected to set policy" (Sandford, 1965, p. 3) and noted that "it will merely be the means of developing alternatives for policy decisions, which ultimately are to be made, in any event, by local and state policymaking bodies. It will furnish the state with the best" (Sandford, 1965, p. 3). ECS was the brainchild of James Conant, president emeritus of Harvard, to create a body working with state governors and disseminate information in support of education. A national conference held in Kansas City, Missouri, framed the goals of the ECS:

> should merely be the means of developing alternatives for policy decisions, which ultimately are to be made, in any event, by local and state policy-making bodies. It should furnish the states with the best available information. It should suggest appropriate goals. It should serve to exchange information, and to advise. It should provide the states with a forum for sharing experiences, improving standards, and debating goals.
>
> *(p. 9)*

Importantly, the ECS articulated actions they would not take, for example, attacking federal funding creating policy, driving a national curriculum, lobbying federal or state government, and replacing existing agencies (p. 11). Included in the materials was the group's governance documents, and the discourse used appeared inclusive as the preamble stated, "the proper education of all citizens is one of the most important responsibilities of the States to preserve a free and open society in the United States" (p. 13). ECS provided reports in 2005, 2011, 2014, and 2016, sharing select information about grade retention studies, although an interpretation was not provided, and without countervailing studies of grade retention. In a review of reading retention, Workman (2014) claimed the ECS reports represented a compilation of state third-grade reading policies. She restated a common, but unproven belief: "the third grade year, is considered a pivotal point in a child's educational career, as a critical shift in learning takes place – one where basic reading skills are established and can be utilized for more complex learning" (p. 1). This statement was followed by another unsupported claim about dropping out of high school, specifically: "often leads to higher rates of unemployment and increased risk of participation in the criminal justice and welfare systems" (p. 1). While appearing to support retention as a reading intervention, she remarked, "retention in this analysis should not be considered an endorsement, but rather a recognition that is an available strategy that some states have chosen to use" (p. 1). Workman listed three major findings from her review of state third-grade reading policies:

• 36 states plus the District of Columbia require a reading assessment in at least one grade, preK-3, with the primary purpose to identify reading deficiencies. The assessments are a mix of state-mandated and locally determined approaches.

• 33 states plus D.C. require or recommend that districts offer some type of intervention or remediation for struggling readers for a P-3 grade. Some states require specific interventions while others let districts choose from a list of suggested interventions.

• 16 states plus D.C. require the retention of third-grade students who do not meet grade-level expectations in reading. Three additional states allow students to be retained based on a recommendation from teacher, parent or superintendent.

(p. 1)

She provided a comparison of laws, annual assessments, interventions, parental notification, and retention requirements and exceptions, by states and the District of Columbia in infographic texts. Missing from the report was information about how states processed requests for exceptions and student demographics to understand whether – and for what reasons – students' requests were granted or denied. Without acknowledging the research reviewed was selective and not comprehensive, Workman concluded:

> The most effective policies must undertake a comprehensive approach that begins with early, high-quality instruction and rapid, effective interventions. A critical component not addressed in this report is the

need for high-quality, well-trained teachers. Some states like Ohio and Connecticut now require that teachers pass a rigorous examination of principles of scientifically research-based reading instruction as a requirement of certification.

(p. 1)

Data presented by states may/may not identify students by race, given Black students' low performance on state standardized reading tests; they are the students most likely to be affected by being retained and focus of contemporary anti-Black literacy laws.

Annie E. Casey Foundation

The history of the early years of the Annie E. Casey Foundation (AECF) revealed the influence and legacy of a widower, Annie E. Casey, after whom the foundation was named. Besides, it described how Jim Casey founded the United Parcel Service (UPS) in 1907 and how he and his siblings established the AECF in 1948. Later in his life, Jim articulated the goal of the foundation:

> What is needed is a renewed determination to think creatively, to learn from what has succeeded and what has failed, and, perhaps most important, to foster a sense of common commitment among all those concerned with the welfare of children.
>
> *(AECF, 2022, para 8)*

Throughout its history, the AECF sought to "use data and evidence as a way of bringing communities together on behalf of children and families" (para 9). However, much like the ECS, in support of laws, policies, programs, etc., their use of data was selective, not comprehensive. In 2010, three publications associated with the AECF were used to spread public concern about the importance of reading by the end of third grade.

First, Lesnick, Goerge, Smithgall, and Gwynne (2010) published a report funded by AECF, *Reading on Grade Level in Third Grade: How Is It Related to High School Performance and College Enrollment?* The report, without citations, opined students who do not read well by the end of third grade find it difficult to comprehend text (p. 1). The study was based on longitudinal data gathered from 26,000 students in Chicago Public Schools. The goal was to understand linkages between third-grade reading performance and educational outcomes of "eighth grade reading performance, ninth grade course performance, high school graduation and college attendance" (p. 1). The authors found students who performed at or above grade level by third grade were more likely to complete high school and attend college. The authors cautioned the findings "do not examine whether low reading performance causes low future educational performance, or whether improving a child's reading trajectory influences future educational outcomes" (p. 1). Among the key findings were:

1. The proportion of students who are below grade level is the highest for male students, for African American students, and for students who have spent time in the foster care system.
2. Students who are above grade level for reading in grade 3 graduate and enroll in college at higher rates versus students who are below grade level.
3. Third-grade reading level is a significant predictor of eighth-grade reading level.

(pp. 2–3)

Second, *Early Warning! Why Reading by the End of Third Grade Matters: A Kids Count Special Report Summary* (2010a) was published by AECF. The report was filled with alarming and unsupported rhetoric about the dangers of failing to read on grade level by the end of third grade. The summary drew heavily from 2009 NAEP reading data without other clear research citations, presented a state-by-state comparison of 2007 NAEP reading results, along with brief discussions of reform efforts under NCLB and CCSSO's Common Core State Standards.

Third, AECF published *Double Jeopardy: How Third-Grade Reading Skills and Poverty Influence High School Graduation* (Hernandez, 2011). The brief provided more research than the prior summative report, albeit the sources are primarily government-funded/supported and AECF's in-house publications. The claims made by Hernandez do not include disconfirming information about the effects of grade retention as the most powerful predictor of failure to graduate from high school or reading scores on achievement tests. Hernandez provided some insights into his data: (a) drawn from the National Longitudinal Survey of Youth (1979), collected by the Bureau of Labor Statistics, reading data was secured beginning in 1985 (four years) based on student performance on a subtest of the Peabody Individual Achievement Tests: Reading Recognition (p. 12). He sought to argue the longitudinal study of students from 1979 to 1989 represented students' reading achievement. However, only four years of reading achievement were used and "reading test scores were used for third grade, *if available*, otherwise tests scores were calculated as the *average of second and fourth grade scores* if both were available, otherwise the second assessed was used if available" (p. 13, emphasis added). Hernandez claimed:

•   One in six children who are not reading proficiently in third grade do not graduate from high school on time, a rate four times greater than that for proficient readers.
•   The rates are highest for the low, below-basic readers: 23 percent of these children drop out or fail to finish high school on time, compared to 9 percent of children with basic reading skills and 4 percent of proficient readers.

- Overall, 22 percent of children who have lived in poverty do not graduate from high school, compared to 6 percent of those who have never been poor. This rises to 32 percent for students spending more than half of their childhood in poverty.
- For children who were poor for at least a year and were not reading proficiently in third grade, the proportion that don't finish school rose to 26 percent. That's more than six times the rate for all proficient readers.
- The rate was highest for poor Black and Hispanic students, at 31 and 33 percent respectively – or about eight times the rate for all proficient readers.
- Even among poor children who were proficient readers in third grade, 11 percent still didn't finish high school. That compares to 9 percent of subpar third-grade readers who have never been poor.
- Among children who never lived in poverty, all but 2 percent of the best third-grade readers graduated from high school on time.
- Graduation rates for Black and Hispanic students who were not proficient readers in third grade lagged far behind those for White students with the same reading skills.

(pp. 3–4)

The multiple caveats needed to accept the study as valid leads to skepticism. AECF found support from a group of corporate executives Business Roundtable (2016), while dismissing a century of research on the ill-fated practice of grade retention; the executives created an action plan to improve literacy rates. Their plan for states included the following: expand access to high-quality pre-K learning opportunities, high-quality full-day kindergarten that ensures a successful transition to elementary school, use of student assessments and data systems to track student progress, equip educators in pre-K–grade 3 to help students become strong readers, require systematic interventions for struggling readers in grades K–3, and coordinate governance of pre-K and grades K–3 to promote efficiency and maximize impact (pp. 2–3). Supporters justified their thinking for each recommendation within a business model and acknowledged the impact of high-stakes reading assessments:

> the numbers are even more troubling for low-income students and students of color. Only 18 percent of black fourth graders, 21 percent of Hispanic fourth graders and 21 percent of lower-income fourth graders … demonstrated proficiency in reading on the 2015 NAEP assessment.
>
> *(p. 11)*

Consistently, supporters of the reading grade retention based their ideas on AECF reports and parroted: students who fail to read on grade level, by the end of third grade, are four times more likely to drop out of school. Not shared were the hundreds of studies suggesting **grade retention**, not **reading ability**, was the primary reason students do not complete high school (Alexander et al., 1994; Grissom & Shepard, 1998).

Several research studies documented grade retention laws along with descriptions of state explanations of laws, policies, and statutes for exemptions. Jimerson and Kaufmann (2003) revealed more requests for exceptions and exemptions were granted to White parents than to parents of students of color. Matthews, Kizzie, Rowley, and Cortina (2010) investigated the intersection of early literacy assessments and social-behavioral variance among Black boys and their peers, given the dismal outlook for early literacy performance among Black boys. Drawing on secondary data from Early Childhood Longitudinal Study–Kindergarten Cohort (ECLS-K), their study investigated the role of classroom behavioral and social factors in literacy development. The authors found learning-related skills accounted for much of the variance between Black students and their peers. The concept centered on "*learning-related skills* (LRS) refers to a cluster of social skills (e.g. task persistence, learning independence, flexible thinking, organization, and attention control) that facilitate active and efficient learning" (Howse, Lange, Farran, & Boyles, 2003, p. 757, italics in the original). They remarked LRS gaps were evident in kindergarten and continued to affect student literacy performance for years. In addition, Matthews et al. (2010) observed:

> SES and home literacy environment were influential for achievement as expected; however, they only explain a fraction of the variance that LRS explains. Within the school setting, punitive disciplinary actions and stringent behavior modification techniques for African American boys have been the primary approach for reducing classroom behavior problems.
>
> *(p. 766)*

Their research was supported by several commentaries, research studies, and reviews about Black students' classroom literacy experiences. Previous studies identifying gender and racial gaps in reading achievement were confirmed, as was the impact of varying social factors in the lives of Black male students. A key finding of this study was the lack of support related to low reading performance and behavioral issues.

Squires (2015) reported Hawaii and Arkansas had the highest retention rates in kindergarten, but they have no stated retention policy for third grade. Most states used test-based assessments for retention based on reading performance from either commercial, local, or state tests. Other states used data from one or more sources including assessments, behavior, and teacher recommendations before making reading retention recommendations. Martorell and Mariano's

(2017) study of non-test casual effects (attendance, discipline, and suspension) of grade retention found grade retention did not have a positive effect on student behavior (p. 25). Weyer (2018) reported the following examples of exemption from retention used by states:

- Been identified as an English language learner with generally less than three years of English instruction
- Been identified as having a disability
- Demonstrated proficiency on an alternative standardized reading assessment or through a portfolio of assessments and classwork
- Been previously retained prior to third grade
- Participated in an intervention, such as a summer reading program
- Received approval for promotion, based on parent, principal, and/or teacher recommendations

Whether students are retained due to failure to pass state reading assessments or teacher recommendations, there are usually appeals processes available. Tavassolie and Winsler (2019) conducted a study of an "ethnically diverse urban sample" of 27,980 students. They found third graders who did not pass the Florida Comprehensive Assessment Test were over-represented by students who were Black and Latinx and received reduced or free lunch. They remarked that appeals by minoritized parents were seldom granted (p. 71) (please see Table 4.2).

NAEP (2019) data also revealed that despite the heavy influence of scientifically based/evidence-based research (science of reading, scientific reading strategies, etc., federal and state government-funded research and school district grants, RTI/MTSS interventions, and third-grade retention laws), nationally students continued to perform poorly on reading assessments.

Lian, Yu, Tu, Deng, Wang, Q, and Zuo (2021) used data from the Program for International Student Assessment (PISA) (2018), including information from 465,146 students in 74 countries, to examine linkages between grade repetition and bullying expressed by students (15–16-year-olds). Their findings indicated, "globally, both boys and girls who repeat a grade are at increased risk of being bullied compared with promoted peers, but girls may experience higher risks than boys of specific types of bullying associated with repeating a grade" (p. 2). The commentaries, studies, and reviews collectively agreed that improvement in reading performance of Black students, school districts, schools, classrooms, and teachers needed to exhibit: less Whiteness, more Blackness, more cultural and linguistic understanding, and less punishment.

The propaganda campaign by AECF and the like, along with state legislators, repeat this lie: third-grade reading retention will help support students academically, improve their reading and reading test performance, and improve

TABLE 4.2 *Third-Grade Reading Retention Laws and Explanations*

State	Law	Retention	Parental Notification	Explanation
Alabama		Required	X	
Alaska	Alaska Stat. Ann. § 14.03.072	Allowed	X	Retention is a local decision.
Arizona	Ariz. Rev. Stat. Ann. § 15–701	Required	X	Third grade retention is required, with good cause exemptions
Arkansas		Required	X	
California	Cal. Educ. Code § 48070.5		X	Third grade retention is required unless the student's teacher determines in writing that retention is not the appropriate intervention.
Colorado	Colo. Rev. Stat. Ann. § 22–7–1205	Allowed	X	Retention is allowed after a meeting with the parent, the student's teacher and other personnel. At that meeting, the group determines if retention is the best intervention strategy.
Connecticut	Conn. Gen. Stat. Ann. § 10–265g	Required	X	Third grade retention is required with good cause exemptions, if a student does not participate in a summer school program.
Delaware	14 Del.C. 153	Required	X	Third grade retention is required with good cause exemptions. Students that score below the standard, level II, on the statewide assessment are provided different exemptions than those that score well below the standard, level I.
District of Columbia	D.C. Code Ann. 38-1803.21, 38-755.03	Required	X	Third grade retention is required with good cause exemptions
Florida	Fla. Stat. Ann. § 1008.25	Required	X	
Georgia	Ga. Code Ann., § 20-2-283	Required	X	

(Continued)

TABLE 4.2 (Continued)

State	Law	Retention	Parental Notification	Explanation
Illinois	105 Ill. Comp. Stat. Ann. 5/10–20.9a	Allowed	X	Students determined by the local district to not qualify for promotion to the next higher grade shall be provided remedial assistance, which may include, but shall not be limited to, a summer bridge program of no less than 90 hours, tutorial sessions, increased or concentrated instructional time, modifications to instructional materials, and retention in grade.
Indiana	511 Ind. Admin. Code 6.2-3.1-3	Allowed	X	If the student does not achieve a passing score on the IREAD-3 assessment.
Iowa	Iowa Code Ann. § 256.7 (31.a)	N/A	X	The state board of education is required to adopt standards that reasonably expect a student's reading progress is sufficient to master fourth grade reading skills prior to promotion to fourth grade.
Kentucky	704 Ky. Admin. Regs. 3:440	Not required	X	
Louisiana			X	
Maine	Code Me. R. tit. 05-071 Ch. 127, § 5	Allowed		Retention is a local decision.
Maryland	Md. Code Ann., Educ. § 7-202	Allowed		Third grade retention is allowed with good cause exemptions. Enrollment in a reading assistance program is an option to avoid retention.
Michigan	Mich. Comp. Laws Ann. § 380.1280f (5.a)	Required	X	Third grade retention is allowed with good cause exemptions.
Minnesota	Minn. Stat. Ann. § 120B.12 (3.b)	Allowed	X	Retention is allowed but is not required.

Mississippi	Miss. Code. Ann. § 37-177-11 Miss. Code. Ann. § 37-177-15	Required	X	Third grade retention is required with good cause exemptions. Intensive acceleration classes are available for students retained in grade three who were previously retained in K-3 Xgrades.
Missouri	Mo. Ann. Stat. § 162.1100 (West) Mo. Ann. Stat. § 167.645	Required	X	Retention is required if a student is not reading at or above one grade level below their current grade level. Students may be considered for conditional promotion if they participate in a summer reading program.
Nevada	Nev. Rev. Stat. Ann. § 392.760 Nev. Rev. Stat. Ann. § 392.765	Required	X	Third grade retention is required with good cause exemptions.
New Jersey	N.J. Stat. Ann. § 18A:35-4.9	Allowed	X	Retention and promotion policies are determined locally.
New Mexico	N.M. Stat. Ann. § 22-2c-6	Allowed	X	Retention is an option based on the teacher and school principal recommendation.
New York		Not Required	X	

(*Continued*)

TABLE 4.2 (Continued)

State	Law	Retention	Parental Notification	Explanation
North Carolina	N.C. Gen. Stat. Ann. § 115C-83.7	Required	X	Third grade retention is required for students who fail to demonstrate proficiency on state-approved standardized tests for reading comprehension. Students that demonstrate reading proficiency by November 1 are eligible for midyear promotion. There is a good cause exemption to mandatory retention that allows students with limited English proficiency, students with disabilities, student who demonstrate proficiency on alternative assessments, students who demonstrate proficiency through reading portfolio, and students who have received reading intervention and have been retained once in kindergarten, first, second, or third grade to be promoted.
Ohio	Ohio Rev. Code Ann. § 3313.608	Allowed	X	School districts have the options to retain a third grade student who does not meet grade level achievement as measured on the state English language arts assessment. The district can also promote the student to fourth grade if the principal and teacher agree that other evaluations of the student's skill in reading demonstrate that the student is academically prepared to be promoted. The district can promote the student to fourth grade but provide the student with intensive intervention services.
Oklahoma	Okla. Stat. Ann. tit. 70, § 1210.508C	Allowed	X	Retention is allowed for students who are not eligible for automatic promotion, with exception for good cause. If the student's Reading Proficiency team unanimously recommends probationary promotion, the student will be advanced to fourth grade. With probationary promotion, the team will continue to review the students reading performance. Retained students can be promoted mid-year, prior to November 1st, upon demonstrating a level of proficiency required to score at grade level on the statewide third-grade assessment.

State	Citation			Description
South Carolina	S.C. Code Ann. § 59-155-160	Required	X	Third grade retention is required for student who fail to demonstrate reading proficiency, with a good cause exemption.
Tennessee	Tenn. Code Ann. § 49-6-3115	Required		Third grade retention is required if the student has not shown a basic understanding of curriculum and demonstration of skills in reading in their grades or standardized test results. If the student participates in an LEA approved research-based intervention prior to the next school year, the student may be promoted.
Texas	Tex. Educ. Code Ann. § 28.0211	Allowed	X	Retention is not required. However, if a student fails to perform satisfactorily on an assessment after three attempts the student shall be retained at the same grade level for the next school year.
Vermont	Vt. Stat. Ann. tit. 16, § 2903	Not Required	X	Retention not required (the cited statute appears to suggest that students who fall behind in third grade receive supplemental instruction in 4th grade instead of being retained).
Virginia	Va. Code Ann. § 22.1 253.13:1	Not required	X	Retention is not required but a student who fails to achieve a passing score on all of the Standards of Learning assessments in grade 3 through 8 must receive intervention services prior to being promoted.
Washington	Wash. Rev. Code Ann. § 28A.655.230	Required	X	Retention is required with a parental exception.
West Virginia	W. Va. Code Ann. § 18-2E-10W. Va. Code R. 126-30-3	Allowed		Classroom teachers may recommend the grade level retention of a student, but it is not required. Participation in an intervention program may be a condition of promotion; however, a teacher may still recommend retention.

State Bill information from © 2021 by the Education Commission of the States (ECS). All rights reserved. ECS is the only nationwide, nonpartisan interstate compact devoted to education. 700 Broadway #810, Denver, CO 80203-3442 their ability to graduate from high school. Students are most likely to drop out, if they are retained, the real culprit for not graduating from high school is grade retention.

Cummings and Turner's (2020) analysis of third-grade reading policies found:

> thirty-seven states and D. C. have policies aimed at getting students reading proficiently by the end of third grade, and 17 of them plus DC require retention of third graders whose assessment scores indicate that they are behind in reading.
>
> *(p. 5)*

They noted "the proliferation of such policies began in 2002, when Florida enacted its third-grade retention law alongside its statewide literacy initiative, just read, Florida!" (p. 5). They also acknowledged Florida's policy has been influential and its model replicated by other states; however, the retention policies are enforced at the local level (p. 5). Controversy arose with state laws mandating retention for students who do not meet third-grade reading standards (p. 7). The idea of retaining students who are not reading on grade level by the end of third grade has been supported by a limited literature base from reading research, irrespective of racial disproportionality in retention rates and the emotional and psychological toll of retention. Yet, 37 states enacted reading retention laws, arguing research indicated reading on grade level by the end third grade was a strong predictor for high school graduation and improved life circumstances. The authors also presented brief explanations that accompanied data on third-grade retention laws and states' position on retention and exemptions.

Oversimplifying the unstated assumptions in read by grade 3 laws:

(1) all children in pre–grade 3 have similar (White-centric) experiences (beliefs, cultures, languages, and religions) and have encountered similar pre-K curricula, instruction, and school environments;

(2) early childhood, after-school, enrichment, and summer school programs, are framed to indoctrinate Black students to act, believe, sound, and think like White people to pass standardized reading assessments and not be retained in grade 3;

(3) profiling Black children (ages 3–5) is an important first step in preventing high school dropouts (irrespective of research that does not support this notion); and

(4) some Black students (ages 5–9) are making an adult-like conscious decision to not learn to read on grade level, so they should be punished and shamed to avoid dropping out of school prior to high school graduation.

Federal government-adjacent agencies, corporate leaders, politicians, and reading researchers have anchored educational policy and supported state laws upon a narrow and unchallenged body of research replicating colonial anti-Black racism and anti-literacy customs, traditions, and statutes. Johnston and Scanlon (2020) recognized the failure of federally funded initiatives, laws, and policies informed by several federal reports and millions of dollars of funded research needed to be explained:

> enthusiasm for the potentially curative benefits of the approach to instruction currently promoted by SOR proponents led to a grand, federally-funded experiment, the Reading First program, that failed to deliver any impact on reading comprehension (the most important target of reading instruction), despite a small but significant increase in word decoding skills. This despite the expenditure of billions of dollars in funding from the US Department of Education over six years.
>
> *(p. 22)*

Among the exemptions allowed by states for families/parents/students seeking an exemption from the third-grade retention laws was a "get of out retention" card. Lists of possible exemptions were not extensive, and most required parental appeals to overturn retention. There was a single exemption that often was used by many families/parents of all ethnic/racial backgrounds, but most successfully by well-to-do White parents: securing a dyslexia referral/designation for their child.

A Caveat: Dyslexia and Third-Grade Reading Retention

Confusion about the definition and characteristics of dyslexia grew from fervent supporters to ardent detractors. The former argued the notion encompassed a range of reading difficulties experienced by readers, and the latter suggested the lack of a clear definition, theory, and research base was sufficient to discard the moniker. Johnston and Scanlon (2020) explained the current support of dyslexia was

> based on a narrow view of science, and a restricted range of research, focused on word learning and, … neurobiology, but paying little attention to aspects of literacy like comprehension and writing, or dimensions of classroom learning and teacher preparation.
>
> *(p. 2)*

They acknowledged the federal government and most states passed laws in support of addressing dyslexia and observed that media restated "a narrative that dyslexia is a central cause of reading difficulty, and that SOR-aligned instruction is necessary, not only for those classified as dyslexic, but for all students" (p. 3).

Elliott (2020) echoed similar sentiments about the "science" used in support of dyslexia; public acceptance of a dyslexia diagnosis; the varying definitions of dyslexia used by educators, parents, and politicians; and resource inequities created by the misrepresentation of reading difficulties identified as dyslexia. He created four categories to explain the differences in dyslexia: (1) "synonymous with the concept of reading disability," (2) a "clinically derived subgroup of poor decoders," (3) "persistent intractability to high-quality intervention," and (4) a "neurodiverse profile" (pp. S62–S64). He observed researchers often used different criteria for diagnosing dyslexia; however, it was not uncommon to find a reference to IQ discrepancy, nowadays considered an outdated, racist, and unused concept. He also argued dyslexia is not as different from people who are poor readers for any number of reasons; however, it had cachet; that is, dyslexia sounded more complex than poor reader: "the value of such a diagnosis is that it identifies a need to cater somewhat differently for small portion of treatment-resistant poor readers for whom evidence based educational approaches have demonstrated limited effectiveness" (p. S64).

Without a clear definition, what it means to be dyslexic and how to address the needs of students "allows schools, clinicians, researchers, or anyone else, to decide who is dyslexic in any valid or reliable way" (Johnston & Scanlon, 2020, p. 5). The lack of a clear definition had been side-stepped by loosely including dyslexia under the 1969 SLDA, later a part of Education of the Handicapped Act (EHA), P. L. 91-230. Dyslexia was not explicitly described in the definition but used by federal and state governments to address reading difficulties. The lack of an agreed-upon definition provided ample opportunity for varying claims about dyslexia and potential solutions. Florida also designated dyslexia as a disability with all inherent rights and funding. Johnston and Scanlon (2020) acknowledged special education's description of students who experienced reading difficulties was later named dyslexia, although "98.5 percent of students deemed to have such a disability were white, and most were middle class" (p. 4). The researchers observed: "… dyslexics are a separate class of individuals, distinct from those experiencing reading problems for other reasons such as intellect, culture, poverty, and/or limited opportunities to learn, coupled with the allusion that dyslexia indicates other exceptional skills" (p. 18). Gabriel (2020) expressed dyslexia was often described as normal and favorably among White males, as "explicitly link dyslexia with giftedness, creativity, and innovation … something to be honored and 'embraced' as a mark of 'great minds' and 'game changers,' rather than as a disability" (p. 324). She observed a common belief among parents and some educators is dyslexia can be understood "as a personal tragedy exacerbated by schools that neither identify nor specifically address it" (p. 311). She also expressed larger socio-political concerns were used in the framing of dyslexia:

> The use of conversion narratives, rather than scientific or economic arguments, signals a move away from accountability era ideas about evidence-based practices or standard protocols for identifying and remediating reading difficulties among all school children. Brand-name programs

sold by for-profit companies are discursively constructed as religions unto themselves, with educators and families publicly declaring allegiance, attributing miraculous turnarounds to their methods, and describing the moment of diagnosis/training in the same terms as a moment of conversion or enlightenment.

(p. 332)

NCES (2010) reported the number of students who identified as receiving Special Education Services has increased over the last decade, especially among students identified as specific learning disabled, not specifically, dyslexic (please see Figure 4.2).

Students identified under the category of SLD grew considerably and were predominated by students of color. NCES articulated the federal definition of a specific learning disability "is a disorder in one or more of the basic psychological processes involved in understanding or using spoken or written language that may manifest itself in an imperfect ability to listen, think, speak, read, write, spell, or do mathematical calculations" (p. 2). Gabriel's (2018) discourse analysis of print media coverage regarding the categorization and education of students identified as dyslexic revealed "arguments were repeatedly constructed in a way that placed individual children (rather than groups of children or members of a certain community or population) as victims of school or government policies" (p. 9). Gabriel (2019) also noted the use of personal narratives filled with emotive language and appeals to support these "taxpaying parents" and frustrated students who were unable to obtain sufficient educational interventions in public schools but found them alternative spaces. She explained how media coverage highlighted individual family cases wherein "dyslexia-specific media coverage constructs an almost disembodied form of literacy that focuses on 'the reading brain' the 'dyslexic mind' and the 'science of reading'" (p. 16). Johnston and Scanlon (2020) summarized the prevailing dyslexia narrative promoted by supporters and the media:

the reasonable premise that a reading problem is not the child's nor the parents' fault, and does not reflect a problem with intelligence or some other hypothetical characteristic like laziness. The narrative's appeal has been enhanced with unfounded claims that dyslexia may also entail an array of exceptional abilities. These claims are supported, not by research, but primarily by anecdotes about prominent, successful public figures, living and dead, who overcame reading difficulties presumed to be due to dyslexia. The experiences of those struggling to overcome reading difficulties, are certainly real. As evidence that dyslexics are more likely to be gifted in various ways, their value is questionable.

(pp. 19–20)

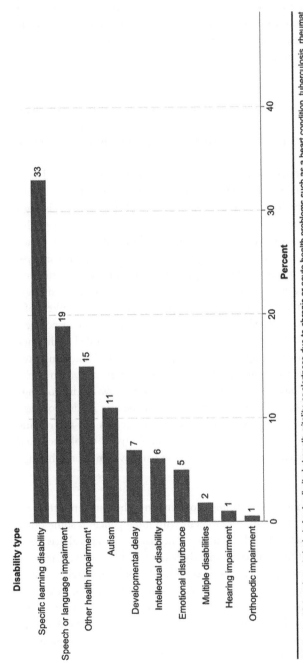

¹ Other health impairments include having limited strength, vitality, or alertness due to chronic or acute health problems such as a heart condition, tuberculosis, rheumat fever, nephritis, asthma, sickle cell anemia, hemophilia, epilepsy, lead poisoning, leukemia, or diabetes.
NOTE: Data are for the 50 states and the District of Columbia only. Visual impairment, traumatic brain injury, and deaf-blindness are not shown because they each acco for less than 0.5 percent of students served under IDEA. Due to categories not shown, detail does not sum to 100 percent. Although rounded numbers are displayed, th figures are based on unrounded data.
SOURCE: U.S. Department of Education, Office of Special Education Programs, Individuals with Disabilities Education Act (IDEA) database, retrieved February 2, 2021 from https://www2.ed.gov/programs/osepidea/618-data/state-level-data-files/index.html#bcc. See *Digest of Education Statistics 2020*, table 204.30.

FIGURE 4.2 Percentage distribution of students ages 3–21 served under the Individuals with Disabilities Education Act (IDEA), by disability type: School year 2019–20.

Credit: National Center for Education Statistics.

Elliott (2020) also expressed concern about the social and political power among lobbying groups to advance their agenda and impact legislation. He argued the nation's political context permitted "this construct has the power to influence government policy, educational practice, and lay perceptions in ways that can lead to increased legislation and resourcing on a scale that would otherwise be difficult to achieve" (p. S69). He articulated:

> dyslexia diagnosis is recognized as having the potential to help those so labeled to gain a more positive picture of themselves, while also encouraging teachers and others to be more understanding, sympathetic, and supportive. However, for struggling readers who lack the label, the suggestion of a greater degree of personal and familial culpability may be an unfortunate consequence.
>
> *(p. S71)*

Likewise, Gabriel and Woulfin (2017) communicated concerns about dyslexia focused on

> the public good of reading assessment, instruction, and intervention as delivered in public schools is deemed insufficient for students with dyslexia labels. Instead, advocates often claim that private assessment and intervention are required to meet the needs of children with dyslexia labels. They therefore argue that schools should be required to provide specific, often branded approaches for identifying and addressing dyslexia.
>
> *(p. 311)*

Gabriel's research noticed connections among lobbying agencies and private vendors to support additional legislation in support of students identified as dyslexic, with some states naming specific approaches or programs, "dyslexia-specific legislation increases the specificity of existing laws, by specifying how dyslexia should be defined, diagnosed, and addressed" (Gabriel, 2018). She observed, "this signals a shift from holding schools accountable for outcomes to prescribing particular remedies, thus creating a market for these tools and approaches with guaranteed demand across the state" (Gabriel, 2020, p. 307). The NCLB accountability requirements tied to scientifically based research required by state laws for reading assessments do not appear required for state-sanctioned private agencies, companies, and programs.

Don't Believe the Hype

In the 70 years since *Brown v. Board of Education* (1954), minoritized students struggled to legally secure their right to an equal education, an undefined concept. The National Equity Project, an organization at the forefront of efforts to improve educational equity in California and beyond, professed: "educational equity means that each child receives what they need to develop to their full academic and social potential" (National Equity Project, 2021, para 1). In recent legal victories plaintiffs, for an equal education have centered on access to literacy, especially appropriate reading instruction.

The history and extant literature of grade-level retention and third-grade reading retention revealed many students who were negatively affected by these laws were Black, Indigenous, and Latinx. Opponents submit the new laws reconstitute White supremacy – under the guise of "states' rights" to make educational decisions and the use of state tests – as a cover for racist literacy policies. Historically, literacy has been weaponized to "remove people of color from economic, political, and social competition" (Browne-Marshall, 2013, p. xxxvi), and the most recent laws, as well as selective waivers, continue the process.

The findings are consistent: The students who were performing below grade level, as measured by state reading standards, were predominately Black and Brown male students and students living in poverty. This created an underclass of students, either unaware of or in defiance of their Fourteenth Amendment rights. Reading retention laws were policy choices, to support a select view of reading and reading assessment over the lives of Black and Brown students. Inoue (2015) suggested if students are doing poorly, it is time to stop and look at the assessment, not the students. The history of reading and reading assessments clearly revealed a persistent gap for Black, Brown, and Native American readers on standardized reading assessments, and begs the question, why are the assessments still used?

Race, Reading, and Grade Retention

Annually, there are hundreds of research studies published with a focus on reading, in general, and reading assessment, in particular. There also are numerous publications produced by agencies, corporations, federal agencies, philanthropic agencies, and proxy-federal organizations. Reading researchers' intervention studies continued along with federally funded reviews of literature. Foorman, Beyler, Borradaile, Coyne, Denton, Dimino, Furgeson, Hayes, Henke, Justice, Keating, Lewis, Sattar, Streke, Wagner, and Wissel (2016), working under the auspices of the Institute for Education Science and the What Works Clearing House, published a guidebook for teachers, *Foundational Skills to Support Reading for Understanding in Kindergarten through 3rd Grade*. The guidebook was produced to address the stagnant reading performance among fourth graders on NAEP reading assessments. The text replicated the findings of *NRP*. Likewise, a study by Wanzek, Stevens, Williams, Scammacca, Vaughn, and Sargent (2018), whose analyses of a variety of intensive interventions lasted from 10 to 50 minutes, one or more times a week, found intensive intervention had positive effects for kindergarten to third-grade students having difficulty learning to read.

Not surprisingly, after two decades of federally sponsored expert reports and recommendations, there has been no significant change in fourth-grade reading proficiency; in fact, proficiency is lower for Black and Latinx students and low-income students as measured on standardized reading assessments. There also is no discussion or accountability for how reading research informed reading assessments, curriculum, and materials; nor how reading interventions influenced third-grade reading retention laws and the racial disproportionality of students placed in special education. An often-cited reason for the lack of reading improvement is the dearth of highly trained teachers and the lack of teacher fidelity to reading programs. The reasoning replicated past responses by politicians and researchers who blamed either Black students (culture/ethnicity, economic status, language, and marital status of parents) or teachers for low reading performance. Yet, many states adopted third-grade reading retention policies and laws, predicated in part on the federal support of reading based on findings from NAEP, *NRP*, and *PRD* along with ongoing funding for reading research, reviews, and surveys, under the pretense that reading by third grade was necessary for future academic/scholastic success. The discourse used in reading retention laws mimicked the language used in reading research studies as well as used in publications written by corporate, philanthropic, and professional journals, seemingly irrespective of countervailing research.

A false dilemma was presented to stakeholders: either students are assessed to be at grade level and promoted and unlikely to graduate from high school, or they are assessed below grade level and retained and more likely to graduate from high school. The exact opposite is true: students who are not retained are more likely to graduate from high school. Studies of reading retention also found students were retained based on low performance on standardized assessments and teacher recommendations. However, White students were more likely to be exempted from state laws on appeal, for a variety of reasons, including being identified as dyslexic. There is an anti-Black literacy throughline from the history of colonial anti-Black literacy laws and the systemic failure of reading research to address Black students' literacy to contemporary anti-Black literacy laws holding Black children – individually and personally responsible – for failure to read on grade level by the end of grade 3. Some states encouraged identifying students as early as preschool as "children who are likely to fail to read on grade level," and extend their preschool participation, thus codifying under the radar a "legal red-shirt" year for many Black students and an additional year of federal school funding for districts. Reading retention laws have punished and criminalized Black eight- and nine-year-old children as well as held them personally accountable for "not" learning to read on grade level as measured by standardized reading assessments, while simultaneously undervaluing what Black students know, and failing to acknowledge any psychological harm they may experience.

5

READING RESEARCH BARRIERS TO BLACK STUDENTS' READING PERFORMANCE

For millions of US citizens, Tuesday, January 17, 2017, began as an ordinary unmemorable day; however, others recalled the day as remarkable and significant because they witnessed politicians use innocuous discourse to build another case for the reform of public education. US Senator Alexander (R-Kentucky), chair of the Senate Education Committee, declared: "Betsy DeVos is on our children's side. On charter schools and school choice, she is in the mainstream" (Alexander, 2017, n.p.). This comment was part of his opening remarks during the first day of hearings on Mrs. DeVos's nomination for US Secretary of Education. His remarks were followed by a selective history of school choice and stereotypical statements about low-income families: "[by] increasing support for giving low-income families more choices of accredited schools, public, private or religious" (n.p.). Further politicizing poverty, his word choice sought to discredit anyone who opposed her nomination, asking: "Would her critics be happier if she had spent her time and her money trying to deny children from low-income families the opportunity to attend schools that wealthy families can choose rather than trying to help them?" (n.p.). Former US Senator Kassebaum (R-Kansas) also praised DeVos's work in schools, claiming DeVos "has dedicated her life to helping children, especially low-income children, have the opportunity to attend a good school" (n.p.). She continued by outlining three criticisms that had been waged against DeVos: "1) her support for more public charter schools; her advocacy for giving lower-income parents more choices; and her considerable wealth to advance effectively those two ideas" (Kassebaum, quoted in Alexander, 2017, n.p.). Finally, Mrs. DeVos proclaimed her support from the then-president-elect Trump before describing her job qualifications. She sketched a past including her own Christian education (having never attended public schools), experiences

DOI: 10.4324/9781003296188-6

with education as a parent (in Christian schools), service as a mentor in public schools, work among government officials, and support of the local control of (public) education. DeVos stated:

> The vast majority of students in this country will continue to attend public schools. ... Every child in America deserves to be in a safe environment that is free from discrimination. Every student in America dreams of developing his or her unique talents and gifts. Every parent in America dreams of a future when their children have access to schools with the rigor, challenges, and safe environments that successfully prepare them for a brighter, more hopeful tomorrow.
>
> *(quoted in Alexander, 2017, n.p.)*

Creating and publicizing support for Betsy DeVos's nomination as US Secretary of Education was important, sending (a) racist dog-whistles to likeminded folks about untapped protentional to change education in the United States in ways consistent with their points of view, (b) repeated old tropes stereotyping Black people and students, and (c) fawning alleged benevolence and offering to help Black and poor students to garner public support. The discourse used by politicians to describe US schooling continued to portray an educational crisis (McQullian, 1998) while focusing on the lack of publicly funded school choice, especially minoritized and low-income students. Statements by Alexander, DeVos, and Kassebaum exemplified how invoking notions of benevolence and "reasonableness" (DeLissovoy, 2016) occluded underlying assumptions of White supremacy. Alexander articulated the need to support "our" children, a phrase suggesting inclusivity. Statements by Alexander, DeVos, and Kassebaum suggested concerns about equalizing opportunities for "low-income children," as if to distance themselves from self-dealing as they were not referencing their own children. These statements represented a deliberate reframing of earlier civil rights discourse about education equity, now proffered in the interest of garnering support for a "solution" (increasing school choice) of an educational crisis (failing schools for children living in poverty), they had named and remedied. None of the speakers' statements referenced the impact of DeVos's charter school campaign in Michigan, where minoritized students composed one third of the total school population. It was an important omission because these campaigns failed miserably in many of Detroit's low-income Black communities. As the city with the largest percentage of charter schools in the nation, it also had a documented history of students' low academic achievement. Henderson (2016) explained how charter schools had been promoted in Michigan and described how the financial clout of the DeVos family, their political action committee, and their support of entrepreneurs had reshaped public education, albeit without significant academic improvement for students.

The anodyne statements by Alexander, DeVos, and Kassebaum, along with the consistently low performance ratings of the charter schools, represented racialized narratives in support of an ideology of White supremacy. The racialized narratives were more than political rhetoric; they were an iteration of systemic racism in education and education reform. In support of DeVos, the then-president Trump asked Congress to fund "school choice for disadvantaged youth, including millions of African-American and Latino children ... families should be free to choose the public, private, charter, magnet, religious or home school that is right for them" (n.p.). To be clear, the racist dog-whistle was heard by people who received millions of taxpayer dollars from charter schools, especially in states where there was little governmental oversight. The pronouncement also legally continued the White hegemonic discourse, framing public education as something for minoritized and poor students. The public education system was in crisis, and those who created the crisis were "prepared" to address education as the "new civil right" by creating a path for racial equity. Historically, the ideas proposed by DeVos and others replicated anti-Black literacy efforts, for example, read-by-third-grade retention laws under local and state control, although "local control, may result in the maintenance of a status quo that will preserve superior educational opportunities and facilities for whites at the expense of blacks" (Bell, 1980, pp. 526–527). The Honorable US Representative Ayanna Pressley (2018) demystified the fallacy underpinning such arguments in a tweet "#Disparities & inequities don't just happen, they are created. They are created by discriminatory laws & predatory actions, & they are preserved by the complicit silence of many" (n.p.).

Anti-Black racism and anti-Black literacy informed read-by-grade-three retention laws and represented/legalized a de facto – by practice – system of racial segregation. For some Black students, there may be underlying economic factors affecting their access to high quality literacy instruction as well as their early reading progress; however, the underlying factors were deliberately created, framed, legalized, and promoted by supporters of White supremacy to forestall Black advancement.

As mentioned in previous chapters, legal attempts at literacy/reading reform echoed White hegemonic discourse to position school choice/charters/vouchers as a logical response: "rather than softening the blow of systemic inequality and marginalization, elite reform efforts (choice schemes, redevelopment, and charterization) end up repackaging and accelerating these processes" (DeLissovoy, 2016, p. 353). Several research studies documented reading retention laws were applied or enforced haphazardly and included exceptions and opportunities for appeals that greatly favored White students and students with economic or social capital. The decision to enforce reading retention laws, or not, replicated colonialist approaches to shield anti-Black racism and reproduced anti-Black literacy.

A consistent narrative among legislative reforms worked as a pretext to normalize the "need" to dismantle public schools and offer alternative schools as a "new normal" way to a more efficient education. Black (2021) succinctly captured this moment:

> Americans like to say that any child willing to work hard can prosper. This isn't true, but we want to believe it, so we say it. Public school systems have for decades labeled Black children inferior and troubled and disadvantaged and underrepresented in ways that determine their scholastic achievement. Few want to admit that often the real problem is the assumptions made about Blackness and its inability to succeed.
>
> *(para 13)*

Soon, there will be fewer White students than Black students in public schools, and it begs the question: Who are reading retention laws harming and who are they helping? For over a century, White supremacy underpinned anti-Black literacy laws, framed reading research, and guided reading assessments as educators, politicians, and stakeholders weaponized literacy for political and personal gain. We know Black students will never be White or White enough to compete as equals on assessments created to maintain White supremacy. How would reading research differ if based on alternative epistemologies and drawing from alternative bodies of research? This chapter presents responses to each query with a focus on Black students as readers, reading research conducted among Black students by Black researchers and allies, and barriers to Black students' reading performance masked as federal investment in equity reading via federal reading grants and a single approach to reading for all students.

Black Literacy Matters

Historical documents and data are not hidden, and ignoring them does not absolve perpetrators from their responsibility to address inequities in reading access, assessment, and research. During the last half-century, there was a lack of concentrated effort to reconceptualize Black students' reading from perspectives and methodologies grounded in Black scholarship. Educational research suffers from the erasure of Black epistemology as Morrison (1984) remarked, "the discredited knowledge' of a discredited people" (p. 342), but it need not be so. Traditionally, "it is only through white thinkers that black thoughts can be understood or philosophical" (Curry, 2008, p. 44). Historically, reading researchers have adopted an aloof stance toward Black readers, unless addressing race was politically expedient and funding was readily available. Moreover, politicians drew from literacy scholarship conducted amongst White students and informed by scientific racism to enact laws.

In 2020, there were multiple educational institutions and school districts decrying the assault on Black lives while not speaking against the reading retention laws in their states and across the nation. P. Williams (1987) warned "unresponsiveness does not make these issues go away. Failure to resolve the dilemma of racial violence merely displaces its power. The legacy of killing finds its way into cultural expectations, archetypes, and isms" (p. 157). The rhetoric about grade retention research being different from reading grade retention laws is an extension of anti-Black racism, as political decisions are made, and the consequences in the lives of Black students are ignored. Read-by-grade-three laws anticipated reading failure among students based on ethnicity/race and economics. Educators, parents, politicians, and reading researchers expressed selective outrage about Black student graduation rates and performance on reading standardized tests while creating barriers to graduating within curriculum as well as state laws and district policies. Repeated calls for the need of additional research to address standardized test differentials among Black, Asian, and White students ring hollow in the constant "this is something we need to work on" closing paragraphs of research studies. It is not enough to make such claims and fail to do so while conceptually and theoretically structuring reading research studies among White students. The current push to retain students who are not reading on grade level by grade 3 is a continuation of past attempts to derail the early reading progress of Black, Brown, and Native students as they are the students who are most often identified as not making sufficient progress. The focus on grade-level progress allowed stakeholders to avoid addressing two fundamental problems: dismantling anti-Black racism in the conceptualization, definition, and assessment of reading; and the use of reading standards based on White racist ideology to inform anti-Black literacy laws. A false dilemma was presented to stakeholders: either students are assessed to be reading at grade level and promoted, or they are assessed below grade level and must be retained. Students can be retained based on low performance on standardized assessments and teacher recommendation, or students can be exempted from a retention recommendation by good cause waivers and/or appeals. Students can be promoted despite a low reading performance if they disagree with a teacher's recommendation through an appeal accompanied by alternative portfolio data. Although students are not solely responsible for their own learning, they are punished, and the adults (corporate executives, hedge fund investors, philanthropists, politicians, reading researchers, reading teachers, state and local administrators) responsible for the assessments, instruction, and laws are not.

Given the reading performance of Black students, as measured by reading assessments at national, state, and local levels had not changed for decades, stakeholders should have been compelled to engage culturally informed epistemologies or to accurately understand language and ways of knowing among Black students. Reading assessments continued to reflect a body of research based on misguided theories informing reading assessments, curriculum, materials, and instruction and thus perpetuating falsehoods about Black student readers.

Reading: Emotional and Psychological Stress

A brief review of research addressed Black reading/literacy achievement and grade retention laws and policies in the lives of Black students. The body of research included Black students' experiences, for example, microaggressions (about communities, cultures, families, income, and language use), and attacks, trauma, and violence (about being retained). The mental health of Black students brought about through reading instruction and test performance was overlooked but should inform literacy approaches among Black children. The "doll test" conducted by Drs. Kenneth and Mamie Clark in the 1940s and cited in the *Brown v. Board* case served as an exemplar of the psychological effects that White dominance and internalized racism had on young children. While the original doll test found Black children preferred White dolls, recent research revealed Black children prefer dolls closer to their own skin tone. Spencer (2010) revealed that most Black children preferred dolls with lighter skin tones, and all students (Black and White) preferred dolls closer to their own skin tone. Similarly, Byrd, Ceacal, Felton, Nicholson, Rhaney, McCray, and Young (2017) conducted a study with 50 participants, roughly half male and half female, 47 Black, 2 Latinx, and 1 White child. Collectively, the children tended to prefer dolls reflective of their skin tone, and Black children exhibited a positive self-image (p. 198). Sturdivant and Alanis (2020) conducted studies that appeared to confirm the results of the Clark study: an emotional and psychological toll of internalized racism within young children. They acknowledged Black female preschoolers preferred to play with non-Black dolls. Sturdivant (2021) analyzed two Black girls at play who seemingly understood notions of privilege afforded non-Black dolls and acted out the differences during play. In sum, the "doll tests" provided cautions about the emotional and psychological well-being of Black students and the importance of addressing their mental health.

Brackett and Simmons (2015) observed a focus on standardized testing performance exacerbated emotional concerns of students and teachers. They identified key factors in support of emotional learning:

> Emotions can either enhance or derail classroom performance. Interest and amusement… harness attention and promote greater engagement. Boredom, anxiety, and fear disrupt concentration and interfere with the ability to learn. Extreme emotions like chronic stress, sometimes arising from trauma or their perception of danger, can result in the persistent activation of the sympathetic nervous system and the release of stress hormones like cortisol. Prolonged release of these hormones affects the brain structures associated with executive functioning and memory hindering the students' ability to learn and thrive in school in life.
>
> *(p. 24)*

Black students, like all students, enter classroom spaces as unique individuals with a life before, after, and beyond school. Their lives consist of varying forms of literacy including communication with multiple people across time and space in ways that may/may not be part of the repertoire of the classroom teacher, literacy coach, or reading specialist. In 2005, IDEIA included behavior under RTI; it permitted school personnel to act upon perceived assumptions about students' behavior and link behavior to economic income, intelligence, and race. M. Alexander (2012) argued the zero tolerance procedures established by schools provided an avenue to a new starting point to begin the school-to-prison pipeline, for Black boys. This positioning concretized efforts to adultify Black students and, as a school district policy, can influence response to student behaviors.

In reading research, many Black boys are similarly profiled as early as in prekindergarten and kindergarten classrooms as in need of socio-emotional support and exhibiting learning difficulties before beginning first grade, where they are identified as "struggling readers." RTI procedures provided school administrators a process to cover or disguise the lack of academic engagement and quality education they deserve (although the moniker shifted from RTI to Multi-Tiered Systems of Support (MTSS), the assumptions on which it was built, and the procedures carried out, have not changed); see also Winn and Behizadeh (2011). The concerns often mentioned in reading research for lack of performance on reading assessments also included behavior as a factor in literacy acquisition and low reading performance. Current reading assessments reflect a body of reading research based on misguided theories informing reading assessments, curriculum, materials, and instruction and thus perpetuating lies about Black students. State reading retention laws are filled with mis/disinformation encoded in anti-Black racism, laws denying or abridging equal educational access in violation of the Fourteenth Amendment. The narratives and research in support of the reading retention laws and the use of a single approach to reading were filled with messages projecting change and suggesting improved outcomes, nine or more years later in the life of a student, that cannot be guaranteed.

The racial demographics of US public school students gathered in 2002 revealed an ever-widening shift:

> Between fall 2009 and fall 2018, the percentage of public-school students who were Hispanic increased from 22 to 27 percent. The percentage of public-school students who were White decreased from 54 to 47 percent, and the percentage of students who were Black decreased from 17 to 15 percent.
> *(Irwin, NCES; Zhang, Wang, Hein, Wang, Roberts, York,*
> *AIR; Bullock Mann, Dilig, & Parker, RTI, 2021, p. 1)*

The percentage of Students of Color were greater than White students, yet state and local groups (governors, politicians, school boards, administrators, etc.) acquiesced to the concerns of White parents, politicians, and students more than any other racial group. As an aggregate racial group, predominately White parents with the support of state laws have worked to promote the use of standardized assessments to retain gifted program status, supported laws to avoid third-grade reading retention (dyslexia diagnosis, unequal approval of appeals), developed advocacy groups and school board candidates to instill their worldview, while working in concert with local, state, and federal and quasi-federal government groups, as well as philanthropic agencies, to push their agendas.

Federal support appeared in Foorman, Beyler, Borradaile, Coyne, Denton, Dimino, Furgeson, Hayes, Henke, Justice, Keating, Lewis, Sattar, Streke, Wagner, and Wissel (2016); working under the auspices of The Institute for Education Science and the What Works Clearing House, they published a guidebook for teachers, *Foundational Skills to Support Reading for Understanding in Kindergarten through 3rd Grade*. The guidebook was produced to address the stagnant reading performance among fourth graders on NAEP reading assessments since 1992. The text replicated findings of federally commissioned reviews of reading research during the 1990s–2000 (Adams, 1990; Snow et al., 1998; *NRP*, 2000): "foundational reading skills that enable students to read words (alphabetics), relate those words to their oral language, and read connected text with sufficient accuracy and fluency to understand what they read" (p. 1). Not all research produced strong support for a narrow view of reading as most were inconclusive and acknowledged the lack of significant change in the reading performance of fourth graders as measured on standardized assessments. Importantly, there were no significant change in fourth-grade reading proficiency, although proficiency among Black and Latinx students and low-income students decreased.

Reasons for the lack of reading improvement was explained as centered on two interrelated factors: few highly trained teachers and the lack of teacher fidelity to reading programs. A recent brief, published by the International Literacy Association (2019), has provided a summative explanation of research on reading assessments and suggested the importance of research along with understanding:

> learning to read is about more than letters and sounds, more than smooth fluent reading, and even more than solid reading comprehension. It is ultimately about providing students with the academic tools, such as learning to read successfully, that allow them to learn what they want and need to learn and to aspire to the life they want to create for themselves and their communities. To achieve that, we need to use the extensive research base on effective reading instruction available today to ensure that teachers, schools, and students are all getting the help they need.
>
> *(p. 6)*

Not surprisingly, the body of research from which these lofty ideas were drawn does not include significant studies conducted by Black scholars among Black students.

Many states adopted third-grade reading retention policies and laws, predicated in part on the federal support of reading research indicating that reading by third grade was necessary for future academic/scholastic success. The state reading retention policies and laws also narrowly defined what reading was and how reading was assessed. There appeared to be a push for political alignment among states as they parroted federalized notions of reading and decisions to evaluate reading proficiency. States that enforced reading retention laws argued research indicated reading on grade level by the end of third grade was a strong predictor for high school graduation and improved life circumstances, although the research suggested by hundreds of studies unequivocally argued that retention was the greatest deterrent to graduation, not reading by third grade.

Knowing Black students perform poorly on standardized reading tests, but requiring grade-level competency for promotion, discriminates against Black students without mentioning or naming race. These laws have been enacted in 37 states, despite data from NAEP revealing little significant change in the reading performance of Black students since 1992, By contrast, special education data revealed a disproportionate number of Black students identified as failing to read on grade level. State-by-state comparison data noted these patterns worked to forestall Black literacy achievement. Although states do not specifically identify Black students as those who are most likely to be retained by the end of third grade, unquestionably low performance on state standardized reading tests suggests Black students will most likely to be affected, and retained. As state policies shift for teachers and some students, despite rhetoric to the contrary, they do not shift in favor of Black students.

Supporters of RTI claimed the approach provided an alternative to IQ tests for consideration of special education placement. The reading assessments and procedures used by RTI included informal and subjective assessments were based on the same fundamental ideological principles of White supremacy and scientific racism and yielded the same results. The outcomes were presented as an abundance of data proving some students needed and were given additional reading support; however, they also continued to lag behind their peers. The twin components of IDEIA and RTI created a double-edged sword legally permitting the constant surveillance of academic performance and student behavior under RTI and have led to Black students' disproportional referral to special education and school suspensions, even among preschoolers. The current read-by-third-grade state laws and policies hold eight- and nine-year-old students accountable for failing to read at a mythical standard of Whiteness crafted and embedded in standardized reading tests.

Who should be held accountable for political decisions with lifelong and incalculable consequences for the lives of Black students? There are racial inequalities in reading assessments, as well as there are racial inequalities in curriculum and instruction. The history of grade retention laws and policies are clear: they do not deter students, they are not an instructional or intervention strategy, and students who are retained are more likely to drop out than students who are socially promoted. Grade retention laws extended legal racial segregation under the law. The results of standardized reading assessments also have long-lasting effects. Moreover, the outcomes of read-by-third-grade laws and policies are highly predictable: Black and Brown students will be retained in grade 3 and exceptions and exemptions are seldom extended to Black and Brown students. The outcomes also magnify existing educational inequalities and the dearth of research focus and interest on Black and Brown students. The grade 3 retention laws are contemporaneous versions of the Black Codes, perpetuating false narratives about people of African descent as without cultures, beliefs, languages, literacies, or religions. Quite the opposite was true: African people were human, with cultures, ethnicities, languages, literacies, and religions, as well, thousands of African people were literate prior to be enslaved in the US.

Knowledge of the rich legacy of Black literacy was unapparent among several members of the current NAGB appointed by former US Secretary of Education, Betsy DeVos, whose efforts in education were based on her personal experiences (although she did not attend public schools nor did her children), support of privatization of education, so-called Christian religious values, and scant understanding of public education. For decades, DeVos fought to protect conservative and White supremacist views. In addition, the NAGB determined, with little regard for Black history and Black literacy in the United States, to install a singular approach to reading, curriculum, materials, instruction, and assessment (how students learn to read, what is read, and how curriculum was taught and tested). Poised as a rebuke of Critical Race Theory (CRT) and portrayed as a rebuke of an indoctrination about the United States as a racist country, several states adopted laws to spare the "feelings of White children" who may learn the truth about the founding of the nation, the horrors of Black enslavement, and the genocide of Indigenous people. Centering education and reading about preserving Whiteness: White parents who have not told their children the truth and White teachers who may be uncomfortable explaining the nation's history. By weaponizing literacy, as part of the battle over the indoctrination of the minds of students, a single view of how to read, what it means to be a reader, and what should be understood and assessed found a convenient foothold. There were alternative bodies of extant research conducted among Black students, by Black researchers and allies, presenting a very different conceptualization of reading and valuing of Black students' culture, language, lives, and race.

Supporting Black Student Readers

Research by S. O. Williams (2007) and Thompson-McMillon (2001) provide contexts to what can happen to Black students who are readers but face implicit racial bias in schools. The longitudinal study by Williams, follows three brilliant Black girls' reading experiences at home and in schools from preschool (where they were beginning readers in English and Spanish) through grade 1 and where the ability to read was secondary to the implicit bias of White teachers who foregrounded their perceptions about classroom behavior above the girls' intellectual and reading abilities. The girls' parents and caregivers also encountered institutional racism as they requested more support for their daughters' education. Her findings are supported by more recent research by Anderson and Martin (2018); Andrews, Brown, Castro, and Id-Deen (2019); Morris (2016); and Wilmot, Migliarini, and Annamma (2021). Thompson-McMillon's study centered on the first-grade reading experiences of two Black boys who were early readers, reading before entering first grade. Their reading experiences in first grade were retarded by teacher behavior expectations and not their ability to read. Their first-grade classroom reading experiences, much like the Black girls', revealed how implicit teacher bias ignored their intellect and reading abilities while applying carceral punishment for classroom behaviors. Her findings are consistent with research among Black students' school experiences (Bryan, 2020; Ferguson, 2010; Hilliard, 1991; Wright & Counsell, 2018). The studies by Williams (2007) and Thompson-McMillon (2001) also noted the emotional and psychological trauma experienced by Black children and their families and parents was an under-researched area of study. The parents of the children in these studies developed home coping systems to deal with the implicit racial bias experienced by their young children after attempts to work with classroom teachers.

Black Students and Reading Assessments

Roderick and Nagaoka (2005) reviewed the Illinois state reading assessment scores of third-grade students in Chicago (1995–1996) and found there were only 5% of third graders who scored below the acceptable level for promotion. Among the students who were retained, they noticed:

> no evidence that retention led to greater achievement growth 2 years after the promotional gate … there is evidence that retaining students under Chicago's promotional policy significantly increased the likelihood of placement in special education.
>
> *(p. 331)*

Brown, Souto-Manning, and Laman (2010) conducted independent case studies to examine the ways in which racism was part of early childhood settings. Souto-Manning's case focused on her own second-grade classroom where a mandated reading program, Accelerate Reader (AR), was the required reading program. Nationally, the program was widely used, and students' progress was tethered to reading books, although no specific books were part of the program. The students who attended the school in which she taught were predominately Black and poor, although there were other minority groups collectively composing over 97% of the student population (p. 520). The school was in an impoverished county without funding to purchase books; thus, students were confined to reading the White-centric books in the school library where multicultural/multiracial books were limited: "when money to purchase books became available, teachers did not have much input. Selections were based on a book's inclusiveness on the AR list. Students' interests and backgrounds were not part of the equation" (p. 520). Thus, there were few incentives for reading diverse texts. Souto-Manning observed that the school practices centered on Whiteness, where the AR "competitive system that further exacerbated ways in which White culture ruled the school. AR fostered independence and individualism, two core values of European American cultures" (p. 521), and not the "collectivism, collaboration, kinship, and interdependence" (p. 521), associated with Black and Latinx cultures.

Research by Thompson (2007) revealed "approximately 60% of the students said that their classes were boring... especially African Americans and Latinx students" (p. 42). She also observed, "student apathy is often caused by low teacher expectations, ineffective instructional practices, a culturally irrelevant curriculum, an over emphasis on standardized tests, weak classroom management skills, and racial tensions at school" (p. 42). Thompson and Shamberger (2015) provided five strategies to improve reading performance among Black students: change beliefs about Black students, create culturally relevant curriculum and instruction, expand instruction and include culturally relevant strategies; engage Black parents, accept the challenge to improve reading performance of Black students. Likewise, Husband's (2012) review of extant literature, including NAEP data, confirmed Black males do not perform well on standardized achievement tests. Like many other researchers, he questioned why the pattern of low performance has persisted over time and suggested the following changes were needed to improve Black male reading performance: increase the culturally relevant literature selections for Black males, use culturally responsive literacy methods as well as attention to cultural understandings, and school personnel should review punitive discipline policies (p. 26).

Griffin and Tackie (2016) drew on data from the 2012 *Schools and Staffing Survey* to recruit Black and Latino teachers. Conceptually, their research was grounded in the idea:

> Teachers of Color bring benefits to classrooms beyond content, knowledge, and pedagogy. As role models, parental figures, and advocates, they can build relationships with students of color that help students feel connected to their schools. ... more frequently hold high expectations for all students and use connections with students to establish structured classroom discipline.

(p. 3)

The goal of their study was to "better understand their unique experiences, why they teach, their perspectives on state of education, and what they believe they bring to the classroom and the field, and challenges they experience in the workplace because of their race" (p. 1). Participants represented the national data base, although most teachers taught in city schools, included teachers across age, subject range, and consisted of 150 Black predominantly female teachers and 30% with more than 15 years of teaching experience. Focus groups' participation consisted of 90-minute audiotaped interviews, which were later transcribed and analyzed. Jones and Mosher (2013) acknowledged multiple studies supported the importance – and positive effects – of a father in the lives of their children. They conducted a study to understand the involvement of fathers with their children based on *National Survey of Family Growth* data (2006–2013) and interviews of four thousand men. An analysis of their data indicated unlike dis/mis/information, Black fathers were involved in the lives of their children at higher rates than White fathers with life activities, that is, helping with bathing, eating, dressing, homework, playing, and reading.

Allen, Davis, Garraway, and Burt (2018) reported the overrepresentation of Black male students in special education classes and the dearth of Black male students in gifted and talented classes. They noted low graduation rates for Black males as well as a high rate of disciplinary referrals and suspensions (p. 7). The over-policing of Black bodies was not limited to Black males, argued Annamma (2018) writing about Black girls with disabilities, referred to this position as a pedagogy of pathologizing (hyper-surveillance, hyper-labeling, and hyper-punishment) created criminals of students who did not fit unspoken and yet desired normative standards (e.g., White, male, able-bodied). The process of pathologizing calls for "marking the origins, causes, developments, consequences, and manifestations of deviation from some imagined norm" (Erevelles, 2014, p. 84).

Reading retention laws did not suddenly arise; there were conditions and events that preceded them. Rogoff (2018) suggested drawing on research highlighting cultural strengths included: "attentiveness to surrounding events, skilled storytelling and narrative, metaphoric thinking, community-mindedness, helpfulness, perspective-taking and consideration, and systems thinking in science" (p. 1). Reading researchers should not racially profile Black students as predetermined subjects who are at risk of reading failure and for whom their research alone can "correct." Black students are people, fellow humans, who deserve respectful and genuine engagement. You also need to know Black people, and Black students, beyond a research project. The one-size-fits-all way of reproducing reading failure needs to be replaced with programs that are both supportive of the communicative and linguistic skills Black students possess as well as malleable to move beyond them. Scripted early reading programs accept as valid only one right answer and may be misaligned with the background knowledges, contexts, experiences, interests, and literacies of Black students and are not helpful predictors or metrics for reading success.

Researchers and teachers seeking one best, nearly right, or right answer often disregard or miss the creativity of students' responses especially those drawing on AAL in playful ways. The language use of Black students was denigrated and misunderstood, as Inoue (2015) and Rosa (2019) noted: Too many researchers and teachers heard race, not language. Countless reading research studies make two indefensible claims when their studies fail to address the needs of Black students: the studies' results had unintended consequences (negatively affecting SOC and students who are poor) and more research was needed to conduct similar research in support of Black students. Equally unjustifiable are politicians and researchers who collaborate to "stack the deck," or "game the system," by repeating the sins of the past – enacting anti-Black literacy laws that require use of White-centric approaches, assessments, instruction, and procedures unfounded as a remedy to improve reading among Black students.

The Importance of Black Teachers in the Lives of Black Students

For over a century, Black people supported access to reading, equitable reading among Black students, and quality reading instruction. Recent research called into question desegregation of Black schools and the hiring of White teachers, as scholars suggested there were improved academic performance among Black students who had Black teachers, including studies in reading research.

Goff, Jackson, Di Leone, Culotta, and DiTomasso (2014) conducted four interrelated studies among urban police officers to better understand attitudes and perceptions of Black children. Their findings indicated Black children were not afforded the innocence of childhood, and Black boys were more often believed to be older and "prematurely perceived as responsible for their actions during a developmental period where their peers receive the beneficial assumption of childlike innocence" (pp. 539–540). Similar findings arose in a study of high school teachers and same/mixed race students by Gershenson, Holt, and Papageorge (2016). The authors noted non–Black teachers hold "significantly lower expectations for Black students, than do Black teachers" (p. 222). Following these concerns, McCarter (2017) reviewed literature on the school-to-prison pipeline (STPP) for social workers. She observed school disciplinary actions were a precursor to the criminal justice system and explained several factors supporting STPP: zero tolerance policies, high-stakes testing, exclusionary discipline, race and ethnicity, sex, sexual orientation and identity, socioeconomic status, disability and mental health, school climate, and SROs (pp. 54–56). All disciplinary actions may have unforeseen consequences; exclusionary discipline "results in grade retention, dropping out or expulsion, and juvenile justice involvement is associated with higher economic costs to schools and communities" (p. 57). Among the effects of STPP also included, "school discipline is disproportionately applied to the most vulnerable: minority students, students with disabilities, and students identifying as LGBTQ" (p. 56). Basile, York, and Black

(2019) also drew on data from a longitudinal, mixed methods study conducted in urban schools in Colorado. The researchers were three men of color who attended one of three schools weekly for over 18 months, where boys of color "comprised half to three quarters of the attendees" (p. 12). Informal interview data were collected from among staff and students. Their findings indicated:

> we found that boys of color arrived at school each day with unwarranted and unjust narratives assigned to them – narratives that deem them to be in need of constant control and punishment. ... this amplification led to boys of color being increasingly over-monitored, subsequently punished more, and then further labeled.
>
> *(p. 21)*

In a follow-up publication, Basile (2021) presented a list of recommendations to honor boys of color to improve their engagement in school.

McKinney de Royston, Madkins, Givens, and Nasir (2020) described a stance often adopted by Black teachers seeking to protect Black students. The researchers purposively selected schools known as "'successful' schools that had large populations of Black student populations and where the sociopolitical contexts outside of schools was mentioned by multiple participants as affecting activities insides of schools" (p. 9). The researchers provided a definition of successful schools "based on an inclusive school climate for Black children as determined by stakeholders and/or normative academic measures" (p. 9). Data were collected using observations of classrooms and 45–60 minutes semi-structured interviews with Black educators, parents, and students. Some students also participated in individual interviews, although focused group interviews were used with elementary students. Research findings revealed: "Black educators conceptualized protection as a central concern, how they articulated the forms of racialized harm from which Black children need protection, and how they identified their Black students as worthy of protection" (p. 14). They articulated, "Black educators' political clarity... about the racialized realities of Black children's lives reflects their awareness that Black children navigate racialized harm, that is, symbolic and physical violence of biases and stereotypes, within schools...."(p. 30). Finally, they explained that racialized harm included

> institutionalized racism as well as interpersonal acts of racialized harm such as daily racial microaggressions (i.e., acts of racism that are no less harmful despite their lack of intentionality or visibility to the perpetuator) ... some teachers holding a color-evasive lens that erases Black children's lived experiences to Black children being stereotyped or institutionally ignored or disregarded. A lack of political clarity about the racialized realities of Black children further exacerbates the complex trauma Black children may

experience and the types of coping, oppositional strategies, or resistant attitudes and behavior they may adopt in response.

(p. 30)

Research by Black scholars provided an alternative epistemological understanding of the lives of Black students in schools. Collectively, they explained how educators, parents, and students understood Black students' schooling experiences and provided knowledge missing from reading research studies conducted by White scholars. Young Black students, children from ages three to eight years, should enter schools and classrooms where their racial sensibilities are not under attack, should not be racially profiled as readers in need of support, and should not be seen as adults. Black students who are learning to read need a healthy, supportive, trusting, and welcoming school climate and classroom in which to thrive. To improve reading performance among Black readers, approaches should be informed by Black epistemology, history, and scholarship by Black researchers and allies. Federal and state reading grants among Black students must require applicants to address Black epistemology, history, and scholarship by Black researchers and allies.

As currently structured, there is a disincentive for federal and state agencies and governments as well as school districts and schools to improve standardized reading performance among Black, Latinx, and Native American students, as it may mean a decrease in federal funds. Moreover, substantial improvement in the standardized reading performance among aggregate racial student groups may result in fewer minoritized students failing standardized reading assessments, and fewer minoritized students identified or referred to special education. Thus, states and school districts will receive fewer federal and state funding subsidies. Historically and contemporaneously, there are examples of customs, laws, policies, and statutes implemented to curtail Black literacy access and performance carried out with "no connection, no compassion, no remorse, no reference …, and no desire to acknowledge" (P. Williams, 1987, p. 128) the impact of these decisions on the lives of Black people.

Black Scholarship in Support of Black Students

The failure to draw upon reading research based on Black ideological and theoretical foundations had consequences for Black students unable to perform well on inequitable reading assessments (see Mathis, 2011), although alternative research existed. There are several asset-based, equity-informed, pedagogical approaches to teaching Black students but were not used or part of the data base used to improve Black education, culturally relevant pedagogy (Ladson-Billings, 1994); culturally responsive teaching Gay (2018); and culturally sustaining pedagogies (Paris & Alim, 2017), among others. A feature they all have in common centers on the dignity of each child and what he/she/they bring to the classroom as well as engaging with students with care. Gay describes it this way:

> Caring, interpersonal relationships are characterized by patience, persistence, facilitation, validation, and empowerment for the participants. Uncaring ones are distinguished by impatience, intolerance, dictations, and control. The power of these kinds of relationships in instructional effectiveness is expressed in a variety of ways by educators, but invariably the message is the same. Teachers who genuinely care about students generate higher levels of all kinds of success than those who do not.
>
> *(p. 47)*

McKinney de Royston, Madkins, Givens, and Nasir (2020) noted the importance of accepting Black children as who they are and discarding learned stereotypes about Black humanity and intelligence, in part because stereotypes result in "lowered expectations, implicit and explicit tracking in schools, disproportionate and harsher disciplinary practices" (p. 71). They argue that teachers should not victimize Black children as "adultification and criminalization of Black children's bodies and actions in schools perpetually" and citing Dansy (2014), they note "deny them to any access to childhood humanity" (p. 71). Finally, Willis et al. (2022) provide empirical, experiential, historical, philosophical, and theoretical groundings drawn from Black scholarship for their approach to Black literacy. The authors methodically build a case for improving Black literacy instruction by drawing on Black scholarship (conceptual, ideological, methodological, and theoretical) as well as providing an overview of the history of anti-Black literacy campaigns in the United States along with Black resistance and triumph in obtaining literacy. Using the acronym CARE, applied specifically to Black students and their families or care givers, they suggested engaging with Black students' lives and literacies to improve literacy. When as follows:

- C Centered on Black Students
- A Awareness of Anti-Blackness – Historical Knowledge and Political Knowledge
- R Racial Equity/Justice
- E Expectations of Personnel in School Districts, Schools, and Classrooms

(p. 150)

They explained that the CARE Framework for Black students' literacy learning means:

- Black parents and guardians will expect that teachers and support personnel will deliver appropriate (culturally, ethnically, linguistically, and racially) and accurate high-quality literacy instruction, free from needless duplication of reading intervention strategies and assessments;

- Black parents and guardians will be active participants in decisions about their child's literacy instruction;
- Black parents and guardians will ask questions about their child's literacy progress;
- Black parents and guardians will be able to voice concerns about the literacy instruction without fear that their child will be retaliated against;
- Black parents and guardians will be provided with accurate and honest information about the specific literacy needs of their child;
- Black parents and guardians will be provided information about specific ways to support literacy learning at home;
- Black parents and guardians will expect that teachers and support staff will adhere to professional literacy standards and that their performance is continually reviewed;
- Black students' literacy progress data/records should be available for review in a responsible time frame;
- Black students' literacy progress will be confidential, and the child's privacy protected
- Black parents and guardians, without retaliation, can and should refuse literacy instruction by researchers, interns, and students in training.

(pp. 157–158)

Research-based options that significantly improved Black students' lives and literacies were not reflected in reading research, federal and state funding streams, or federal and state laws. In concert with anti-Black literacy law, federally funded reading grants purported as a national investment seeking to improve reading and equity as well as federal and state requirements endorsing a single approach to reading, have not proven to significantly improve reading for Black students.

Federal Reading Grants: A Barrier to Black Literacy

Several federal government grants use discretionary funds earmarked to advance literacy and improve the literacy performance of low performers, the on-going *Striving Readers Comprehensive Literacy* (2010+) and proposed the Literacy Education for All, Results for the Nation Act (LEARN)/H.R.2706 (2013–2014). Such legislative efforts were meant to convey the federal government's investment and desire to create equitable literacy access. The research used in support of the grants drew from multiple sources of research that aligned with ideas drawn from federally commissioned reviews of literature that have not proven to significantly improve literacy among low-performing students: a narrow set of "scientific and evidence-based" criteria and teachers' lack of fidelity to reading programs as the culprit for approaches that do not present reading improvement. The research base underpinning the grants remained anchored in scientific racism. At the center of these efforts remained the unspoken anti-Black literacy narrative, portraying Black students negatively as reluctant literacy learners and decrying how federal funds were not making a difference (the implication is low performers are biologically/genetically and mentally lower functioning). For example, LEARN, H.R.2706 (please see Appendix G, page 288) was a federal grant program based on anti-Black racism and called for evidence-based research – a wink-and-nod to scientific racism – framed largely on White, English-dominant, middle-to-upper-middle class students and the needs of White students. Educators were being forced to adopt the ideological and theoretical foundations to pursue a career in teaching.

Rhode Island, LEARN

The state of Rhode Island recently passed the Rhode Island Right to Read Act (§ 16-11.4-6, (2019)), that required the following for educators:

> No later than 2025, the following shall have proficient knowledge and skills to teach reading consistent with the best practices of *scientific reading instruction and structured literacy instruction*:
>
> (1) A person who completes a state-approved educator preparation program; and
> (2) A person seeking teacher licensure by reciprocity or by adding an endorsement.
>
> … no later than 2025, a person who completes a state-approved educator preparation program, other than a teacher of elementary education program, shall demonstrate an awareness of the *best practices of scientific reading instruction and structured literacy instruction*.
>
> *(para 2–5, emphasis added)*

Thus, the state of Rhode Island forced teacher education programs to require teacher candidates to adopt and teach a select view of reading. The licensure requirement foregrounded systemic racist structures, processes, and procedures embedded within an ideology of White supremacy attendant to reading, reading instruction, and reading assessments.

Other grants offered through discretionary funds, for example, the Innovative Approaches to Literacy Program (2018), sought to

> … support the development of literacy skills in low-income communities, including programs that (1) develop and enhance effective school library programs, which may include providing professional development for school librarians, books, and up-to-date materials to high-need schools; (2) provide early literacy services, including pediatric literacy programs

through which, during well-child visits, medical providers trained in research-based methods of early language and literacy promotion provide developmentally appropriate books and recommendations to parents to encourage them to read aloud to their children starting in infancy; and (3) provide high-quality books on a regular basis to children and adolescents from low-income communities to increase reading motivation, performance, and frequency.

(https://www2.ed.gov/programs/innovapproaches-literacy/index.html)

Another grant, *The Comprehensive Literacy State Development* (CLSD), ESEA Sections 2222–2225, was the 2020 iteration of the former. The Office of Elementary and Secondary Education website stated:

The purpose of the CLSD discretionary grants is to create a comprehensive literacy program to advance literacy skills, including pre-literacy skills, reading, and writing, for children from birth through grade 12, with an emphasis on disadvantaged children, including children living in poverty, English learners, and children with disabilities.

(https://www2.ed.gov/programs/clsd/index.html)

And much like reading retention laws that do not mention race, the grants are purposed to improve the reading performance of racialized minorities on standardized tests and for promotion; not mentioning race does not mean race and racism do not exist within the laws and grants. These broadly framed literacy grants also drew from centuries-old ideas about the needs of people living under economic stress, which students needed academic support, and the type of supported needed to replicate Whiteness. Hall (2003) observed:

One-sided explanations are always a distortion. Not in the sense that they are a lie about the system, but in the sense that a "half truth" cannot be the whole truth about anything ... You will thereby produce an explanation which is only *partially* adequate. And in that sense, "false."

(Hall, 2003, p. 37, italics in the original)

The discourse used to demographically identify Black students was implied in the descriptive character list of students in need of support, without a specific reference to Black students; "disadvantaged, living in poverty, and children with disabilities" are all terms that had been used in education research and reading laws. For some Black students, there were underlying economic factors affecting access to early reading progress and high-quality literacy instruction; as a result, some Black students had been placed in special education classes. The underlying factors, however, were deliberately created, framed, legalized, and promoted by supporters of White supremacy. The discourse sought to portray concern for

Black readers but suggested anti-Black racism and literacy underpinned stated concerns about the inability of reading research to adequately direct attention to Black readers were not new. Transformative social change would require action, not dreams or platitudes or statements about goals for future reading research.

Bensimon (2018) insightfully warned, "the authentic exercise of equity and equity mindedness requires explicit attention to structural inequality and institutionalized racism and demands system-changing responses" (p. 97). When considering the reading assessments administered to young children (5–9-year-old students), also required an acknowledgment that, "whiteness circulates through structures, policies, practices, and values that are typically assumed to be fair in neutral" (p. 97). Despite discourse suggesting otherwise, state legislators' glowing words about "all students" fails to demonstrate knowledge about Black students, a tactic recentering White students as more valued.

Ties That Bind

US Supreme Court cases that engaged explicit race-based education policies were ruled unconstitutional, as in *Parents Involved in Community Schools v. Seattle School District No. 1, et al.; Crystal D. Meredith, Custodial Parent and Next Friend of Joshua Ryan McDonald v. Jefferson County Board of Education, et al.*, 2007). Similarly, state laws on grade retention disproportionally negatively affect Black students "the architects of today's reforms are solutions worn out of mindsets that are predominantly male, white, and liberal" (Bensimon, 2018, p. 96).

The lack of attention to racial justice and equity in literacy required working through a legal system for supporters and waiting for racial justice in literacy research to pass for opponents. Inoue (2015) observed, "waiting is complicity in disguise… Any denial of racism … is a white illusion" (p. 24). He continues, "It upholds a white hegemonic set of power relations that is the status quo. It is in the imagination of those too invested in a white racial habitus, regardless of their racial affiliation" (p. 24). The equity and reading performance reforms made by state politicians appear as reactions to the most recent crisis with actions taken, allegedly done in the best interest of the crisis and seeking a solution that is at best temporary, and portend to do "something." State laws and policies written to punish eight- and nine-year-old children by retaining them in third grade for not reading on grade level fail to "problematize Whiteness" (Bensimon, 2018, p. 97) from the assumptions on which reading is defined and assessments measured, institutional racism makes possible the reproduction of racial inequality (p. 97). While systemic racism and implicit bias exists, stakeholders made conscious decisions to use a singular reading approach, continue the use of standardized reading tests, although historically Black students do not perform well on standardized reading assessments. Begging the question: how are the new reading laws and policies as well as reading assessments supportive of anti-Black racism and forestalling Black literacy?

A Single Approach to Beginning Reading: Barrier to Black Literacy

Baldwin (1966) proffered "I can't believe what you say … because I see what you do" (para 26). There was an explosion of anti-Black literacy laws in the late twentieth century, as well as the first two decades of the twenty-first century extending the practice of establishing what appeared as race-neutral laws, anchored in scientific racism. State read-by-grade-three retention laws and federally funded reading grants were joined by new state-level reading instruction requirements for a single approach to reading creating a legal de facto – by practice – system of racial segregation. For decades, some reading researchers promoted a single approach to beginning reading instruction, or a one-size-fits-all approach, confirmed and reconfirmed by multiple federally commissioned reviews of literature and used as a metric for federal funding. Collectively, the studies produced "proven methods" of teaching reading: the five key components of reading phonemic: awareness, phonics, vocabulary, comprehension, and fluency).

Brooks (2022) wrote a pithy review of current debates surrounding phonics and the teaching of phonics. He observed there are varying definitions and explications for teaching phonics, only some of which are consistent with the definitions used. His definition of *phonics* stated, "phonics is a method of teaching people to read and spell (and therefore write) in an alphabetic writing system by associating symbols (letters/graphemes) with sounds (phonemes)" (para 10). He observed varying definitions of phonics and approaches to teaching phonics (analytic, onset-and-rime, synthetic) are used by governmental agencies as well as teachers. Brooks mentioned factors that limit the "mandated" (para 143) use of evidence-based phonics research used in required reading programs as "most such data come from follow-up testing of children within research studies" (para 57). Brooks acknowledged the effectiveness of phonics instruction in early reading while questioning its effectiveness as an intervention and suggested the use of longitudinal research studies of the same children overtime were more reliable sources for building effective phonics programs. Although he does not unpack the continued use of the much-maligned IQ tests used to assess student reading performance, it remains a consistent feature or dog-whistle, used by government agencies and reading researchers to describe students: low-achievers, poor readers, reading disabled, and struggling. His striking conclusions were: "systematic phonics teaching is effective for teaching children to read and spell in English. The combination of systematic phonics teaching and literature-/meaning-based approaches is probably more effective than either alone" (para 39).

Although saying it over and over does not make it so, in this case, repeated exposure to the same idea made it nearly impossible for alternative perspectives to gain a foothold in reconceptualizing reading and bring the literacy of Black students to the fore. As in the past, the assumptions undergirding reading research and instruction needed for "all" students were understood to mean upper-to-middle-class, Standard English, and White students. Supporters proffered a singular approach, if conducted properly, would work for other students. If not, the students who failed to learn to read by the approach would need to adjust, or their teachers were not well trained. None of the research significantly used in support of a singular approach, included or reviewed research, that proved effective among Black students. To be clear, irrespective of the moniker, the body of research was grounded in an ideology of White supremacy and scientific racism.

Racist Discourse of Experimental Research in Education

Foundational Anti-Black Literacy Beliefs	White people are superior to all other ethnic/racial people
	White people are human, Black people are not human
	The differences between White people and Black people are biological and genetic
	Black people are incapable of rational thought
	Laws are needed to prevent Black people from learning to read and write
	Scientific research, conceptualized in White supremacy and conducted among predominately White people, proves Black people are not as intelligent as White people
	White and Black students should be taught in separate schools and classrooms
	Black students should be placed in separate special education classes due to mental retardation, lack of intellectual acuity, and anti-social behavior
	New laws are needed to identify students (predominately Black) who should be referred to special education
Current Anti-Black Literacy Beliefs	Scientific research grounded in White supremacy and conducted among predominately White students proves they are better readers than Black students
	There are biological and genetic reasons that explain why some people (White) read better than other (Black) people
	White people are more intelligent as measured on standardized reading tests based in research conducted among predominately White people
	Laws are needed to identify students (predominately Black) who should be referred to special education (based on reading and behavior)
	New laws are needed to identify students (predominately Black) who should be retained in grade 3 to improve their performance on state standardized reading tests

Shortly after NCLB went into effect, reading researchers began replacing the notion of "scientifically based" with evidence, or "evidence-based," research, to suggest multiple research studies were used to "prove" reading outcomes, among young children (preschool to grade 3) based on the "abundance of research," were possible if the correct steps were taken.

Recently, the concept of science of reading (SoR) re-emerged as a new addition to the mythical "reading war" saga; neither the concepts underpinning SoR or reading wars are new. Amanda P. Goodwin and Robert T. Jimenez (2020), editors of special issues of *Reading Research Quarterly*, focused on SoR and proffered a definition used by the International Literacy Association (n.d.): "a corpus of objective investigation and accumulation of reliable evidence about how humans learn to read and how reading should be taught" (p. S7). Reading research in support of anti-Black literacy, predecessors of this approach also drew on similar assumptions about human biology, cognitive science, genetics, and scientific/objective evidence to deny literacy access to Black students and drew from similar foundational roots of scientific racism underpinning psychology (American Psychological Association, 2021a, 2021b, 2021c, 2021d, para). Such reading models were not required to acknowledge or engage sociocultural and linguistic influences on reading and did not address implicit bias and racism within schooling (curriculum, instruction, and materials).

Beginning with the word "science" in SoR, a definition of *science* was provided to distinguish it from colloquial understandings as "the intellectual and practical activity encompassing the systematic study of the structure and behaviour of the physical and natural world through observation and experiment" (quoted in Gabriel, 2020, p. 15). Reading researchers, especially psychologists (cognitive, education, neuro), drew from guidelines offered by The National Institute of Sciences and the What Works Clearing House (WWC). The latter agency was established in 2002 by the US Department of Education and in part to address NCLB legislation requirements for the support of "scientifically based programs" and in part to cull research and programs. Polanin, Caverly, and Pollard (2021) clarified the WWC "strives to produce high-quality resources to support education professionals in making evidence-based decisions" (p. 3). In 2015, under the *Every Child Succeeds Act*, the definition of evidence-based decisions was reviewed, and updated in 2017. A more concise definition, aligned with federal law, described four tiers of evidence: strong, moderate, promising, and rationale. Theoretically, evidence-based research remained moored to experimental studies defined as "a study that is designed to compare outcomes between two groups of individuals (such as students) that are otherwise equivalent except for their assignment to either a treatment group receiving the project component or control group that does not" (slide 3). Experimental studies remained the "gold standard" of education research, and the distinction of "evidence-based" remained tethered to the discourse of its racist history as "evidence" used to make decisions was drawn from the same well of scientific racism and White supremacy. These processes reflect a thinly veiled attempt to instantiate Whiteness and validate its place in the social order as a requirement to perform well on reading assessments. The background knowledge a reader possesses was only deemed accurate if it aligned with Whiteness. The approach to reading should center on the needs of the person being taught to read.

Seidenberg (n.d.) stated that SoR "is a body of basic research in developmental psychology, educational psychology, cognitive science, and cognitive neuroscience on reading, one of the most complex human behaviors, and its biological (neural, genetic) bases" (para 1). Advocates and devotees of the SoR do not all share the same definition and the approach to reading. Nevertheless, most implied and argued that when the approach was followed with fidelity, students "magically" learn to read. However, if students do not magically learn to read, either (a) the steps are not followed correctly or (b) the students' needs are beyond reading, that is, poverty. Some researchers, in a workaround strategy of appropriating the monikers of culturally relevant, culturally responsive, culturally sustaining, and (the under-defined yet ubiquitous) diversity implied their presence while not reconceptualizing the theoretical foundation of their approach to reading. The whitewashing of these terms suggested a lack of respect for the theories on which they are established and a dishonest attempt to engage Black literacy scholarship. To be clear, epistemologically and methodologically, SoR replicated scientific racism, and narratives used in promoting SoR –by conservatives and conservative think tanks – focused on "research-based reading methods." The notion of research-based evidence was used to anchor the approach to science, without using the word science; however, "research-based evidence" consisted mainly of notions borne in scientific racism: psychological, experimental, and quasi-experimental studies.

As with previous one-size-fits-all reading approaches, there was no attempt to provide a substantive body of "evidence" that the approach was effective among Black students. Reading research continued with research agendas as "scientific study" while failing to acknowledge the scientific racism that grounds the research, and comfortable with Black students experiencing so called 'unintended consequences.' Reading researchers often countered that, their goal is to support all readers. Not seeking to do harm does not mean harm does not occur in the lives of those affected by the research; innumerable Black students experienced the disparate impact of anti-Black racism and anti-Black literacy. Scott (2021) provided a legal definition for succinctly capturing this phenomenon, *disparate impact*:

> refers to the result of the application of a standard, requirement, test or other screening tool used for selection that—though appearing neutral— has an adverse effect on individuals who belong to a legally protected class. The US Congress has incorporated disparate impact concepts in antidiscrimination laws, including statutes dealing with civil rights, education, housing, and employment.

(para 1)

Scott also articulated, "federal statutes and regulations authorize the use of disparate impact analysis to identify unlawful discrimination" (para 4). The disparate impact of anti-Black literacy laws in the lives of Black students, as early as preschool, is impossible to fathom. New state anti-Black literacy and anti-CRT laws have the potential to adversely affect all children.

During the 2019–2021 school years, some states suspended standardized state-level testing, in part because of the undue mental stress upon students and in part because of the economic digital divide among students with access to the internet. Many students who lived in poverty or impoverished communities had limited access to consistent, functional, regular Internet and/ or to electronic devices to attend virtual classrooms. The lull in education and testing created an opportunity for politicians and school administrators to erect a new anti-Black literacy barrier. New state laws and local school policies were enacted requiring SoR coursework or training for classroom teachers, school administrators, and reading specialists. And required administrators and teachers to use the approach as part of curriculum oversight. In some cases, classroom observations of teachers were added to ensure the SoR was being implemented. The licensure requirement in Rhode Island, for example, continued to foreground the century-long systemic racist structures, processes, and procedures embedded within an ideology of White supremacy, attendant to reading, reading instruction, and reading assessments based on pseudoscientific racism and the myth of meritocracy (North Carolina and Texas have similar requirements.)

The approach to reading, as framed by SoR, re-emerged to obfuscate anti-Black literacy by repeating an old narrative: (a) cognition is universal, (b) the theories informing cognitive research in reading and researchers were unbiased, and (c) substantive research among Black students and their reading prowess was ignored. Stunningly, state politicians, school board leaders, and reading researchers continued to codify and justify SoR despite its roots in scientific racism. The tactic, reminiscent of the support of RTI/MTSS presented a new name, but the same root problem of unacknowledged, unaddressed, unchallenged, unmentioned, and unresolved – anti-Black racism. In fact, the laws and policies created a toxic brew of pending failure as an extension of reading retention laws, moving from late third grade, when students were identified as failing, to *several years earlier, during Pre-K, to identify students in need of additional supports* (as opposed to locating programs working effectively among Black students).

Over the last two years, for example, several Republican-led states began to require school personnel complete training in SoR, attend summer training or year-round workshops, and require pre-service methods courses include SoR as the preferred approach to reading. Collectively, they were strategically silent about its grounding in scientific racism, lack of evidence to support reading improvement among Black students, the disproportionate number of Black students retained by the end of third grade who received SoR instruction, and the disproportionate number of Black students who received SoR instruction and were referred to special education. The pattern of *strategic silence* or *strategic inaction* among literacy researchers, politicians, and stakeholders to address racism reflected

> ...the conscious and purposeful process whereby organisations fail to pub-licise or mention a material fact. This can either be a negative material fact ranging from support for a political party to hiding an accident or spillage, or a positive material fact like gaining a certification or endorsement.
>
> *(The Oxford Review Encyclopaedia of Terms, 2022)*

Strategic silence appeared planned, as an omission, error, or administrative over-sight. Supporters positioned the approach as if protecting reading research from any culpability when students did not learn to read while simultaneously ignoring scientific racism-fueled anti-Black literacy. Several states also instituted require-ments for classroom teachers, reading specialists, and school administrators to adopt the SoR approach to reading, varying by the commercial and research sources used, and connections to testing industry. Adding to the variety of pos-sible SoR understandings was the lack of consensus among reading research-ers about the definitions of the terms evidence-based and science, although Seidenberg and Borkenhagen (2020) readily admitted the term SoR was a buzz-word and held little actual meaning (p. 4). For states and school districts who are promoting and requiring the SoR approach, a working definition is warranted.

Old Wine in New Wineskins: Anti-Black Literacy

The new laws and policies also obfuscated another way to understand their effect: high-jacking early literacy among Black students, identifying them as young children, and forestalling their scholastic lives years before they take the state-required third-grade reading tests. The discriminatory impact of these laws on the lives of Black students, especially Black males and students living in poverty, are unknown. White supremist viewpoints gaslighted the public into believing the SoR approach and RTI/MTSS were likely to improve reading among students, but especially among Black and poor students, and diminish racial disproportionality in special education placement. Predictably, the oppo-site occurred: SoR and RTI/MTSS continued the use of cognitive science and educational psychology to reproduce reading approaches effective among White students that have not significantly improved reading performance for Black stu-dents while simultaneously increasing the number of Black students identified/referred to special education.

Institutional structures (academic, corporate, and political) have systemati-cally failed to adequately provide equal high quality literacy access to meet the needs of Black students. The legacy of failed laws and policies does not mask the ideology of White supremacy codifying laws and erecting anti-Black literacy barriers. The veiled attempts to address Black literacy performance as measured by standardized tests consistently failed Black students and eroded trust in the willingness to conceptualize literacy beyond Whiteness.

Sleeter (2021) challenged how notions of colonialism and racism are portrayed by academics and the media. She reviewed and described multiple ethnic studies and programs that successfully have impacted and raised the academic achievement of minoritized students. She makes the claim by examining the academic achievement of minority students through a focus on ethnic studies and colonialism, employing counter historical narratives to explain how racism is enacted. She noted a strong push emerged from conservative White power elites to dismantle the programs and to mischaracterize them as destructive or "dangerous discourses" (p. 57). Au (2021) also revealed, "multicultural and anti-racist education leads to higher engagement and academic achievement for students of color" (p. 106). There also were fears within the reading/literacy field about the racist historical roots of reading research and the legacy of all who have benefited from the lies being revealed; many do not want to acknowledge loss (grantsmanship, income, status, etc.), and some do not have the political will or moral compass to address what to do about the lack of equity in reading approaches, assessments, concepts, curriculum, definitions, materials, methods, and research.

If the goal of federal, state, and local educational entities was ever to improve Black students' education and literacy the starting point would be Black epistemology, history, and scholarship. To prioritize and structure effective Black literacy, there must be appreciation, acceptance, knowledge, and valuing of Black students' (cultures, languages, and ways of knowing), along with institutional and instructional engagement of multi-pronged approaches to Black literacy. Given the reluctance of federal laws and policies to set precedent for research among Black readers, alternative ancillary federal agencies became structures used to establish reading assessment and research standards for predominately White students, without accountability. Federal formal and informal networks helped to present a consistent mischaracterization of the literacy needs of Black students and students who lived in poverty as rhetorical tools when messaging the exceptional nature of charter and choice schools, although not supported by research as expert opinions gave way to political dog-whistles. The evolution of governance informing education in place of educators and experts can be found in a case study of the state of Florida, where the state's governance crafted and passed anti-Black literacy laws, becoming ever-more restrictive while not mentioning race yet targeting Black students.

6

FAULT LINES

Florida's Anti-Black Literacy Laws

An overview of Florida's history of customs, laws, policies, and statutes and their intersection with anti-Black racism and anti-Black literacy presented a cautionary tale. Importantly, the state's governance and cyclical restructuring of governance serve politically powerful believers in White supremacy and supportive alignment among state and local power brokers. The political actions created solid front for restrictive anti-Black racism and anti-Black literacy reading laws.

An Evolution of Florida's Anti-Black Literacy Laws

The landmass known as Florida was originally part of Spain. The Treaty of Adams-Onís (1819) and the Transcontinental Treaty (1821) ceded the land to the United States. The landmass agreement was much larger than obtaining Florida and was influenced by the expansion of the US version of chattel enslavement of people of African descent. Florida's Slave Codes (1782) were unlike those in other areas of the South. Chattel enslavement consisted of tasks; when completed, enslaved people were permitted more freedom, military service, and children born to mixed-race parents were not automatically enslaved (Thompson, 1992). In 1828, Floridians adopted An Act relating to Crimes and Misdemeanors committed by Slaves, free Negroes, and Mulattoes, creating Slave Codes more aligned with those in other Southern states and thus more restrictive. Thompson's (1992) review of Florida's Slave Codes, 1821–1861, suggested that they were "more humane" (p. 324), and legal "precautionary measures designed to forestall the likelihood of slave insurrection, petty thievery, miscegenation, escapes, and countless other infractions associated with the frustrations of an oppressed people ... and to control both slaves and masters" (p. 324). The Slave Codes, 63 in total, included anti-Black racist and anti-literacy laws, forbidding "reading, writing, set type, any sort of

DOI: 10.4324/9781003296188-7

FIGURE 6.1   The State Flag of Florida

reading material where formidable legal barriers intended to prevent potentially seditious literature from reaching the bondsman" (p. 325). A decade later, while still a territory, Florida adopted the *St. Joseph Compromise*, mimicking earlier US laws: census counts would recognize Black people as 3/5s a person; free and enslaved people could be brought into the state; and only White people were considered citizens, and thus, only White people were permitted to vote. When Florida became a state in 1845, it adopted a defensive stance against the emancipation of Black people and adopted harsh Black Codes.

The notion of White supremacy was engrained in the thinking of many White people who could not envision Black people as equally human, preferring to view them as a source of free labor (Richardson, 1969). White politicians elected to ignore the racial equity changes to the US Constitution, believing they had "a duty to perform – the protection of our wives and children from threatened danger, and the prevention of scenes which may cost the extinction of an entire race" (quoted on p. 368). In deliberations about changes to the Florida Constitution, arguments against changes cited in the *Dred Scott* decision:

> to prove that the Negro was not a citizen and that Congress had no power to make him such. After praising the institution of slavery and reminding the legislature that it had been destroyed without their concurrence, the committee members recommended legislation which would "preserve as many as possible" of the "better features of slavery."
>
> *(Richardson, 1969, p. 373)*

The Florida State Constitution (1885) forbade Black and White children from attending the same schools, an idea extended in the 1895 Constitution to include:

> a Penal offense for any persons to conduct any school, any grade, either public or private where whites and blacks are instructed or boarded in the same building or taught in the same class by the same teachers.

Penalty: Between $150 and $500 fine, or imprisonment in the county jail between three and six months.

(n.p.)

During the Jim/Jane Crow era in Florida, anti-Black and anti-Black literacy customs, laws, statutes, and traditions were rampant. Florida Atlantic University (n.d.) provided "A Map of Jim Crow America," including a 1913 Education statute, declaring it "unlawful for white teachers to teach Negroes in Negro schools, and for Negro teachers to teach in white schools" (para 14). A similar law was passed in 1927; it was "a criminal offense for teachers of one race to instruct pupils of the other in public schools" (para 15). Given Florida's long history of resistance to racial equity in all aspects of life including education, it was not surprising that Floridian politicians struggled to reconcile Supreme Court decisions regarding race, *Brown v. Board* (1954); Civil Rights Act (1964); *Green v. School Bd. of. New Kent Co, 391 US 430*, (1968); and *Swann v. Charlotte-Mecklenburg Bd. of Education*, 402 US 1. (1971), and revisions to the Florida State Constitution of 1968 continued into 2016. Nonetheless, because of these collective legal decisions, Floridians were forced to implement desegregation education (Orfield & Ee, 2017). The current iteration began with the candidacy of J. Bush for governor in the mid-1990s. As Kupscznk (2020) articulated:

long focused on accountability for schools and teachers, without fulfilling its reciprocal upwards accountability. Throughout the nation, between the 1970s and the 1990s, the accountability movement replaced desegregation and equity as the primary driver of education reform … policymakers have no excuses not to recognize the contexts that make teachers, students and their schools "fail."

(p. 314)

Florida was among the states leading attempts to erase (e-race) the anti-Black history of the United States as well as the lives, experiences, and intergenerational fallout of White supremacy, seeking to repeat and retell convenient, inaccurate lies about the past to comfort White feelings of guilt and privilege and to whitewash and invisibilize the truth, when what was needed are accurate historical narratives that demystify the past and tell the truth. Much like Colson Whitehead's (2019) Pulitzer Prize–winning novel, *The Nickel Boys*, was based on the state-run institution Florida State Reform School, later renamed the Dozier School for Boys, in Marianna, Florida (1900–2011). Black men who survived the abuse, beatings, and whippings have shared their stories with the media.

In this chapter, the history of reading retention and ancillary laws in Florida reveal the most recent iterations of anti-Black racism and anti-Black literacy which permit holding children accountable for not learning to read. Florida's revolving door of education legislation continued the use of decades–old approaches, processes, and procedures that ignore racial inequity and legal racism, finding Black readers' performance on standardized reading assessments a path of least resistance. Attempts to address racial differences in reading achievement and performance on standardized reading assessments has been expanded to include early childhood education/universal pre-kindergarten, summer intensive reading programs, and most recently, the alleged abandonment of end-of-year standardized testing (replaced by more surveillance of students through "progress monitoring"). The latter provided a greater lack of transparency whereby implicit biases, language policing, and macro/microaggressions may suck the life out of Black students. Thus, progress monitoring becomes a lethal form of death by a thousand cuts through the unexamined psychic toll on Black students, by literacy coaches/interventionists/teachers.

Twentieth-Century Florida Reading Retention Laws

John Ellis (Jeb) Bush moved to Florida in the mid-1980s, where he quickly became a fixture in the Republican Party, before entering politics as Florida's commerce secretary (1987–1988). The *Orlando Sentinel* published an article by Mitchell and Van Gieson (1993), noting his campaign for the office of governor in Florida, and in a 1994 interview, he declared:

> I would abolish the Department of Education as it now exists, reducing the 2,000-person bureaucracy to about 50 to administer federal education funding and maintain minimum academic standards in Florida's schools.

Although he was unsuccessful in his first bid for governor, J. Bush was a political insider and drew upon his family's political acumen to inform his second run for governor. While planning for a second candidacy for governor, in 1996, he started a nonprofit, Foundation for Florida's Future, and became a co-founder of the first charter school in Florida (National Governors Association, 2022, para 1). Jeb Bush and the Commissioner of Education, Frank Brogan, also maneuvered to administer the state's education policy. The State of Florida's constitution, Amendment X was revised in 1998 as follows:

> The education of children is a fundamental value of the people of the State of Florida… to make adequate provision for the education of all children residing within its borders. Adequate provision will be made by law for a uniform, efficient, safe, secure, and high-quality system of free public schools.
>
> *(quoted in Herrington & Weider, 2001, p. 524)*

The state constitutional amendment "shifted more control over education policy to the governor" (Kupscznk, 2020, p. 6), a decision reflecting the governor of Texas, George W. Bush, his brother. Governor J. Bush was a longstanding supporter of school choice and the charter school movement, and under his leadership, the state expanded and endorsed a voucher program (an idea supported by his father, G. H. W. Bush) as well higher academic standards and the use of assessments were instituted (an idea supported by his brother, G. W. Bush). As governor, J. Bush (1999–2007) exerted his authority and revamped Florida's education system.

The Florida Formula: Changing Florida Education

As governor, J. Bush implemented the "Florida formula," alleging a statewide education program based on principles of increasing accountability and expanded parental choice. DiCarlo (2015) summarized the policies as follows:

1. Hold schools accountable: "A–F" school grading system, attached to rewards and consequences;
2. School choice: charter schools and different forms of private school choice programs;
3. High expectations: retention/remediation of low-scoring third graders, higher graduation standards;
4. Funding for school and student success: tying funding to performance and more flexibility in how districts can spend money;
5. Quality educators: alternative teacher certification and new teacher evaluations.

(p. 1)

Infamously, the Florida Formula stated, "8-year old's, will be retained." Emma (2017) exposed nuances in the Florida Formula that privileged charter and private education to: "adopt vouchers, expand charter schools, and implement education savings accounts, which allow parents to use taxpayer dollars for a full menu of options, including private schools, online courses, textbooks and tutoring" (para 23).

Governor J. Bush also created an accountability system and evaluated/graded schools in Florida from A–F; this action was like the test-based accountability system that his brother, the then-Governor of Texas George W. Bush, used. In Florida, Brogan began using public school rankings and annually published lists of the lowest-performing schools "which connected a large bundle of policy reforms to student performance on the FCAT" (Kupscznk, 2020, p. 6). The Florida grading scale was created based primarily on student scores on standardized tests. Third graders who did not pass the state reading test could be retained and made to attend an intensive summer camp for additional help with reading. Teachers were eligible to receive bonuses for student growth or an "A" rating, which means extra funding for those schools and teachers already working on par. In addition, students who attended poorly ranked schools could receive a voucher to attend a private or religious school.

During the J. Bush governorship, there was a deliberate attempt to create laws and policies that appeared to be race-neutral. The absence of the word "race" and other words associated with race does not mean, as in numerous federal documents, racism was absent. Discourse used in this way obfuscated race and racism in education policies and conflated race and poverty (free-and-reduced lunch, low-income, under-resourced schools) as synonyms. Orfield and Ee (2017) reviewed desegregation patterns in Florida:

> In the 2000s, racial concerns were replaced with accountability and school choice policies including *No Child Left Behind* and *Race to the Top*. With intense pressure on schools to increasing perform on high stakes state testing programs, segregation became a diversion and, even worse, an excuse. When the schools did not perform, and a very disproportionate share of schools with double segregation by race and poverty were branded with "D's" or "F's", the state, under the leadership of Gov. Jeb Bush, blamed them, sanctioned them and encouraged the growth of charter and voucher schools. Without attention on segregation and its remedies, the goal of racial diversity was ignored.
>
> *(p. 7)*

Governor J. Bush used his grading system against failing schools, as he "blamed them, sanctioned them and encouraged the growth of charter and voucher schools" (p. 7). Several civic organizations joined the NAACP as plaintiffs in the *Holmes et al. v. Bush et al.* (2000), challenging the vouchers for private schooling as in violation of the Florida state constitution. The lawsuit was filed against Governor J. Bush and the State of Florida, as the plaintiffs argued the Florida Constitution did not permit the use of public funds/taxpayer funds to support voucher programs for students who wanted to attend private schools. After presenting their case, the judge ruled:

> relying on the canon, *expressi exclusio alterius* [to express one excludes alternative] Smith ruled, that on its face, the Opportunity Scholarship Program (or voucher program) was unconstitutional... the education article identifies the system of schools as the method by which the state is to provide high quality education to the children of Florida.
>
> *(Herrington & Weider, 2001, p. 529)*

In the fall of 2001, Governor J. Bush signed an Executive Order Number 01-260, *Just Read Florida!*, containing a list of belief statements and a request for the Florida Department of Education to make recommendations for improving reading (please see Appendix H, page 290). The *Just Read, Florida!* initiative was pronounced as "a comprehensive, coordinated reading initiative aimed at helping every student become a successful, independent reader, is hereby initiated" (p. 1). Section 3 of the EO stated:

A. early-reading instruction strategies and reading screenings or assessments for K–2 students;
B. reading intervention strategies for students who read below grade level;
C. reading course requirements for middle school and high school students who are not reading at grade level;
D. reading activities in teacher preparation and professional development programs;
E. leveraging technology to improve reading proficiency and integrating online professional development with existing and traditional training;
F. utilizing teacher reading academies and/or schools within schools to teach effective reading strategies;
G. planning for integration, coordination and effective investment of antici- pated federal funds from President Bush's Reading First Initiative, and for the 21st century Community Learning Centers;
H. developing ongoing public–private partnerships aimed at increasing reading proficiency and providing supplemental books to students;
I. recognizing outstanding reading teachers and schools at which students are making significant progress in reading;
J. increasing parental and family involvement in teaching and encouraging reading;
K. encouraging family literacy practices and programs through innovative inte- gration of adult literacy and elementary and secondary school programs; and
L. utilizing, supporting, and training mentors and volunteers to help children and adults learn to read.

(p. 2)

Importantly, given the shift in administration of the Florida Department of Education, an additional educational office, *Just Read Florida!*, was opened, teth- ered to a research university and accountable to the Commissioner of Education, under Florida Statute 100.215:

> Work with the Florida Center for Reading Research to identify scientifi- cally researched and evidence-based reading instructional and intervention programs that incorporate explicit, systematic, and sequential approaches to teaching phonemic awareness, phonics, vocabulary, fluency, and text com- prehension and incorporate decodable or phonetic text instructional strat- egies. Reading intervention includes evidence-based strategies frequently used to remediate reading deficiencies and includes, but is not limited to, individual instruction, multisensory approaches, tutoring, mentoring, or the use of technology that targets specific reading skills and abilities.

(para 9)

Importantly, the statute codified an approach to reading based on earlier research funded by the United States government. These collective actions reflected how, after the passage of NCLB, some states bolstered their approach to reading by mimicking the language of reading research, in "evidence-based assessments", concepts, and methods; and passed reading retention laws. Florida passed the following reading retention law:

(a) Any student who exhibits a substantial deficiency in reading, based upon locally determined or statewide assessments conducted in kindergarten or grade 1, grade 2, or grade 3, or through teacher observations, must be given intensive reading instruction immediately following the identification of the reading deficiency. The student's reading proficiency must be reassessed by locally determined assessments or through teacher observations at the beginning of the grade following the intensive reading instruction. The student must continue to be provided with intensive reading instruction until the reading deficiency is remedied.

(b) If a student's reading deficiency is not remedied by the end of grade 3, as demonstrated by scoring Level 2 or higher on the statewide, standardized assessment required under s. 1008.22 for grade 3, the student must be retained. (Fla. Stat. Ann. § 1008.25)

Pam Stewart (2002), Florida's commissioner of education, published the *Read to Learn* guidelines to explain reading retention law:

> Florida law … says that third graders who do not have a score of Level 2 or above on the statewide Florida Standards Assessment- English Language Arts (FSA-ELA) must be retained (not promoted to grade 4)… children who demonstrate the required reading level through a state-approved alternative standardized reading test or through a student portfolio can be granted a good cause exemption and be promoted to grade 4. A student will only be retained in grade 3 once.
>
> *(para. 2, readtolearn.pdf)*

She also provided an explanation of "good cause" exemption requirements:

> Some students with disabilities, some English language learners (ELL), and some students who have already been retained can receive a good cause exemption and be promoted even though they are not reading at the required level. If your child is not eligible for the good cause exemption, you will be notified as to why your child is not eligible.
>
> *(para 4)*

Incoherently, she continued:

> Retention does not mean that the child has failed. It does not mean that
> teachers or parents are not working hard enough. It does mean that the
> child needs more instructional time and help to catch up and meet grade
> 3 reading performance levels. The purpose of retention is to give chil-
> dren who have substantial reading deficiencies more time and the intensive
> instruction they need to catch up in reading.
>
> *(para)*

Within her explanation, she sought to reassure citizens, deflecting the scourge
of retention using disinformation and misdirection about the meaning of retention and parental care. The excerpt also served to assure citizens, without data
or research, that more time in a grade would help students "catch up" with their
peers. The research does not confirm her assertion. Next, she offered information about what must be done by the school to request grade retention, and the
process for approval of "good cause exemption" conducted by the school (other
possible options, mid-year promotion, and transitional classes were not included):

- The student's teacher must submit documentation to the principal;
- The principal must review the documentation and decide whether or not
  the student should be promoted. If the principal determines that the student
  should be promoted, the principal must make the recommendation to the
  school district superintendent; and
- The school district superintendent must accept or reject the principal's recommendation that the student be promoted.

(para 28)

The State also issued criteria for promotion and retention more than a decade
later, with similar criteria: "scores Level 2 or greater on the Florida Standards
Assessment (FSA) for English Language Arts" (p. 80). In addition, there were
eight "good cause exemption" options: assessments (alternative, mid-year, portfolio, summer), ELL participant, ESE alternative assessment, and previous reten-
tion/ESE previous retention (p. 80). Moreover, guidelines for using alternative
standardized reading assessments were published, under Good Cause Promotion
(please see Appendix I, page 293).

Widening the Reach: Early Childhood Education as an Intervention

After the third-grade reading retention law was in effect, other measures were
taken to address reading performance. Governor J. Bush and educators agreed to
improve early childhood education in the state, in part, to prevent reading problems in grades K–3. He signed HB-1A into law in 2005, and Florida initiated

an early childhood learning program, Voluntary Pre-Kindergarten, or VPK. The idea of "universal high-quality preschool education" appeared noteworthy when it was established in Florida in 2005. The program was free for all four-year-old children who lived in Florida and born before September 1 of the year they enrolled in the program. The Florida Department of Education secured oversight of the program, implemented the initial class in the 2005–2006 school year, created learning standards, and cyclically evaluated the program. There were no stated conceptual or theoretical bases for VPK programs, although in the United States, "universal" and "high-quality" were synonyms for English dominant, White, middle-classness.

There was a body of literature demonstrating positive and lifelong effects of high-quality preschool education, and many states used preschool education to prevent later educational problems. The idea of "universal high-quality preschool education" appeared noteworthy; however, Chatterji's (2006) review of the Early Childhood Longitudinal Study found that achievement gaps existed in kindergarten among students of various ethnic/racial groups and expanded in first grade:

> Children of different minority groups exhibited different patterns of reading achievement in first grade. Compared with the specified reference groups, gaps in reading became clearly discernable in three groups as formal reading instruction began in first grade—African Americans, boys, and high-poverty children. In all three groups, minor differences at *kindergarten entry increased and appeared to consolidate as children completed first grade.*
> *(p. 504, emphasis added)*

Bassok, Miller, Galdo, and Johnson (2014) presented a review of Florida's program, and while complimentary found areas in need of improvement. According to the Florida Department of Education website, the State was required, pursuant to Section 1002.69, Florida Statutes (F. S.), to "adopt a statewide screening instrument that assesses the readiness of each student for kindergarten based on performance standards adopted by the state under section 1002.67(1), F.S., for the Voluntary Prekindergarten Program (VPK)" (para 1). All students who attended a VPK program needed a pre/post assessment, and the Florida Administrative Code, under Rule 6A-1.09433, identified the assessment tools to be administered.

Gilliam, Maupin, Reyes, Accavitti, and Shic's (2016) study of preschool teacher's implicit bias found that teachers' focused attention on Black children and indicated they watched for bad behavior, especially the behavior of Black boys. The authors revealed that when teachers and students were of the same race, less strident differences in expectations occurred. Thus, noting as early as preschool, Black students, particularly boys, were hyper-surveilled for behavior which at the preschool level can result in a misdiagnosis of readiness for kindergarten.

During the 2017–2018 school year, the state selected an online assessment tool, *Renaissance's Star Early Literacy Assessment* (n.d.), and provided a flier, *FLKRS Test Design Summary and Blueprint.* The program was recognized as an assessment tool for early literacy and "designed to measure the early literacy skills of beginning readers" (para 5). *The Star Early Literacy* assessed the alphabetic principle, concept of word, visual discrimination, phonemic awareness, phonics, vocabulary, and early numeracy. The early literacy assessments were based on federally funded research recommendations. Sources including research studies that were not representative of all students, suggested limited reading skills, and failed to engage support of reading as a communicative skill where words convey meaning of text or comprehension. Students' awareness of, comfort with, and technical skill on computers was not considered.

Gray-Lobe, Pathak, and Walters (2021) suggested, "preschool enrollment improves post-secondary outcomes" (p. 3). Their study confirmed that student test performance is not sustained. They also noted, "positive long-term impacts for an intervention that improves adolescent behavioral outcomes, but not test scores" and "highlight the importance of considering non-test score and long-term outcomes when assessing the effectiveness of education programs" (p. 5). Similar findings were reported by McKenzie, S., Jordan, E., and Wood, C. (2021) who examined data from four-year-old students who participated in a state-sponsored public pre-kindergarten program with students who did not participate in the program in third and fourth grades. Their findings indicated low-income students who participated in the program, predominantly Black and Latinx, by third grade "outperform similar peers on math and reading achievement tests in 3rd grade in three of four cohorts. These findings suggest this program has the potential to set students up for lasting academic success" (p. 4), although the findings by fifth grade were less robust.

Gullo and Impellizeri (2021) examined data from the Early Childhood Longitudinal Study Kindergarten Class of 2010–2011 to determine whether teacher observations of early literacy and mathematics competencies provided insight into students' academic progress in grades three and four. Their findings indicated that students leave kindergarten with many and varied skills, and teacher observations are important indicators but not predictors of future academic and behavioral competencies. Hong and Hong's (2021) analysis of data from Early Childhood Longitudinal Study Kindergarten Class of 1998–1999 revealed third-grade reading retention policies did not increase reading instructional time. They also found the policies appeared effective for students who had slightly undercut scores but not for students who were low performers: "just below the average ability and therefore were likely at the margin of being retained. Interestingly, students whose prior ability was in the middle tier also appeared to benefit from test-based promotion in reading" (p. 11). To be clear, the research did not document or report implicit bias.

Following his tenure as governor, J. Bush established the Foundation for Excellence in Education, a nonprofit think tank, that received large donations and grants from the Bill Gates Foundation, Michael Bloomberg, and Betsy DeVos, among others. J. Bush and Betsy DeVos shared likeminded ideas on education and worked closely to divert taxpayer dollars from public education to fund charter schools and private education. Additionally, former President Trump proposed support of a 20 billion dollar school choice program – with help of DeVos' American Federation for Children agency while also pushing for a nine million dollar cut from the US Department of Education budget.

Review of Florida Read by Grade 3 Laws

Greene and Winters's (2007) initial study of the effectiveness of Florida's third-grade reading retention for academic years 2001–2002 and 2004–2005 revealed that students who were retained increased their reading performance. They argued, in part, third-grade reading retention was preferable to social promotion. Greene and Winters (2009) conducted an additional study of the effectiveness of Florida's third-grade reading retention for academic years 2000–2001 and 2003–2004, with a focus on student demographics. Their findings of student performance, two years after the initial testing, revealed: "minority students are more likely to be retained under Florida's test-based retention policy after controlling for other factors, including baseline academic proficiency" (p. 141). In Florida, Black students were more likely than all other ethnicities/races of students to be retained, initially retained students outperformed students who were granted exemptions. Importantly, Schwerdt, West, and Winters (2017) reviewed Florida's third-grade reading retention policy over time and found little effect on the completion of high school.

Florida Formula and NAEP

Governor J. Bush (2011) advanced the Florida Formula for literacy; however, Mathis (2011) critiqued the "Florida formula," popularized by Governor J. Bush and used by him as representative of his nonprofit, The Foundation for Educational Excellence. Mathis acknowledged that former Governor J. Bush sought to instill educational reforms and recognized Bush presented "a selective misrepresentation of test score data...ignores less favorable findings" (para. 1). The critique reviewed six of Bush's education reforms, including comments on third-grade retention and reading. Mathis found the presented assessment data consisted largely of NAEP scores and changes with comparisons between 1992 and 1994 to show current rates as improvement, although the nature and procedures for NAEP changed over time. Governor J. Bush asserted the improved reading performance on NAEP was a consequence of grade retention

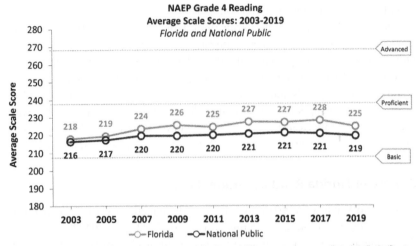

FIGURE 6.2 NAEP Fourth Grade Reading Assessment for Florida 2003–2019

policies, without corroborating evidence. Mathis argued a more accurate explanation lay in understanding "fourth-grade test scores are artificially inflated by Florida's grade-retention policy, first by the removal of low-scoring children and later by the inclusion of more mature students" (p. 7). He concluded, "considering the overwhelming evidence that retention is ineffective (if not harmful), it is troubling to see Mr. Bush endorse such an approach. Finally, Florida's real problems of inequitable and inadequate education remain unaddressed" (para 1). Disentangling the data for the state of Florida was fraught with difficulties, as the data were not presented in the same matter across time. For example, while 1992 NAEP data provided state-by-state analysis, 2000 NAEP data was presented by geographical regions. In other examples, reading scores for gender were not disaggregated by race, and economic status was broadly defined only by students who received free and reduced lunch (all data presented above are average scores) (please see Figure 6.2).

Florida Literacy Plan (2011), a Striving Readers initiative, re-declared Florida's commitment to ensure all students learn to read and successfully passed the end-of-the-year annual standardized reading test. The plan was drawn from federally supported research and argued in sync with federal government reading research that it "provides systematic, high-quality instruction that focuses on the essential components of reading instruction: phonemic awareness, phonics, fluency, comprehension, and vocabulary" (p. 2). Additionally, the plan restated IDEIA (2004) notions of RTI

> assessment to guide reading instruction (screening, diagnostic, and progress monitoring). We believe that Initial Instruction (ii) must be grounded in

scientifically based reading research and aligned with the Sunshine State Standards for reading. Finally, we are committed to the idea that many children will require Immediate Intensive Intervention (iii) to make adequate progress in learning to read.

(p. 2)

Rose and Schimke (2012), working with ECS, presented a selective overview of research on grade three policies in their brief, *Third Grade Literacy Policies: Identification, Intervention, Retention*. They also provide examples from research, although their conclusions mimicked those of Hernandez (2011). Their review of Florida's third-grade retention law listed key components:

- Strong early identification and intervention are a crucial components of any retention policy.
- States can expect a jump in K–3 retention rates in the first years of policy implementation.
- As the benefits of early identification and intervention are felt, test scores are likely to improve, and retention rates likely to decline.
- A mandated retention policy with identification and intervention guidelines provides urgency around 3rd grade reading and leads to earlier assessment and intervention.
- Good-cause exemptions allowing students to demonstrate proficiency through alternative assessments and/or portfolios appear to adequately screen for children who would benefit from promotion, despite low scores on statewide assessments.
- Strong school leadership is important to the success of an early identification, intervention and retention policy. Particularly helpful are setting high expectations for children, communicating goals and processes clearly to teachers, and providing adequate support to staff.

(p. 7)

Much like other authors of ECS briefs, the authors proposed steps to encourage states to improve early reading:

1. create a sense of urgency around third-grade reading, emphasizing the benefits of early identification and intervention.
2. expand access to quality pre-K and full-day kindergarten programs to give young learners ample opportunities and assistance to develop literacy skills.
3. ensure all early learning opportunities are built around language-rich, rigorous, and engaging curricula to develop students' knowledge, vocabulary, and skills.

(p. 9)

Additional ideas suggested identifying "struggling readers," the use of evidence-based intervention strategies, supporting school administrators and teachers, and enlisting support from families and communities. Finally, they advised states to include "good cause exemptions" for low-performing students on statewide assessments like those used in Florida.

Extant Literature and Alternative Findings

Missing from Rose and Schimke's brief/review of exemptions were the findings by Greene and Winters (2009) acknowledging students most likely to be affected by high-stakes testing for promotion and who receive exemptions upon appeal were White and middle-to-upper middle class, while minoritized students' appeals were most often denied.

Balkcom's (2014) review of research on Florida' third-grade reading retention policy likewise sought to explain why the retention law existed and how the law benefited students, relying heavily on data from the AECF and NAEP. She connected the need for improved standardized testing to NCLB and cited several studies appearing to confirm improved reading performance of retained students over time. She did not include a single study that disputed grade retention in general or third-grade reading retention laws, specifically. Balkcom strongly indicated that students' reading performance improved as fourth graders and as recorded on fourth-grade NAEP scores. Her review supported Floridian advocates of grade retention who claimed, "by catching up on prerequisite skills, students should be less at risk for failure when they go on to the next grade" (Shepard and Smith, 1990, p. 84), although there was little solid research to support the claim.

Robinson-Cimpian (2015) reviewed Florida's reading retention law supported by the National Education Policy Center, and much like Chatterji (2010) and Mathis (2011), he debunked the claims of Florida's fourth grade students, acknowledging the results reflected an extra year of schooling. He exposed the findings of positive effects of reading retention laws and revealed "how less sophisticated methods … can lead to underestimates of the retention effects, due to not accounting for factors unobserved by researchers" (p. 3). He also noted that students' reading performance on standardized tests are confounded by state requirements for intensive interventions (p. 10), and "the generalizability of the effects is very limited to students in Florida at or very near the statewide third-grade test threshold for retention" (p. 10). Thus, he concluded:

> students in Florida who are retained in third-grade because they just barely failed to attain the state's threshold performed better than students of the same age on next year's tests of math and reading. The study also admitted the purported benefits fade over time.
>
> *(p. 3)*

LiCalsi, Ozek, and Figlio's (2019) review of Florida's third-grade reading retention law sought to determine whether it reinforced socioeconomic inequalities.

Their findings suggested the education of mothers appeared to be a determinator of whether third graders were retained:

> Students are also more likely to be retained due to the policy if their mother is foreign born, if they qualify for free or reduced-price lunch, or if they are black. We also ... that students from high-SES families are more likely to be granted an exemption even after we control for exemption eligibility. These findings are robust to various model specifications and hold true for different student, teacher, and school subgroups of interest.
>
> *(p. 22)*

Tavassolie and Winsler (2019) also provided a review of the enforcement among school districts of the mandatory third-grade reading law in Florida. They found that although school districts were mandated to retain students who failed the reading assessment on the FCAT, not all students who failed were retained, and some of who were promoted did so with a code attached. They also recognized Black and Latinx students were more likely to be recommended for retention than their White peers (p. 71). Their findings and those of other researchers whose results focused on racial disproportionality and inequity were ignored by politicians, and research promoters of reading retention – who appear in a never-ending search for a variable other than race/racism on which to append variances in standardized testing performance.

Egalite, Kisida, and Winters (2015) examined teachers, not their mothers, to determine a teacher's role in grade retention. They acknowledged "student math and reading achievement is significantly, positively influenced by the race/ethnicity of their teacher" (p. 45). The researchers used student-level demographic information located in FCAT databases from 2001–2002, 2008–2009, and student performance on reading and math standardized state assessments for "over 2.9 million students linked to 92,000 teachers" in the dataset (p. 46). Their findings indicated, "teachers of the same race/ethnicity could theoretically narrow the performance gap between students of different races/ethnicities by serving as high-quality, academic role models or because they are more inclined to hold high expectations for a student's potential" (p. 51). It was not clear whether the Florida Department of Education or governors considered increasing the number of teachers of color in grades K–3 to improve reading performance.

Governance of Education 2.0: A Carousel of New Legislation

Governor R. DeSantis (2019) issued an Executive Order 19–23 to dismiss Common Core State Standards and replaced the standards with the Florida Department of Education's state assessment, Benchmarks for Excellent Student Thinking (B.E.S.T.) for English Language Arts and Mathematics. A state website outlined the Benchmarks for Excellent Student Thinking and included links to K–12 comprehensive evidence-based reading plan forms for districts to complete.

Section 11b (11) Assessment, Curriculum, and Instruction 6A- 6. 053(11). F. A. C., notably replicated concepts found in federal government reports, President G. W. Bush's (2002), Executive Order 13, and IDEIA (2004) response to intervention. Moreover, K–12 reading instruction aligned with Florida's Revised Formula for Success (please see Appendix J, page 296).

The interventions replicated RTI/MTSS approaches that instantiated racial discrimination and have been unable to dismantle racial disproportionality. Missing in the explanation like others which preceded it was the fourth tier of RTI, special education, as well as a viable means of tracking racial disproportionality in special education placement. The state forms requested percentages of students' scores on state-level reading assessments for grades 3–10 but no other demographic information about students, although additional information was mandated by federal law.

A review of the B.E.S.T. was conducted by Friedberg, Shanahan, Fennell, Fisher, and Howe (2020). The researchers acknowledged that the report was funded by the Bill & Melinda Gates Foundation and the Thomas B. Fordham Foundation. Their evaluation noted that the new ELA standards were coherent and rigorous:

> Major strengths include clear definitions and expectations relative to teaching students to read complex texts, including useful examples of what constitutes appropriate texts and reasonably clear "learning progressions" for foundational skills and for the comprehension/analysis/interpretation of reading and writing that, if accomplished, should assure college and career readiness in these abilities by the time students complete high school.
>
> *(p. 9)*

They also described strengths and weaknesses under the categories "clarity and specificity" and "content and rigor," acknowledging some standards needed to be revised, and made recommendations. Their final assessment of English Language Arts Standards recommended "significant and immediate revisions. Standards are not suitable until and unless these revisions occur" (p. 16). A temporary halt to address the recommendations and make revisions occurred during the onset of a worldwide pandemic. Later, on September 14, 2021, new legislation was under consideration to

> eliminate the common-core based, end-of-year Florida Statewide Assessment and create the new Florida Assessment of Student Thinking (F.A.S.T.). By creating the F.A.S.T. plan, Florida is becoming the first state in the nation to fully implement progress monitoring instead of end-of-year standardized testing, and will fully eliminate Common Core.
>
> *(para 1, https://www.fldoe.org/fast/)*

The proposed F.A.S.T. assessments were shorter tests to be administered three times a year, in a form of "progress monitoring." The Florida Department of Education website promoted the new assessments by suggesting they "will restore the ability for parents and teachers to have impactful conversations about students' growth," borrowing heavily from similar rhetoric used in support of RTI:

- Eliminating the Florida Statewide Assessment.
- Protecting Florida's #1 position in the nation accountability system, which has lifted Florida to the top 3 in the nation and has done more to protect low-income families, African American and Hispanic students, and children with unique abilities.
- Utilizing progress monitoring to empower educators, parents, and most importantly students to a level never seen before.
- Becoming the first state in the nation to switch from end-of-the-year assessments to state standards-aligned progress monitoring for accountability.
- Reducing testing time, and minimizing the stress of testing to three much shorter "check-in" assessments in the Fall, Winter and Spring.

*(para 2, https://www.fldoe.org/accountability/
assessments/k-12-student-assessment/best/)*

The proposal appeared to be an amalgamation of previous approaches beginning with recommendations of former federally funded and sanctioned approaches to reading. There was no explicit information in support of several claims listed on the site. First, what agency, institution, or organization recognized Florida as the number one state for accountability, what criteria was used to evaluate accountability, and when did the ranking occur? Second, what data was used in support of the claim that Florida has done more to protect low-income families, African American and Hispanic students, and children with unique abilities?" The research reviewed herein suggests otherwise. There also was no discussion of how the elimination of FCAT affected current laws requiring districts to retain students who are not reading on grade level by the end of third grade. Nonetheless, the site explained why the new format for testing was needed:

- Takes days to administer, and means less learning time
- High-stakes test
- Encourages narrow focus on tests
- Based in Common Core
- Not customizable to each student
- Fails to give parents timely information to support their children at home
- Too late for meaningful conversations between parents, students, and teachers to modify instruction

*(para 1, https://www.fldoe.org/core/fileparse.php/
20007/urlt/FAST-One-Pager-V2.pdf)*

It is not clear whether the new assessment format eliminated the fundamental flaws in standardized assessments or if the new format was a rebranding of the former B.E.S.T. program. Nor was it clear whether the concerns and recommendations made by Friedberg et al. (2020) were included in the new assessment.

Death by a Thousand Cuts: Progress Monitoring

In 2017, an amendment to Florida's 2001 reading retention law, H. B. 131, proposed to remove the mandatory retention of students whose reading performance on statewide assessments did not meet requirements; however, it was defeated. The new ongoing progress monitoring, under FAST, created a "death-by-a-thousand-cuts" scenario with untold potential to harm and injure Black students, through implicit biases, microaggressions, and racism or what P. Williams (1987) called spirit-murder, where racism

> resembles other offenses against humanity whose structures are so deeply embedded in culture as to prove extremely resistant to being recognized as forms of oppression … where the victim is forced to convince others that he or she was not at fault.
>
> *(p. 129)*

Progress monitoring can begin during pre-kindergarten; the youngest and most vulnerable Black students' lives are at risk among an 80% White teaching force, who may constitute White listeners of Black language. As Rosa and Flores (2015) submitted, White listeners must broaden their understanding of culture and language, forego linguistic hierarchies, and adopt linguistic ideologies that are inclusive, ideas absent from many teacher education programs and reading licensure.

The new state assessment format was announced early in the 2021–2022 school year to be implemented beginning 2023–2024 school year. As the state transitions to the new test, before the new standards are established, the old assessment were used, before a pause in testing. How students will be assessed, and reading retention laws enforced, are unclear. Equally unclear are the next steps and may be part of a larger unannounced strategy by the Florida Education Commissioner, Richard Corcoran, and Governor DeSantis, who set the education policy.

Specific Learning Disabilities and Dyslexia

The US legal definition of SLD (1969) names dyslexia as a potential cause of SLD. Special education advocates lobbied state governments to pass exclusions for "legitimate" claims of dyslexia knowing the clock would run out on the racially disproportionate and uneven application of RTI (RTI was never a law), although written as part of IDEIA (2004) and as such, worked as a temporary substitute to extend unequal educational access and racial disproportionality of students referred to special education. The determination of dyslexia was among the list of exemptions permitted to avoid being retained under the third-grade reading retention law. There was a special case made for students identified as dyslexic, including a redefinition of dyslexia in the state of Florida. The Florida State Board of Education Rule 6A-6.03018, Florida Administrative Code, Exceptional Student Education Eligibility for Students with Specific Learning Disabilities (2009) specifically defined dyslexia, under SLD, in Florida:

> Dyslexia is a type of reading disability, dysgraphia is a type of written language disability, and dyscalculia is a type of math disability. Eligibility for special education has always been twofold in that 1) the existence of a disability must be evident and 2) the student's need for resources available through special education must be evident. Not all students who are diagnosed with a disability meet SLD eligibility criteria, or require the resources provided through special education services in order to progress adequately and meet grade level expectations.
>
> *(p. 1)*

The National Center on Improving Literacy (2021) reported on the newly defined use of specific learning disabilities and dyslexia HB7029, State Board of Education Rule 6A-6.03018, and HB7069:

> HB7029 provides that students with dyslexia are eligible for a scholarship to attend a school other than the one assigned. HB7069 amends several pre-existing education laws, some of which are related to literacy and dyslexia. The law allocates funds to provide an additional hour of research-based reading instruction to the 300 lowest performing elementary schools based on state assessment results, as well as certain supplementary objectives.
>
> *(e.g., professional development to provide intervention)*

A special focus was the new law on reading instruction and assessment aligned with grade 3 reading laws, RTI/MTSS, and special education:

> Annually, school districts shall submit a K–12 comprehensive reading plan. The plan must describe reading intervention strategies. Statewide kindergarten screening shall provide objective data concerning each student's readiness for kindergarten. Any student in kindergarten through grade 3 who exhibits substantial reading deficiency as determined in paragraph 5(a) must be covered by a federally required plan (e.g., IEP), an individual progress monitoring plan, or both. Parents shall be notified in writing if their child has been identified as having a substantial reading difficulty, and the current and potential options

for Remediation. The law also eliminates social promotion, except for good cause (e.g., student received intensive reading instruction for 2 or more years); calls for the revision of professional development standards and teacher preparation practices; and sets requirements for core instructional materials.

(para 1, https://improvingliteracy.org/state-of-dyslexia/florida)

Several key features of the law were warranted: (a) taxpayer money permitting students to attend schools outside of their area and (b) pre-service teacher training requiring:

Scientifically researched and evidence-based reading instructional strategies that improve reading performance for all students, including explicit, systematic, and sequential approaches to teaching phonemic awareness, phonics, vocabulary, fluency, and text comprehension and multisensory intervention strategies.

(para 4)

Thus, the law echoed previous notions of scientific reading research. The most problematic portion of the law, Section 11, conflated reading deficiencies and special education:

"Students with Reading Deficiencies" of HB7029, Florida requires statewide screening in kindergarten that must be used to identify students in need of intervention and support pursuant to FS 1008.25. However, this screening is for kindergarten readiness and is not dyslexia specific.

(para 3)

Some school districts went to great lengths to ensure students were identified as in need of special education services broadly under the notion of dyslexia and thereby were not affected by read by grade 3 guidelines. Among White wealthy parents, there was a push to have their children designated as special needs, specifically dyslexic. In doing so, they could sidestep grade-level reading retention in a "Get Out of Reading Retention Card," which was listed under waivers or good faith clauses. This is not to suggest a conspiracy theory or some coordinated effort to amplify and promote the low performance of BIPOC students while excusing White students with cultural capital to claim "legitimate" dyslexia. Joe Solochek (2021), a journalist with the *Tampa Bay Times*, exposed and reported on how quickly changes can occur. In this case, there was a change to how special needs students were determined:

Board members spent six minutes on the proposal, which defined the students' disabilities in a way that would suddenly take away the academic help many had received for years. They spent three minutes hearing a staff presentation, two minutes listening to one public speaker, and another minute unanimously approving the measure without asking a question or making a comment.

(para 5)

The new rule was instituted to comply with the guidelines under the federal 2015 *Every Child Succeeds Act*, permitting 1% of the state's student population can participate in Florida's alternative tests, although the rule was extended to students who were too young for statewide tests (para 10, para 14). The Florida State Board of Education redefined the guidelines for the "most significant cognitive disability" and included IQ levels for compliance (para 13). In addition, "children must demonstrate their inability to make progress on general education standards even with added assistance over two grading periods" (para 13). The language used to identify students and the use of IQ tests as a metric were troubling, as was the potential for continued anti-Black literacy. Selena of @SelenaCarrion (Jan. 18, 2022) asked: "How is the very same school system that caused 'at-risk' students to 'fall behind' and into an 'achievement gap', supposedly the best place to 'accelerate' their learning now?"

Despite Florida's history and practice of grade retention, the Florida Association of School Psychologists (FASP) issued a paper, *Position statement on the practice of grade retention and social promotion*, in 2015, strongly encouraging all stakeholders to

abandon the practice of grade retention in favor of evidenced-based supports and interventions for children and youth that demonstrably improve educational outcomes long-term. Conversely, the practice of promotion in the absence of such targeted supports and interventions is not an acceptable, research-supported alternative to grade retention.

(para 1)

School psychologists also expressed concern about long-term negative impact of grade retention, noting: "retention ranks 148th out of 150 educational practices for the effect size it has on student achievement" (para 2); ...the call by the National Association of School Psychologists' call to abandon the practice due to "numerous negative effects of grade retention for students both academically and socially-emotionally" (para 4);... and "minorities, particularly African Americans/Blacks, are more likely to be retained than Whites, and male students are more likely to be retained than females" (para 4). School districts, however, continued the practice of grade retention, which persisted after the National Association and Florida State Association of School Psychologist reviewed the research, acknowledged the disproportionate number of Black and Brown students retained, and noted the negative emotional impact and land lack of academic progress in the practice.

Carceral Use of Student Data

In Florida, the use of student scholastic achievement was extended beyond the school doors, as Bendi and McGrory (2020) reported on the alleged use of private student data by a local sheriff's office. The authors cited a Pasco County Sheriff's Department intelligence report:

> identifying at risk youth who are destined to life of crime and engaging them to prevent them from developing into prolific offenders ... has significant crime prevention potential. Accurate identification prevention of at-risk youth set them on the right path.
>
> *(quoted on p. 13)*

The intelligence report continued by suggesting selected factors of a students' life predisposed them to a potential life as a criminal. In a follow-up story, McGrory and Weber (2021) revealed the US Department of Education had opened an investigation:

> The US Department of Education's Student Privacy Policy Office has opened an investigation into the alleged violation of the Family Educational Rights and Privacy Act of 1974 by Pasco County Schools regarding the potential non-consensual disclosure of personally identifiable information from student education records to the Pasco County Sheriff's Office. To protect the integrity of our investigation, we will not provide any details about the investigation and will not respond to further inquiries until the investigation is concluded, unless we are required by law to do so.
>
> *(para 24)*

Davison (2021) confirmed that the school district was under federal investigation for the possible misuse of private student information and sharing the information with the sheriff's office as the information was used "to compile a list of students who could potentially become criminals—a claim the sheriff's office denies" (para 2).

Decoding Florida's Education Initiatives

During 2021, Governor DeSantis, the Florida House and Senate, and the Education Department were engaged in multiple legislative actions directly affecting reading and student achievement. First, there was a debate over a new proposed law, the New Worlds Reading Initiative Tax Credit (2021), which would deliver books to the homes of elementary school children. The pending bill would permit Governor DeSantis to release funds for free children's books for students:

> Establishing the New Worlds Reading Initiative under the Department of Education; requiring the administrator, in consultation with a specified entity, to develop a selection of books; requiring the administrator to coordinate monthly book distribution to certain students; requiring the administrator to assist with local implementation of the initiative, requiring that a certain notification include information about the initiative, etc.
>
> *(New Worlds Reading Initiative Tax Credit, 2022)*

The law centered on the importance of learning to read while offering Florida taxpayers a break. It linked Florida's early childhood initiative, VPK, by offering a select set of books (from the B. E. S. T. Standards), that may indoctrinate young readers into conservative, right-winged notions of a whitewashed history of the US. There were other quirks with the law limiting it to students attending charter schools in grades kindergarten through fifth. In addition, the law adds legal weight to prejudge which students may not be reading on grade level. Although the law was characterized as an additional intervention to avoid grade 3 retention, by delivering books directly to students at their home/residence, there were opportunities for implicit bias or racism for Black students who because of their culture, language, race, or social economic status could be identified and retained before grade 3. The eligibility requirements are:

> Any student who has been identified as having a substantial deficiency in reading if any of the following criteria are met in accordance with Rule 6A-6.053 subsection 12: The student scores at the lowest achievement level/benchmark as identified by the publisher during a universal screening period, on an assessment listed in the district's approved District K-12 Comprehensive Evidence-based Reading Plan; The student scores at the lowest achievement level/benchmark as identified by the publisher during *progress monitoring administration at any time during the school year*, on an assessment listed in the district's approved District K-12 Comprehensive Evidence-based Reading Plan; or The student has demonstrated, through consecutive formative assessments or teacher observation data, minimum skill levels for reading competency in one or more of the areas of phonological awareness; phonics; vocabulary, including oral language skills; reading fluency; and reading comprehension.
>
> *(New Worlds Reading Initiative Tax Credit, 2022, paras 2–3, emphasis added)*

These processes described and supported scientific racism and a limited approach to reading framed by research conducted primarily, but not exclusively, among English dominant, middle-class, White students. Ample research existed to support the use of cultural and linguistic knowledge among Black students, an idea not apparent in the stated standards. When children are reading text including cultural and linguistic concepts, experiences, and ideas they are familiar with, they enjoy reading, and their reading improves. Books are to be delivered nine times a year and published in English, Haitian Creole, and Spanish. Agreeably, research indicated readers are more engaged with text when reading about something familiar (culture, ethnicity, and language) and score higher on standardized reading tests.

Throughout the history of literacy in Florida, stakeholders in reading have been (business and corporate investors, politicians, school administrators, teachers, reading researchers, and reading specialists) who conceptualized, defined, and measured reading should NOT be the people to ameliorate concerns for anti-Black literacy by renaming and promoting the similar approaches, assessments, concepts, and theories founded on scientific racism and effective among White students. When reading results have been challenged, concerns are deflected away from ideological positioning, by pointing to Black cultural, economic status, familial, and linguistic differences, as the most likely reason for low performance on reading assessments. The use of progress monitoring used to identify and recommend grade retention suggests increased oversight of students, which means Black males are likely to be profiled and surveilled.

The narrative discourse often projected Black students – as young three-year-old preschoolers – were the most likely to be labeled as students at-risk, struggling, or who potentially may fail to read on grade level by the end of third grade as measured on state standardized tests. With impunity, stakeholders were less likely to acknowledge that the ideology of White supremacy informed their thinking and obfuscated notions of power and control of literacy by (a) dehumanizing and profiling Black students; (b) defining literacy as synonymous with Whiteness; and (c) permitting the denial of access to high-quality Black literacy that celebrates Black accomplishments, cultures, ethnicities, genders, languages, joys, religions, and sorrows. In short, the bill exemplified how anti-Black literacy laws were established for students to be retained (in Florida that means Black students and students living in poverty), by creating a way to retain Black students **before** grade 3 and possibly identify them for special education.

The bill was introduced along with other bills that politicized education curricula and restricted discussions of systemic racism and race as well as discussions of gender and LBGTQAI+ issues. As such, the implication was that the selected books would be exemplars and not address these issues and help to tamp down public outcry over the alleged troubling curriculum in schools. The bill and rhetorical stance communicated to the public replicated actions undertaken by the United Daughters of the Confederacy, a group that held tremendous power over school boards adoption of texts with flattering remembrances of the "Lost Cause," from the perspective of Southern Whites. By contrast, Mechanic (2021) expressed concern:

> most grade-school kids aren't exposed to anything resembling a comprehensive, inclusive version of their history. And while the white parents picketing school boards say they don't want their kids to feel bad about their skin color, what of all the nonwhite children who are made to feel self-conscious or inferior about their own skin color at school or work? Are we to leave them ignorant of the hell this nation inflicted on their ancestors? And do we deprive white kids of an honest view of our history simply because the complicity of their forebears might make them uncomfortable?
>
> *(para 12)*

Smith (2021), a Black author and scholar, provided personal memories as a Black male child attending school and learning lessons about Black people. He shared memories of his experiences, his education, and the inaccurate portrayal of Black history:

> I remember feeling as I silently wondered why every enslaved person couldn't simply escape like Douglass, Tubman, and Jacobs … had they not tried hard enough? Didn't they care enough to do something? Did they *choose* to remain enslaved? This, I now realize, is part of the insidiousness of white supremacy that illuminates the exceptional in order to implicitly blame those who cannot, despite the most brutal circumstances, attain superhuman heights. It does this instead of blaming the system, the people who built it, the people who maintained it … This is its own quiet violence.
>
> *(p. 64)*

Smith's remembrance demonstrated how the zeal to protect White students' comfort, fragility, guilt, and sanity had come at the cost of devaluing Black history, lives, and well-being. The version of US history promoted and read in schools, assured the horrific treatment of Black people would continue to be discounted, ignored, and unrecognized. Smith's memories may be typical of Black people educated in the United States and forced to learn an inaccurate account of Black history. The history of anti-Black racism, its disparate effects on the lives of Black people, and anti-Black literacy laws enacted in Florida unashamedly support White supremacy. Nearly a century ago, Drs. Clark & Clark revealed the psychological and emotional toll that racism has on Black children, and it has been over 70 years since a similar finding was acknowledged in Brown v Board. Whether deliberately or unwittingly, reading approaches and assessments enacted in Florida continue to ignore Black cultures, languages, and ways of knowing as they inflict emotional and psychological harm on Black students through reading retention.

7

LINKING THE PAST TO THE PRESENT ANTI-BLACK RACISM AND ANTI-BLACK LITERACY

The histories of anti-Black racism and anti-Black literacy access in the United States provides a critique of the ideological roots of White supremacy and the false narrative framing the democratic stance of the nation: the importance of Anglo-Saxon, culture, language, literacy, and values and the unfiltered mischaracterizations about People of Color as less-than-human, unintelligent, and without culture, language, literacy, and value. Glaude (2016) argues these ideas reflect a fundamental belief that White people are more valued than all other people and underpin US democracy. The idea resurfaced as I watched and listened to the nearly non-stop coverage of the trial of Kyle Rittenhouse (a young White man who killed two White protestors in Wisconsin). While the jury was deliberating, a commentator projected that he would likely be acquitted, in part because the predominately White jury looked at him and saw themselves. Surprisingly, the verdict came as a video exposed how two teens, fighting at a mall in NJ, were treated differently. In a video, a White teen is beating a younger Black teen as two White police officers rush to the scene. First, one officer gently guides the White teen to sit alone on a sofa. Second, the other officer throws the Black teen – who is not resisting – to the ground and kneels on his back to handcuff him, while the first officer joins the take-down and handcuffing the Black teen.

There are other incidents of Black anti-racism daily on social media memes; for example, one circulating meme juxtaposes the photos of eight White people who were armed and had murdered Black people but were arrested without incident, against photos of eight Black people who were unarmed, living their lives, and murdered by White people (ordinary citizens and police officers). On the one hand, although the videos are telling, people are cautioned by local police officials not to believe what they see as well as by television outlets; you may only see a portion of the tape, and there will be an internal investigation.

DOI: 10.4324/9781003296188-8

It is reminiscent of how White newspapers renamed the destruction of Black property and the murders of Black people as "riots," employing language to convey that Black people deserved the injustices they experienced before, during, and after the "riots." By contrast, Black newspapers, covering the same events, employed language to convey Black people as victims and White perpetrators as murderers, although they seldom were convicted of property destruction or mass murder. Current access to technology and social media seeks to capture events in real time and describe the unprovoked killings of Black people, parishioners of Mother Emmanuel AME church in Charleston, SC, and Saturday-afternoon grocery shoppers in Buffalo, NY, as mass murders. Several major US newspapers, on the other hand, have admitted their role in support of White supremacy (support of Black enslavement, racial segregation, racist tropes, suppression of voting rights as well as exoticizing and stereotyping non-White communities, and sensationalizing headlines about Black people), beginning in 2020 with the *Los Angeles Times* and *Kansas City Star* along with the *Baltimore Sun* and *Philadelphia Inquirer* (2022), among others.

As noted throughout this book, the past is not past – as actions, beliefs, and values – continue to affect the present. So too are the histories, laws, and policies as well as social structures created to re-enslave Black minds and bodies to work for White people. Before we can replace anti-Black racism and anti-Black literacy, we must understand their true roots and legacies. This chapter revisits several historical events resurfacing, in part to reveal the legacies of White supremacy and in part to understand how the ideology of White supremacy continues to evolve and influence anti-Black racism and literacy access in the twenty-first century. Woven throughout the chapter are statements published by the American Psychological Association (2021a, 2021b, 2021c, 2021d, please see Appendices K, L, M, and N in Support Materials at www.routledge.com/9781032275000) in juxtaposition to contemporary commentary, literacy laws and policies, and reading research efforts to concretize a single approach to reading. The APA statements also debunk efforts to whitewash US history by restricting select books, discussions, and media from addressing issues of race/racism. In the first part of this chapter, remnants of the legacy of Black enslavement and anti-Black racism in the twenty-first century are examined. The second part of the chapter discusses the legacy of efforts to privatize education along with the effect on literacy. The third part of the chapter describes authoritarianism in the special case of Florida laws as an aggressive anti-Black literacy effort. The chapter concludes with closing remarks.

Anti-Black Racism: The Struggle Continues

On this colonized land, inequality exists and is particularly harsh for people of African descent in the United States (this is not to suggest other people of color were/are unaffected). The goal of colonizers is to have a ready workforce to help them retain wealth and power. The failure to acknowledge why and how

Black people were enslaved, and forbidden to learn literacy, redounds within the nation replicating the past and framing the present. Traditional histories of the United States, as taught in schools, consistently have tried to whitewash the crimes against humanity enacted during chattel enslavement and the role of White people in seeking to sustain enslavement, by other names and processes over time. No one is alive to provide firsthand accounts or to record the atrocities foisted upon Black people; although the Federal Writers' Project (1936–1940) collected accounts that are available online, these sources are seldom used. As you listen to the accounts, you become acutely aware that the history of the United States differs significantly when expressed by formerly enslaved Black people who experienced the horrors of enslavement. In this section, contemporary understandings of Black enslavement are discussed.

Evolving Re-Enslavement of Black People

Chattel slavery was an abuse of human rights, and for some people, intergenerational trauma persists. Black people, free and enslaved, daily faced the possibility of beating, death, murder, rape, starvation, and unjust incarceration. Within the first six months of his presidency, President Biden declared Juneteenth a federal holiday and signed it into law on June 17, 2021. The holiday is meant to remember that some enslaved Black people remained enslaved two years after they were legally free.

Butler (2009) interviewed children of formerly enslaved Black people and learned of their bravery as well as their commitment to their families and progeny. She reports the lives and hardships were not often shared with the next generation, not because they were unknown but because families desired their children to seek greatness and believed knowing the past hardships might make them bitter and angry. Black enslavement is believed to have ended in 1863, in the United States; however, for some Black people, it continued into the twentieth century (Blackmon, 2008). Anti-Black racism and anti-Black literacy fueled the continuation of Black enslavement in the form of the peonage system where Black people – who were unable to read or write – signed contracts to work the land in hope of one day paying off their debts and owning the land on which they worked; however, that was never the plan by White landowners. The latter sought continuous free Black labor without land compensation.

The 'new'forms of slavery continued anti-literacy, murders, along with mass murders, lynchings, and constant surveillance. Formerly enslaved Black people sought to negotiate their labor; however, White landowners' fear and vigilante White mobs intimidated Black people (Ager, Boustan, & Eriksson, 2019), and some Black people were re-enslaved without recourse as the legal system failed to protect them. Given that many politicians were descendants of White enslavers (Ager et al., 2019), they created "contracts" for illiterate Black people to sign with a mark in lieu of signature (Pope, 2010). The contracts were used to force formerly enslaved Black people into involuntary servitude. In addition, White local power elites, law enforcement, and judges created a cheap labor market for US corporations through a contract lease program that also served to disenfranchise Black people. In his Pulitzer Prize–winning book, *Slavery, by Another Name: The Re-enslavement of Black Americans: From the Civil War to World War II*, David A. Blackmon (2008) succinctly and powerfully captures this scheme, as he describes why Green Cottenham, a formerly enslaved Black man, was arrested in 1908 for vagrancy:

> Vagrancy, the offense of a person not being able to prove at a given moment that he or she is employed, was a new and flimsy concoction dredged up from legal obscurity at the end of the nineteenth century by the state legislatures of Alabama and other southern states. It was capriciously enforced by local sheriffs and constables, adjudicated by mayors and notaries republic, recorded, haphazardly or not at all in court records, and, most tellingly in a time of massive unemployment among all southern men, was reserved almost exclusively for black men. Cottenham's offense was blackness.
>
> *(p. 1)*

Mr. Cottenham was found guilty, his 30-day sentence extended, and his death imminent. Innumerable formerly enslaved Black people were defenseless and forced to produce bricks, mine coal, create turpentine, or make steel. Black re-enslavement as involuntary servitude, peonage, or sharecropping, occurred as Black people who were unable to read or write, were left to their own understanding of the law lies told by White people, and the will of White law enforcement and politicians. In a self-published text, Harrell (2014) draws from the National Archives to research incidents of involuntary servitude of Black people – not only by White enslavers but also by major US corporations. Her review suggested the practice was known by judges (local, state, and members of the US Supreme Court); politicians (local mayors, state governors, and US presidents); as well as the NAACP. Peonage and "contractual" servitude were other forms of Black enslavement used throughout the South in violation of the Thirteenth Amendment.

The remnants of Slave Codes also remain within racial discrimination based on Black hair, where White people continue to seek control of Black people's bodies and use customs, traditions, and legal power to do so. After a decade an Act was before the US Congress, the Creating a Respectful and Open World for Natural Hair Act of 2022 (C.R.O.W.N.) to stop discrimination of Black bodies but was defeated by Republicans. Mechanic (2021) summarizes the failure of US history to address the legacy of anti-Black racism:

> Slavery, of course, was merely one phase of a long and violent campaign by white Americans to enrich themselves – and later to protect their political power and economic advantages – at the expense of the powerless. Beyond

even the Black Codes, the Jim/Jane Crow statutes, the racial pseudoscience, lynchings, land seizures, and a 13th Amendment loophole that encouraged convict leasing and the groundless incarceration of the newly emancipated, virtually every government initiative designed to help families build intergenerational wealth – the Homestead Acts, the National Housing Act of 1934, the Social Security Act, the GI Bill, etc. – left Black people on the sidelines.

(para. 3)

His comments occurred during the COVID-19 pandemic, during which news commentors and political pundits often described the stark reality and an alleged "sudden awareness" of the history of inequality in the United States among economic classes and ethnic/racial groups.

The Ark of the Moral Universe

After more than a century, on January 5, 2022, Louisiana governor John Bel Edwards signed a posthumous pardon for Homer Plessy. He acknowledged the anti-Black racism and Jim/Jane Crow injustice:

The stroke of my pen on this pardon, while momentous, it doesn't erase generations of pain and discrimination. It doesn't … fix all of our present challenges. We can all acknowledge we have a long ways to go. But this pardon is a step in the right direction.

(Waxman, 2022, para 3)

In attendance were descendants of Homer Plessy and US District Judge John Ferguson, who have formed the Plessy and Phoebe Ferguson Foundation. Also in attendance was a descendant of US Supreme Court Judge John Harlan (a former slave holder), who cast the only dissenting vote. His great-great-granddaughter, Amy Dillingham, a celebrated cellist, fittingly played *Lift Every Voice and Sing*, during the ceremony.

Lynching Outlawed

Bryan Stevenson's research reveals the traumatizing lynching of Black people during 1880–1940, or what he calls "terror lynchings." He has documented the states in which multiple lynchings occurred: Alabama, Arkansas, Florida, Georgia, Illinois, Indiana, Kansas, Kentucky, Louisiana, Maryland, Mississippi, Missouri, North Carolina, Ohio, Oklahoma, South Carolina, Tennessee, Texas, Virginia, and West Virginia (Equal Justice Initiative, p. 3). He also observes these crimes were public; "terror lynchings" were "horrific acts of violence whose perpetrators were never held accountable. Indeed, some public spectacle lynchings were attended by the entire White community and conducted as celebratory acts of racial control and domination" (para 8). For over a century, there have been numerous attempts to outlaw lynching, and on March 29, 2022, the Emmett Till Antilynching Act was signed by President Biden.

Importantly, many of the lynchings were related to Black people exercising their right to vote; although the right to vote for Black men was guaranteed in the Constitution, the Fifteenth Amendment, it included a caveat: "except as punishment for crime," thus, federal and state laws were created alleging crimes and re-enslaving Black men and denying them the right to vote.

Black Disenfranchisement Revisited

Anti-Black racism and anti-literacy historically have been part of Black voter suppression. Currently, some states are determined to set parameters on who can vote and under what conditions, reminiscent of voter suppression tactics in the nineteenth and twentieth centuries. The landmark 1965 Voting Rights Act (VRA) protects people from racial discrimination as they seek to register and to vote. A key protection in the VRA, Section 2, 52 U.S.C. § 10301, is a federal law protecting voters from discrimination based on color, race, or membership in a language minority group (as defined in Sections 4(f)(2) and 14(c)(3) of the Act, 52 U.S.C. §§ 10303(f)(2), 10310(c)(3)). Section 2 also prohibits the denial of equal access for all citizens in state-created voting laws or practices adopted or maintained to discriminate against the voting rights of citizens (US Justice Department, 202, para 1).

Blacksher and Guinier (2014) argue forcefully against the unproven notion of "equal sovereignty" (wherein states determine citizenship, not the federal government) in the *Shelby County v. Holder* case. They claim it is a reinstatement of Chief Justice Taney's majority decision in the Dred Scott case, characterizing Black people as non-citizens, and thus did not have the right to vote. In the *Shelby County v. Holder* case, the Supreme Court's majority decision, written by (current) Justice John Roberts, "held that the 'equal sovereignty' of the State of Alabama takes precedence over Congress's exercise of its explicit constitutional power to enforce the voting rights of the descendants of slaves" (p. 39). The ruling

> suggests that the Supreme Court majority is attempting to head off congressional reconsideration of the right to vote as one of the fundamental privileges and immunities endowed by the Constitution on every person who becomes a citizen of the United States.
>
> *(p. 42)*

The ruling gutted Section 4 of the Civil Rights Act 1965, requiring federal preclearance due to past racial voting discrimination. Blacksher and Guinier also claim: "It is up to us, the American people, to demand that Congress carry out its constitutional duty in ways that unmistakably acknowledge that the descendants of slaves are full and equal members of the sovereign people" (p. 69).

Their concerns are a cautious warning against threats to democracy and growing skepticism of the voting process and results. Following the 2020 presidential race, the insurrection of the US Capitol, and the ongoing misguided search for voter fraud, states enacted several laws to hamper and suppress the right to vote with a disparate impact on Black citizens, including gerrymandering. Moreover, some states have instituted suppressive laws to restrict registering and voting. 19 states have passed laws to suppress – and in some cases intimidate – voters, while 25 states have expanded voting rights. The Honorable State Representative, Ayanna Presley, notes, "oppression, the disenfranchisement of voters, of an electorate, of communities is not something that just happens in the ether, it is created by policy." The proposed legislation, For the People Act (SB1) & the John Lewis Act (SB2), is designed to combat voter suppression tactics and shore up the voting rights for all, but the Senate has failed to pass both acts.

Critical Race Theory: Hijacked in the Service of White Supremacy

Critical race theory (CRT) is a construct that emerged out of the Civil Rights Movement and Critical Legal Studies, during the mid-1980s (Bell, 1980; Curry, 2008). CRT provides an explanation for racial inequality that does not dehumanize Black people, as it focuses on White supremacy and systemic racism used to retain privilege and power.

Anti-Black Racism and Anti-CRT: Retrenchment from Racial Equity

An often-used tactic of White supremacy is to create, pronounce, and project a problem where one does not exist, as a rallying cry and racist dog-whistle to likeminded folk. A 2020 EO by then-president Trump was written, in part, as a response to the *1699 Project* and in part as a response to CRT – a perspective *not* taught in schools – but taught in law schools that proffer racism in the United States is institutional, structural, and systemic. The aim of *The Times*'s 1619 Project was "to reframe the country's history by placing the consequences of slavery and the contributions of Black Americans at the very center of our national narrative" (Hannah-Jones, 2019, para 2). The response by many White Americans drew on state legislative powers to restrict the teaching of literacy; to avoid teaching an accurate and truthful history of the United States, in favor of a history that repeats the notion of Black inferiority. The EO (*Federal Register*), Section 2, provided definitions of "divisive concepts":

> (a) "Divisive concepts" means the concepts that (1) one race or sex is inherently superior to another race or sex; (2) the United States is fundamentally racist or sexist; (3) an individual, by virtue of his or her race

or sex, is inherently racist, sexist, or oppressive, whether consciously or unconsciously; (4) an individual should be discriminated against or receive adverse treatment solely or partly because of his or her race or sex; (5) members of one race or sex cannot and should not attempt to treat others without respect to race or sex; (6) an individual's moral character is necessarily determined by his or her race or sex; (7) an individual, by virtue of his or her race or sex, bears responsibility for actions committed in the past by other members of the same race or sex; (8) any individual should feel discomfort, guilt, anguish, or any other form of psychological distress on account of his or her race or sex; or (9) meritocracy or traits such as a hard work ethic are racist or sexist, or were created by a particular race to oppress another race. The term "divisive concepts" also includes any other form of race or sex stereotyping or any other form of race or sex scapegoating.

(para 16)

The idea of "divisive concepts" sought to upend notions of inclusion – as un-American and dangerous – while simultaneously and erroneously seeking to gaslight the public into believing that the lack of inclusiveness was inclusion and thus more patriotic/American. The idea of "divisive concepts" appeared fixated on seeking to re-define CRT on its own terms and as an umbrella buzzword and talking point by supporters and in the media about the history of race and racism in the nation, centering on whose narrative should be taught in schools. Groups rallied in support of the EO; anti-CRT collations were created; books, curriculums, and school libraries were under siege; and redesigns were legislated. Supporters of the EO and anti-CRT were determined to whitewash the curriculum and present a favorable view of the role of White people throughout US history, while diminishing all White produced negative events, irrespective of historical accuracy. In some states, supporters demanded a review of all books, lesson plans, materials, and videotaping of teaching in classrooms. Under new state laws, students were not permitted to *read* about the illegal *Wander* and *Clotilda* slave ships that brought enslaved Africans to the United States; chattel slavery; anti-Black literacy laws; the Civil War; President Lincoln's White supremacist stance during debates with Stephen A. Douglas, and his plan to deport all Black Americans; Juneteenth (Emancipation Day); United Daughters of the Confederacy narrative of the "Lost Cause" and its influence on US education; the separate-but-equal outcome of the Homer Plessey lawsuit; massacres of Black people and burning of businesses, churches, homes, and schools; attempts throughout history to deport Black people, as in the 1920 removal of all Black people from the state by the Mississippi state Senate; *Brown v. the Board of Education I, II*; the Civil Rights movement; the Voting Rights Act; the presidency of Barak Obama; and many other events in US history. Although these historical events continue to have an impact on the lives of Black people in the

United States, the goals of anti-CRT supporters have misrepresented the theory to include all racial concerns and issues, except when – in their minds – White people are portrayed as benevolent, Christian, intelligent, upstanding, moral citizens, and "saviors" of the world.

Despite the seemingly benign title, the EO is an extension of White supremacy and has influenced 54 proposed state bills, 48 directly applying to K–12 public schools and 24 having become law (PEN, 2022). Some state laws center on public outcries to "protect White students" from discussing, learning, and reading about issues of race and racism and learning an accurate US history. The concerns are not new; James Baldwin (1963) wrote about them in the 1960s:

> What is upsetting the country is a sense of its own identity. If, for example, one managed to change the curriculum in all the schools so that Negroes learned more about themselves and their real contributions to this culture, you would be liberating not only Negroes, you'd be liberating white people who know nothing about their own history. And the reason is that if you are compelled to lie about one aspect of anybody's history, you must lie about it all.
>
> *(p. 3)*

Some people who are vocal opponents of CRT also have a limited understanding of the founding fathers, many who were not the virtuous people American history teaches. Leonardo (2009) understands the stance as one which "encompasses a 'pedagogy of amnesia,' [that] encourages students to consider the nation's founding fathers as benign heroes rather than participants in the construction of racist practices" (p. 173). Glaude (2021) calls this phenomenon *white innocence*:

> the refusal to know the world that racism creates in order to avoid responsibility for that world… the intricate rituals of denial and self-deception that define how we deal and have dealt with matters of race in this country.
>
> *(para 3)*

For example, most of the founding fathers were enslavers, and elected to continue servitude, even the enslavement of their own progeny. Some are fearful their children may learn a more accurate history, and others are concerned their children will learn how White supremacy sustains their White privilege. Ironically, these are parents who need not fear what is being taught in school, as they employ White privilege and their children are seeing it enacted in real time, at home. Not specifically mentioning CRT, race and racism does not mean the concepts are not fueling a desire to erase anti-Black racism in history. Failing to acknowledge racism reinserts Whiteness at the expense of Black history (chattel slavery, deportations, genocides, land and property thefts, lynchings, mass incarcerations, mob violence, rapes, starvation, sterilizations, etc.).

Co-opting the Truth

The pretext of White aggrievement issued an opportunity for likeminded legislation at state and local levels. Aiding the effort was the Manhattan Institute, originally named the International Center for Economic Policy Studies, founded in 1977 by Anthony Fisher and William J. Casey. In the anti-CRT movement at Manhattan Institute, two 'fellows' were active frontrunners in seeking to discredit and dismantle CRT, establish anti-CRT curricula in public-schools teaching about racism in the United States, and providing legislative guidance. First, Christopher Rufo's (2021) 806-word opinion in the *Wall Street Journal* seeks to explain and justify concerns about CRT from a limited conservative, fascist, right-wing perspective. He uses a popular set of conservative right-wing tropes, to blame academics, left-wing media, liberals, progressives, and politicians for support of CRT. He misidentifies as the essence of CRT "promoting critical race theory's core concepts, including race essentialism, collective guilt and racial superiority" (para 2). From his perspective, he dismisses CRT as "a radical ideology that seeks to use race as a means of moral, social and political revolution" (para 5) that views "America is an irredeemably racist nation and that the constitutional principles of freedom and equality are mere 'camouflages,'" (para 5). Rufo submits anti-CRT advocates are mainstream, multiracial, and nonpartisan without providing supporting documentation. Then, he argues school curriculum should ban − what he refers to as − CRT-inspired curricula and seeks to rebut the retrenchment to whitewashed curricula. He alleges the goals of state legislation banning CRT is to

> *simply prohibit* teachers from compelling students to believe that one race "is inherently superior to another," that one race is "inherently racist, sexist, or oppressive," or that an individual "bears responsibility for actions committed in the past by other members of the same race."
>
> *(para 7, emphasis added)*

He suggests discussions about the nation's history of racism is still part of the curriculum if no racial group is harmed in the process.

There are multiple alarms within the Rufo text, beginning with the opening sentence seeking to invoke the notion of culture wars as opposed to a war on truth. He also positions the anti-CRT movement as a backlash to global support of racial equity in the United States (the fear of some White people that a focus on the history and contemporary inequitable treatment of minoritized people will erode White dominance). Next, he misrepresents CRT and its key tenants to fit his argument. Then, he attempts to soften his anti-racist position, in a "*move toward innocence*" (Mawhinney, 1998, quoted in Tuck & Yang, 2012, p. 3, italics in the original) by including non-White racial groups in his opinion. Finally, as he supplies misinformation, he issues a call to action to address and "combat misinformation" (para 8).

Second, James Copland's (2021) brief relies heavily on Rufo's text, presents a rational against CRT, and provides a legislative template for government agencies. Copland's critique of CRT draws on surveys conducted by three separate groups who are led predominately by White people, an overview of CRT and CRT in education, inclusion of texts produced by members of the Manhattan Institute, and a list of "dos" and "don'ts" for constructing legislation. He supplies a rationale for the brief

> to add some light by elucidating basic principles that policymakers should consider in crafting legislative and other responses and by presenting model legislation, drawn from existing templates in many states, that should conform to these principles and pass constitutional muster.
>
> *(p. 3)*

When discussing education, he makes clear differences between legislation needed for public schools and exemptions for charter and private schools. He establishes a binary of good/bad legislation, where anti-CRT is "good" along with the admonition to avoid "value-laden judgments[;] particularly those involving individual identity," should steer clear of "so-called lived experience over objective deductive and inductive analysis" (p. 8). He expresses the need for legislation to address whether an "individual *should* feel discomfort, guilt, anguish, or another form of psychological distress solely because of the individual's race or sex" and includes "only normative-laden judgments premised on identity" (p. 9, emphasis in the original). Importantly, he includes a template to guide writers in framing anti-CRT legislation.

The threats against academic freedom, free speech, and public education have been addressed by the National Education Association (NEA), professional educational organizations, and university research centers. Bouie (2022) identifies Rufo's goal is to destroy public education in the United States, and restates Rufo's plan "to get universal school choice you really need to operate from a premise of universal public-school distrust. It's not subtle" (para 6-7). The threat is real as school districts, schools, and classroom teachers may lose funding or their teaching license. Bouie (2022) warns "these are not just attacks on individual teachers and schools; … they are the foundation for an assault on the very idea of public education, part of the long war against public goods and collective responsibility" (para 13). NEA (2018) provides a template to counter anti-CRT attacks. The bold, racist, and unambiguous assault on education reminds us of Woodson's notion of schools being the starting point of lynching Black bodies, as Givens (2019) proffers "the violence inflicted upon Black bodies began at the level of ideas and knowledge" (p. 1465). Further, he argues:

> the knowledge system of schools constructed Black people as ahistorical subjects, obscured historical systems of oppression, and taught students

to look to White–Eurocentric colonial ideology as a human standard…
Schools failed to offer African American students any cogent social analysis
of their historically constructed oppression, no alternative system of representation to interpret Black life.

(p. 1465)

Givens also interprets Woodson's scholarship to mean Black people understood
how White supremacy functioned in society and in education, as the "ideology
shaping school content and practices offered moral justification for the daily ter-
rors of anti-Blackness, … Students needed a new epistemology to interpret the
world, new semantics for understanding their own subjectivity" (Givens, 2019,
p. 1465). Unfortunately, anti-Blackness and anti-CRT laws are working in concert to resurrect – if not amplify – past White supremacist educational practices.

Table 7.1 provides a quick overview of new anti-CRT laws although most
laws do not reference CRT, preferring to draw on language akin to "divisive concepts"; not so coincidentally, several state laws specifically name *The
1619 project* as the reason for implementing bills, although few have much to
say about added concerns over sexual discussions (LGBTQAI+) and teaching

TABLE 7.1 Anti-CRT and Reading by Grade 3 Retention

State	Anti-CRT Legislation	Third Grade Reading Retention Laws
Alabama	HB8 Rep. Chris Pringle (R) prefiled a bill for next legislative session that would ban schools from "teaching certain concepts regarding race or sex, such as critical race theory."	Retention Required
Arizona	HB2898In late June, Gov. Doug Ducey, a Republican, signed a law restricting how teachers can discuss race and sex in the classroom. If educators or schools are found to be in violation of this law, the school district could be fined up to $5,000. In May, a separate bill that would have fined teachers $5,000 for promoting one side of a controversial topic failed to pass the Senate.	Retention Required
Arkansas	HB 1218 In March, Republican legislators withdrew their bill that would have prohibited teaching that promotes "division" between groups or "social justice." Arkansas passed a law in May that prohibited "divisive concepts" in state agency training, though this does not apply to public schools.	Retention Required

(Continued)

TABLE 7.1 (Continued)

State	Anti-CRT Legislation	Third Grade Reading Retention Laws
Florida	The state board of education voted to approve a rule that prohibits schools from teaching critical race theory and the 1619 Project.	Retention Required
Georgia	In June, the governor-appointed state board of education adopted a resolution against lessons that "indoctrinate" students or "promote one race or sex above another." The resolution also opposes awarding credit for student service learning with advocacy groups. These restrictions have not been codified into rules, however.	Retention Required
Idaho	HB 377 Gov. Brad Little, a Republican, signed a law in April limiting the ways that teachers can discuss race and gender and banning what the legislation called tenets of critical race theory.	N/A
Iowa	HF 802 In June, Gov. Kim Reynolds, a Republican, signed a law limiting the ways that teachers can discuss race and gender.	N/A
Kentucky	Bill requests 60 and 69 Republican legislators have pre-filed two bills for the 2022 session that would prohibit teaching certain concepts related to race, sex, and religion, and would subject teachers who violate the law to disciplinary action.	N/A
Louisiana	HB 564 In April, Rep. Ray Garofalo (R) voluntarily deferred a bill that would ban teaching of "divisive concepts," after criticism from other Louisiana lawmakers and state education officials.	N/A
Maine	LD 550 In February, Rep. Meldon Carmichael (R) introduced a bill that would prohibit public school teachers from "engaging in political, ideological or religious advocacy in the classroom."	Allowed
Michigan	SB 0460 In May, Republican legislators introduced a bill that would direct school boards to ensure that curriculum does not include critical race theory, the 1619 Project, or "anti-American and racist theories."	Retention Required
Missouri	HB 952 Rep. Brian Seitz (R) introduced a bill that would ban teaching of critical race theory and use of specific curricula, including the 1619 Project. The Missouri legislative session ended in May.	Retention Required

(Continued)

TABLE 7.1 (Continued)

State	Anti-CRT Legislation	Third Grade Reading Retention Laws
Montana	At the request of Superintendent of Public Instruction Elsie Arntzen (R), Montana Attorney General Austin Knudsen (R) issued an opinion in May that prevents schools from asking students to reflect on privilege and bans teaching that assigns characteristics to individuals based on their race or sex. The opinion is legally binding.	N/A
New Hampshire	HB 2 In June, Republican Gov. Chris Sununu signed the state budget into law. The budget bill included language banning teachers from discussing race, gender, and other identity characteristics in certain ways in class. This provision was added to the budget after a separate bill seeking to ban the teaching of "divisive concepts" died earlier this spring.	N/A
North Carolina	H324 In May, the House passed a bill that would prevent teachers from promoting certain concepts related to race or sex. The bill is now in Senate committee. A separate Senate bill would delay the implementation of new social studies standards, which would require that students learn about racism in American history.	Retention Required
Ohio	HB 322 HB 327 In May and June, Republican legislators introduced two bills: One would prohibit discussion of certain topics related to race and sex and forbid schools from awarding credit for student service learning with advocacy groups. If teachers promote any banned ideas, their classes cannot count toward graduation requirements for the students present. The other would prevent classroom conversations regarding "divisive concepts."	Retention Required
Oklahoma	HB1775 In May, Gov. Kevin Stitt, a Republican, signed a law limiting the ways that teachers can discuss racism and sexism in class.	Allowed
Pennsylvania	HB 1532 In June, Rep. Russ Diamond (R) introduced a bill that would limit how teachers can discuss racism and sexism and ban schools from hosting speakers or assigning books that advocate "racist or sexist concepts."	N/A

(Continued)

TABLE 7.1 (Continued)

State	Anti-CRT Legislation	Third Grade Reading Retention Laws
Rhode Island	HB 6070 Rep. Patricia Morgan (R) introduced a bill in March that would prohibit the teaching of "divisive concepts" related to race or sex. A House committee recommended that the bill be held for further study.	N/A
South Carolina	HB 4325 HB 4343 In May, Republican lawmakers introduced two bills: one that would prohibit schools from compelling students to "personally affirm, adopt, or adhere to the tenets of critical race theory," and another that would ban the use of the 1619 Project and require schools to list the materials they use on their website.	Retention Required
South Dakota	HB 1157 In February, Republican legislators withdrew a bill they had introduced that would ban schools from using materials that encourage the overthrow of the US government or promote social justice for particular groups. In May, Gov. Kristi Noem signed the "1776 Pledge" which opposes critical race theory in schools.	N/A
Tennessee	HB 0580 Gov. Bill Lee, a Republican, signed a law in May that limits how teachers can discuss racism and sexism in the classroom.	Retention Required
Texas	HB 3979 In May, the state legislature passed a bill that prohibits schools from awarding credit for student service learning with advocacy groups or requiring teachers to discuss controversial issues.	Allowed
Utah	At the request of the legislature, the Utah State Board of Education approved a new rule in June that would limit how teachers can discuss racism and sexism.	N/A
West Virginia	SB 618 HB 2595 In February and March, Republican legislators introduced two bills that would prohibit schools from teaching "divisive concepts" relating to race and sex.	Allowed
Wisconsin	SB 411 A bill introduced in June would prevent teachers from promoting "race or sex stereotyping" and withhold 10% of state aid from schools that violate this prohibition. It would also require that schools publish a list of all curricula they use.	N/A

https://www.k12dive.com/topic/50-states-education-policy/
https://www.edweek.oreg/policy-politics/map-where-critical-race-theory-is-under-attack/
2021/06 (July 12, 2021)

about White privilege (individual state contexts and understandings of the historical, political, and social contexts that informed the creation of state laws).

Some state laws permit vigilante justice, like Virginia's snitch-line and bounties to be paid for a violation. The laws encourage people to report violations of new laws – which could lead to an investigation of school personnel (administrators, staff, teachers) and people losing their jobs. The latter has caused some librarians and school personnel to self-regulate in fear of loss of income. Some states also threaten to withhold funding if schools defied the state law. Pollack et al.'s (2022) analysis of state and local anti-CRT data reveals an interconnected network of likeminded individuals:

> The anti "CRT" effort is a purposeful, nationally/state interconnected, and locally driven conflict campaign to block or restrict proactive teaching and professional development related to race, racism, bias, and many aspects of proactive diversity/equity/inclusion efforts in schools, while — for some — gaining political power and control. Strategy, language, terminology and tactics are shared and encouraged across localities through networking fueled by powerful conservative entities (media, organizations, foundations, PACs, and politicians) that exploit and foment local frustration and dissent over what should be taught and learned in schools. Targets include both school district policy and state law, and local educators themselves.
>
> *(p. vii)*

It is unclear in the repeated discourse used across state laws how the new laws diminish White privilege. There are several troubling outcomes: (1) parents, politicians, and school administrators are willing to whitewash history, irrespective of accuracy, completeness, and the truth; (2) due to vagueness of the law, threats of retaliation, public school teachers and school administrators may self-censure to avoid losing their jobs, licensure, tenure, and pension; and (3) the legislation appears to be a pretext for the ongoing plans to privatize public education. The authors note the goals of the anti-CRT campaigns "seeks to expose restrict, ban, 'abolish' censor, and control a wide set of school conversations on race and inclusion" (Pollack et al., 2022, p. vii). Thus, public campaigns and state laws continue the history of "protecting" White students' privilege and possible feelings of discomfort as laws are enacted irrespective of the possible depriviledging and psychological harm experienced by Black students and other students of color. The outcome of such laws demonstrate how historically "powerful brilliant men and women have produced racist ideas in order to justify the racist policies of their era, in order to redirect the blame for their era's racial disparities away from those policies and onto Black people" (Kendi, 2016, p. 9).

Anti-CRT and Curriculum

In the fervent push to outlaw CRT, the American Historical Association (AHA) issued a joint statement with the American Association of University Professors, the Association of American Colleges & Universities, and PEN America, that was signed by over 150 professional organizations, although none was affiliated with literacy (AHA, 2021a) (please see Appendix O, page 302). The collective body reviewed many of the state bills focused on restricting the racist history of the United States, as in a pending Oklahoma House Bill 2988, which states:

> An Act relating to education; prohibiting the use of the *1619 Project* in certain institutions; prohibiting teaching certain concepts pertaining to America and slavery; providing penalties for violation; preempting field of study; nullifying subsequent federal action; providing for codification; and providing an effective date.
>
> *(p. 1)*

A letter from AHA (2021b) questioned limiting how teachers taught and discussed:

> certain concepts pertaining to America and slavery (para 1). They cautioned that limiting an understanding of slavery would be "harmful to the youth of Oklahoma, leaving students ignorant of basic facts of American history and poorly prepared for the critical thinking and interpretive skills required for career and civic accomplishment.
>
> *(para. 3)*

AHA makes clear that restrictions diminish students' learning:

- the US Constitution prohibited Congress from abolishing US participation in the international slave trade for two decades;
- the *Plessy v. Ferguson* decision legalized racial segregation;
- the overwhelming majority of slave holders in the United States identified as White; and
- slavery was abolished three decades later in the United States than in most of the British Empire.

The state of Louisiana drafted a similar law in 2021 to stop the teaching of CRT (although it is not taught in the state's K–12 schools). The state's evolving resistance to accurately teach the history of racism in the United States and the state had been brewing for years, and its response provides a cautionary tale.

Louisiana State Representative, Ray Garofalo Jr. (R), introduced legislation to Louisiana House Bill 564, deeming some events and ideas might be contentious and suggesting that chattel enslavement was not all bad; there was some "good" to slavery (a comment he later tried to clarify). Fortunately, the bill did not pass. The bill entitled "Provides relative to training with respect to certain concepts related to race and sex in elementary and secondary schools and post-secondary education institutions" appears innocuous. Louisiana has less obvious but equally inaccurate educational materials for students as found in the online program, *Louisiana Reads!* a free, state-sponsored curriculum. It includes *The Classic Tales of Brer Rabbit* (J. C. Harris, 2008) as a mentor text for third graders; a text, listed among the multicultural offerings, that was not happenstance. The website fails to mention the origin of folktales within narratives of African and Native American people and fails to explain Chandler profited from their publication. Alice Walker reflected on the offensive version of *The Complete Tales of Uncle Remus* (J. C. Harris, 1955) and expressed regret revered African American tales were exploited, noting his versions "stole a good part of my heritage … By making me feel ashamed of it" (Walker, 2012, p. 637). Overt messages provide the teacher a chance to clarify misunderstandings, while subtle messages do not, which only serves to perpetuate stereotypes. Nonetheless, the failed attempt in 2021 has been resuscitated, and in 2022, a new bill by Garofalo will be discussed.

The nation has witnessed how quickly ill-informed state legislative bodies and local school boards moved in response to the concerns of White parents. There continues to be an attempt to invisibilize race, as Bonilla-Silva (2003) observed, new ideas act as a barrier and gatekeeper for Black people "without ever being explicitly about race" (p. 272), "as they are rearticulated in new, non-racial terms" (p. 272). Some states have proposed that anti-CRT state laws include colleges and universities, entities receiving federal funding, and workplaces. New Hampshire, for instance, passed the "Right to Freedom From Discrimination in Public Workplaces and Education" (N.H. Rev. Stat. § 354-A:29), on June 2, 2021. Due to the vagueness of the law, teachers were unsure of the boundaries and expressed concerns about their professional ethics, freedom, and knowledge.

A nationwide group leading challenges includes Moms for Liberty, a well-organized nonprofit that began in Florida and replicates tactics used by the United Daughters of the Confederacy to whitewash an imagined history of the United States. The former group believes that Southerners were the victors and victims of the Civil War – both groups hold that their efforts must ensure US history portrays White people as benevolent, equitable, God-fearing, and heroes while not addressing the history of racism and impact of racism. As a conservative, well-financed, and politically connected group, they work to abolish CRT, culturally relevant instruction, and social-emotional learning from schools. They find particularly abhorrent accurate descriptions, discussions, texts, and videos about Black enslavement, the deportment and internment of Asian Americans, as well as Native American genocide and land displacement. These conservative groups are connected to powerful political allies and strategically engage local politicians, school board members, and textbook publishers. They support banning books – primarily but not exclusively – written by minoritized authors and discussions about White privilege.

Anti-CRT State Laws

Nationally, anti-CRT laws and "protecting our children" rallies have galvanized White backlash and potential right-leaning voters. Opportunities to protest and respond emboldened some supporters who claim they are "saving US public education," while other supporters envisage the opportunities as another step toward privatizing education in the United States. Not all anti-CRT-proposed bills have become law; some are pending, and others vetoed as in North Carolina. A White minority of public-school parents are insisting on changes to how history and literacy are taught in multiple states, despite representing less than half the student population in public schools (Irwin et al., 2021).

Less well publicized are left-leaning civil rights groups (Migdon, 2022), "blue" suburban mothers groups (Gowen, 2022), and organizations such as the College Board (CB) that oppose anti-CRT state laws (proposed laws) and divisive concepts/topics – so named to include any concern or topic that presents alternative views of Whiteness as pure and morally just as well as homophobic topics. The CB has threatened to remove high school courses that do not address divisive concepts. According to Zach Goldberg of the CB, banned courses may result in removal of the course from "AP Course Ledger provided to colleges and universities" (quoted in Stump, 2022, para 4). His statement aligns with the CB principles: "if a school bans required topics from their AP courses, the AP Program removes the AP designation from that course and its inclusion in the AP Course Ledger provided to colleges and universities" (para 5). Supporters have exposed the White supremacist ideology seeking to maintain White and sanitized versions of race and racism, especially subjects like English and US history. The concerns voiced center on the feelings of school children, albeit what is really meant is the feelings of White school children, revealing their "racial double standards" (Beinart, 2022, para 9), as there is little concern for the feelings of Black school children and other minoritized students. This is amazing, unfortunate, and preventable. In response, the CB added an African American Studies pilot course to its offerings, a decision fraught with controversy.

The Seeds of Privatizing Education and Their Effect on Anti-Black Literacy

Former president George H. W. Bush argued for improving public education and touted providing vouchers to students attending poorly performing or under-resourced schools as a foil (more wealthy students took advantage of vouchers than students living in poverty) and sought not to "overburden White taxpayers" (Walsh, 2021, n.p.) with support of failing schools. His notion of improving education was carried further by his sons, George W. Bush as governor of Texas and president of the United States, and Jeb Bush, as governor of Florida. The dog-whistle reveals the tacit assumption that only White people are taxpayers and everyone else, especially Black people, benefit from their labor. Besides being historically and factually inaccurate, the notion of "taxpayer" is – as Walsh argues – coded language appearing race-neutral but meant as a rallying call among White people: "the taxpayer myth has deep roots, and throughout history it has been intertwined with the idea that all forms of resources from the government belong to white people, to do with as they please" (n.p.). Walsh proffers: "an identity had been created, racialized but still outwardly race-neutral, uniting white people across classes in a privileged public category designed to naturalize inequality" (n.p.). He also acknowledges that historically, Black people have paid taxes at a disproportionate rate under laws enacted by President Bush, as Black people continue to pay taxes for public education disproportionately funding White students' access to vouchers used for private schools. A promoted "common-sense" logic is that taxpayer dollars are being used wisely to educate all students, although some are not learning to read well. Thus, it is best to retain students who are not reading on grade level by grade 3 and "fix" the reading problems so students do not become a future burden on the tax system. Tangentially, there is the unspoken notion that if White people are paying the bulk of taxes, schools should give them every possible advantage to be successful, including, but not limited to, special programs for the gifted and talented, a cache of "approved" programs that identify their children as dyslexic (if needed), and tax dollars to pay for private school education (an identification also to avoid being retained in grade 3 current laws). Arguments in support of school choice, under these considerations, replicate White supremacist ideology underpinning school choice as a solution to educational inequity to insiders with knowledge about true efforts whereby so-called "reforms" are a protective cover for legalizing education re-segregation. US Senator Patty Murray (2017) voices concern about school choice following the release of President Trump's 2018 budget. She argues the budget "request commits to diverting public funds from bipartisan education programs for school privatization efforts ... to increase 'school choice,' in reality, privatization presents a false choice for parents, students, and communities" (n.p.). Murray's online post includes a letter to Senate colleagues and a lengthy memo that explicates concerns over the "false choice" labeled as school choice. She clearly explains the differences in geographical areas where school choice is non-existent or exceedingly burdensome and where vouchers are not a realistic option; use of vouchers for private and religious schooling; and considerable differences between wealthy and less wealthy school districts. The memo does not include a discussion of the role race/ethnicity and poverty played in school choice in the United States.

As governor of Texas, George W. Bush pushed for accountability in education, a salvo used when he was president of the United States to reauthorize
ESEA as NCLB. A catalyst for the passage of NCLB was to improve the reading
performance on standardized reading tests, especially among students identified
as disabled, impoverished, or minorities, with a goal of all students reading on
grade level by the end of third grade. As common in educational research, concerns of racism were diminished and explained with an educational mélange of
culture, ethnicity, and language, and race to push for funding and political support. The body of federally funded research and reports (1990, 1998, 2000) used
to address reading was the same body of research referenced by states in support
of reading retention laws that disproportionately harm Black students.

An under-recognized section of IDEIA (2004) is the idea to provide students
with 'universal, 'high-quality education, which is a long way of saying universal-
izing education supports Whiteness as the center of education. Reading instruction in schools is based on multiple inequalities (cultures, ethnicities, genders,
languages, races, and religions) as approaches, curriculum, materials, procedures,
and structures mimic White-centric attitudes, beliefs, experiences, and values.
Many non-White students are taught to read in ways that are *not* affirming and
reflective of their diverse communities and families. Reading instruction in
schools also is based on the idea that educators (school administrators, classroom
teachers, and literacy coaches) do not exhibit implicit racial bias and internalized
anti-Black racism while teaching Black students to read.

Appropriate and authentic universal, high-quality instruction should include
multiple cultures, genders, languages, social classes, values, beliefs, races, ethnicities, religions, epistemologies, etc. Given, the penchant for US education and
literacy to default to the concerns of White parents and the literacy needs of
White students, there is little hope "universal" or high-quality literacy instruction, includes text varieties that represent abilities, cultures, ethnicities, genders,
languages, races, and religions. In light of these shortcomings, the APA (2021b)
issued a public apology: *Apology to People of Color for APA's role in promoting, perpetuating, and failing to challenge racism, racial discrimination, and human hierarchy in
the United States*:

> **Whereas** the field of psychology has not historically supported research
> on communities of color by not adequately reporting and including them,
> minimally reporting them as a demographic data point, and/or interpret-
> ing results based on Eurocentric research standards, thereby perpetuating
> invisibility and resulting in a lack of quality research that can inform prac-
> tices and policies that impact communities of color …
>
> *(para 18)*

> **Whereas** these views have often been centered in research used to advance
> the careers of White researchers who became "experts" with respect to the

ethnically diverse studied group, without providing any follow up to that community or insight into the data findings and the implications for the researched community ...

(para 19)

Whereas psychologists created and promoted the widespread application of psychological tests and instruments that have been used to disadvantage many communities of color ... contributing to the overdiagnosis, misdiagnosis, and lack of culturally appropriate diagnostic criteria to characterize the lived experience and mental health concerns of people of color ...

(para 22)

Whereas APA and its leadership failed to take concerted action in response to calls from Black psychologists (many of whom later formed ABPsi) for an end to the misuse of testing and assessment practices (including standardized assessments) and interventions in education and the workplace developed by psychologists and others that perpetuated racial inequality ...

(para 23)

APA acknowledges an ideology of White supremacy is embedded within its field, is based in scientific racism, and has inflicted harm on People of Color. An ideology of White supremacy has not been acknowledged in reading research; however, herein an ideology of White supremacy is identified as embedded within reading research (assessment, concepts, curriculum, definitions, instruction, research, recommendations, standardized tests, and teacher education), has been chronicled, and is demystified as the source of anti-Black literacy (Table 7.2).

TABLE 7.2 Intersection of Psychology and Reading Research

American Psychological Association (2021a, 2021b, 2021c, 2021d)	Reading Research
American Psychological Association acknowledges it role in perpetuating racism	
American Psychological Association apologizes for the organization's role in perpetuating racism	
American Psychological Association chronicles the organization's role in perpetuating racism	
...eugenicists focused on the measurement of intelligence, health, and capability, concepts which were adopted by the field of psychology and used systemically to create the ideology of White supremacy and harm communities of color	X

(Continued)

TABLE 7.2 (Continued)

American Psychological Association (2021a, 2021b, 2021c, 2021d)	Reading Research
Since its origins as a scientific discipline in the mid-19th century, psychology has, through acts of commission and omission, contributed to the dispossession, displacement, and exploitation of communities of color. This early history of psychology, rooted in oppressive psychological science to protect Whiteness, White people, and White epistemologies, reflected the social and political landscape of the US at that time. Psychology developed under these conditions, helped to create, express, and sustain them, continues to bear their indelible imprint, and often continues to publish research that conforms with White racial hierarchy	
…psychologists established, participated in, and disseminated scientific models and approaches rooted in scientific racism when the discipline was first founded	X
White male leadership, many of whom contributed to scientific inquiry and methods that perpetuated systemic racial oppression, including promoting the ideas of early 20th century eugenics; Eugenics is defined as the idea that racial differences and hierarchies are biologically based and fixed, and was used to support segregation…	X
Results from a century's worth of psychological studies of individual difference were interpreted as evidence of innate, hereditary difference in ability between racial and ethnic groups, Historically, groups found to score differently on assessments designed by White psychologist and normalized on White populations were deemed inferior based on those results. These interpretations have created and upheld existing racial stereotypes and prejudice against people of color and reinforce the belief White supremacy. Such believes sound strong support in the 20th century among psychologist and other social scientist, particularly those involved in eugenics movement	X
…some prominent psychologists historically have perpetuated, and others continue to perpetuate racism through pseudoscientific theories that postulate racial differences in intelligence, propensity to violence, limits on educability, and other psychological characteristics, thereby contributing to eugenics and other racist movements in the United States and abroad	X
…psychologists created, sustained, and promulgated ideas of human hierarchy through the construction, study, and interpretation of racial difference, and therefore contributed to the financial wealth gap and social class disparities experienced by many communities of color	X

(Continued)

TABLE 7.2 (Continued)

American Psychological Association (2021a, 2021b, 2021c, 2021d)	Reading Research
Psychological data have been used by psychologist and others to justify social policies that harm people of color, including racial segregation, diminished educational opportunities, restrictions on immigration, institutionalization, forced sterilization, and anti-miscegenation laws. Psychology has a standing field to challenge research practice and policy frameworks rooted in white normativity that supported the continued belief and White superiority.	X
… psychology has minimized and marginalized psychologists from communities of color and their contributions to the field	X
…the field of psychology has historically contributed to the belief in human hierarchy through allowing—or not challenging—racial bias throughout the discipline and profession, such as in peer review, publishing, research motivated by racism, racial disparities in psychological research, and the valuation of certain types of research), as well as in Eurocentric models of clinical practice, including psychological assessment…	X
American Psychological Association issues a resolution to address the organization's role in perpetuating racism and announces actions to affect change moving forward	

Underlying the unvoiced assumption about solving the problem of low reading performance on standardized reading test is victimization of the individual – in this case – students who are Black and students who live in poverty. The reasons given for low reading performance are Black attitudes toward education, culture, community, family, language, and poverty. Among the 'solutions' to low reading performance has been the promise of school choice campaigns.

By contrast, the National Education Association (2018) suggests that equity concepts need to be redefined. They also offer guidelines for Racial Equity Impact Assessment (REIA):

> a systematic examination of how different racial and ethnic groups will likely be affected by a proposed action or decision. REIAs are used to minimize unanticipated adverse consequences in a variety of contexts, including the analysis of proposed policies, institutional practices, programs, plans and budgetary decisions. The REIA can be a vital tool for preventing institutional racism and for identifying new options to remedy long-standing inequities.

(p. 42)

Anti-Black Literacy and Anti-Black Racism in Literacy Research

In the field of reading, there is a mythical debate, publicized nationally as reading/literacy wars that often serve as a bellwether to usher in new education reforms. A recurring focus has been which approach to reading will ensure more students are reading on grade level by the end of third grade (balanced reading, phonics, science of reading, SOR). It is not enough to project such "war claims" and fail to follow-up, while continuing to conceptually and theoretically conduct reading research studies among White students as if their beliefs, culture, language, and values reflect the lives of all students. Several states have instituted summer programs and teacher literacy academies for all personnel involved in K–3 teaching of reading. Among the tactics being used to deflect concerns about BLM and racial inequity and to induce teachers are (a) misidentifying alternative approaches, for example, Calkins's unit of study and Reading Recovery as supportive of CRT, and (b) strongly suggesting a required reading approach will help Black students to improve reading performance although there is limited research (by any standard) to suggest this is true. The promotion of SoR and the required training are framed on a circular argument: Supporters of SoR claim to have identified the "problem" (low reading scores) – although the low reading score is, in part, a consequence of over 30 years of studies of reading instruction based on reading research grounded in scientific racism. Supporters also claim to have identified a "solution" for low reading performance – more SoR – despite 30 years of instruction and NAEP assessments that do not reveal significant change in reading performance.

Schwartz (2022) reports that more than half of the states require teachers use the "science of reading" framework, "the body of research on how children learn to read text. Many of the practices that schools currently use, and that are promoted by popular reading programs, do not align with this evidence base, in early reading instruction" (para 2). She notes the framework places an "emphasis on foundational skills instruction—teaching students how to recognize the different sounds in words, how to link those sounds to letters, and how to blend those letters together to read words" (para 13) – and is much more than teaching phonics. Her review of the "science of reading" framework finds

1. States' number one priority? Professional development
2. Teachers can't do it alone. Systems matter
3. The "science of reading" isn't just about phonics
4. Educators must fundamentally reimagine their practice. And old habits can be hard to shake
5. Follow-up support and coaching could make a big difference

Although some states require teachers to learn to teach reading using the SoR approach, for example, North Carolina, others are less prescriptive. Granados (2021) summarizes several legislative actions undertaken by the North Carolina

General Assembly: Bill 755, Academic Transparency (pending); Bill 324, ensuring dignity & nondiscrimination/schools (vetoed); and passed, Bill 387, Excellent Public Schools, that identifies and requires training and use of SoR (see Fofaria, 2021). There may be networking, if not duplicity, among book companies, corporate leaders, curriculum developers, federal funding agencies, institutions of higher education, independent education providers, politicians, review boards, and the testing industry, as there is a considerable amount of money available to support reading improvement. To be clear, in the academy, SoR is characterized as:

> evidence-based reading instruction practices that address the acquisition of language, phonological and phonemic awareness, phonics and spelling, fluency, vocabulary, oral language, and comprehension that can be differentiated to meet the needs of individual students.
>
> *(North Carolina Senate Bill 387, p. 1, emphasis in text)*

How differentiation for individual students occurs is unclear. SoR can be found in 24 state laws and policies and the District of Columbia, have training requirements that may include denigrating references to diversity, equity, race, and social justice as the "real problem." In the 2022–2023 school year, for instance, SoR is promoted as an anecdote to CRT, extending the ill-conceived anti-CRT rhetoric while simultaneously referencing other reading approaches that are not grounded in CRT.

The promotion of the "science of reading" framework as a "scientific" response to early reading is reminiscent of the promotion of science as a failsafe determiner of achievement, intelligence, and merit. Foundational to the "science of reading" is the belief that science is sacrosanct, and the science of reading is built on evidence-based scientific research. SoR extends notions about early reading that emerged in the 1990s followed by similar pronouncements of skills needed to develop reading, although none of the approaches have significantly improved reading acquisition for Black students. SoR resurrects with a slight-of--hand, and under the cover of evidence-based research, scientific racism as a key to progress. The "evidence" references the use of the science/experiments and quasi-experiments root in racism; not saying it out loud does not mean it does not exist. The ideological assumptions in support of White supremacy continue to underpin the conceptualization, definition, instruction, and assessment of literacy. The insistence on a singular approach to reading, SoR, supports an indoctrination of Whiteness in contemporary reading retention laws while limiting the cultures, languages, and literacies of Black readers, thus diminishing the quality of literacy instruction they receive. A singular (conceptual/ideological/philosophical/theoretical) approach to addressing literacy is tantamount to a "one-size-fits-all" approach. Clearly, some people will fit, and others will not; the focus is seldom on those who fit because they move forward, and those who do not fit are seen as somehow deficient. If the approach does not work for Black students, change the approach; do not try a new variation of the same approach, but a completely new approach not reliant on research conducted among White-centric students.

The redoubled effort and legislative support of SoR in state laws and policies is used as a counterattack and defense against acknowledgment of White supremacy, scientific racism, and racially discriminatory practices while dismissing Black scholarship that indicates literacy growth when instruction and materials are asset-based. There also is a resurgence in the idea that some students are more "at-risk" of reading failure because of culture/ethnicity/race, economics, language, and poverty. The risk factors identified are enacted to maintain White supremacy. Unlike their colonial antecedents that criminalized Black people for learning to read, new laws criminalize Black student readers for *not* learning to read, in a specific way and timeframe. Flores (2022) pointedly suggests renaming so-called "risk factors" as "indicators of oppression" (n.p.). All anti-Black literacy laws are foundational to retaining White supremacy.

Variation on a Theme

Standardized tests have long been gatekeepers to post-secondary college admissions and workplace entre'. The underperformance of some non-White people on standardized tests supports a false narrative, concocted by eugenicists and White supremacists to justify the creation of laws, policies, and statutes to highjack equitable and equal literacy education.

Apology, Chronology, and Resolution by the American Psychological Association

The APA (2021a) admits and chronicles the organization's roots in White supremacy and scientific racism and supports racial inequities through testing:

> WHEREAS, the field of psychology has historically contributed to the belief in human hierarchy through allowing—or not challenging—racial bias throughout the discipline and profession, …as well as in Eurocentric models of clinical practice, including psychological assessment …
>
> *(para 13)*

> WHEREAS some prominent psychologists historically have perpetuated, and others continue to perpetuate racism through pseudoscientific theories that postulate racial differences in intelligence, propensity to violence, limits on educability, and other psychological characteristics, …
>
> *(para 14)*

The ideology of White supremacy continues to evolve although some psychologists know it is a lie and, for reasons untold, refuse to tell the truth. The organization also published an *Apology to People of Color for APA's role in promoting, perpetuating, and failing to challenge racism, racial discrimination and human hierarchy in the United States* (2021b):

Whereas …since its origins as a scientific discipline in the mid-19th century, psychology has, through acts of commission and omission, contributed to the dispossession, displacement, and exploitation of communities of color. This early history of psychology, rooted in oppressive psychological science to protect Whiteness, White people, and White epistemologies, reflected the social and political landscape of the US at that time. Psychology developed under these conditions, … continues to bear their indelible imprint, and often continues to publish research that conforms with White racial hierarchy …

(para 8)

APA (2021c) also traces the organization's support of scientific racism and White supremacy, support bolstered by eugenicists (including reading researchers and ideas reflected in the history of reading assessments):

Historically, groups found to score differently on assessments designed by White psychologist and normalized on White populations were deemed inferior based on those results. These interpretations have created and upheld existing racial stereotypes and prejudice against people of color and reinforce the belief White supremacy…

(para 15)

Psychological data have been used by psychologist and others to justify social policies that harm to people of color, including racial segregation, diminished educational opportunities, restrictions on immigration, institutionalization, forced sterilization, and anti-miscegenation laws. Psychology has a standing field to challenge research practice and policy frameworks rooted in white normativity that supported the continued belief and White superiority.

(para 16)

The organization does not stand alone in fighting anti–Black racism in education and policy. During the first decade of the twenty-first century, colleges and universities began to abandon the use of standardized admission tests such as the ACT and SAT because of perceived class, ethnic/racial, and linguistic biases. Some colleges and universities offer the option of taking standardized admissions tests (ACT/SAT) or applying for admission without taking the tests, for example, the University of California system and all colleges and universities in the state of IL. Following the 2020 summer of racial reckoning, David G. Payne, vice president and COO of ETS, sent an email explaining:

We at ETS stand in unity over the call to end structural and systemic racism and inequities that continue to plague our society, and we are intensely committed to fulfilling our purpose as an education nonprofit in ways that can help address these issues.

The mission of ETS for 70 years has been "to advance quality and equity in education by providing fair and valid assessments as well as research and related services … for all people worldwide." Toward that end, we conduct extensive research on educational access and opportunity from preschool through adulthood, suggest federal and state policy changes, and have made progress in collaboration with organizations dedicated to improving equity.

We also work to make our tests free from bias, including:

- following the highest psychometric standards for test quality and fairness, including those jointly developed by the American Educational Research Association (AERA), the National Council on Measurement in Education (NCME) and the American Psychological Association (APA)
- forming diverse teams to review test questions
- training all employees on fairness procedures
- eliminating test questions that psychometric analyses indicate may unfairly bias any particular group of test takers

(para 1–4)

He concludes by stating, "this work is more important than ever as standardized testing has become an issue in discussions about the advancement of access and equity" (para 5). As altruistic as his comments are, ETS did not alter its production of standardized tests, nor acknowledge the roots of scientific racism on which they are created. Instead, the organization's website, filled with smiling BIPOC notes their renewed efforts to promote the notion of evidence, implying that outcomes of standardized testing are based on the gathering of evidence. The tactics are meant to rebuff concerns of racial inequity embedded in standardized tests with the notion "people of color work here and appear happy," and evidence is an anticipated and fair product of testing, while not addressing the roots of psychological testsing based on scientific racism. The College Board (CB), by contrast, has been outspoken since a loss in status of the once beloved SAT finds 1,000 colleges and universities do not require their test for admission. A group of scholars waged concerns captured in the text *Disfigured History: How the College Board Demolishes the Past* (Randall, 2020), making clear their animus for the CB presentation of history citing the *1619 Project* and calling for social justice. Over the last decade, however, many colleges and universities have abandoned the admission tests because of perceived class, ethnic/racial, and linguistic biases.

In another example of reform, a suit was filed on behalf of students required to take standardized college admission examinations and those seeking scholarships within the University of California system. Superior Court Judge Brad Seligman issued an injunction to halt the use of standardized tests on September

244 Linking the Past to the Present

2020, in part because of the lack of access for students with disabilities during the COVID-19 pandemic (Wantabe, 2021, para 3). Speaking on behalf of the plaintiffs in the landmark federal lawsuit, Mark Rosenbaum remarked:

> The SAT and ACT are dead and gone as far as the UC system is concerned,... historic decision puts an end to racist tests that deprived countless California students of color, students with disabilities, and students from low-income families of a fair shot at admissions to the UC system.
>
> *(quoted in Wantabe, 2021, para 7)*

Michael Brown, Provost of the massive University of California system, in 2021, informed the Board of Regents, following three years of study, that no standardized tests would be required because all produced biased results. An alternative test by Smarter Balance, a company used for statewide K–12 testing, was considered, but found to reflect "racial and economic disparities" (Wantabe, 2021, para 17), and it was vetoed. Mary Gauvin, UC Riverside professor, observed the state test resulted in a "modest incremental value" after high school, while simultaneously "reflecting and reproducing inequality" (quoted in Wantabe, 2021, para 15). The decision not to require any standardized tests has resulted in an increased enrollment of BIPOC, and in the UC system consideration for admission will include a variety of factors along with anti-bias training for reviewers of student applications. The decision extends the number of colleges and universities nationwide not requiring entrance exams, for example, Georgia and Illinois give students the option to take and use their scores on the ACT or SAT. There also are states reconsidering and revising standardized testing use among K–12 students as well as elite public schools under increasing scrutiny when White students are not admitted because alternatives to standardized tests are used to openly screen applicants in large school districts, for example, New York City and Chicago, among others. Cullotta (2022) reports in the *Chicago Tribune* discussions are underway to eliminate standardized testing and replace the annual tests with three tests throughout the school year in IL.

Standardized Reading Tests

The ideology of White supremacy infuses all aspects of US thought, including those of early psychologists seeking to understand reading (APA, 2021c). Standardized reading tests began in the late 1800s and continue to be used in the United States, to understand how reading occurs, to prove the superiority of White students (eugenics, individual differences, and the inheritability of intelligence), and to perpetuate the myth of White racial superiority.

Given the apology and chronology by APA (2021a, 2021c) and the history of standardized reading tests framed by research in educational psychology, it is disheartening to read whitewashed histories of reading and contemporary reading research as ecumenical attempts to help all children. There is a great deal of silence in the field of reading about the history of racism and little to no acknowledgment of the role it has played and continues to play. For example, although there is no "scientific" basis for claims of biological and racial differences in intelligence testing and in standardized reading tests, "race as *biology* makes it easy to believe that many of the divisions, we see in society are natural. But race, like gender and disability, is socially constructed" (Sensoy & DiAngelo, 2017, p. 121, emphasis in the original) Thus, there remains unchallenged reporting of performance on standardized reading tests, by race, as a determiner of student ability, achievement, intelligence, and performance.

Recall, *Gray's Oral Reading Test* (Wiederholt and Bryant, 2012), originally developed and used in the early 1900s, and, now revised, remains a popular staple in reading assessment of oral reading accuracy, comprehension, fluency, and rate. The results, then and now, for Black students and Black students who are AAL speakers reveal they do not perform as well as their White peers. Some reading researchers continue to argue for its use, although they are uncertain which factors prevent Black students from performing well on the test (Champion et al., 2010). What happens when these children are "tested" for fluency, oral reading, retellings, and word identification – and the person *hearing* them expects Standard English? One researcher suggests "children whose language is not as developed as their peers just do not sound right" (Caldwell, 2014, p. 128). Given the extensive linguistic and sociolinguistic research (Alim & Smitherman, 2012, 2020; Baugh, 2000; Lanehart et al., 2015; Richardson, 2003; Rickford & Rickford, 2000), validating AAL as a rule-governed language, Black students' performance on oral reading assessments continues to reflect racialized misunderstandings about AAL and is characterized as a "reading difficulty" damning some students to special education. Some Black students have not performed well on oral reading tests, in part because of English language variations. What continues to fuel the mischaracterizations and misunderstandings of AAL in reading assessment, research, and teacher preparation?

Mass and social media outlets have used alarmist language to portray learning loss of nine-year-old students as caused by the pandemic while drawing on NAEP reading and math outcomes. The pandemic amplified and exacerbated problems already in existence, the lack of achievement for all racial demographic groups and widening achievement gaps between Black and White students. The media foci (approaches to reading, pandemic learning loss, and racial achievement gaps in reading performance) are distractions from addressing the scientific racism that underpins reading approaches, assessments, and research.

Grade Retention

In a 2021 publication by the Education Commission of the States, they include data about local decision making, at the classroom, school, and district levels used in some states to make recommendations for grade retention. Kelley, Weyer, McCann, Broom, and Keily (2021) have produced an updated comparison of state K–3 polices for the ECS that reveals:

- Nineteen states and the District of Columbia require that children attend kindergarten.
- Seventeen states and the District of Columbia require full-day kindergarten, and 39 states plus the District of Columbia require districts to offer kindergarten either full or half day.
- Twenty-three states and the District of Columbia have policies in place to guide the transition process from pre-K to kindergarten, with 17 states requiring family engagement in this process.
- Thirty-seven states and the District of Columbia require assessments outside of the federally required third-grade assessments, including screeners, diagnostic, summative, and formative assessments.
- Twenty states have literacy instruction requirements for teacher training and professional development, ranging from passing an assessment to receiving job-embedded training.
- Seventeen states and the District of Columbia require grade retention for nonproficient third graders, with good cause exemptions, and an additional 10 states allow for grade retention.
- Seventeen states have a provision in the statute or regulation limiting the suspension or expulsion of students in pre-K through third grade. (para 3)

Despite narratives that appear cloaked in racial equity, collectively such laws, policies, and statutes continue to normalize and seek to codify contemporary versions of anti-Black racism and literacy.

Reading Retention

A history of reading should acknowledge how the ideology of White supremacy influences, frames, and informs state anti-literacy laws and is supported by proxy federal agencies. The anti-literacy laws reveal a conscious and intentional choice to compromise literacy equity for Black students at the behest of White students – by supplementing and promoting an incremental façade of racial progress. Such attempts to legalize racial equality have not resulted in equity as innumerable legal and political maneuvers are used to dismantle, ignore, and sidestep laws that unambiguously address anti-Black racism and anti-Black literacy. Inconceivably, support for anti-Black literacy laws that knowingly could harm a child emotionally and psychologically and fracture a sense of self have been passed since 1998. The laws drew from the White supremacy playbook, creating a hierarchy of reading based on student performance on standardized reading tests or teacher recommendations: students who are reading on grade level or beyond by the end of third grade, students who are not reading on grade level by the end of third grade and are retained, students who are struggling to read on grade level by the end of third grade, but labeled dyslexic and will not be held back, and students who are not reading on grade level by the end of third grade but are likely to successfully appeal retention. The effects of COVID-19 on the nation's school children were severe as economic and racial inequities were pronounced, including food insecurity and lack of access to the internet and technological devices. Au (2021) notes the increased pressure to perform well on standardized tests has been detrimental to every student's learning but has been especially detrimental to non-White students who attend high-poverty and under-resourced public schools where policies have been implanted to "increase time spent on reading" (p. 106). Nonetheless, some states initially planned to continue end-of-year assessments and enforce reading retention laws.

Research conducted by Cummings and Turner (2020) articulate "the most controversial third-grade reading policies are those that mandate retention for students who do not meet a pre-defined measure of proficiency" (p. 7). They confirm many previous findings: the effects of reading grade retention "were short-lived and not statistically significant," (p. 7), and "could negatively affect high school graduation rates, and disproportionately affected minoritized students" (p. 7). In addition to an uneven application of reading retention laws, caveats may or may not be shared with all parents and guardians (please see Table 7.3). Research continues to note appeals on behalf of middle- to upper-class White students are most likely to be granted, whereas appeals on behalf of students of color, primarily Black students and students who are poor, are least likely to be granted. The uneven enforcement of reading retention laws creates a legal pathway to discriminate against Black students as they are disproportionately affected by the uneven enforcement of reading retention laws. Much like the anti-literacy laws of the nineteenth century, and school segregation laws of the twentieth century, under the shadow and blessing of reading retention laws, schools have created inequitable access to high-quality literacy.

State and local school districts used reading retention laws, compelling nine-year-old students to be retained, as if students willfully decide not to learn to read. Should school districts, administrators, teachers, and reading specialists also be held accountable for failing to teach a student to read on grade level by the end of third grade? The entire cabal begs the questions: Why do these laws exist, who benefits from the laws, and why have the laws not been abrogated or repealed? Are politicians and school administrators willfully ignorant as they continue to campaign and promote dis/mis/information about reading and high school graduation – given the research unequivocally notes students who are *retained*

TABLE 7.3 Literacy Interventions Were Not Widely Addressed in States' COVID-19 Guidance

Table 1. State Third-Grade Reading Policies

State	Third-Grade Reading Policy	Retention	Diagnostic/Screening Assessments	Parental Notification	Interventions	Literacy Coaches/Reading Specialists
Alabama	Yes	Required	X	X	X	X
Alaska	Yes	Allowed	X	X	X	
Arizona	Yes	Required	X	X	X	
Arkansas	Yes	Required	X	X	X	
California	Yes	Required	X	X	X	
Colorado	Yes	Allowed	X	X	X	
Connecticut	Yes	Required	X	X	X	X
Delaware	Yes	Required	X	X	X	
District of Columbia	Yes	Required	X	X	X	X
Florida	Yes	Required	X	X	X	X
Georgia	Yes	Required	X	X	X	
Hawaii	No	N/A				
Idaho	Yes	N/A	X	X	X	
Illinois	Yes	Allowed	X	X	X	X
Indiana	Yes	Required	X	X	X	
Iowa	Yes	N/A	X	X	X	
Kansas	No	N/A	X		X	
Kentucky	No	N/A	X	X	X	X
Louisiana	Yes	N/A	X	X	X	
Maine	Yes	Allowed	X		X	
Maryland	Yes	Allowed	X			

State					
Massachusetts	Yes	N/A	X		
Michigan	Yes	Required	X	X	X
Minnesota	Yes	Allowed	X	X	
Mississippi	Yes	Required	X	X	X
Missouri	Yes	Required	X	X	
Montana	No	N/A			
Nebraska	Yes	N/A	X	X	
Nevada	Yes	Allowed	X	X	X
New Hampshire	No	N/A			
New Jersey	Yes	Allowed	X	X	
New Mexico	Yes	Allowed	X	X	
New York	Yes	N/A	X	X	
North Carolina	Yes	Required	X	X	
North Dakota	No	N/A	X	X	X
Ohio	Yes	Required	X	X	
Oklahoma	Yes	Allowed	X	X	
Oregon	No	N/A			
Pennsylvania	No	N/A			
Rhode Island	No	N/A	X		
South Carolina	Yes	Required	X	X	X
South Dakota	No	N/A			
Tennessee	Yes	Required		X	

(Continued)

TABLE 7.3 (Continued)

Table 1. State Third-Grade Reading Policies

State	Third-Grade Reading Policy	Retention	Diagnostic/ Screening Assessments	Parental Notification	Interventions	Literacy Coaches/ Reading Specialists
Texas	Yes	Allowed	X	X	X	X
Utah	Yes	N/A	X	X	X	X
Vermont	No	N/A		X	X	
Virginia	No	N/A	X	X	X	
Washington	Yes	Required	X	X	X	
West Virginia	Yes	Allowed	X		X	
Wisconsin	No	N/A	X	X		
Wyoming	Yes	N/A	X		X	
Total	37 + D.C.	17 + D.C. Require; 12 Allow	42 + D.C.	35 + D.C.	40 + D.C.	12

Source: Cummings, A., & Turner, M. (2020). Policy brief. Covid-19 and third-grade reading policies: An analysis of state guidance on third-grade reading policies in response to Covid. Education Policy Innovation Collaborative ..... pp. 6–7.

are more likely **not** to complete high school? Grade retention can now include pre-K children, innocent Black youngsters who may experience state-sanctioned trauma and violence (three-year-old children being expelled or suspended from preschool and six-year-old students being handcuffed by police). And, where failure to read on grade level by the end of third grade is criminalized with additional schooling that may not support graduation from high school. Why are children being treated as if adults, as if they are making an intentional and personal choice not to learn? Schools and classrooms should create contexts for learning by addressing the learning needs of the children in the room. Each child is an individual, who is unique and worthy of being provided high-quality literacy instruction. Whose interests are served by anti-Black grade reading retention laws or policies, and who benefits?

Without an acknowledgment of the legacy of systemic racism and accompanying statements and plans for reform, discourses in support of new state laws rely on the "reasonableness" of proposed changes to reading laws that may appear as value-neutral but are in fact embedded in racism. The language is used to preserve Whiteness within the laws and "signal" protection to people who have cultural, economic, and linguistic cache. Laws presented as race-free or race-neutral, but using language of "reasonableness," to appear objective and culture-free. Given the APA's statements and resolution, it is surprising that a closer examination of racial bias in standardized reading tests/assessments and laws, policies, and statutes is not under review. Besides, where are the histories acknowledging how scientific racism in literacy research has harmed Black students while simultaneously ignoring alternative findings in Black scholarship? Reading researchers and politicians have played the long game to dishonor, dismiss, and ignore all reading research contrary to the narrative they project, especially about Black people and Black literacy achievement. Moreover, they have established and enforced laws contrary to decades of reading research among Black students as well as the potential for substantive literacy improvement with the application of culturally, ethnically, linguistically, and racially informed instruction.

One would think there would be acknowledgments, admissions, and a chronicling of racist actions and extensive replacement of misinformed reading research used to inform federal, state, and local laws about standardized reading tests. Changes, however, focus on a singular approach to reading, school curriculum, and instruction as well as books and materials and how they are used. Some states permit in-class video surveillance of instructions and parental and community oversight of curricula that calls for placing an entire year's lesson plans online during the late spring for the following year.

Peter P. v. Compton Unified School District

Change, substantive radical change, must begin long before the student/teacher interactions. It begins when teachers understand the history of anti-Black racism and anti-Black literacy embedded within the United States and how structural racism worked to thwart human rights – including literacy – from Black people. A case in California, *Peter P. v. Compton Unified School District* (2015–2021), addressed schooling, beyond literacy, was decided on behalf of families who fought to address the trauma of racism experienced by students. Radhakrishnan (2021) reports:

> the suit was filed in Los Angeles by Public Counsel and Irell & Manella LLP in 2015 on behalf of a class of students and three teachers, seeking Compton Unified School District to incorporate proven practices that address the barriers to learning caused by trauma-in the same way public schools have adapted and evolved in past decades to help students who experience physical or other barriers to learning.
>
> *(para 3)*

The plaintiffs' counsel also contextualizes the concerns of the parents and students:

> Compton Unified School District serves students who are disproportionately affected by racism and poverty, and are therefore particularly likely to be affected by complex trauma, a condition in which someone is exposed to multiple traumatic events that can be interpersonal, invasive, and continue for a long period of time. *Unaddressed complex trauma can profoundly affect a young person's ability to learn, think, read, concentrate, and communicate, and social science has linked complex trauma with academic, behavior, and attendance challenges.*
>
> *(Radhakrishnan, 2021, para 6, emphasis added)*

Rosenbaum, director of Public Counsel's Opportunity Under Law Project, shared "because of the heroic work of the Compton School District and leading trauma experts in the nation, students and teachers will have assistance in their schools to help address the trauma attendant to racism, poverty, police abuse, and bullying" (Radhakrishnan, 2021, para 1).

Authoritarianism and Anti-Black Literacy in Florida

Florida's governor DeSantis signed HB 1213, effective July 1, 2020, that requires teaching about the Holocaust and consideration of how schools should provide instruction about the 1920 racial massacre (he referenced it as a riot) in Ocoee, FL. Given vigilante White mobs beat, burned, destroyed, and murdered innumerable Black people (1901 and 1920 Jacksonville fires; Perry (1922) and Rosewood (1923) massacres), it is unclear why the Ocoee massacre was selected and considered important but not required as part of the state-sanctioned curriculum.

Governor DeSantis and the Florida Board of Education, quickly adopted a narrow view of US history for public schools on January 13, 2021, when he endorsed Florida HB 241, the Florida Parents' Bill of Rights (signed into law on June 29, 2021). The bill required "each district school board to develop and adopt a policy to promote parental involvement in the public school system; providing requirements for such policy; defining the term 'instructional materials'" (p. 1). Importantly, Section 5, Section 1014.04, Florida Statutes, declares, "the right to direct the education and care of his or her minor child" and "the right to direct the upbringing and the moral or religious training of his or her minor child" (p. 4). Likewise, Section 6, Section 1014.05, Florida Statutes, proclaims parents' have a right to "learn about his or her minor child's course of study, including the source of any supplemental education materials" (p. 7). Under 1006.28(2)(a)2., parents have a right "to object to instructional materials and other materials used in the classroom. Such objections may be based on beliefs regarding morality, sex, and religion or the belief that such materials are harmful" (pp. 7–8). These ideas align with efforts by the Florida-based Moms for Liberty organization and are filled with disinformation about CRT and other concerns. The bill fails to acknowledge that CRT is not taught in schools, is not a means to valorize people of color, does not teach anti-Whiteness, and does not ask people to become unpatriotic. All such bills are written to address White discomfort and White fragility about discussions remotely related to race, racism, and inclusion. In support of the new bill, prior to it becoming law, DeSantis (2021) argues:

> We won't allow Florida tax dollars to be spent teaching kids to hate our country or to hate each other. We also have a responsibility to ensure that parents have the means to vindicate their rights when it comes to enforcing state standards. Finally, we must protect Florida workers against the hostile work environment that is created when large corporations force their employees to endure CRT-inspired "training" and indoctrination.
>
> *(para 2)*

He expresses an ill-conceived understanding of CRT and provides a way to prosecute those who break the law. The new Florida laws appear unconcerned about historical accuracy or truthfulness regarding the legacy of racism within the United States. The concerns that an accurate and truthful history of this nation will reveal the depth of White supremacy as well as the legal, psychological, and violent tactics used to maintain unearned White privilege, are not loss in their silence. Ironically, predominately White women are using their privilege to protest discussions of White privilege.

Some commentators claim DeSantis was following a national conservative attack on CRT, arguing in part CRT is an attempt to rewrite history. Goldberg (2021) counters by observing, conservatives were attempting to "neoliberalize racism: to reduce it to a matter of personal beliefs and interpersonal prejudice" (para 20). He continues, "on this view, the structures of society bear no responsibility, only individuals" (para 20). CRT is not the root of the problem for DeSantis and likeminded conservatives; their fear is that unabashed White privilege, supremacy, and nationalism will be challenged along with everyone who supports it. Crenshaw (2021) insightfully observes the focus of such state laws are the emotional and intellectual needs of White people: community members, parents, but especially students. The FL Citizens' Alliance, for example, sent a rallying Tweet:

> On Monday June 7th, Collier County Public Schools will be holding a special hearing to adopt K-5 English Language Arts textbooks that are full of Critical Race Theory (CRT) and its many tentacles (ex. "equity", "diversity", BLM, 1619 project, social emotional learning, etc.).
>
> *(Tweet Fl Citizens' Alliance, n.p.)*

The incendiary Tweet is filled with misinformation and illustrated the lack of understanding about CRT as well as language associated with equity, racism, and social justice. The organizers did not acknowledge Black students have been indoctrinated by White supremacy throughout the education system in the United States. On November 17, 2022, Chief US District Judge Mark E. Walker blocked Florida's so-called 'Stop W.O.K.E. Act' enforcement at public colleges and universities. There are likely to be appeals given Governor DeSantis re-election earlier in the month. As disturbing as the current CRT rhetorical crises is, it reminds us this tactic has been used throughout US history to demonize Black people "in the process of devaluing its image of black people, the general white population seems to have been socialized to blind itself to the horrors inflicted by white people" (Williams, 1987, p. 152).

Florida laws have continued to evolve as Solochek (2022) reports (HB 7, HB 1467, HB 1557; SB 1054) additional laws also affected public school students (see Copland, 2021) (please see Table 7.4). Given the governance structure and the Republican majority in their House/Senate, a new bill allegedly focused on "individual freedom" was introduced on January 13, 2021. It prohibited schools and workplaces from using instructional material to teach, among other things, a person's status as "privileged or oppressed is necessarily determined by his or her race, color, national origin, or sex" (Jones, 2022, para 5). Ironically, the language of the new laws demanded instruction promote "equality" – no individual or group is superior under US law. Solochek (2022) noted the majority of new education laws were written for students attending public schools as "the Florida Statutes chapter relating to district school board powers, a section from which charter schools are exempted" (para 5). Thus, under certain conditions, charter and private school students are permitted to learn about the nation's racist past.

TABLE 7.4 Florida Education Laws (2021–2022)

Common Name	Focus	Signed
Home Book Delivery for Elementary Students CS/SB 1372	Providing credits against oil and gas production taxes and sales taxes payable by direct pay permitholders, respectively, under the New Worlds Reading Initiative Tax Credit; providing a credit against the corporate income tax under the New Worlds Reading Initiative Tax Credit; establishing the New Worlds Reading Initiative under the Department of Education, etc. (https://www.myfloridahouse.gov/Sections/Bills/billsdetail.aspx?BillId=72182&)	April 6, 2021
Financial Literacy Bill SB1054	this act as the "Dorothy L. Hukill Financial Literacy Act"; revising the requirements regarding financial literacy for the Next Generation Sunshine State Standards; revising the required credits for a standard high school diploma to include one-half credit of instruction in personal financial literacy and money management and seven and one-half, rather than eight, credits in electives; modifying the requirements for the award of a standard high school diploma for Academically Challenging Curriculum to Enhance Learning options, etc. (https://www.flsenate.gov/Session/Bill/2022/1054)	March 22, 2022
Curriculum Transparency Bill CS/HB 1467	K-12 Education; Establishing term limits for school board members; deleting a requirement that district school boards maintain a specified list on their websites; requiring certain meetings relating to instructional materials to be noticed and open to the public; revising district school board requirements for the selection and adoption of certain materials, etc. (https://www.flsenate.gov/Session/Bill/2022/1467)	March 25, 2022

(Continued)

TABLE 7.4 (Continued)

Common Name	Focus	Signed
Parental Rights in Education CS/CS/ HB 1557	Requires district school boards to adopt procedures that comport with certain provisions of law for notifying student's parent of specified information; requires such procedures to reinforce fundamental right of parents to make decisions regarding upbringing & control of their children; prohibits school district from adopting procedures or student support forms that prohibit school district personnel from notifying parent about specified information or that encourage student to withhold from parent such information; prohibits school district personnel from discouraging or prohibiting parental notification & involvement in critical decisions affecting student's mental, emotional, or physical well-being; prohibits classroom discussion about sexual orientation or gender identity in certain grade levels; requires school districts to notify parents of healthcare services; authorizes parent to bring action against school district to obtain declaratory judgment; provides for additional award of injunctive relief, damages, & reasonable attorney fees & court costs to certain parents. (https://www.flsenate.gov/Session/ Bill/2022/1557)	March 28, 2022
Individual Freedom CS/HB 7	Providing that subjecting any individual, as a condition of employment, membership, certification, licensing, credentialing, or passing an examination, to training, instruction, or any other required activity that espouses, promotes, advances, inculcates, or compels such individual to believe specified concepts constitutes discrimination based on	April 22, 2022

(*Continued*)

TABLE 7.4 (Continued)

Common Name	Focus	Signed
	race, color, sex, or national origin; revising the requirements for required instruction on health education; prohibiting instructional materials reviewers from recommending instructional materials that contain any matter that contradicts certain principles, etc." (https://www.myfloridahouse.gov/Sections/Bills/billsdetail.aspx?BillId=76553)	

A proposed amendment to teach US history: 6A-1.094124 Required Instruction Planning and Reporting, in Section 1003.42(2), F.S. revealed:

> (b) Instruction on the required topics must be factual and objective, and may not suppress or distort significant historical events, such as the Holocaust, slavery, the Civil War and Reconstruction, the Civil Rights movement and the contributions of women, African American and Hispanic people to our country as already provided in section 1003.42 of Florida Statutes. Examples of theories that distort historical events and are inconsistent with State Board approved standards include the denial or minimization of the Holocaust and the teaching of "critical race theory," meaning the theory that racism is not merely a product of prejudice, but that racism is embedded in American society and its legal systems to uphold the supremacy of white persons. Instruction may not utilize material from the *1619 Project* and may not define American history as something other than the creation of a new nation based largely on universal principles stated in the Declaration of Independence.

Instruction must include the US Constitution, the Bill of Rights, and subsequent amendments.

As such, HB 7 appeared to revise and restate ideas from earlier laws, as if in response to Manhattan Institute's admonishments, to provide narrow and restrictive definitions. Ceballos, Brugal, and Solochek (2022) tracked Florida's ever-evolving public school curriculum, with a focus on civics and aligned with the passage of HB7, the Individual Freedom Act. In summer sessions of the Civics Literacy Excellence Initiative, teachers participated in a short course with pay (a paid longer extended course was also an option). Many teachers voiced concerns about the approach, naming it a Christian fundamentalist indoctrination and the inaccurate historical discussions. Among the texts discussed, two former presidents, Washington and Jefferson, it is alleged, without support, sought to outlaw enslavement. However, there is no mention of them as enslavers and as men who profited from the enslavement of Black people.

Two additional bills may lead to further restrictions of education: the Curriculum Transparency Bill (CS/HB 1467: K-12 Education), allowed parents an oversight of educator's curriculum decisions and whitewashing of education, and the Financial Literacy Act, also known as the CS/SB 114: High School Graduation Requirements/Dorothy L. Hukill Financial Literacy Act, now a requirement for graduation and may also be a bellwether of additional retention.

The history and resources likely to improve reading engagement among students of color are being banned, under state laws (Sleeter & Zavala, 2020). Numerous studies have shown asset-based approaches (culturally relevant pedagogy/teaching, culturally responsive teaching, and culturally sustaining pedagogies) improve the academic achievement of Black students, however, the exclusion of these approaches denies every student the opportunity to learn about contributions to our nation made by people of color.

Florida Revamps Standardized Reading Assessment

On March 15, 2022, Governor Ron DeSantis signed into law CS/SB 1048: Student Assessments to replace the state's standardized program, *Next Generation Sunshine State Standards*. The new law amended as a single end-of-year statewide assessment in English language arts and mathematics, replaced by three tests per year, or "progress monitoring" assessments (FL SB 1048) to occur at the beginning, middle, and end of the school year, beginning in 2022–2023. Both laws are much more biting and painful in practice and continue the legal and political anti-Black literacy campaign, in part because the laws are undergirded by scientific racism. As the APA (2021a) apology admits the calls for scientific and evidence-based research in support of education writ large, here in reading, as founded on the ideology of White superiority and the testing industry has been built to sustain it. The legislation alleges progress monitoring of student academic performance in grades 3–9 permits more timely interventions for students who need additional learning supports. An early childhood version of progress monitoring is included in the law for students who participated in VPK – grade 3. The final progress monitoring assessment, also known as the comprehensive end-of-year progress monitoring assessment, merely renamed the annual standardized state assessment. Under section 5, Reading Deficiency and Parental Notification, the law states:

> Any student in kindergarten through grade 3 who exhibits a substantial deficiency in reading based upon screening, diagnostic, progress monitoring, or assessment data; statewide assessments; or teacher observations

must be provided intensive, explicit, systematic, and multisensory reading interventions immediately following the identification of the reading
deficiency.

(p. 23)

Importantly, schools need not wait until the end of the year assessment, as they
can provide reading interventions sooner if deemed necessary. For example, for
students who are identified as dyslexic:

> evidence-based interventions for a student whose parent submits docu-
> mentation from a professional licensed under chapter 490 which demon-
> strates that the student has been diagnosed with dyslexia.

(p. 23)

Grade promotion of third graders, a combination of the first two progress
monitoring assessments, or use of the final assessment, can be used to promote
students to grade 4. The results made possible additional support for third-grade
students reading at or above level or acceleration for select students. Moreover,
reading on grade level by the end of third grade portion of the law remained,
except for "good cause" exemptions. Students with "good cause" exemptions
must receive intensive reading interventions. The research focusing on "good
causes exemptions" reveals that exemptions are extended more often to White
students, and students identified as dyslexic are under-reported. The discourse
surrounding good cause exemptions begs the questions (1) for whom are the
exemptions "good" and (2) for whom is the "cause" applicable, given Florida
re-classified dyslexia?

Students in VPK who exhibit early reading deficiencies may be referred for
reading interventions prior to kindergarten. Once in kindergarten, students can
be identified for reading interventions based on their initial (beginning of the
year) progress-monitoring assessment as well as identified as exhibiting "characteristics of dyslexia or having other learning disorders" (p. 29). In short, students could be identified as needing reading interventions, and perhaps special
education, within the first few months of attending kindergarten, perhaps as
a five-year-old. The notion of progress monitoring or the tracking of student
learning over time on the surface appears more benevolent than a one-time,
end-of-the-year test could potentially change the life of a five-year-old. Progress
monitoring, however, provides numerous opportunities for students and par-
ents/guardians to fall through the cracks of a new system. There is far too much
wiggle room and subjectivity, and there is no monitoring of teachers or administrators. Who monitors implicit racial bias or macro/microaggressions toward
Black students (culture, language, ways of knowing) among school personnel?
There is the potential for abuse, as the new laws and policies extend systemic

racism through replication of an ideology of White supremacy and scientific racism. The opportunities for misinterpretations of the law come at the expense of the most vulnerable students in Florida schools, Black students and students who live in poverty. The new laws, like their predecessors, exist to delimit literacy access and control Black minds and bodies. Given the laws extend into VPK and kindergarten, some young Black students are unknowingly fodder for an inequitable and unjust educational system:

> Whites, it must frankly be said, are not putting in a similar mass effort to reeducate themselves out of their racial ignorance. It is an aspect of their sense of superiority that the white people of America believe they have so little to learn. The reality of substantial investment to assist Negroes into the twentieth century, adjusting to Negro neighbors and genuine school integration, is still a nightmare for all too many white Americans...These are the deepest causes for contemporary abrasions between the races. Loose and easy language about equality, resonant resolutions about brotherhood fall pleasantly on the ear, but for the Negro there is a credibility gap he cannot overlook. He remembers that with each modest advance the white population promptly raises the argument that the Negro has come far enough. Each step forward accents an ever-present tendency to backlash.
>
> *(Martin Luther King, Jr., 1967, p. 10)*

Parents of potential VPK students received a letter outlining the goals of VPK, an explanation of the new state assessments, and a parental guide to support student learning (*First Teacher: A Parent's Guide to Growing and Learning 4-Year-Olds*). The assessment uses a computer program that reads to students, poses questions, and depending on their responses either decreases or increases difficulty. The guidebook includes multiple subjects as well as emotional, physical, and social benchmarks. Ideally, young children who attend VPK will be better prepared for kindergarten instruction in reading and math. The children who are most vulnerable are least likely to have an enhanced VPK program, are familiar with schooling, or have access and comfortability with computers. It is not clear how the VPK programs are monitored, reviewed, or evaluated. As such, young children will be screened and progress monitoring will occur as part of early literacy and math programs per s. 1002.67(1)(a), F.S. and s. 1002.68, F.S., respectively. When you consider that early reading assessments are primarily oral, it is imperative to ask what role does raciolinguisitics (Rosa & Flores, 2015) play in literacy assessments (oral reading fluency assessments, identification and use phonemes and phonics). Why are the listeners held harmless for their inability to hear Black readers? What have literacy instructors, especially those working with young children, been taught about African American language?

Given the swiftly shifting demographics of students in public schools as more culturally, ethnically, linguistically, and racially diverse than in the past, how does anti-CRT laws, banning books by minoritized authors, early RTI/MTSS interventions, and sanctioning of SoR, engage all readers and construct equitable assessments reflecting inclusivity? New laws and school policies replicate how White supremacist ideology and actions use "strategies to remove involvement in and culpability for systems of domination" (Tuck & Yang, 2012, p. 9). These actions include:

(1) establishing state anti-CRT laws to forbid discussions of concerns of race and diminish culturally, ethnically, linguistically, and racially diversity concerns;

(2) establishing state laws and school district requirements to be learn, train, and use SoR to teach reading thus re-instantiating a White-centric view of reading;

(3) retain ties with the testing industry to use scientifically racist tests as measures of reading performance.

As more BIPOC become the majority population in public schools, there are aggressive efforts to discredit and destroy public education in support of privatizing and monetizing (charter schools) education by elites. Greene (2019), for instance, reports that former US Secretary of Education, DeVos, "founded and funded, American Federation for Children, $2.4 billion was put into … voucher programs in the US, and $956 million of that was spent in Florida…ranked only behind California, Texas and Arizona for total number of charter schools" (para 2). Contemporary anti-Black literacy laws continue to dismiss the humanity of Black people and wrestle with sharing the power of literacy, through the mischaracterization of Black people's culture, humanity, intelligence, language, and racial oppression. Beginning this process among the youngest Black students is heartbreakingly inhumane.

Conclusion

President Biden in his first few days in office issued a series of executive orders including one addressing systemic racism and pushing toward equity for all Americans. His actions, as well as a press conference held by his Domestic Policy Advisor, Susan Rice, are meant to reassure the public of the seriousness of his actions, as well as to make clear to all Americans the current administration will redress inequalities in all areas of life, including education. They center their actions, thoughts, and work in racial equity. Moreover, they emphasize that as a nation we will not tolerate xenophobia toward Asian American and Pacific Islanders, people of the Jewish faith, or Native Americans. Seeking educational equity in higher education, and beyond education in politics, society, and the workforce, takes intentional and sustained effort. Bensimon (2018) provides a definition of *equity* and its role in higher education. She proffered:

equity has a very strong and distinct meaning. It is rooted in achieving racial proportionality in all educational outcomes and in critically assessing whiteness at the institutional and practice levels. It is about acknowledging and addressing racism in our educational systems.

(p. 98)

President Biden (2021) also issued Executive Order 13985, Advancing Racial Equity and Support for Underserved Communities Through the Federal Government, to address the nation's systemic racism and to build toward equity for all people. It is not clear if this EO has changed the many federal government agencies influence reading issues. High-stakes testing and teaching to the reading curriculum are not transformative change, and as currently conceptualized and constructed, instantiate Whiteness.

Under the EO all governmental agencies are expected to review their policies. NAEP, for instance, although tasked with reframing a national reading assessment, a charge that began before the EO, has experienced resistance and retrenchment efforts that forestall addressing forthrightly expressed concerns of reading experts' (Forzani et al., 2022) attempts to create future NAEP reading assessments that are culturally and linguistically more equitable by abandoning initial announcements to address sociocultural foci in reading assessments and revising the use of technology to help readers fill in background knowledge. The forthcoming NAEP Reading Framework (2023) reflects an over-reliance on ideologies of White supremacy embedded in coded language to obscure attempts to retain the illusion of White intellectual superiority by drawing conservative public commentaries about reading, standardization, and testing as well as selective whitewashed disciplinary knowledge (Forzani et al., 2022, pp. 25–28). Not surprisingly, there is no acknowledgment of the APA statements and chronology of racist ideologies and actions, nor the complicity of reading researchers, the dearth of Black achievement and Black scholarship informing NAEP assessments, and reproduction of anti-Black literacy assessments that have not proven to improve Black literacy performance, thus causing harm to some Black students. Power elites in federal government agencies, like CCSSO, NCES, NCIL, NCR, NGA, NSGSB, IES, continue to draw on White supremacy and scientific racism in shaping grants and framing standardized tests, some out of ignorance, others out of self-interest. Other federal adjacent agencies and nonprofit organizations, like ACEF, CB, and ECS, remain mute with regard to APA's apology, chronology, and resolution, as they continue to suggest their stance is acultural, evidence-based, and objective. Standardized reading tests used by most states are based on NAEP, and states also have been strategically silent about issues of equity and constructing equitable reading assessments.

If Black Lives Matter, how is reading research addressing and improving reading achievement among Black students? Too often, reading achievement among Black children is presented as an additive task that will require "additional research." For over a century, the additional research has *not* been the focus of research funding or the abysmal read by the end of third-grade laws. Black parents/caregivers do not send their children to school to fail, or to be treated as failures, and their children "cannot be taught by anyone whose demand, essentially, is that the child repudiate his experience and all that gives him sustenance, and enter into a limbo in which he will no longer be black" (Baldwin (1997, p. 6). How are states and school districts responding? Why is there little outrage – where is the recognition of the long game – to keep a ready Black source of cheap labor? Who will speak for innocent Black children who enter school hopeful to become literate in a system structured for them to fail and poised to blame them for failing to read at grade level by the end of grade 3? Would these circumstances be different if the students most likely to be retained were White – would the narrative be 'America's children are failing to read?' Given the history of reading reforms, the outcome of anti-Black literacy laws and policies will find harm done to a disproportionate percentage of Black students, as "often there's people from backgrounds of privilege who become lawyers, or become politicians and make the law, but it's the poorest people in our societies who disproportionately feel the impact of the law" (McLean quoted in Cooper, 2020). Former US Secretary of Education, William Bennet (1995), quipped, "if this were happening to White kids it would end tomorrow" (n. p.). Any history narrative about literacy that fails to offer an accurate and truthful account of racism in the United States is an attempt to rewrite history.

AFTERWORD

An earlier draft of this book began to crystalize in the summer of 2021, after the murders of several Black people (Ahmaud Arbery, Sandra Bland, Carlos Carson, Angelo Crooms, George Floyd, Casey Goodsen, Atatiana Jefferson, Tony McCade, Elijah McClain, Breonna Taylor, and Sincere Pierce, among others unaccounted) "we are living through a very dangerous time" (Baldwin, 1963, p. 1). As noted in this book, unprovoked murders of Black people were not unknown to occur in the United States, nor were news reports that sought to characterize Black peoples' lives by drawing on education/school records to paint them as troubled, if not criminal, youth. As well, some reports drew untethered stereotypical connections to their educational attainments, occupations, or presumed intelligence. M. Alexander (2012) argues this is how White supremacy functions to envisage and hold accountable

> black youth as black criminals … is essential to the functioning of mass incarceration as a racial caste system. For the system to succeed – that is, for it to achieve the political goals black people must be labeled criminals before they are formally subject to control. The criminal label is essential, for forms of explicit racial exclusion are not only prohibited but widely condemned.
>
> *(p. 200)*

What was new was the actions, in many cases caught on video, of law enforcement. The collective murders of Black people fueled a global backlash as protestors insisted that Black Lives Matter (BLM). Garza, Cullors, and Tometi (2013) created the movement in acknowledgment and recognition of "the precarious nature of Black lives in the United States … [where Black people] face special

DOI: 10.4324/9781003296188-9

challenges that must all be attended to in order for all Black people to attain equality in the United States and in order for the United States to truly say it is an egalitarian and free society" (Bunyasi & Smith, 2019, pp. 1–2). The guide-book by Bunyasi and Smith clarifies that it is "important to address ideological and structural systems of contemporary American racism … until Black lives begin to matter, the United States of America will never be a liberal, egalitarian democracy" (p. 2). BLM is often succinctly expressed as "all lives will not mat-ter until Black Lives Matter." Global support for BLM galvanized calls to address racial inequity and systemic racism in education, government, institutions, poli-tics, and society. The global support for BLM – demanding the world address anti-Black racism and seeking racial equity in all aspects of life - although largely performative – sent shock waves and heightened fears among advocates of White supremacy fearful of losing control and power over Black bodies and minds. National support for BLM began to acknowledge the history of systemic racism within the United States as well as how laws and the judicial system functioned to criminalize Black people.

Businesses, colleges and universities, companies, corporations, newspapers, professional organizations, school boards, and school districts posted announce-ments in support of BLM – kind and welcoming words of support for Black people, acknowledgment of a US history of racial inequity and injustice – and descriptions of a commitment to equity, diversity, inclusion, and racial and social justice. Some entities pledged to address systemic racism within their realm of influence, for example, the American Academy of Pediatrics, the American Medical Association, the American Psychological Association, and the Educational Testing Services as most – at some level – admitted their racist foundations and the perpetuation of racism. Others acted as several prestigious universities dropped their dependence on college admission exams, ACT and SAT, or made them optional. And literacy organizations (the National Council of Teachers of English, the International Literacy Association, and the Literacy Research Association) joined the cacophony of voices and issued statements in support of diversity, equity, and inclusion. Despite what appeared to be commit-ments to change, there has been little substantive change.

The combined global and national support for BLM also caused a reaction-ary movement. Crenshaw (2021) "racism, reform, and retrenchment" (para. 15) occur historically when racism is identified, reforms are suggested, before retrenchment begins. Once racism is identified, reforms are planned, but remain unrealized as White resentment emerges. The cycle of identifying racism, reform, and retrenchment is reflective of the national ethos – to mask the racist actions, beliefs, experiences, and laws of the past. Attacks on BLM, and all discussions demythologizing White domination, power, superiority, and the maintenance of systemic racism under US laws, are rooted in anti-Black racial resentment.

In education and the politics of education, redoubled efforts have been undertaken to install additional oversights and standardization of curriculum and assessments, seeking to sanitize the curriculum and insisting students regurgitate a singular view of US history that valorizes Whiteness, thereby indoctrinating all students to believe untruths glorifying the actions, beliefs, and values of White people, without mentioning how Black people (and other people of color) were abducted, abused, beaten, burned, disenfranchised, displaced, killed, lynched, raped, and starved. As well, there are attempts to wrest the true aggrievements of Black Lives under centuries of White supremacy and replace them with the pretense of aggrievement and projections about the psyches of White children. These projected fears center on the urgent need to protect the emotional and psychological well-being of White children and grandchildren from discussing, hearing, learning, and reading an accurate history of systemic racism in the United States, from the horrific – unspeakable – traumas of Black enslavement and the unearned and relished advantages of White privilege. Seemingly innocent requests have been heard and attended to as evidenced by new education laws throughout the nation, in addition to bull-horn pronouncements that reignited White fears of race-mixing, replacement theories, and the so-called 14 words: "We must secure the existence of our people and a future for white children." These efforts are reminiscent of the logic used in the 1700s to create anti-Black literacy laws, as White people feared for their lives as Black people rebelled against chattel enslavement. As a result, state and school local districts have ramped up efforts to recenter Whiteness in the curriculum and assessments.

Contemporaneous Anti-Black Literacy Laws

The history of anti-Black literacy reveals a throughline of White supremacy and anti-Black racism, demonstrated by deliberate efforts to demonize and vilify Black people to maintain economic and political power; preserve White privilege, structural inequality; and supremacy. Any history of literacy that fails to include an accurate and truthful account of the role of anti-Black racism and anti-Black literacy in the United States

> naturalizes and dehistoricizes difference, mistaking what is historical and cultural for what is natural, biological, and genetic. The moment the signifier black is torn from its historical, cultural, and political embedding and lodged into a biologically constituted racial category, we valorize, by inversion, the very ground of racism we're trying to deconstruct.
>
> *(Hall, 1993, p. 111)*

Such historical accounts are an attempt to rewrite history. Ignoring and obfuscating the racist history of reading access, assessment, funding, and research does not absolve stakeholders from their responsibility to address inequities in reading research and assessment. When anti-Black literacy laws were abolished as legal barriers, the ideology of White supremacy fueled scientific racism (eugenics, individualism, inheritability of intelligence, and meritocracy) and created additional barriers: admission tests, merit awards, and standardized test performance that were codified into novel anti-Black literacy laws:

- the ideology of White supremacy is foundational to anti-literacy laws,
- anti-literacy laws are anti-Black literacy laws,
- support of anti-Black literacy laws is a response to White people's fear of Black resistance and intellectual acumen,
- anti-Black literacy laws and policies are created to justify barriers to literacy and Black advancement,
- anti-Black literacy laws are used, deliberately and strategically, to control Black people's economic, educational, and intellectual reach,
- anti-Black literacy laws reflect the material danger of White supremacy and are a threat to Black economic and educational advancement,
- an ideology of White supremacy foments anti-Black literacy laws and is ever-evolving.

Several questions emerge from the history of anti-Black racism and literacy: Why would a nation knowingly apply scientifically racist reading research and permit laws to be enacted that harm innocent Black children and criminalize them for not learning to read? Why would a nation continue to fund reading research conceptually grounded in scientific racism yet expect improved reading performance among Black students while holding them responsible for low reading performance? Who is harmed by anti-Black literacy laws that restrict Black students from equal access to culturally informed and high-quality literacy instruction, and why?

Historically, the process derives from an effective and thinly veiled pattern of intentionally enacting legal barriers of anti-Black racism and anti-Black literacy: reading retention laws, for instance, along with a host of unacknowledged and ever-evolving anti-Black literacy campaigns (federally funded reading/literacy grants, a single approach to reading), frame rhetorical narratives justifying changes to reading approaches, assessments, curriculums, initiatives, and programs allegedly to help, improve, intervene, monitor, and support Black reading achievement. Recent state laws reflect such anti-Black literacy campaigns:

(1) prohibiting asset-based, culturally based, ethnic, and equity-based pedagogical approaches to learning and literacy, although many have proven to be effective approaches among Black learners,
(2) requiring SoR training (pre-service and in-service teachers and school personnel), although its use among Black students has not proven to significantly improve reading achievement,

(3) encouraging interventions (RTI/MTSS) albeit they have not improved literacy achievement among Black students and are linked to increase Black students identified as SLD and placed in special education;

(4) supporting progress monitoring (a feature of RTI/MTSS), which increases the use of formal and informal testing (grounded in scientific racism), relies heavily on teacher recommendations while failing to address or identify implicit racial bias among teachers/administrators; and

(5) use of RTI/MTSS to identify behavioral concerns leading to increased labeling, referrals, and surveillance, as well as incarceration of Black students as young as six

To be clear, the current ideological assumptions underpinning reading will not be sufficient to move us forward; the concepts and definitions of reading that have worked for some but not for others are not sufficient to move everyone forward; no benevolence, magic, or mathematical formula is sufficient to address racism; and those in positions of power who made the current reading status possible – intentionally or not – should not be tasked to move the field forward.

What might new reading laws look like, if instead of placing the legal weight of accountability, performance, and responsibility on young Black children for failing to read on grade level by the end of grade 3, the legal accountability, performance, and responsibility were aimed at book and curriculum publishers, politicians, reading researchers, teachers, and state and local administrators? As new state literacy/reading policies shift for teachers and students, despite rhetoric to the contrary, they do not shift in favor of Black students. Although narrative discourse among state legislators and school administers use glowing words about "all students," they are disregarding research findings that clearly demonstrates students who are Black as well as students who are low income are most often affected by state reading retention policies and laws, static federally funded reading grants, as well as culturally and linguistically misinformed reading approaches.

A singular reading crisis exists: an ideology of White supremacy that determines when and where literacy is taught, to whom, and under what conditions (curriculum, instructional approach, materials, and assessments). The crisis exposes individual and institutional efforts to forestall Black literacy; federal, state, and local laws are enacted to eviscerate Black advancement through literacy; and attempts are made to derail Black economic, educational, and political advancement. Educators, politicians, and reading researchers often distract attention away from racial inequity and the racist roots of standardized reading assessments by proposing a panacea or novel approach to reading that promises to produce improved performance on standardized reading assessments for low-performing Black students: No approach grounded in White supremacy will magically autocorrect centuries of anti-Black racism and anti-Black literacy.

The narratives and research attending contemporary anti–Black literacy laws intentionally project change and suggest improved outcomes although the opposite is more likely. Academics, business leaders, corporate executives, educators, politicians, and reading researchers continue to endorse the status quo: White supremacist ideological positioning of reading research, mischaracterization of Black people, and discourses used to editorialize and catastrophize the languages, literacies, and lives of Black people. Reading approaches, assessments, curricula, initiatives, and interventions embracing the "fix-them" motif of White supremacy hold Black students responsible for misperceptions about languages, lives, and literacies, with absolution from harm enacted in the lives of Black students.

Given what is known about the emotional and psychological effects of internalized racial oppression and young children unconsciously (Clark & Clark, 1950; Davis 2005), state laws choose to ignore the effect on the lives of Black students have made a strategic and hurtful choice. The framers of the new state laws have disingenuously argued all people will be treated fair, and no one will be made to feel inferior, without explaining how this can be accomplished in a society based on racism. The new state literacy laws suggest otherwise: Black students' literacy does not matter. The American Psychology Association (2021) admitted the organization's past support of scientific racism and White supremacy, presented a detailed chronology of its past racist actions, and proposed steps to ameliorate systemic racism. APA acknowledges their history of dismissive actions toward Black achievement and Black scholarship, actions taken in their self-interest, harmed people of color, and actions to be taken moving forward. The organization also presents a historic chronology and guidelines to dismantle racism in the field. Many of the historic racist actions or failures to act, and people within psychology and psychological testing – including reading research and reading assessments – have been discussed herein. Numerous Supreme Court cases ruling in support of Black children's education and literacy make specific references to their psychological well-being. The US Department of Health & Human Services defines *historical trauma* and recognizes

> multigenerational trauma experienced by a specific cultural, racial or ethnic group. It is related to major events that oppressed a particular group of people because of their status as oppressed, such as slavery, the Holocaust, forced migration, and the violent colonization of Native Americans. While many in such a group will experience no effects of the historical trauma, others may experience poor overall physical and behavioral health, including low self-esteem, depression, self-destructive behavior, marked propensity for violent or aggressive behavior, substance misuse and addiction, and high rates of suicide and cardiovascular disease. … Compounding this familial or intergenerational trauma, historical trauma often involves the additional challenge of a damaged cultural identity.
>
> *(Sotero, 2006)*

Given the research findings, why are states rushing to codify laws that are likely to induce emotional harm among Black students, instead of preventing anti-Black literacy trauma? There are literacy approaches successful with Black students; why are they not adopted, adapted, and implemented to improve Black students academic and literacy achievement?

New anti-Black literacy state laws do not pretend to protect Black students from psychological harm, yet new literacy requirements create immeasurable opportunities for emotional and psychological harm. To restate, innocent, vulnerable, Black children as young as three years old are being profiled, and young children can be retained in kindergarten under progress monitoring and teacher recommendations, as they are simultaneously indoctrinated into Whiteness and criminalized through retention. These actions are indefensible: state curriculum guidelines banning books by Black authors, preventing discussions of racism, promoting universalism/Whiteness, and whitewashing US history provide opportunities for students to internalize racial oppression

> If you can control a man's thinking, you don't have to worry about his actions. If you can determine what a man thinks, you do not have to worry about what he will do. If you can make a man believe that he is inferior, you don't have to compel him to seek an inferior status, for he will seek it for himself. If you make a man think that he is justly an outcast, you don't have to order him to the back door, he will go without being told; and if there is no back door, his very nature will demand one.
>
> *(Woodson, 1933, p. xiii)*

Not a single professional literacy/reading organization has acknowledged the racist history of reading research nor announced plans to dismantle anti-Black racism and anti-Black literacy. Their collective and strategic silence supports by fiat the disinformation about Black literacy underway and assures a way to retain the power to conceptualize, define, and measure reading and reading research. Silence is complicity, and subversion reveals a lack of effort help to sustain anti-Black literacy.

Now is the time to reconceptualize how reading is defined, end efforts that obfuscate systemic racism, and demand institutional change. Reading research must address its rootedness within scientific racism, and embrace the moral obligation to correct history, conceptualize and define reading without racial bias inclusive of cultures/ethnicities/races and languages, and conduct research without bias. These steps will require intense unlearning of the past, forsaking the anti-Black racist theoretical and methodological foundations of reading (approaches, assessments, curricula, materials, and standardized reading tests), investment in reading research that is conceptualized and conducted without anti-Black racial bias. Political activism is needed to write inclusive literacy laws that include and embrace Black epistemology and scholarship among Black children (asset, culturally, linguistically and racially based).

The Future Is Now

As this complex history of reading/literacy among Black people in the United States reveals, literacy represents more than the ability to read and write, because interwoven are cultural, linguistic, political, racial, and social factors that have influenced federal, state, and local anti-Black literacy laws. We can only imagine what Black literacy achievement would look like if: (1) the humanity of Black students is acknowledged; (2) Black students are taught in ways that value their cultures, languages, literacies, race, and ways of knowing; and (3) literacy assessments are conceived, constructed, and measured in ways that are inclusive of Black culture, epistemology, history, language, and literature.

Honest concern about the reading prowess of Black readers starts with knowing who Black readers are and centering on their strengths. It is morally corrupt to request additional funding from the federal government and philanthropic groups to conduct similar research studies, knowing that there will be similar findings. Although the history of reading, reading assessment, and reading research began in psychology and likewise sought to anchor itself to science, there have been no clear admissions of its past and contemporary racist moorings by institutions, organizations, or politicians. The silence is strategic as it appears to "hold harmless" advocates and supporters of the past and current evidence-based and scientifically based concepts, definitions, strategies, and procedures. And it permits advocates and supporters of White supremacy to proceed without seeking to persuade corporate leaders, educators, and politicians, otherwise. Given the conceptual and ideological foundations of research, advocates are reticent to call it into question, knowing the foundation in scientific racism, the immorality of the laws it frames, and the disparate impact on Black literacy learners. To admit that a history of racism exists implies an awareness of the racist past, the need to eliminate it, as well as the responsibility to create a new more racially equitable and just agenda. Governor Gretchen Whitmer, for example, in 2023, signed Senate Bill 0012, repealing Michigan's Read by Grade Three law.

I believe as a nation and field of inquiry, we have the capacity to make real, significant, life-altering change in how reading is conceptualized, defined, and assessed for Black readers. We can prevent failures by reconceptualizing reading, deprioritizing Whiteness, and enacting and enforcing federal and state literacy laws that value racial equity. The decision to create, design, administer, and score more equitable reading/literacy assessments is not a hard choice, although it is an ethical and moral choice. So, too, are decisions to assess, conceptualize, define, and instruct reading differently and inclusively – let us choose wisely.

Black literacy is wealth, intergenerational knowledge, and beliefs that have incalculable value. Literacy always has been a source of freedom, liberation, and power – cherished as if currency among Black people as we share our creativity, knowledge, imagination, independence, and intellect with the world.

APPENDIX A

Missouri (1847): An Act Respecting Slaves, Free Negroes, and Mulattoes

NEGROES AND MULATTOES.

AN ACT respecting slaves, free negroes and mulattoes.

§ 1. Negroes or mulattoes not to be taught to read or write.
2. Where preacher is negro or mullato; certain officers to be present at service.
3. Certain specified meetings unlawful; how suppressed.

§ 4. No free negro or mulatto to emigrate to this State.
5. Punishment for violation of this act.
6. Free negroes and mulatoes under twenty-one years; for certain causes, not to be bound out in this State.

Be it enacted by the General Assembly of the State of Missouri, as follows:

§ 1. No person shall keep or teach any school for the instruction of negroes or mulattoes, in reading or writing, in this State.

NEGROES AND MULATTOES.

§ 2. No meeting or assemblage of negroes or mulattoes, for the purpose of religious worship, or preaching, shall be held or permitted where the services are performed or conducted by negroes or mulattoes, unless some sheriff, constable, marshal, police officer, or justice of the peace, shall be present during all the time of such meeting or assemblage, in order to prevent all seditious speeches, and disorderly and unlawful conduct of every kind.

§ 3. All meeting of negroes or mulattoes, for the purposes mentioned in the two preceding sections, shall be considered unlawful assemblages, and shall be suppressed by sheriffs, constables, and other public officers.

§ 4. No free negro or mulatto shall, under any pretext, emigrate to this State, from any other State or territory.

§ 5. If any person shall violate the provisions of this act, he shall, for every such offence, be indicted and punished by fine not exceeding five hundred dollars, or by imprisonment not exceeding six months, or by both such fine and imprisonment.

§ 6. Free negroes and mulattoes who are under the age of twenty-one years, and who would not be entitled to receive from the county court a license to remain in this State, if they were twenty-one years old, shall not be bound out as apprentices in this State.

Approved February 16, 1847.

APPENDIX B

Dred Scott v. Sandford, 60 US 393 - Supreme Court 1857 (Excerpt)

60 US 393 (____)

19 How. 393

DRED SCOTT, PLAINTIFF IN ERROR, v. JOHN F.A.
SANDFORD.

Supreme Court of United States.

It was now argued by Mr. Blair and Mr. G.F. Curtis for the plaintiff in error, and
by Mr. Geyer and Mr. Johnson for the defendant in error.

Mr. Chief Justice TANEY delivered the opinion of the court.

This case has been twice argued. After the argument at the last term, differences of opinion were found to exist among the members of the court;
and as the questions in controversy are of the highest importance, and the
court was at that time much pressed by the ordinary business of the term, it
was deemed advisable to continue the case, and direct a re-argument on some
of the points, in order that we might have an opportunity of giving to the
whole subject a more deliberate consideration. It has accordingly been again
argued by counsel, and considered by the court; and I now proceed to deliver
its opinion.

There are two leading questions presented by the record:

1. Had the Circuit Court of the United States jurisdiction to hear and deter-
    mine the case between these parties? And
2. If it had jurisdiction, is the judgment it has given erroneous or not?

The plaintiff in error, who was also the plaintiff in the court below, was, with his
wife and children, held as slaves by the defendant, in the State of Missouri; and

he brought this action in the Circuit Court of the United States for that district, to assert the title of himself and his family to freedom.

The declaration is in the form usually adopted in that State to try questions of this description, and contains the averment necessary to give the court jurisdiction; that he and the defendant are citizens of different States; that is, that he is a citizen of Missouri, and the defendant a citizen of New York.

The defendant pleaded in abatement to the jurisdiction of the court, that the plaintiff was not a citizen of the State of Missouri, as alleged in his declaration, being a negro of African descent, whose ancestors were of pure African blood, and who were brought into this country and sold as slaves.

To this plea the plaintiff demurred, and the defendant joined in demurrer. The court overruled the plea, and gave judgment that the defendant should answer over. And he thereupon put in sundry pleas in bar, upon which issues were joined; and at the trial the verdict and judgment were in his favor. Whereupon the plaintiff brought this writ of error.

Before we speak of the pleas in bar, it will be proper to dispose of the questions which have arisen on the plea in abatement.

That plea denies the right of the plaintiff to sue in a court of the United States, for the reasons therein stated.

If the question raised by it is legally before us, and the court should be of opinion that the facts stated in it disqualify the plaintiff from becoming a citizen, in the sense in which that word is used in the Constitution of the United States, then the judgment of the Circuit Court is erroneous and must be reversed.

It is suggested, however, that this plea is not before us; and that as the judgment in the court below on this plea was in favor of the plaintiff, he does not seek to reverse it, or bring it before the court for revision by his writ of error; and also that the defendant waived this defence by pleading over, and thereby admitted the jurisdiction of the court…

The question is simply this: Can a negro, whose ancestors were imported into this country, and sold as slaves, become a member of the political community formed and brought into existence by the Constitution of the United States, and as such become entitled to all the rights, and privileges, and immunities, guarantied by that instrument to the citizen? One of which rights is the privilege of suing in a court of the United States in the cases specified in the Constitution.

It will be observed, that the plea applies to that class of persons only whose ancestors were negroes of the African race, and imported into this country, and sold and held as slaves. The only matter in issue before the court, therefore, is, whether the descendants of such slaves, when they shall be emancipated, or who are born of parents who had become free before their birth, are citizens of a State, in the sense in which the word citizen is used in the Constitution of the United States. And this being the only matter in dispute on the pleadings, the court must be understood as speaking in this opinion of that class only, that is, of those persons who are the descendants of Africans who were imported into this country, and sold as slaves.

...In the opinion of the court, the legislation and histories of the times, and the language used in the Declaration of Independence, show, that neither the class of persons who had been imported as slaves, nor their descendants, whether they had become free or not, were then acknowledged as a part of the people, nor intended to be included in the general words used in that memorable instrument.

It is difficult at this day to realize the state of public opinion in relation to that unfortunate race, which prevailed in the civilized and enlightened portions of the world at the time of the Declaration of Independence, and when the Constitution of the United States was framed and adopted. But the public history of every European nation displays it in a manner too plain to be mistaken.

They had for more than a century before been regarded as beings of an inferior order, and altogether unfit to associate with the white race, either in social or political relations; and so far inferior, that they had no rights which the white man was bound to respect; and that the negro might justly and lawfully be reduced to slavery for his benefit. He was bought and sold, and treated as an ordinary article of merchandise and traffic, whenever a profit could be made by it. This opinion was at that time fixed and universal in the civilized portion of the white race. It was regarded as an axiom in morals as well as in politics, which no one thought of disputing, or supposed to be open to dispute; and men in every grade and position in society daily and habitually acted upon it in their private pursuits, as well as in matters of public concern, without doubting for a moment the correctness of this opinion.

And in no nation was this opinion more firmly fixed or more uniformly acted upon than by the English Government and English people. They not only seized them on the coast of Africa, and sold them or held them in slavery for their own use; but they took them as ordinary articles of merchandise to every country where they could make a profit on them, and were far more extensively engaged in this commerce than any other nation in the world.

The opinion thus entertained and acted upon in England was naturally impressed upon the colonies they founded on this side of the Atlantic. And, accordingly, a negro of the African race was regarded by them as an article of property, and held, and bought and sold as such, in every one of the thirteen colonies which united in the Declaration of Independence, and afterwards formed the Constitution of the United States. The slaves were more or less numerous in the different colonies, as slave labor was found more or less profitable. But no one seems to have doubted the correctness of the prevailing opinion of the time.

The legislation of the different colonies furnishes positive and indisputable proof of this fact.

https://scholar.google.com/scholar_case?case=3231372247892780026&q=Dred+Scott+v.+Sandford,+60+U.S.+393+(1857).&hl=en&as_sdt=400006&as_vis=1

APPENDIX C
Civil War Amendments

The 13th Amendment

Section 1: "*Neither slavery nor involuntary servitude, except as a punishment for crime whereof the party shall have been duly convicted, shall exist within the United States, or any place subject to their jurisdiction.*"

Section 2: "*Congress shall have power to enforce this article by appropriate legislation.*"

The 14th Amendment

Section 1: "*All persons born or naturalized within the United States, and subject to the jurisdiction thereof, are citizens of the United States and of the state wherein they reside. No state shall make or enforce and lay which shall abridge the privileges or immunities of citizens of the United States; nor shall any state deprive any person of life, liberty, or property, without due process of law; nor deny to any person within its jurisdiction the equal protection of the laws.*"

Section 2: "*Representatives shall be apportioned among the several states according to their respective numbers, counting the whole number of persons in each state, excluding Indians not taxed. But when the right to vote at any election for the choice of electors for President and Vice President of the United States, Representatives in Congress, the executive and judicial officers of a state, or the members of the legislature thereof, is denied to any of the male inhabitants of such state, being twenty-one years of age, and citizens of the United States, or in any way abridged, except for participation in rebellion, or other crime, the basis of representation therein shall be reduced in the proportion which the number of such male citizens shall bear to the whole number of male citizens twenty-one years of age in such state.*"

Section 3: "*No person shall be a Senator or Representative in Congress, or elector of President and Vice President, or hold any office, civil or military, under the United States, or under any state, who, having previously taken an oath, as a member of Congress, or as an officer of the United States, or as a member of any state legislature, or as an executive or judicial officer of any state, to support the Constitution of the United States, shall have engaged in insurrection or rebellion against the same, or given aid or comfort to the enemies thereof. But Congress may by a vote of two-thirds of each House, remove such a disability."*

Section 4: *"The validity of the public debt of the United States, authorized by law, including debts incurred for payment of pensions and bounties for services in suppressing insurrection or rebellion, shall not be questioned. But neither the United States not any state shall assume or pay any debt or obligation incurred in aid of insurrection or rebellion against the United States, or any claim for the loss or emancipation of any slave; but all such debts, obligations and claims shall be held illegal and void."*

Section 5: *"The Congress shall have power to enforce, by appropriate legislation, the provisions of this article."*

The 15th Amendment

Section 1: *"The right of citizens of the United States to vote shall not be denied or abridged by the United States or by any state on account of race, color, or previous condition of servitude."*

Section 2: *"The Congress shall have power to enforce this article by appropriate legislation."*

https://www.law.cornell.edu/constitution/amendmentxv

APPENDIX D

Sec. 300.320 Definition of Individualized Education Program

Statute/Regs Main » Regulations » Part B » Subpart D » Section 300.320
300.320 Definition of individualized education program.

(a) General. As used in this part, the term individualized education program or IEP means a written statement for each child with a disability that is developed, reviewed, and revised in a meeting in accordance with §§300.320 through 300.324, and that must include—

  (1) A statement of the child's present levels of academic achievement and functional performance, including—

    (i) How the child's disability affects the child's involvement and progress in the general education curriculum (i.e., the same curriculum as for nondisabled children); or
    (ii) For preschool children, as appropriate, how the disability affects the child's participation in appropriate activities;

  (2)

    (i) A statement of measurable annual goals, including academic and functional goals designed to—

      (A) Meet the child's needs that result from the child's disability to enable the child to be involved in and make progress in the general education curriculum; and
      (B) Meet each of the child's other educational needs that result from the child's disability;

    (ii) For children with disabilities who take alternate assessments aligned to alternate academic achievement standards, a description of benchmarks or short-term objectives;

(3) A description of—

    (i) How the child's progress toward meeting the annual goals described in paragraph (2) of this section will be measured; and

    (ii) When periodic reports on the progress the child is making toward meeting the annual goals (such as through the use of quarterly or other periodic reports, concurrent with the issuance of report cards) will be provided;

(4) A statement of the special education and related services and supplementary aids and services, based on peer-reviewed research to the extent practicable, to be provided to the child, or on behalf of the child, and a statement of the program modifications or supports for school personnel that will be provided to enable the child—

    (i) To advance appropriately toward attaining the annual goals;

    (ii) To be involved in and make progress in the general education curriculum in accordance with paragraph (a)(1) of this section, and to participate in extracurricular and other nonacademic activities; and

    (iii) To be educated and participate with other children with disabilities and nondisabled children in the activities described in this section;

(5) An explanation of the extent, if any, to which the child will not participate with nondisabled children in the regular class and in the activities described in paragraph (a)(4) of this section;

(6)

    (i) A statement of any individual appropriate accommodations that are necessary to measure the academic achievement and functional performance of the child on State and districtwide assessments consistent with section 612(a)(16) of the Act; and

    (ii) If the IEP Team determines that the child must take an alternate assessment instead of a particular regular State or districtwide assessment of student achievement, a statement of why—

        (A) The child cannot participate in the regular assessment; and

        (B) The particular alternate assessment selected is appropriate for the child; and

(7) The projected date for the beginning of the services and modifications described in paragraph (a)(4) of this section, and the anticipated frequency, location, and duration of those services and modifications.

(b) Transition services. Beginning not later than the first IEP to be in effect when the child turns 16, or younger if determined appropriate by the IEP Team, and updated annually, thereafter, the IEP must include—

(1) Appropriate measurable postsecondary goals based upon age appropriate transition assessments related to training, education, employment, and, where appropriate, independent living skills; and
(2) The transition services (including courses of study) needed to assist the child in reaching those goals.

(c) Transfer of rights at age of majority. Beginning not later than one year before the child reaches the age of majority under State law, the IEP must include a statement that the child has been informed of the child's rights under Part B of the Act, if any, that will transfer to the child on reaching the age of majority under §300.520.
(d) Construction. Nothing in this section shall be construed to require—

(1) That additional information be included in a child's IEP beyond what is explicitly required in section 614 of the Act; or
(2) The IEP Team to include information under one component of a child's IEP that is already contained under another component of the child's IEP.

[71 FR 46753, Aug. 14, 2006, as amended at 72 FR 61307, Oct. 30, 2007]
https://sites.ed.gov/idea/regs/b/d/300.320)
Last modified on Jul. 12, 2017

APPENDIX E

Fact Sheet: Preventing Racial Discrimination in Special Education

What Is the Dear Colleague Letter on Preventing Racial Discrimination in Special Education?

The Office for Civil Rights (OCR) at the US Department of Education issued the Dear Colleague Letter on Preventing Racial Discrimination in Special Education on December 12, 2016, to help ensure that all students, regardless of race, color, or national origin, have equitable access to high-quality general and special education instruction.

The letter provides a brief legal summary of Title VI of the Civil Rights Act of 1964 (Title VI), the Individuals with Disabilities Education Act (IDEA), and Section 504 of the Rehabilitation Act of 1973 (Section 504), and explains, through analysis and illustrative examples, the Title VI requirement that students of all races, colors, and national origins have:

- equitable access to general education interventions and to a timely referral for an evaluation for disability and special education and/or related aids and services under the IDEA or Section 504; and
- equitable treatment in the evaluation process, in the quality of special education services and supports they receive, and in the degree of restrictiveness of their educational environment.

How Can a School District Prevent Racial Discrimination in Special Education?

- **Referral** – Districts and schools must not discriminate on the basis of race, color, or national origin in referring students for evaluation. Racial discrimination in referrals can result in under-identification for special education of students who need services and over-identification for special education of students who do not actually need services.

- One common method that is used in an effort to improve student achievement and school climate and/or reduce inappropriate special education referrals is the implementation of *evidence-based intervention strategies* to provide help and support, within the general education setting, to students who need such support.
- An intervention framework must not, however, serve as a substitute, or a precondition, for an evaluation for students believed to need such an evaluation.
- If a district has reason to believe a student has a disability and needs special education or related services because of that disability, Section 504 requires the district to timely evaluate the student, regardless of whether the student has received any general education intervention services.

- *How Can a School District Prevent Racial Discrimination in Special Education? (continued)*

  - *Evaluation* – Whether pursuant to Section 504 or the IDEA, districts must ensure that they comply with the nondiscrimination requirements of Title VI. For example, districts must not treat similarly situated students of different races differently in the type of evaluation procedures used by the district, unless the district has a legitimate, nondiscriminatory reason for the difference in treatment. Districts also must avoid treating similarly situated students of different races or national origins differently in the amount and type of documentation supporting educational placement decisions. A district must not use an evaluation or testing procedure that has a disproportionate adverse impact on a racial or ethnic group if there is a comparably effective evaluation or testing procedure that accomplishes the district's important educational goal with less adverse impact (e.g., less over-identification or under-identification).
  - *Special Education Services* – Districts must not discriminate against students based on race, color, or national origin in the provision of special education or related aids and services under Section 504 or in the implementation of an individualized education program under the IDEA. Districts must give students equitable access, without regard to race, color, or national origin to the most integrated setting appropriate for the student.

How Can I Get Help From OCR?

- *Requesting More Information.* With questions or for more information, including technical assistance on civil rights compliance, please contact the US Department of Education's Office for Civil Rights (OCR) customer service team at 1-800-421-3481 (TDD 1-800-877-8339) or ocr@ed.gov or visit OCR's website at www.ed.gov/ocr.

- *Filing a Complaint.* Anyone who believes that a school that receives Federal financial assistance has discriminated against someone based on race, color, national origin, sex, disability, or age, can file a complaint of discrimination with OCR within 180 days of the alleged discrimination. For more details, please visit www.ed.gov/ocr/complaintintro.html or contact OCR's customer service team at 1-800-421-3481 (TDD 1-800-877-8339).

APPENDIX F
California Assembly Bill No. 1626

Assembly Bill No. 1626
CHAPTER 742
An act to add Sections 48070.5 and 60648 to the Education Code, relating to education.
[Approved by Governor September 22, 1998. Filed with Secretary of State September 23, 1998.]
LEGISLATIVE COUNSEL'S DIGEST
AB 1626, Wayne. Pupil promotion and retention.

(1) Existing law requires the governing board of each school district and each county superintendent of schools to adopt policies regarding pupil promotion and retention, and requires a pupil to be promoted or retained only as provided according to those policies. This bill would, in addition to the policies adopted pursuant to those provisions, require the governing board of each school district and each county board of education to approve a policy regarding the promotion and retention of pupils between specified grades, and would require that policy to provide for the identification of pupils who should be retained or who are at risk of being retained in their current grade level on the basis of specified factors. The bill would require the policy to be based on various other considerations. By imposing new duties on school districts regarding the adoption of this policy, the bill would impose a state-mandated local program.
(2) Existing law, known as the Leroy Greene California Assessment of Academic Achievement Act, requires the Superintendent of Public Instruction to design and implement a statewide pupil assessment program that includes, among other things, a plan for producing individual pupil scores based on both the achievement test that is part of the Standardized Testing and Reporting

(STAR) Program and the statewide assessment of pupil performance in the core curriculum areas. This bill would require the Superintendent of Public Instruction to recommend, and the State Board of Education to adopt, levels of pupil performance for the achievement tests administered under the STAR Program in reading, English language arts, and mathematics for each grade level, and would require that those performance levels identify and establish the level of performance that is deemed to be the minimum level required for satisfactory performance in the next grade.

(3) The California Constitution requires the state to reimburse local agencies and school districts for certain costs mandated by the state. Statutory provisions establish procedures for making that reimbursement, including the creation of a State Mandates Claims Fund to pay the costs of mandates that do not exceed $1,000,000 statewide and other procedures for claims whose statewide costs exceed $1,000,000. This bill would provide that, if the Commission on State Mandates determines that the bill contains costs mandated by the state, reimbursement for those costs shall be made pursuant to these statutory provisions.

...

SEC. 2. Section 48070.5 is added to the Education Code, to read:

48070.5.

(a) In addition to the policy adopted pursuant to Section 48070, the governing board of each school district and each county board of education shall, in those applicable grade levels, approve a policy regarding the promotion and retention of pupils between the following grades:

   (1) Between second grade and third grade.
   (2) Between third grade and fourth grade.
   (3) Between fourth and fifth grade.
   (4) Between the end of the intermediate grades and the beginning of middle school grades which typically occurs between sixth grade and seventh grade, but may vary depending upon the grade configuration of the school or school district.
   (5) Between the end of the middle school grades and the beginning of high school which typically occurs between eighth grade and ninth grade, but may vary depending upon the grade configuration of the school or school district.

(b) The policy shall provide for the identification of pupils who should be retained and who are at risk of being retained in their current grade level on the basis of either of the following:

   (1) The results of the assessments administered pursuant to Article 4 (commencing with Section 60640) of Chapter 5 of Part 33 and the minimum

levels of proficiency recommended by the State Board of Education pursuant to Section 60648.

(2) The pupil's grades and other indicators of academic achievement designated by the district.

(c) The policy shall base the identification of pupils pursuant to subdivision (b) at the grade levels identified pursuant to paragraph (1) and (2) of subdivision (a) primarily on the basis of the pupil's level of proficiency in reading. The policy shall base the identification of pupils pursuant to subdivision (b) at the grade levels identified pursuant to paragraphs (3) through (5) of subdivision (a) on the basis of the pupil's level of proficiency in reading, English language arts, and mathematics.

(d) (1) If either measure identified in paragraph (1) or (2) of subdivision (b) identifies that a pupil is performing below the minimum standard for promotion, the pupil shall be retained in his or her current grade level unless the pupil's regular classroom teacher determines in writing that retention is not the appropriate intervention for the pupil's academic deficiencies. This written determination shall specify the reasons that retention is not appropriate for the pupil and shall include recommendations for interventions other than retention that in the opinion of the teacher are necessary to assist the pupil to attain acceptable levels of academic achievement. If the teacher's recommendation to promote is contingent upon the pupil's participation in a summer school or interim session remediation program, the pupil's academic performance shall be reassessed at the end of the remediation program, and the decision to retain or promote the pupil shall be reevaluated at that time. The teacher's evaluation shall be provided to and discussed with the pupil's parent or guardian and the school principal before any final determination of pupil retention or promotion...

APPENDIX G
Literacy Education for All, Results for the Nation (LEARN) Act

Research demonstrates that a high-quality, literacy-rich environment is an important prerequisite for academic success—this is especially true in early childhood when children are developing the foundation upon which future learning is built.

Research also shows that low-income children are less likely to have access to high-quality, literacy-rich environments. These same children perform 40% lower on assessments of literacy achievement even before they start kindergarten.

These challenges become greater as children enter and progress through elementary and high school. More than 5 million high school students do not read well enough to understand their grade level material. According to the National Assessment of Educational Progress, 26% of these students cannot read essential materials such as such as road signs, newspapers, and bus schedules. To be successful in today's 21st Century global economy, students must develop oral language, reading, and writing abilities.

The Literacy Education for All, Results for the Nation (LEARN) Act will ensure that all students receive high-quality literacy instruction beginning in early childhood and continuing through high school graduation.

The LEARN Act responds to the clear need for literacy instruction and high quality support for students at all age, development and grade levels. This legislation provides for a strong federal investment in high-quality literacy instruction that will help states improve programs to strengthen the literacy skills of all students.

Specifically LEARN supports high literacy for all students from birth through high school by:

- Providing Federal support to States to develop, revise, or update comprehensive literacy instruction plans that when implemented, ensure high-quality instruction and effective strategies in reading and writing from early education through grade 12
- States provide subgrants to early childhood education programs and school districts and their public or private partners to implement evidence based programs to ensure high-quality comprehensive literacy instruction for students most in need
- Comprehensive literacy programs include explicit, systematic and intentional instruction in phonological awareness, phonic decoding, vocabulary, language structure, reading fluency, and reading comprehension.
- Providing high-quality, research-based professional development opportunities for instructional staff and financial support for literacy coaches.

https://www.ncld.org/wp-content/uploads/2015/11/LEARN-Act.pdf

APPENDIX H

Florida EXECUTIVE ORDER NUMBER 01-260 (September 7, 2001)

WHEREAS, the Florida Constitution provides that the education of children is a fundamental value of the people of the State of Florida and instructs the Executive and Legislative branches to make adequate provision for the education of "all children" residing within the State's borders; and

WHEREAS, reading is the most powerful common denominator in education and paramount to an individual's success; and

WHEREAS, research strongly indicates that failure to read proficiently is the most compelling reason children are retained in the same grade, assigned to special education, or given long-term remedial services; and

WHEREAS, Florida's students are making progress in acquiring necessary reading skills and have demonstrated increases in reading scores in recent years; however, only about half of Florida's fourth graders read at or above grade level, only four in ten of our middle school students read at or above grade level, and fewer than four in ten of our high school students read at or above grade level; and

WHEREAS, there are a variety of existing efforts in Florida to improve reading skills and the State of Florida has taken many recent actions to improve reading proficiency, including, but not limited to: expanding the required courses regarding the reading process for freshmen entering teacher programs; appropriating $5 million this year for the Family Literacy and Reading Excellence Center, which prepares master teachers to train their colleagues to teach reading more effectively; the Reading Adoption Process, which for the first time this fall will ensure that all Florida reading curricula and instructional methods will support the Sunshine State Standards; and continuing the Governor's Family Literacy Initiative, which has awarded over $2 million in Family Literacy Grants to start or expand 50 literacy programs throughout Florida; and

WHEREAS, Florida's ultimate goal is that every student read at or above grade level; and WHEREAS, parents, families, neighbors and mentors play a crucial role in helping children learn to read; and

WHEREAS, teachers need improved access to innovative, creative, and effective strategies to help children learn to read proficiently; and

WHEREAS, with a more comprehensive and coordinated effort from the State, additional assistance, and encouragement from families and communities, many more students can become successful readers, pursue their dreams, and improve the quality of life in Florida; and

NOW, THEREFORE, I, JEB BUSH, Jeb Bush, as Governor of the State of Florida, and pursuant to the power vested in me by law, do hereby promulgate the following executive order, effective immediately:

Section 1.

Just Read, Florida!, a comprehensive, coordinated reading initiative aimed at helping every student become a successful, independent reader, is hereby initiated.

Section 2.

The Florida Department of Education, working with local school districts, is hereby requested to:

1. inventory and review reading programs utilized in Florida schools to provide an assessment of the effectiveness of these programs and determine the cost per student of these programs; and
2. recommend statewide standards for reading programs based on the latest scientific research. The department will gain input from and work with successful reading teachers, the Florida Reading Association, school administrators, superintendents, parents, legislators, business and community leaders, and university researchers. These standards should support the work of successful teachers and reflect the findings of the National Reading Panel and the National Institute of Child Health and Human Development (NICHD).

Section 3.

The Florida Department of Education is hereby requested to address and make recommendations, in consultation with the Florida Board of Education, regarding at least the following areas:

1. early-reading instruction strategies and reading screenings or assessments for K–2 students;
2. reading intervention strategies for students who read below grade level;
3. reading course requirements for middle school and high school students who are not reading at grade level;

4. reading activities in teacher preparation and professional development programs;

5. leveraging technology to improve reading proficiency and integrating online professional development with existing and traditional training;

6. utilizing teacher reading academies and/or schools within schools to teach effective reading strategies;

7. planning for integration, coordination and effective investment of anticipated federal funds from President Bush's Reading First Initiative, and for the 21st Century Community Learning Centers;

8. developing ongoing public-private partnerships aimed at increasing reading proficiency and providing supplemental books to students;

9. recognizing outstanding reading teachers and schools at which students are making significant progress in reading; increasing parental and family involvement in teaching and encouraging reading;

10. encouraging family literacy practices and programs through innovative integration of adult literacy and elementary and secondary school programs; and

11. utilizing, supporting, and training mentors and volunteers to help children and adults learn to read.

https://www.fldoe.org/core/fileparse.php/7539/urlt/just_read_florida_executive_order.pdf

APPENDIX I

Alternative Standardized Reading Assessment and Use of Student Portfolio for Good Cause Promotion

6A-1.094221 Alternative Standardized Reading Assessment and Use of Student Portfolio for Good Cause Promotion.

(1) Pursuant to Section 1008.25(6), F.S., relating to the statewide public school student progression law eliminating social promotion, students who score at Level 1 on the grade three statewide English Language Arts Florida Standards Assessment may be promoted to grade four if the student:

    (a) Scores at or above the 45th percentile on the Reading SAT-10;

    (b) Demonstrates an acceptable level of performance on an alternative standardized reading assessment approved pursuant to subsection (2) of this rule; or

    (c) Demonstrates reading on grade level as evidenced through mastery of the Language Arts Florida Standards in reading equal to at least Level 2 performance on the grade three statewide English Language Arts Florida Standards Assessment through a student portfolio pursuant to subsection (3) of this rule.

(2) The Department of Education shall review and approve the use of alternative standardized reading assessments to be used as a good cause exemption for promotion to fourth grade and will provide a list of approved alternative assessments to districts.

    (a) The approval of an alternative standardized reading assessment must be based on whether the assessment meets the following criteria:

        1. Internal consistency reliability coefficients of at least 0.80;

2. High validity evidenced by the alignment of the test with nationally recognized content standards, as well as specific evidence of content, concurrent, or criterion validity;

3. Norming studies within the last five (5) to ten (10) years, with norming within five (5) years being preferable; and,

4. Serves as a measure of grade three achievement in reading comprehension.

(b) Districts may submit requests for the approval of alternative standardized reading assessments to be used as a good cause exemption for promotion to fourth grade. Once an assessment has been approved by the Department of Education, the assessment is approved for statewide use.

(c) The Department of Education shall approve the required percentile passing score for each approved alternative standardized reading assessment based on an analysis of Florida student achievement results. If an analysis is not feasible, students must score at or above the 50th percentile on the approved alternative standardized reading assessment.

(d) The earliest the alternative assessment may be administered for student promotion purposes is following administration of the grade three statewide English Language Arts Florida Standards Assessment. An approved standardized reading assessment may be administered two (2) times if there are at least thirty (30) days between administrations and different test forms are administered.

(3) To promote a student using a student portfolio as a good cause exemption there must be evidence that demonstrates the student's mastery of the Language Arts Florida Standards in reading equal to at least a Level 2 performance on the grade three statewide English Language Arts Florida Standards Assessment. Such evidence shall be an organized collection of the student's mastery of the Language Arts Florida Standards that are assessed by the grade three statewide English Language Arts Florida Standards Assessment. The student portfolio must meet the following criteria:

(a) Be selected by the student's teacher,

(b) Be an accurate picture of the student's ability and only include student work that has been independently produced in the classroom,

(c) Include evidence that the standards assessed by the grade three statewide English Language Arts Florida Standards Assessment have been met. Evidence is to include multiple choice items and passages that are approximately sixty (60) percent literary text and forty (40) percent information text, and that are between 100–700 words with an average of 500 words. Such evidence could include chapter or unit tests from the district's/school's adopted core reading curriculum that are aligned with the Language Arts Florida Standards or teacher-prepared assessments.

(d) Be an organized collection of evidence of the student's mastery of the Language Arts Florida Standards that are assessed by the grade three statewide English Language Arts Florida Standards Assessment. For each standard, there must be at least three (3) examples of mastery as demonstrated by a grade of seventy (70) percent or above on each example, and,

(e) Be signed by the teacher and the principal as an accurate assessment of the required reading skills.

Rulemaking Authority 1008.25(9) FS. Law Implemented 1008.25(6) FS. History– New 5-19-03, Amended 7-20-04, 3-24-08, 2-1-09, 4-21-11, 11-4-14, 6-23-16.

APPENDIX J
Florida's Revised Formula for Success

- Six components of reading: oral language, phonological awareness, phonics, fluency, vocabulary, and comprehension;
- Four types of classroom assessments: screening, progress monitoring/formative assessment, diagnosis, and summative assessment;
- Core instruction (Tier 1): is standards-aligned; includes accommodations for students with a disability, students with an Individual Educational Plan (IEP), and students who are English language learners; provides print-rich explicit and systematic, scaffolded, and differentiated instruction; builds background and content knowledge; incorporates writing in response to reading; and incorporates the principles of Universal Design for Learning as defined in 34 C.F.R. 200.2(b)(2)(ii);
- Immediate intervention (Tier 2): is standards-aligned; includes accommodations for students with a disability, students with an IEP, and students who are English language learners; provides explicit, systematic, small-group teacher-led instruction matched to student need, targeting gaps in learning to reduce barriers to students' ability to meet Tier 1 expectations; provides multiple opportunities to practice the targeted skill(s) and receive feedback; and occurs in addition to core instruction; and
- Immediate intensive intervention (Tier 3): is provided to students identified as having a substantial deficiency in reading; is standards-aligned; includes accommodations for students with a disability, students with an IEP, and students who are English language learners; provides explicit, systematic, individualized instruction based on student need, one-on-one or very small-group instruction with more guided practice, immediate corrective

feedback, and frequent progress monitoring; and occurs in addition to core instruction and Tier 2 interventions. In accordance with Section 1008.25(4) (c), F.S., students identified with a substantial reading deficiency must be covered by a federally required student plan, such as an IEP or an individualized progress monitoring plan and receive intensive interventions from teachers who are certified or endorsed in reading.

APPENDIX K

APA RESOLUTION on Harnessing Psychology to Combat Racism: Adopting a Uniform Definition and Understanding

To access this resource, please visit https://www.apa.org/about/policy/resolution-combat-racism.pdf or this book's Support Material at www.routledge.com/9781032275000.

APPENDIX L

Apology to People of Color for APA's Role in Promoting, Perpetuating, and Failing to Challenge Racism, Racial Discrimination, and Human Hierarchy in US.

To access this resource, please visit https://www.apa.org/about/policy/racism-apology or this book's Support Material at www.routledge.com/9781032275000.

APPENDIX M

Historical Chronology. Examining Psychology's Contributions to the Belief in Racial Hierarchy and Perpetuation of Inequality for People of Color in US.

To access this resource, please visit https://www.apa.org/about/apa/addressing-racism/historical-chronology or this book's Support Material at www.routledge.com/9781032275000.

APPENDIX N

Role of psychology and APA in dismantling systemic racism against People of Color in US.

To access this resource, please visit https://www.apa.org/about/policy/dismantling-systemic-racism or this book's Support Material at www.routledge.com/9781032275000.

APPENDIX O

Joint Statement on Legislative Efforts to Restrict Education about Racism and American History

We, the undersigned associations and organizations, state our firm opposition to a spate of legislative proposals being introduced across the country that target academic lessons, presentations, and discussions of racism and related issues in American history in schools, colleges and universities. These efforts have taken varied shape in at least 20 states; but often the legislation aims to prohibit or impede the teaching and education of students concerning what are termed "divisive concepts." These divisive concepts as defined in numerous bills are a litany of vague and indefinite buzzwords and phrases including, for example, "that any individual should feel or be made to feel discomfort, guilt, anguish, or any other form of psychological or emotional distress on account of that individual's race or sex." These legislative efforts are deeply troubling for numerous reasons.

First, these bills risk infringing on the right of faculty to teach and of students to learn. The clear goal of these efforts is to suppress teaching and learning about the role of racism in the history of the United States. Purportedly, any examination of racism in this country's classrooms might cause some students "discomfort" because it is an uncomfortable and complicated subject. But the ideal of informed citizenship necessitates an educated public. Educators must provide an accurate view of the past in order to better prepare students for community participation and robust civic engagement. Suppressing or watering down discussion of "divisive concepts" in educational institutions deprives students of opportunities to discuss and foster solutions to social division and injustice. Legislation cannot erase "concepts" or history; it can, however, diminish educators' ability to help students address facts in an honest and open environment capable of nourishing intellectual exploration. Educators owe students a clear-eyed, nuanced, and frank delivery of history, so that they can learn, grow, and confront the issues of the day, not hew to some state-ordered ideology.

Second, these legislative efforts seek to substitute political mandates for the considered judgment of professional educators, hindering students' ability to learn and engage in critical thinking across differences and disagreements. These regulations constitute an inappropriate attempt to transfer responsibility for the evaluation of a curriculum and subject matter from educators to elected officials. The purpose of education is to serve the common good by promoting open inquiry and advancing human knowledge. Politicians in a democratic society should not manipulate public school curricula to advance partisan or ideological aims. In higher education, under principles of academic freedom that have been widely endorsed, professors are entitled to freedom in the classroom in discussing their subject. Educators, not politicians, should make decisions about teaching and learning.

Knowledge of the past exists to serve the needs of the living. In the current context, this includes an honest reckoning with all aspects of that past. Americans of all ages deserve nothing less than a free and open exchange about history and the forces that shape our world today, an exchange that should take place inside the classroom as well as in the public realm generally. To ban the tools that enable those discussions is to deprive us all of the tools necessary for citizenship in the twenty-first century. A whitewashed view of history cannot change what happened in the past. A free and open society depends on the unrestricted pursuit and dissemination of knowledge.

Signed,

American Association of University Professors

American Historical Association

Association of American Colleges & Universities

PEN America

REFERENCES

Adams, M. J. (1990). *Beginning to read: Thinking and learning about print.* MIT Press.

Ager, P. Boustan, L. P., & Eriksson, K. (2019, September). The intergenerational effects of a large wealth shock: White Southerners after the Civil War. National Bureau of Economic Research. Working Paper, 25700. https://www.nber.org/papers/w25700

Alexander, E. (2009). *Praise song for the day.* Graywolf Press.

Alexander, K. L., Entwisle, D. R., & Dauber, S. L. (1994). *On the success of school failure: A reassessment of the effects of retention in the primary grades.* Cambridge University Press.

Alexander, L. (2017, January 17). Betsy DeVos is on our children's side. U. S. Senate Committee Health, Education, Labor, & Pensions. https://www.help.senate.gov/chair/newsroom/press/alexander-betsy-devos-is-on-our-childrens-side

Alexander, M. (2012). *The new Jim Crow: Mass incarceration in the age of colorblindness* (rev. ed.). New Press.

Alim, H. S., & Smitherman, G. (2012). *Articulate while Black: Barack Obama, language, and race in the U.S.* Oxford University Press.

Alim, H. S., & Smitherman, G. (2020). "Perfect English" and white supremacy. In J. McIntosh & N. Mendoza-Denton (Eds.), *Language in the Trump era: Scandals and emergencies* (pp. 226–236). Cambridge University Press.

Allan, L. (1937). *Strange fruit.* Commodore.

Allen, K. M., Davis, J., Garraway, R. L., & Burt, J. M. (2018). Every student succeeds (Except for black males) act. *Teachers College Record, 120,* 1–20.

Allen, R. (1983). "Liberty further extended": A 1776 antislavery manuscript by Lemuel Haynes. *The William and Mary Quarterly,* Third Series, *40*(1), 85–105.

Allensworth, E. M. (2005). Dropout rates after high-stakes testing in elementary school: A study of the contradictory effects of Chicago's efforts to end social promotion. *Educational Evaluation and Policy Analysis, 27*(4), 341–364.

Alryyes, A. (2011). *A Muslim slave: The life of Omar ibn Said.* University of Wisconsin Press.

Althusser, L. (1971). *Lenin and philosophy and other essays. Monthly Review Press* (translated, A. Blunden, originally published 1970).

America. (2000). An education strategy sourcebook. https://eric.ed.gov/?id=ED327985

American History Association. (2021a, June 6). Joint statement on legislative efforts to restrict education about racism in American History. https://www.historians.org/divisive-concepts-statement

American History Association. (2021b, December 22). AHA sends letter opposing Oklahoma bill that would limit teaching of race and slavery in America. https://www.historians.org/news-and-advocacy/aha-advocacy/aha-letter-opposing-oklahoma-bill-that-would-limit-teaching-of-race-and-slavery-in-america-(december-2021)

American Life Histories: Manuscripts from the Federal Writers' Project, 1936 to 1940. (2022). https://www.loc.gov/collections/federal-writers-project/about-this collection/

American Psychological Association. (2021a, February, 27). Resolution on harnessing psychology to combat racism: Adopting a uniform definition and understanding. https://www.apa.org/about/policy/resolution-combat-racism.pdf

American Psychological Association. (2021b, October 29). Apology to people of color for APA's role in promoting, perpetuating, and failing to challenge racism, racial discrimination, and human hierarchy in U.S. https://www.apa.org/about/policy/racism-apology

American Psychological Association. (2021c, October 29). Historical chronology. Examining psychology's contributions to the belief in racial hierarchy and perpetuation of inequality for people of color in U.S. https://www.apa.org/about/apa/addressing-racism/historical-chronology

American Psychological Association. (2021d, October 29). Role of psychology and APA in dismantling systemic racism against people of color in U.S. https://www.apa.org/about/policy/dismantling-systemic-racism

Anderson, B. N., & Martin, J. A. (2018). What K–12 teachers need to know about teaching gifted black girls. *Gifted Child Today, 41*(3), 117–124.

Anderson, G. E., Jimerson, S. R., & Whipple, A. D. (2005). Student ratings of stressful experiences at home and school: Loss of parent and grade retention as superlative stressors. *Journal of Applied School Psychology, 1*, 1–20.

Anderson, J. D. (1988). *The education of Blacks in the South, 1860–1935.* University of North Carolina Press.

Andrews, D. J. C., Brown, T., Castro, E., & Id-Deen, E. (2019). The impossibility of being "perfect and white": Black girls' racialized and gendered schooling experiences. *American Educational Research Journal, 56*(6), 2531–2572.

Annamma, S. A. (2018). *The pedagogy of pathologization: Dis/abled girls of color in the school-prison pipeline.* Routledge.

Annamma, S. A., Connor, D., & Ferri, B. (2013). Dis/ability critical race studies (DisCrit): Theorizing at the intersections of race and dis/ability. *Race Ethnicity and Education, 16*(1), 1–31.

Annie E. Casey Foundation. (2010a). *Early warning! Why reading by the end of third grade matters. A kids count special report from the Annie E. Casey Foundation.* https://www.aecf.org/resources/early-warning-why-reading-by-the-end-of-third-grade-matters https://www.aecf.org/resources/early-warning-why-reading-by-the-end-of-third-grade-

Annie E. Casey Foundation. (2010b). *Early warning! Why reading by the end of third grade matters: Summary.* https://old.ed.psu.edu/goodlinginstitute/pdf/Special_Report_Executive_Summary.pdf

Annie E. Casey Foundation. (2022). About us: Our history. https://www.aecf.org/about/history

Artiles, A. J. (2013). Untangling the racialization of disabilities: An intersectionality critique across disability models. *Du Bois Review, 10*(2), 329–347.

Artiles, A. J., Kozleski, E. B., Trent, S. C., Osher, D., & Ortiz, A. (2010). Justifying and explaining disproportionality, 1968–2008: A critique of underlying views of culture. *Exceptional Children, 76*(3), 279–299.

Au, W. (2007). High-stakes testing and curricular control: A qualitative metasynthesis. *Educational Researcher, 36*(5), 258–267.

Au, W. (2013). Hiding behind high-stakes testing: Meritocracy, objectivity and inequality in U.S. education. *The International Education Journal / Comparative Perspectives, 12*(2), 7–19.

Au, W. (2016). Racial justice is not a choice: White supremacy, high-stakes testing, and the punishment of Black and Brown students. In D. Watson, J. Hagopian & W. Au (Eds.), *Teaching for black lives* (pp. 243–250). Rethinking Schools Press.

Au, W. (2021). Testing for Whiteness? How high-stakes, standardized tests promote racism, undercut diversity, and undermine multicultural education. In H. P. Baptiste & J. H. Writer (Eds.), *Visioning multicultural education: Past, present, future* (pp. 99–111). Routledge.

Baldwin, J. (1963, December 21). A talk to teachers. *The Saturday Review*.

Baldwin, J. (1965). The white man's guilt. *Ebony, 20*(10), 47–48.

Baldwin, J. (1966, July 11). A report from occupied territory. https://www.thenation.com/article/archive/report-occupied-territory-2/

Baldwin, J. (1997). If Black English isn't a language, then tell me what is. *Black Scholar, 27*(1), 5–6.

Balkcom, K. (2014). Bringing sunshine to third-grade readers: How Florida's third-grade retention policy has worked and is a good model for other states considering reading laws. *The Journal of Law Education, 43*(3), 443–454.

Banks, J. A., & Banks, C. A. M. (2019). *Multicultural education: Issues and perspectives* (10th ed.). Wiley.

Barksdale, R., & Kinnamon, K. (1972). *Black writers of America: A comprehensive anthology*. Prentice Hall.

Barrett-Tatum, J., Ashworth, K., & Scales, D. (2019). Gateway literacy retention policies: Perspectives and implications from the field. *International Journal of Policy and Leadership, 15*(10). http://journals.sfu.ca/ijepl/index.php/ijepl/article/view

Basile, V. (2021). Decriminalizing practices: Disrupting punitive-based racial oppression of boys of color elementary school classrooms. *International Journal of Qualitative Studies in Education, 34*(3), 228–242.

Basile, V., York, A., & Black, R. (2019). Who is the one being disrespectful? Understanding and deconstructing the criminalization of elementary school boys of color. *Urban Education, 57*, 1–29.

Bassok, D., Miller, L. C., Galdo, E., & Johnson, A. J. (2014). *Florida's voluntary pre-kindergarten program - An Overview of the largest state pre-school program in the nation*. EdPolicyWorks_Report_1_FL_VPK.pdf

Baugh, J. (2000). *Beyond Ebonics: Linguistic pride and racial prejudice*. Oxford University Press.

Beinart, P. (2022, March 7). We can support Ukraine and admit the racism in US foreign policy at the same time. https://peterbeinart.substack.com/p/we-can-support-ukraine-and-admit?s=r

Bell, B. (1987). *The Afro-American novel and its tradition*. University of Massachusetts Press.

Bell, D. A. (1980). *Brown v Board of Education* and the interest convergence dilemma. *Harvard Law Review, 93*, 518–533.

Benchmark for Excellent Student Thinking. (2021). *Benchmarks for Excellent Student Thinking (B.E.S.T.) Standards – English Language Arts, 2021*. https://www.fldoe.org/core/fileparse.php/18736/urlt/EnglishLanguageArts.pdf

Bendi, N., & McGrory. K. (2020, November 19). Pasco's sheriff uses grades and abuse histories to label schoolchildren potential criminals. The kids and their parents don't know. *Tampa Bay Times*. https://projects.tampabay.com/projects/2020/investigations/police-pasco-sheriff-targeted/school-data/

Bensimon, E. M. (2018). Reclaiming racial justice in equity. *Change, 50*(3) (May–August), 95–98.

Biden, J. R. (2021, January 26). Condemning and combating racism, xenophobia, and intolerance against Asian Americans and Pacific Islanders in the United States [Memorandum]. Department of Justice. https://www.whitehouse.gov/briefing-room/presidential-actions/2021/01/26/memorandum-condemning-and-combating-racism-xenophobia-and-intolerance-against-asian-americans-and-pacific-islanders-in-the-united-states/

Bill of Rights of the State of Oregon. (1857). https://sos.oregon.gov/archives/exhibits/constitution/Documents/transcribed-1857-oregon-constitution.pdf

Black, D. (2021). The Capitol attack was White supremacy, plain and simple. https://www.cnn.com/2021/01/10/opinions/capitol-attack-white-supremacy-daniel-black/index.html

Blackmon, D. A. (2008). *Slavery by another name: The re-enslavement of Black Americans from the Civil War to World War II*. Doubleday.

Blacksher, J., & Guinier, L. (2014). Free at last: Rejecting equal sovereignty and restoring the constitutional right to vote Shelby County v Holder. *Harvard Law & Policy Review, 8*(1), 39–69.

Blain, K. N. (2022). To fight attacks on "Critical Race Theory," look to Black history. https://www.thenation.com/article/society/crt-black-teachers-resist/

Blakemore, E. (2022, January 11). How dolls helped win *Brown v. Board of Education*: Deceptively simple doll tests helped convince the Supreme Court to strike down school segregation. https://www.history.com/news/brown-v-board-of-education-doll-experiment (originally published, 2018, March 27).

Blow, C. (2021, July 28). Opinion. The "Lost Cause" is back. https://www.nytimes.com/2021/07/28/opinion/republicans-race-debate.html

Bly, A. (2011). In pursuit of letters: A history of the Bray schools for enslaved children in colonial Virginia. *History of Education Quarterly, 51*(4), 429–459.

Bond, G., & Dykstra, R. (1964). *Conference on coordination of accepted proposals for the Cooperative research program in first grade reading instruction*. Final report. (Report Number CRP-F-062). University of Minnesota. (ERIC Document Reproduction Service No. ED 003 422.

Bond, G., & Dykstra, R. (1967). The cooperative research program in first-grade reading instruction. *Reading Research Quarterly, 2*, 5–142.

Bond, H. M. (1924). Intelligence tests and propaganda. *The Crisis, 28*, 63–64.

Bond, H. M. (1927). Some exceptional Negro children. *The Crisis, 34*, 257–259.

Bonilla-Silva, E. (2003). "New racism", color-blind racism, and the future of whiteness in America. In A. W. Doane & E. Bonilla-Silva (Eds.), *White out: The continuing significance of racism* (pp. 271–284). Routledge.

Boone, J., & Adesso, V. (1974). Racial differences on a black intelligence test period. *Journal of Negro Education, 43*(4), 429–436.

Boozer, B. (1978). And alternative to intelligence testing for minority children. *Journal of Negro Education*, 414–418.

Bouie, J. (2022, April 22). Opinion: Democrats, you can't ignore the culture wars any longer. *New York Times.* https://www.nytimes.com/2022/04/22/opinion/red-scare-culture-wars. html?referringSource=articleShare

Bourque, M. L. (2009). A history of NAEP achievement levels: Issues, implementation, and impact, 1989–2000. Paper Commissioned for the 20th anniversary of the National Assessment Governing Board, 1988–2008. Washington, DC.

Brackett, M. A., & Simmons, D. (2015). Emotions matter. *Educational Leadership,* 22–27.

Brigham, C. (1923). *A study of American intelligence.* Princeton University Press.

Brooks, G. (2022). Current debates over the teaching of phonics. *Oxford Reference Research Encyclopedias.* https://doi.org/10.1093/acrefore/9780190264093.013.1543

Brown v. Board of Education I, 347 U.S. 483 (1954).

Brown v. Board of Education II, 349 U.S. 294 (1955).

Brown, S., Souto-Manning, M., & Laman, T. T. (2010). Seeing the strange in the familiar: Unpacking racialized practices in early childhood settings, *Race Ethnicity and Education, 13*(4), 513–532.

Browne-Marshall, G. J. (2013). *Race, law, and American Society 1607-present* (2nd ed.). Routledge.

Bryan, N. (2020). Shaking the bad boys: Troubling the criminalization of black boys' childhood play, hegemonic white masculinity and femininity, and the school playground-to-prison pipeline. *Race Ethnicity and Education, 23*(5), 673–692.

Bryant, P. (1998, May, 22). *A review of the reading program of the Mississippi Department of Education.* Office of the State Auditor, Performance Audit Division.

Bucholtz, M., Casillas, D. I., & Lee, J. S. (2017). Language and culture as sustenance. In D. Paris & H. S. Alim (Eds.), *Culturally sustaining pedagogies: Teaching and learning for justice in a changing world* (pp. 43–59).

Bunch, L. G., & Burns, K. (2020). History is now: What is America's story? Webinar. https://millercenter.org/news-events/events/history-now-what-americas-story

Bunyasi, T. L., & Smith, C. W. (2019). *Stay woke: A people's guide to making All Black Lives Matter.* New York University Press.

Bureau of Refugees, Freedmen, and Abandoned Lands. (1865–1866).

Bush, G. W. (1999, September 3). Excerpts from Bush's speech on improving education. The *New York Times.* https://www.nytimes.com/1999/09/03/us/excerpts-frombush-s-speech-on-improving-education.html

Bush, G. W. (2002a). President's Commission on Excellence in Special Education (PCESE). www2.ed.gov/inits/commissionsboards/whspecialeducation/reports/summ.html

Bush, G. W. (2002b). Radio address by the President to the nation. https://georgewbush-whitehouse.archives.gov/news/releases/2002/01/20020119.html

Bush, J. E. (2001). Executive Order. 01-260. Just Read Florida. https://www.fldoe.org/core/fileparse.php/7539/urlt/just_read_florida_executive_order.pdf

Business Roundtable. (2016). Why reading matters and what to do about it. https://www.businessroundtable.org/why-reading-matters-and-what-to-do-about-it

Butler, S. (2009). *Sugar of the crop: My journey to find the children of slaves.* Lyons Press.

Byrd, D., Ceacal, Y. R., Felton, J., Nicholson, C., Rhaney, D. M. L., McCray, N., & Young, J. (2017). A modern doll study: Self concept. *Race, Gender & Class, 24*(1–2), 186–202.

Cabral, L. B. (2006). Dissertation: *Letters from four antebellum black women educators to the American Missionary Association, 1863–1870 (Blanche Virginia Harris, Clara C. Duncan, Sallie Louise Daffin, Edmonia Goodelle Highgate).* University of Massachusetts, Boston.

Caldwell, J. S. (2014). *Reading assessment: A primer for teachers and coaches* (3rd ed.). Guilford.

Caldwell, O., & Courtis, S. (1924). *Then and now in education.* World Book Company.

California Assembly Bill. (1998a). 1626. http://leginfo.ca.gov/pub/97-98/bill/asm/ ab_1601-1650/ab_1626_bill_19980923_chaptered.html

California Assembly Bill. (1998b). 1639. www.leginfo.ca.gov/pub/97-98/bill/asm/ ab_1601-1650/ab_1639_bill_19980831_enrolled.html

Capellaro, C. (2004). Blowing the whistle on the Texas miracle. *Rethinking Schools, 19*(1), 17–18.

Carnine, D. (2003). IDEA: Focusing on improving results for children with disabilities. Testimony before the Subcommittee on Education Reform. Hearing before the Subcommittee on Education Reform of the Committee on Education and the Workforce. House of Representatives, One Hundred Eighth Congress, First Session. https://archive.org/stream/ERIC_ED482635/ ERIC_ED482635_djvu.txt

Case, S. H. (2002). The historical ideology of Mildred Lewis Rutherford: A Confederate historian's New South creed. *The Journal of Southern History, 68*(3), 599–628.

Castro-Villarreal, F., Villarreal, V., & Sullivan, J. R. (2016). Special education policy and response to intervention: Identifying promises and pitfalls to advance social justice for diverse students. *Contemporary School Psychology, 20,* 10–20.

Cattell, J. M. (1890). Mental tests and measurements. *Mind, 15,* 373–381.

Cattell, J. M. (1896). Address of the president before the American Psychological Association, 1895. *Psychological Review, 3,* 134–148.

Ceballos, A., Brugal, S., & Solochek, J. (2022, June 28). Some teachers alarmed by Florida civics training approach on religion, slavery. https://www.tampabay.com/news/florida-politics/2022/06/28/some-teachers-alarmed-by-florida-civics-training-approach-on-religion-slavery/

Center for Research on Education Outcomes. (2009). Multiple choice: Charter school performance in 16 states. Stanford University. http://credo.stanford.edu/reports/ MULTIPLE_CHOICE_CREDO.pdf

Center for Research on Education Outcomes. (2013). National charter school study 2013. Stanford University. https://credo.stanford.edu/wp-content/uploads/2021/08/ ncss_2013_final_draft.pdf

Chall, J. (1967). *Learning to read: The great debate.* McGraw Hill.

Champion, T. B., Rosa-Lugo, L. I., Rivers, K. O., & McCabe, A. (2010). A preliminary investigation of second- and fourth-grade African American students' performance on the *Gray Oral Reading Test*—Fourth edition. *Topics in Language Disorders, 30*(2), 145–153.

Chatterji, M. (2006). Reading achievement gaps, correlates, and moderators of early reading achievement: Evidence from the Early Childhood Longitudinal Study (ECLS) kindergarten to first grade sample. *Journal of Educational Psychology, 98*(3), 489–507.

Children with Specific Learning Disabilities Act. (1969). https://www.ldonline.org/ ld-topics/about-ld/timeline-learning-disabilities

Chotiner, I. (2020, June 1). Bryan Stevenson on the frustration behind the George Floyd protests. https://www.newyorker.com/news/q-and-a/bryan-stevenson-on-the-frustration-behind-the-george-floyd-protests

Civil Rights Act of 1866. https://history.house.gov/Historical-Highlights/1851-1900/ The-Civil-Rights-Bill-of-1866/

Civil Rights Act of 1870. www.antibiaslaw.com/list/civil-rights-act-of-1870

Civil Rights Act of 1875. https://www.senate.gov/artandhistory/history/common/ generic/CivilRightsAct1875.htm

Civil Rights Act of 1964, Pub. L. 88-352, 78 Stat. 241 (1964).

Clark, K. B., & Clark, M. P. (1950). Emotional factors in racial identification and preference in Negro children. *The Journal of Negro Education, 13*(3), 341–350.

Coddington, J., & Fairchild, H. F. (2012). *Special education and the mis-education of African American children: A call to action. Position paper of the Association of Black Psychologists.* https://www.abpsi.org/pdf/specialedpositionpaper021312.pdf

Cong. Rec. 16 April 1997.

Cooper v. Aaron. (1958). https://www.oyez.org/cases/1957/1%20MISC

Copland, J. (2021, August 26). How to regulate critical race theory in schools: A primer and model legislation. https://www.manhattan-institute.org/copland-critical-race-theory-model-legislation

Council of Chief State Officers. (2019). *Report third grade reading laws: Implementation and impact.* https://ccsso.org/resource-library/third-grade-reading-laws-implementation-and-impact

Council of Chief State School Officers. (2022). https://ccsso.org/about

Courtis, S. (1914). Standard tests in English. *Elementary School Teacher, 14*(4), 374–392.

Craft, W. (1969). *Running a thousand miles for freedom: Or, the escape of William and Ellen Craft from slavery.* Mnemosyne Pub. Co. (originally published 1860, William Tweedie).

Cramer, L. (2015). Inequities in intervention among culturally and linguistically diverse students. *Urban Education, 12*(1), 1–10.

Cramer, S. C. (1996). Looking to the future. In S. C. Cramer & W. Ellis (Eds.), *Learning disabilities: Lifelong issues* (pp. 297–304). Paul H. Brookes.

Cramer, S. C., & Ellis, W. (Eds.). (1996). *Learning disabilities: Lifelong issues.* Paul H. Brookes.

Creating a Respectful and Open World for Natural Hair Act (C.R.O.W.N.). (2022).

Crenshaw, K. (2021, July 1). The panic over critical race theory is an attempt to whitewash U. S. history. *The New York Times,* Digital.

Culatta, R. (2022). Grit and persistence. www.instructionaldesign.org/concepts/grit/

Cullotta, K. A. (2022, May 4). Illinois educators, union leaders demand end to standardized student testing: "This is a racist relic of the past." https://www.chicagotribune.com/news/breaking/ct-illinois-student-standardized-testing-opposition-20220504-v7uxp6dqind5vmr4q7mtswuory-story.html

Cummings, A., & Turner, M. (2020). *Policy brief. Covid-19 and third-grade reading policies: An analysis of state guidance on third-grade reading policies in response to Covid.* Education Policy Innovation Collaborative.

Curry, T. (2008). Saved by the Bell: Derrick Bell's racial realism as pedagogy. *Philosophical Studies in Education, 39,* 35–46.

Dalton, K. C. C. (1991). "The Alphabet Is an Abolitionist" literacy and African Americans in the emancipation era. *The Massachusetts Review, 32*(4), 545–580.

Dancy, T. E. (2014). The adultification of Black boys: What educational settings can learn from Trayvon Martin. In K. J. Fasching-Varner, R. E. Reynolds, K. A. Albert, & L. L. Martin (Eds.), *Trayvon Martin, race, and American justice: Writing wrong* (pp. 49–55). Springer.

Dao, J. (2000, September 26). The 2000 Campaign: The Texas Governor; Bush expands on education theme, saying a reading crisis endangers the economy. https://www.nytimes.com/2000/09/26/us/2000-campaign-texas-governor-bush-expands-education-theme-saying-reading-crisis.html

Darwin, C. (1979). *Origin of the species: Or the preservation of favorite races in the struggle for life* (Foreword, P. Horan). Avenel Books (original work published in 1859).

Davis, J. (1860). Speech before 36th Congress, 1st sess., *Congressional Globe, 106,* 1682.

Davis, K. (Director). (2005). *A girl like me* [Documentary]. Reel Works Teen Film-making. https://vimeo.com/59262534

Davison, L. (2021, April 19). Pasco sheriff, school district push back on school district data sharing allegations. Phttps://www.baynews9.com/fl/tampa/news/2021/04/19/pasco-sheriff--schools-push-back-on-student-data-share-allegations

DeLissovoy, N. (2016). Race, reason, and reasonableness: Toward an "unreasonable" ped agogy. *Educational Studies, 52,* 346–362.

Della Vecchia, G. P. (2020). Don't leave us behind: Third-grade reading laws and unin-tended consequences. *Michigan Reading Journal, 52*(2), 7–16.

Dennis, D. V., Kroeger, D. C., O'Byrne, W. I., Meyer, C. K., Kletzein, S. B., Huddleston, A. P., & Gilrane, C. (2012). Test-based grade retention. (Policy brief). www.literacyresearchassociation.org/publications/LRATestBasedRetentionPBFinal.pdf

DeSantis, R. (2019). Executive order 19-23. https://www.flgov.com/2019/01/31/governor-ron-desantis-issues-executive-order-19-32/

DeSantis, R. (2021, December 15). Governor DeSantis announces legislative proposal to stope W.O.K.E activism and critical race theory in schools and corporations. https://www.flgov.com/2021/12/15/governor-desantis-announces-legislative-proposal-to-stop-w-o-k-e-activism-and-critical-race-theory-in-schools-and-corporations/

DiCarlo, M. (2015). The evidence on the "Florida Formula" for education reform. Report Albert Shanker Institute. https://www.shankerinstitute.org/resource/evidence-florida-formula-education-reform

Diouf, S. (2019, February, 05). Conversation on Omar ibn Said collection. Library of Congress. https://www.loc.gov/item/webcast-8638

Douglass, F. (1845). *Narrative of the life of Frederick Douglass: An American slave, written by himself.* Antislavery Office.

Douglass, F. (1852). What to the slave is the fourth of July? https://teachingamericanhistory.org/library/document/what-to-the-slave-is-the-fourth-of-july/

Douglass, F. (1864). Speech. "The mission of the war." https://www.blackpast.org/african-american-history/1864-frederick-douglass-mission-war/

Dred Scott v. Sandford, 60 U.S. 394 (1856).

Dreeben, R. (1987). Closing the divide: What teachers and administrators can do to help Black students reading their reading potential. *American Educator, 22*(4) 28–35.

Du Bois, E. B. (1890). *The Suppression of the African Slave-Trade to the United States of America, 1638–1870.* [Dissertation]. Harvard University.

Du Bois, E. B. (1940). *Dusk of dawn: An autobiography of the race concept.* Kraus-Thomson Organization.

Du Bois, W. E. B. (1905). Resolution of the Niagara movement. In H. Brotz & B. W. Austin (Eds.), *African American social and political thought* (p. 538). Routledge.

Du Bois, W. E. B. (1966). The propaganda of history. In W. E. B. Du Bois (Ed.), *Black reconstruction in America: An essay toward the history of the part which Black folk played in the attempt to reconstruct democracy in America.* Russell & Russell.

Du Bois, W. E. B. (1996). Of our spiritual strivings. Chapter one, *The souls of Black folk.* Project Gutenberg (original publication 1903).

Duckworth, A. L., Peterson, C., Matthews, M. D., & Kelly, D. R. (2007). Grit: Perseverance and passion for long-term goals. *Journal of Personality and Social Psychology, 92*(6), 1087.

Duckworth, A. L., Quinn, P., & Tsukayama, E. (2012). What No Child Left Behind leaves behind: The roles of IQ and self-control in predicting standardized achievement test scores and report card grades. *Journal of Educational Psychology, 104,* 439–451.

Dunn, L. M. (1968). Special education for the mildly retarded: Is much of it justifiable? *Exceptional Children, 35,* 5–22.

Duster, M. (2021). *Ida B. the queen: The extraordinary life and legacy of Ida B. Wells.* Simon & Schuster.

Education of the Handicapped Act (EHA) (n.d.). P. L. 91-230.

Education Sciences Reform Act, P.L. 107-27. (2002).

Egalite, A. J., Kisida, B., & Winters, M. A. (2015). Representation in the classroom: The effect of own-race teachers on student achievement. *Economics of Education Review, 45,* 44–52.

Elementary and Secondary Education Act, Public Law 89-10. (April 11, 1965). https://www2.ed.gov/about/offices/list/oii/nonpublic/eseareauth.pdf

Ella T. v. California. (2019).

Elliot, M., & Hughes, J. (2019, August 18). The 1619 project. *New York Times* magazine. https://www.nytimes.com/interactive/2019/08/19/magazine/history-slavery-smithsonian.html

Elliott, J. G. (2020). It's time to be scientific about dyslexia. *Reading Research Quarterly, 55*(S1), S61–S75.

Ellis, W., & Cramer, S. C. (1995). *Learning disabilities: A national responsibility.* National Center for Learning Disabilities.

Ellyson, J. T., Goode, J., & Montague, A. J. (1901). Broadside. https://encyclopediavirginia.org/no-white-man/

Emma, C. (2017, January 2). Jeb Bush's consolation prize. https://www.politico.com/story/2017/01/jeb-bushs-consolation-prize-233097

Emmitt Till Antilynching Act. (2022). https://www.congress.gov/bill/117th-congress/house-bill/55/cosponsors

Erevelles, N. (2014). Crippin' Jim Crow: Disability, dis-location, and the school-to-prison pipeline. In L. Ben-Moshe, C. Chapman, & A. C. Carey (Eds.), *Disability incarcerated* (pp. 81–99). Palgrave Macmillan.

Erickson, A. T. (2012). Building inequality: The spatial organization of schooling in Nashville, Tennessee, after Brown. *Journal of Urban History, 38,* 247–270.

Every Student Succeeds Act, 20 U.S.C. § 6301 (2015). https://www.ed.gov/essa?src%3Drn

F.A.S.T. Florida's Assessment of Student Thinking. (2021). https://www.fldoe.org/core/fileparse.php/20007/urlt/FAST-One-Pager-V2.pdf

Ferguson, A. A. (2010). *Bad boys: Public schools in the making of Black masculinity.* The University of Michigan Press.

Ferri, B. A., & Connor, D. J. (2005). In the shadow of Brown: Special education and the overrepresentation of students of color. *Remedial and Special Education, 26,* 93–100.

Finkelman, P. (2011). Slavery, the Constitution, and the origins of the Civil War. OAH. *Magazine of History, 25*(2), 14–18.

FL Citizens' Alliance. (2021, June 3). Tweet.

Flesch, R. (1968). *Why Johnny can't read.* William Morrow Paperbacks.

Flores, N. (2022, July 1). Tweet. https://twitter.com/nelsonlflores/status/1542869604661448704

Florida Administrative Code. (2009). Exceptional student education eligibility for students with specific learning disabilities.

Florida Administrative Code. (2021). Voluntary prekindergarten pre- and post-assessments. Rule 6A-1.09433. https://www.law.cornell.edu/regulations/florida/Fla-Admin-Code-r-6A-1-09433

Florida Association of School Psychologists. (2015). *Position statement on the practice of grade retention and social promotion.* https://www.nasponline.org/assets/Documents/Research%20and%20Policy/Position%20Statements/GradeRetentionandSocialPromotion.pdf

Florida Atlantic University. (n.d.). Map of Jim Crow America. https://www.fau.edu/artsandletters/pjhr/chhre/pdf/sjc-map-jim-crow-america-florida.pdf

Florida B.E.S.T. Standards, (2021). www.fldoe.org/standardsreview

Florida Constitution. (1885). http://library.law.fsu.edu/Digital-Collections/CRC/CRC-1998/conhist/1885con.html

Florida Constitution. (1968). https://files.floridados.gov/media/693801/florida-constitution.pdf (amended, 2016).

Florida Formula for Success. (n.d.) (Rev.) Fla. Admin. Code R. 6A-6.053. https://casetext.com/regulation/florida-administrative-code/department-6-department-of-education/division-6a-state-board-of-education/chapter-6a-6-special-programs-i/section-6a-6053-district-k-12-comprehensive-evidence-based-reading-plan

Florida Literacy Plan. (2011). Striving readers. https://www.fldoe.org/core/fileparse.php/7539/urlt/strivingreaders.pdf

Florida Senate Bill. (2021). HB 241. Parents' Bill of Rights. https://www.flsenate.gov/Committees/billsummaries/2021/html/2475

Florida Senate Bill. (2022). CS/SB 114: High school graduation requirements Dorothy L. Hukill Financial Literacy Act. https://www.flsenate.gov/Session/Bill/2019/114/BillText/c1/PDF

Florida Senate Bill. CS/HB 1467: K-12 Education. (n.d.) https://www.flsenate.gov/Session/Bill/2022/1467

Florida Senate Bill. FL SB 1048. (n.d.) Student Assessments. https://www.flsenate.gov/Session/Bill/2022/1048

Florida Senate. (2016a). 2016 Florida Statutes. 1002.69 Statewide kindergarten screening; https://www.flsenate.gov/laws/statutes/2016/1002.69

Florida Senate. (2016b). 2016 Florida Statutes. 1002.67 Performance standards. https://www.flsenate.gov/Laws/Statutes/2016/1002.67

Florida State. (n.d.) HB7069.

Florida. (n.d.) HB7029, State Board of Education Rule 6A-6.03018

Fofaria, R. R. (2021, April 6). What does this science of reading bill really mean, and how did we get here? https://www.ednc.org/2021-04-06-science-reading-bill-nc-north-carolina-instruction-explain-educators-teacherss/

Foorman, B. R., Francis, D. J., Fletcher, M., Schatschneider, C., & Mehta, P. (1998). The role of instruction in learning to read: Preventing reading failure in at-risk children. *Journal of Educational Psychology, 90,* 37–55.

Foorman, B., Beyler, N., Borradaile, K., Coyne, M., Denton, C. A., Dimino, J., Furgeson, J., Hayes, L., Henke, J., Justice, L., Keating, B., Lewis, W., Sattar, S., Streke, A., Wagner, R., & Wissel, S. (2016). *Foundational skills to support reading for understanding in kindergarten through 3rd grade* (NCEE 2016–4008). National Center for Education Evaluation and Regional Assistance (NCEE), Institute of Education Sciences, U.S. Department of Education. http://whatworks.ed.gov

For The People Act (SB1). https://www.congress.gov/bill/117th-congress/senate-bill/1/text

Forten, C. (1861–1864). Life on the sea Islands. *The Atlantic Monthly*. https://www.theatlantic.com

Forzani, E., Afflerbach, P., Aguirre, S., Brynelson, N., Cervetti, G., Cho, B-Y., Coiro, J., García, G. E., Greenleaf, C., Guthrie, J. T., Hain, B., Hinchman, K., Katz, M-L., Lee, C. D., Pacheco, M., Pearson, P. D., Ross, A., Skerrett, A., & Uccelli, P. (2022). Advances and missed opportunities in the development of the 2026 NAEP Reading Framework. *Literacy Research: Theory, Method, and Practice*, *71*(1), 153–189.

Frankenberg, E., & Taylor, K. (2015). ESEA and the Civil Rights Act: An interbranch approach to desegregation. *The Russell Sage Foundation Journal of the Social Sciences*, *1*, 32–49.

Franklin, B. C. (1931). The Tulsa race riot and three of its victims. https://transcription.si.edu/project/37850. Smithsonian. National Museum of African American History and Culture, 2022.

Franklin, J., & Moss, A. (1994). *From slavery to freedom: A history of African Americans*. McGraw Hill.

Friedberg, S., Shanahan, T., Fennell, F., Fisher, D., & Howe, R. (2020). *The state of the sunshine state standards.* https://fordhaminstitute.org/national/research/state-sunshine-states-standards-florida-best-edition

Fuchs, D., & Fuchs, L. S. (2006). Introduction to response to intervention: What, why, and how valid is it? *Reading Research Quarterly*, *41*, 93–99.

Fuchs, D., Fuchs, L., Compton, D. L., Bouton, B., Caffrey, E., & Hill, L. (2007). Dynamic assessment as response to intervention: A scripted protocol to identify young at-risk readers. *Teaching Exceptional Children*, *39*, 58–63.

Fuchs, D., Fuchs, L., Mathes, P. G., & Simmons, D. C. (1997). Peer-assisted learning strategies: Making classrooms more responsive to diversity. *American Educational Research Journal*, *34*, 174–206.

Fuchs, L. S., & Fuchs, D. (1998). Treatment validity: A unifying concept for reconceptualizing the identification of learning disabilities. *Learning Disabilities Research & Practice*, *13*, 204–219.

Fuchs, L. S., & Fuchs, D. (2007). A model for implementing responsiveness to intervention. *Council for Exceptional Children*, *39*, 14–20.

Gabriel, R. (2018). Dyslexia legislation: A brief history. *Journal of Reading Recovery*. *17*(2) 25–34.

Gabriel, R. (2019). Rights, responsibilities and learning to read: Contrasting claims to a "right to read." A paper presented at the Literacy Research Association, Tampa, FL, December 2019.

Gabriel, R. (2020). Converting to privatization: A discourse analysis of dyslexia policy narratives. *American Educational Research Journal*, *57*(1), 305–338.

Gabriel, R., & Woulfin, S. (2017). Reading and dyslexia legislation: The confluence of parallel policies. In J. Lester, C. Lochmiller, & R. Gabriel (Eds.), *Discursive perspectives on education policy and implementation* (pp. 197–218). Palgrave.

Gadsden, V. L. (1994). Understanding family literacy: Conceptual issues facing the field. *Teachers College Record*, *96*(1), 58–86.

Gamse, B. C., Jacob, R. T., Horst, M., Boulay, B., & Unlu, F. (2008). Reading first impact study. Final report. Executive summary. NCEE 2009-4039. Institute of Education Sciences (ED), National Center for Education Evaluation and Regional Assistance.

Garza, A., Cullors, P., & Tometi, O. (2013). Black lives matter. Herstory. https://blacklivesmatter.com/herstory/

Gardner, D. P., National Commission on Excellence in Education (ED), W. C., & And, O. (1983). *A nation at risk: The imperative for educational reform. An open letter to the American people. A report to the nation and the Secretary of Education.*

Gary, B. v. Snyder (2016).

Gary, B. v. Whitmer - 957 F.3d 616 (6th Cir. 2020).

Gates, H. L. (2011). *Life upon these shores: Looking at African American history, 1513–2008.* Knopf.

Gay, G. (2018). *Culturally responsive teaching: Theory, research, and practice* (3rd ed.). Teachers College Press.

Gershenson, S., Holt, S. B., & Papageorge, N. W. (2016). Who believes in me? The effect of student dash teacher demographic match on teacher expectations. *Economics of Education Review 52*, 209–224.

Gersten, R., Darch, C., & Gleason, M. (1988). Effectiveness of a direct instruction academic kindergarten for low-income students. *The Elementary School Journal, 89*, 227–240.

Gersten, R., & Dimino, J. A. (2006). RTI (response to intervention): Rethinking special education for students with reading difficulties (yet again). *Reading Research Quarterly, 41*, 99–108.

Gilder Lehrman Institute of American History. (2021). Lord Dunmore's proclamation, 1775. https://www.gilderlehrman.org/history-resources/spotlight-primary-source/lord-dunmores-proclamation-1775

Gilliam, W. S., Maupin, A. N., Reyes, C. R., Accavitti, M., & Shic, F. (2016). *Do early educators' implicit biases regarding sex and race relate to behavior expectations and recommendations of preschool expulsions and suspensions?* Yale Child Study Center.

Givens, J. R. (2019). "There would be no lynching if it did not start in the schoolroom": Carter G. Woodson and the occasion of Negro History Week, 1926–1950. *American Educational Research Journal, 56*(4), 1457–1494.

Givens, J. R. (2021). *Fugitive pedagogy: Carter G. Woodson and the art of Black teaching.* Harvard University Press.

Glaude, E. (2016). *Democracy in black: How race still enslaves the American Soul.* Crown.

Glaude, E. (2021). Opinion: The Kyle Rittenhouse verdict is American madness incarnate. https://www.washingtonpost.com/opinions/2021/11/22/kyle-rittenhouse-verdict-white-innocence-american-delusion/

Goals. (2000). https://clinton.presidentiallibraries.us/exhibits/show/education-reform/goals-esea

Goff, P. A., Jackson, M. C., Di Leone, B. A. L., Culotta, C. M., & DiTomasso, N. A. (2014). The essence of innocence/consequences of dehumanizing Black children. *Journal of Personality and Social Psychology, 106*(4), 526–545.

Goldberg, D. T. (2021, May 7). The war on critical race theory. *Boston Review.* http://bostonreview.net/race-politics/david-theo-goldberg-war-critical-race-theory

Gong Lum v. Rice. (1927). *Gong Lum v. Rice,* 275 U.S. 78. https://supreme.justia.com/cases/federal/us/275/78/

Goodwin, A. P., & Jimenez, R. T. (2020). The science of reading: Supports, critiques, and questions. *Reading Research Quarterly, 55*(S1), S7–S16.

Gordon, R. A., & Rudert, E. E. (1979). Bad news concerning IQ tests. *Sociology of Education, 52*, 174–190.

Gould, S. (1996). *The mismeasure of man.* Norton (originally published 1981).

Gowen, A. (2022, February 9). "Blue" suburban moms are mobilizing to counter conservatives in fights over masks, book bans and diversity education. https://www.washingtonpost.com/nation/2022/02/09/suburban-women-voters-organize/

Graff, H. (1979). *The literacy myth: Literacy and social structure in the nineteenth-century city.* Academic Press.

Graff, H. (1991). *The literacy myth: Cultural integration and social structure in the nineteen-century.* Transaction Publishers (originally published in 1979).

Graff, H. (1995). *The labyrinths of literacy: Reflections on literacy past and present* (rev. ed.). University of Pittsburgh Press.

Granados, A. (2021, December 14). On COVID, posting lesson plans, testing, race, and more: How this legislature dealt with education. https://www.ednc.org/2021-12-14-a-legislative-recap-what-happened-this-long-session-of-the-general-assembly/#critical-race-theory

Gray, W. S. (1917). *Studies of elementary school reading through standardized tests* (Supplemental Educational Monograph, Number 1). University of Chicago Press.

Gray-Lobe, G., Pathak, P., & Walters, C. (2021). Long term effects of universal preschool. MIT School Effectiveness & Inequality Initiative. Discussion Paper #2021.05.

Green v. School Bd. of. New Kent Co, 391 U.S 430. (1968). https://www.oyez.org/cases/1967/695

Green, E. L. (2019, March 8). DeVos illegally delayed special education rule, judge says. https://www.nytimes.com/2019/03/08/us/politics/betsy-devos-special-education.html

Greene, J. P., & Winters, M. A. (2007). Revisiting grade retention: An evaluation of Florida's test-based promotion policy. *Education Finance and Policy, 2*(4), 319–340.

Greene, J. P., & Winters, M. A. (2009). The effects of exemptions to Florida's test-based promotion policy/Who is retained? Who benefits academically? *Economics of Education Review, 28*(1), 135–142.

Greene, P. (2019). Will Florida abolish the Common Core? (Spoiler alert: Probably not). https://www.forbes.com/sites/petergreene/2019/02/06/will-florida-abolish-the-common-core-spoiler-alert-probably-not/?sh=41d5f9a4752c

Greenidge, K. (2021, March 5). Black spirituals as poetry and resistance. https://www.nytimes.com/2021/03/05/t-magazine/black-spirituals-poetry-resistance.html20

Griffin, A., & Tackie, H. (2016). *Through our eyes: Perspectives and reflections from Black teachers.* The Education Trust.

Griggs v. Duke Power Co., 401 U.S. 424. (1971).

Grissom, J., & Shepard, L. (1998). Repeating and dropping out of school. In L. Shepard & M. Smith (Eds.), *Flunking grades: Research and policies on retention* (pp. 34–63). Falmer Press.

Gullo, D. F., & Impellizeri, W. E. (2021). Kindergarten teachers' ratings of children's behavioral and learning competencies: Predictive impact on children's third and fourth grade achievement trajectories. *Early Childhood Education Journal, 50,* 304–314.

Hall, S. (1980). Encoding/decoding. In S. Hall, D. Hobson, A. Low, & P. Willis (Eds.), *Culture, media, language* (pp. 129–138). Centre for Contemporary Cultural Studies (original work published 1973).

Hall, S. (1993). What is this "black" in black popular culture? *Social Justice, 20*(1/2) 104–114.

Hall, S. (2003). The problem of ideology: Marxism without guarantees. In D. Morley & K. Chen (Eds.), *Stuart Hall: Critical dialogues in cultural studies* (pp. 25–47). Routledge.

Hannah-Jones, N. (2019, August 14). *The 1669 project.* https://www.nytimes.com/interactive/2019/08/14/magazine/1619-america-slavery.html

Harper, F. E. W. (1854). Slave auction. In F. E. W. Harper, …. https://poets.org/poem/slave-auction

Harper, F. E. W. (1893). *Sketches of southern life.* Ferguson Bros., CO. & Printer.

Harrell, A. (2014). *Department of Justice: Slavery, peonage, and involuntary servitude.* Antoinette Harrell.

Harris, C. (1993). Whiteness as property. *Harvard Law Review, 106,* 1707–1791.

Harris, J. C. (1955). *The complete tales of Uncle Remus.* Houghton.

Harris, J. C. (2008). *The classic tales of Brer Rabbit.* Running Press Kids.

Harris, V., & Willis, A. I. (2016). William Edward Burghardt Du Bois. In J. Palmer (Ed.), *Fifty key contemporary thinkers on education* (pp. 212–219). Routledge.

Haynes, L. (1776). *Liberty further extended: Or free thoughts on the illegality of slave-keeping.*

Heath, S. B. (1983). *Ways with words: Language, life, and work in communities and classrooms.* Cambridge University Press.

Heffernan, H. (1969). The school curriculum in American education. In E. Fuller & J. B. Pearson (Eds.), *Education in the states: Nationwide development since 1900* (pp. 215–286). National Education Association.

Henderson, S. (2016, December 3). Besty DeVos and the twilight of public education. *Detroit Free Press.* www.freep.com/story/opinion/columnists/stephen-henderson/2016/12/03/betsy-devos-education-donald-trump/94728574/

Hernandez, D. J. (2011). *Double jeopardy: How third grade reading skills and poverty influence high school graduation.* Annie E. Casey Foundation www.aecf.org/m/resourcedoc/AECF-DoubleJeopardy-2012-Full.pdf

Herrington, C. D., & Weider, V. (2001). Equity, adequacy and vouchers: Past and present school finance litigation in Florida. *Journal of School Finance, 27,* 517–534.

Hilliard, A. (1991). Do we have the will to educate all children? *Educational Leadership, 49*(1), 31–36.

Holmes et al., v. Bush et al. (2000). WL 527694 (Fla. Cir. Ct.) Case no. 99-3370.

Homestead Act. 1862. https://www.archives.gov/milestone-documents/homestead-act

Homestead Act. 1866. https://www.senate.gov/artandhistory/history/common/civil_war/Homestead_Act.htm

Hong, G., & Yu, B. (2007). Early-grade retention and children's reading and math learning in elementary years. *Educational Evaluation and Policy Analysis, 29*(4), 239– 261.

Hong, Y., & Hong, G. (2021). With test-based promotion-effects on instructional time allocation and student learning in grade 3. *AERA Open, 7,* 1–15.

Horowitz, S. H., Rawe, J., & Whittaker, M. C. (2017). *The state of learning disabilities: Understanding the 1 in 5.* National Center for Learning Disabilities.

Hosp, J. L., & Madyun, N. (2007). Addressing disproportionality with response to intervention. In S. Jimerson, M. Burns, & A. VanDerHeyden (Eds.), *Handbook of response to intervention: The science and practice of assessment and intervention* (pp. 172–181). Springer.

Howse, R. B., Lange, G., Farran, D. C., & Boyles, C. D. (2003). Motivation and self-regulation as predictors of achievement in economically disadvantaged young children. *Journal of Experimental Education, 71,* 151–174.

Huddleston, A. P. (2014). Achievement at whose expense? A literature review of test-based grade retention policies in U.S. school. *Education Policy Analysis Archives, 22*(18). http://dx.doi.org/10.14507/epaa.v22n18.2014

Huey, E. B. (1908). *The psychology and pedagogy of reading; With a review of the history of reading and writing and of methods, text, and hygiene in reading.* Macmillan.

Hughes, J. N., Chen, Q., Thoemmes, F., & Kwok, O. (2010). An investigation of the relationship between retention in first-grade and performance on high stakes tests in third grade. *Educational Evaluation and Policy Analysis, 32*(2), 166–182.

Hurston, Z. N. (1927). Cudjo's own story of the last African slaver. *The Journal of Negro History, 12*(4), 648–663.

Hurston, Z. N. (2018). *Barracoon: The story of the last "Black Cargo."* Amistad.

Husband, T. (2012). Why can't Jamal read? *Phi Delta Kappan, 93*(5), 23-27.

Individuals with Disabilities Education Improvement Act of 2004, Pub L. No., 08-446, 118.

Innovative Approaches to Literacy Program. (2018). https://www2.ed.gov/programs/innovapproaches-literacy/index.html

Inoue, A. B. (2015). *Antiracist writing assessment ecologies: Teaching and assessing writing for a socially just future.* WAC Clearinghouse and Parlor Press.

Intercultural Development Research Association. (2019). Failing-in grade retention. www.idra.org

International Literacy Association. (2019). Brief: Children experiencing reading difficulties: What we know and what we can do. https://www.literacyworldwide.org

Irwin, V., NCES, Zhang, J., Wang, X., Hein, S., Wang, K., Roberts, A., York, C., AIR, Barmer, A., Bullock Mann, F., Dilig, R., & Parker, S., RTI. (2021). *The condition of education 2021.* https://nces.ed.gov/pubsearch/pubsinfo.asp?pubid=2021144

Jacob, R. T., Stone, S., & Roderick, M. (2004). *Ending social promotion: The response of teachers and students.* Consortium on Chicago School Research.

James, J. F. (Ed.). (1925). Autobiography of Omar ibn Said, Slave in North Carolina, 1831. *The American Historical Review, 30*(4), 787–795.

Jefferson, T. (1774). Instructions to virginia's delegates to the first continental congress. https://founders.archives.gov/documents/Jefferson/01-01-02-0090

Jefferson, T. (1776). A declaration by the representatives of United States of America, in General Congress Assembled. https://www.pbs.org/wgbh/aia/part2/2h33t.html

Jenkins, J. R., & O'Connor, R. E. (2002). Early identification and intervention for young children with reading/ learning disabilities. In R. Bradley, L. Danielson, & D. P. Hallahan (Eds.), *Identification of learning disabilities: Research to practice* (pp. 99–150). Erlbaum.

Jenkins, M. D. (1936a). Case studies of Negro children of Binet IQ 160 and above. *Journal of Negro Education, 19*(3), 322–332.

Jenkins, M. D. (1936b). A socio-psychological study of Negro children of superior intelligence. *Journal of Negro Education, 5*(2), 189–190.

Jensen, A. R. (1969). How much can we boost I.Q. and scholastic achievement? *Harvard Educational Review, 33*, 1–123.

Jensen, A. R. (1972). *Genetics and education.* Harper & Row.

Jensen, A. R. (1973). *Educability and group differences.* Harper & Row.

Jimerson, S. R. (2001a). Meta-analysis of grade retention re-search: Implications for practice in the 21st century. *School Psychology Review, 30*, 420–437.

Jimerson, S. R. (2001b). A synthesis of grade retention research: Looking backward and moving forward. *The California School Psychologist, 6*, 47–59.

Jimerson, S. R., Anderson, G. E., & Whipple, A. D. (2002). Winning the battle and losing the war: Examining the relationship between grade retention and dropping out of high school. *Psychology in the Schools, 39*, 441–457.

Jimerson, S. R., Ferguson, P., Whipple, A. D., Anderson, G. E., & Dalton, M. J. (2002). Exploring the association between grade retention and dropout: A longitudinal study examining socio-emotional, behavioral, and achievement characteristics of retained students. *The California School Psychologist, 7*, 51–62.

Jimerson, S. R., & Kaufmann, A. M. (2003). Reading, writing, and retention: A primer on grade retention research period. *The Reading Teacher, 56*(7), 622–635.

John Lewis Act. (n.d.) https://www.congress.gov/bill/116th-congress/senate-bill/4263

Johnson, C. (1923). The mental testing of Negro groups. *Opportunity, 1,* 21–28.

Johnson, J. W., & Johnson, J. R. (1900). *Lift every voice and sing.* Edward B. Marks Music Corp.

Johnson, K. R., & Simons, H. D. (1972). Black children and reading: What teachers need to know. *The Phi Delta Kappan, 53*(5), 288–290.

Johnson, W. (1999). *Soul by soul: Life inside the antebellum slave market.* Harvard University Press.

Johnson, W. B. (1991). A Black teacher and her school in Reconstruction Darien: The correspondence of Hettie Sabattie and J. Murray Hoag, 1868–1869. *The Georgia Historical Quarterly, 75*(1), 90–105.

Johnston, P., & Scanlon, D. (2020). *Literacy research report: An examination of dyslexia research and instruction, with policy implications.* Literacy Research Association.

Jones, J., & Mosher, W. D. (2013). Fathers' involvement with their children in the United States, 2006–2010. *National Health Statistics Report, 71,* 1–22.

Jones, L. V. (1996). A history of the national assessment of educational progress and some questions about its future. *Educational Researcher, 25*(7), 15–22.

Jones, Z. C. (2022, March 10). Florida legislature passes "Stop WOKE Act," second controversial education bill this week. https://www.cbsnews.com/news/florida-critical-race-theory-education-stop-woke-act/

Judd, C. (1913). Educational news and editorial comment. *Elementary School Teacher, 15,* 1–2.

Kaestle, C., Damon-Moore, H., Stedman, L., Tinsley, K., & Trollinger, W., Jr. (1991). *Literacy in the United States: Readers and reading since 1880.* Yale University Press.

Karier, C. J. (1972). Testing for order and control in the corporate liberal state. *Educational Theory, 22*(2), 154–180.

Karier, C. J. (1986). *The individual, society, and education: A history of American educational ideas* (2nd ed.). Free Press (original publication, 1970).

Katzmann, M. T., & Rosen, R. S. (1970). The science and politics of the National Educational Assessment. *The Record, 71*(4), 571–586.

Kelley, B., Weyer, M., McCann, M., Broom, S., & Keily, T. (2021). 50-state comparison: State K-3 policies. https://www.ecs.org/doctype/50-state-comparison/

Kendi, I. X. (2019). *How to be an antiracist.* One World.

Kennedy, W., Van de Riet, V., & White, J. (1963). A normative sample of intelligence and achievement of Negro elementary school children in the Southeastern United States. *Monographs of the Society for Research in Child Development, 28,* 1–112.

Kidder, W. C., & Rosner, J. (2002). How the SAT creates built-in-headwinds: An educational and legal. *Santa Clara Law Review, 43*(1), 131–211.

Kim, H., & Bauer, S. S. (2018). Effect of Early grade retention on school completion: A prospective study. *Journal of Educational Psychology, 110*(7), 974–991.

King, J. (2016). *Fact sheet: Preventing racial discrimination in special education.* U.S. Department of Education, Office of Civil Rights. https://www2.ed.gov/about/offices/list/ocr/docs/dcl-factsheet-racedisc-special-education.pdf

King, M. L. (1963). Speech. "I have a dream." https://www.americanrhetoric.com/speeches/mlkihaveadream.htm

King, M. L. (1967). *Where do we go from here: Chaos or community?* Beacon Press.

Koretz, D., & Diebert, E. (1996). Setting standards and interpreting achievement: A cautionary tale from the National Assessment of Educational Progress. *Educational Assessment, 3*(1), 53–81.

Kratochwill, T. K., Clements, M. A., & Kalymon, K. M. (2007). Response to intervention: Conceptual and methodological issues in implementation. In S. R. Jimerson, M. K. Burns, & A. M. VanDerHeyden (Eds.), *Handbook of response to intervention: The science and practice of multi-tiered systems of support* (pp. 25–52). Springer.

Kupscznk, L. A. (2020). *How does grading schools impact Florida's teachers and Students? The need for a new approach to school accountability.* [Doctoral Dissertation]. Scholar Works at UMass Boston. University of Massachusetts Boston.

Ladson-Billings, G. (1994). *The dreamkeepers: Successful teachers of African American children.* Wiley.

Lanehart, S. L., Bloomquist, J., & Malik, A. M. (2015). Language use in African American communities: An introduction. In S. L. Lanehart, J. Bloomquist, & A. M. Malik (Eds.), *The Oxford handbook of African American language* (pp. 1–21). Oxford.

Langemann, E. C. (2000). *An elusive science: The troubling history of education research.* University of Chicago Press.

Larry P. v. Riles. C-71-2270 FRP. Dist. Ct. (1979 & 1986).

Leonardo, Z. (2009). *Race, whiteness, and education.* Routledge.

Leonardo, Z. (2012). The race for class: Reflections on a critical raceclass theory of education. *Educational Studies, 48,* 427–449.

Lesnick, J. Goerge, R. M., Smithgall, C., & Gwynne, J. (2010). Report to the Annie E. Casey Foundation. *Reading on grade level in third grade: How is it related to high school performance and college enrollment?* Chapin Hall at the University of Chicago.

Lhamon, C. E. (2016). *Dear colleague letter: Preventing racial discrimination in special education.* U.S. Department of Education. https://www2.ed.gov/about/offices/list/ocr/letters/colleague-201612-racedisc-special-education.pdf

Lian, Q., Yu C., Tu, X., Deng, M., Wang, T., Su, Q., & Zuo, X. (2021). Grade repetition and bullying victimization in adolescents: A global cross-sectional study of the Program for International Student Assessment (PISA) data from 2018. *PLoS Med, 18*(11), 1–17.

LiCalsi, C., Ozek, U., & Figlio, D. (2016). The uneven implementation of universal school policies/maternal education and florida's mandatory grade retention policy. Working Paper 167 (later published in *Education Finance and Policy,* 2019).

Lincoln, A. (1865, March 4). Abraham Lincoln's second inaugural address. https://www.battlefields.org/sites/default/files/atoms/files/Lincoln%20Second%20Inagural%20Address.pdf

Lindo, E. J. (2006). The African American presence in reading intervention experiments. *Remedial and Special Education, 27,* 148–153.

Lippman, W. (1922). Tests of hereditary intelligence. *The New Republic,* 328–330.

Literacy Education for All, Results for the Nation Act. (2013). https://www.ncld.org/wp-content/uploads/2015/11/LEARN-Act.pdf

Literacy Research Association. (2012). Policy brief. Test-base grade retention.

Lloyd, D. N. (1974). Analysis of sixth grade characteristics predicting school dropout or graduation. *JSAS Catalog of Selected Documents in Psychology, 4,* 90.

Lloyd, D. N. (1978). Prediction of school failure from third-grade data. *Educational and Psychological Measurement, 38,* 1193–1200.

Lloyd, G., & Martinez, J. S. (2021). Common interpretation: The slave clause. https://constitutioncenter.org/interactive-constitution/interpretation/article-i/clauses/761

Long, H. (1923). Race and mental tests. *Opportunity, 1,* 22–25.

Long, H. (1925). On mental tests and racial psychology: A critique. *Opportunity, 2,* 134–138.

Lorence, J. (2014). Third-grade retention and reading achievement in Texas: A nine-year panel study. *Social Science Research, 48*, 1–19.

Lorence, J., & Dworkin, A. G. (2006). Elementary grade retention in Texas and reading achievement among racial groups, 1994–2002. *Review of Policy Research, 5*, 999–1033.

Louisiana House Bill 564. (2021). Provides relative to training with respect to certain concepts related to race and sex in elementary and secondary schools and postsecondary education institutions. https://legiscan.com/LA/text/HB564/2021

Love, B. J. (2004). Brown Plus 50 counter-storytelling: A critical race theory snalysis of the "Majoritarian achievement gap" story. *Equity and Excellence in Education, 37*(3), 227–246.

Loyola, M. (2016). Almost a miracle. https://www.city-journal.org/html/almost-miracle-14734.html

Lyon, G. R. (1996). The state of research. In S. C. Cramer & W. Ellis (Eds.), *Learning disabilities: Lifelong issues* (pp. 3–64). Paul H. Brookes.

MacMillan, D. L., & Reschly, D. J. (1988). Overrepresentation of minority students: The case for greater specificity or reconsideration of the variables examined. *Journal of Special Education, 32*, 15–24.

MacMillan, D. L., Siperstein, G. N., & Gresham, F. M. (1996). A challenge to the viability of mild mental retardation as a diagnostic category. *Exceptional Children, 62*, 356–371.

Marsh, J. A., Gershwin, D., Kirby, S. N., & Xia, N. (2009). *Retaining students in grade: Lessons learned regarding policy design and implementation* (Technical Report No. 677). RAND Education.

Martorell, P., & Mariano, L. (2017). The causal effects of grade retention on behavioral outcomes. *Journal of Research on Educational Effectiveness, 11*(2), 192–216.

Massachusetts Historical Society. (1848). Long road to justice: Sarah C. Roberts vs. City of Boston. www.longroadtojustice.org/topics/education/sarah-roberts.php

Mathis, W. (2011). *Review of Florida formula for student achievement: Lessons for the nation*. National Educational Policy Center. https://nepc.colorado.edu/thinktank/review-florida-formula

Matthews, J. S., Kizzie, K. T., Rowley, S. J., & Cortina, K. (2010). African Americans and boys. Understanding the literacy gap, tracing academic trajectories, and evaluating the role of learning-related skills. *Journal of Educational Psychology, 102*(3), 757–771.

Mawhinney, J. (1998). "Giving up the ghost": Disrupting the (re)production of white privilege in anti-racist pedagogy and organizational change. [Masters thesis]. Ontario Institute for Studies in Education of the University of Toronto. www.collectionscanada.gc.ca/obj/s4/f2/dsk2/tape15/PQDD_0008/MQ33991.pdf

McCarter, S. (2017). The school-to-prison pipeline: A primer for social workers. *Social Worker, 62*(1), 53–61.

McGrory, K., & Weber, N. (2021, April 19). Feds investigating Pasco schools giving student data to sheriff. *Tampa Bay Times.* https://www.tampabay.com/investigations/2021/04/19/feds-investigating-pasco-schools-giving-student-data-to-sheriff/

McHenry, E. (1996). "Dreaded eloquence": The origins and rise of African American literary societies and libraries. *Harvard Library Bulletin, 6*(2), 32–56. http://nrs.harvard.edu/urn-3:HUL.InstRepos:42665394

McKenzie, S., Jordan, E., & Wood, C. (2021). Early access: Elementary school outcomes for Arkansas Better Chance public pre-kindergarten participants. *Arkansas Education Report, 18*(5), 1–35.

McKinney de Royston, M. M., Madkins, T. C., Givens, J. R., & Nasir, N. S. (2020). "I'm a teacher, I'm gonna always protect you": Understanding Black educators' protection of Black children. *American Educational Research Journal, 58*(1), 68–106.

McLaughlin, E. C. (2021). Critical race theory is a lens. Here are 11 ways looking through it might refine your understanding of history. https://www.cnn.com/2021/05/27/us/critical-race-theory-lens-history-crt/index.html

McMillon, G. M. T. (2001). A tale of two settings: African American students' literacy experiences at church and at school. [Unpublished doctoral dissertation]. Michigan State University.

McNamara, R. (2020, August 7). Ida B. Wells. http://thoughtco.com/ida-b-wells-basics-1773408

McQuillan, J. (1998). *The literacy crisis: False claims real, solutions.* Heinemann.

Mechanic, M. (2021, August 13). America still hasn't processed its original sin. https://www.motherjones.com/media/2021/08/black-author-america-original-sin-legacy-slavery-clint-smith-book-how-word-passed/

Meeropol, A. (1937). Bitter Fruit. *The New York Teacher*, January, 17.

Meyer, L. H., Park, H-S., Bevan-Brown, J. M., & Savage, C. (2015). Culturally responsive special education in inclusive schools. In J. A. Banks & C. A. Banks (Eds.), *Multicultural education: Issues and perspectives* (pp. 235–256), Wiley.

Michigan Senate. (2023). Senate bill 0012. http://legislature.mi.gov/doc.aspx?2023-SB-0012

Migdon, B. (2022, March 1). Texas civil rights groups demand school district return over 100 books to library shelves. https://thehill.com/changing-america/respect/diversity-inclusion/596335-texas-civil-rights-groups-demand-school-district

Miller, H. A. (1923). The myth of superiority. *Opportunity*, 1, 288–289.

Mitchell, P., & Van Gieson, J. (1993). Jeb Bush's thesis: Get rid of the Education Department. https://www.orlandosentinel.com/news/os-xpm-1993-10-31-9311010245-story.html

Monaghan, E. J. (2005). *Learning to read and write in colonial America.* University of Massachusetts Press.

Monaghan, J. E. (1998). Reading for the enslaved, writing for the free: Reflections on liberty and literacy. *Proceedings of the American Antiquarian Society, A Journal of American History and culture through 1876, 108*(2), 309–341.

Montagu, M. F. A. (1945). Intelligence in northern negroes and southern whites in the first world war. *American Journal of Psychology, 58,* 161–188.

Morphett, M. V., & Washburne, C. (1931). When should children learn to read? *The Elementary School Journal, 31*(7), 496–503.

Morris, M. W. (2016). *Pushout: The criminalization of black girls in schools.* The New Press.

Morris, R. C. (1976). *Reading, 'riting, and reconstruction: The education of freedmen in the South, 1861.* University of Chicago Press.

Morrison, T. (1975, May 30). Portland State University's Oregon Public Speakers Collection: "Black Studies Center public dialogue. Pt. 2," May 30, 1975. https://pdxscholar.library.pdx.edu/orspeakers/90/

Morrison, T. (1984). Rootedness: The ancestor as foundation. In M. Evans (Ed.), *Black women writers (1950– 1980)* (pp. 339–345). Anchor.

Morse, W. (1919). Lemuel Haynes. *The Journal of Negro History, 4*(1), 22–32.

Moten, D. E. (1999). Racial integrity or "race suicide": Virginia's eugenic movement, W.E.B. Du Bois, and the work of Walter A. Plecker. *Negro History Bulletin, 62*(2/3), 6–17.

Murray, J. (1775). Lord Dunmore's proclamation, 1775. https://www.gilderlehrman.org/history-resources/spotlight-primary-source/lord-dunmores-proclamation-1775

Murray, P. (2017, March 22). Memorandum: *Real choice vs. false choice: The repercussions of privatization programs for students, parents, and public schools.* https://www.help.senate.gov/imo/.../Murray_Privatization%20Caucus%20Memo.pdf

Mutua, K. (2008). Counternarrative. In L. M. Given (Ed.), *The SAGE encyclopedia of qualitative research methods* (p. 133). SAGE.

NAACP Legal Defense and Educational Fund, Inc. (2022). *Brown v. Board*: The significance of the "Doll test." https://www.naacpldf.org/ldf-celebrates-60th-anniversary-brown-v-board-education/significance-doll-test/

National Assessment Governing Board. (2022). *Reading framework for the national assessment of educational progress: 1992–2000.* Author.

National Assessment Governing Board. (2022). Reading framework https://www.nagb.gov/content/dam/nagb/en/documents/publications/frameworks/reading/2026-reading-framework/naep-2026-reading-framework.pdf

National Association for the Advancement of Colored People. (1969). *Is it helping poor children? Title I and ESEA: A report.* Washington Research Project.

National Association of School Psychologists. (2011). Position statement. https://www.nasponline.org/assets/Documents/Research%20and%20Policy/Position%20Statements/GradeRetentionandSocialPromotion.pdf

National Center for Education Statistics. (1992). *National assessment of educational progress: The nation's report card: Reading 1992.* National Center for Education Statistics, Institute of Education Sciences, U.S. Department of Education. https://files.eric.ed.gov/fulltext/ED369067.pdf

National Center for Education Statistics. (1994). *National assessment of educational progress: The nation's report card: Reading 1994.* National Center for Education Statistics, Institute of Education Sciences, U.S. Department of Education.

National Center for Education Statistics. (1994). National assessment of educational progress. The 1994 national assessment of educational progress in reading. http://nces.ed.gov.nationsreportcard

National Center for Education Statistics. (2000). *National assessment of educational progress: The nation's report card: Reading 1994.* U.S. Department of Education. https://nces.ed.gov/nationsreportcard/pdf/main2000/2001499.pdf

National Center for Educational Statistics (2002). *National assessment of educational progress: The nation's report card: Reading 2002.* U.S. Department of Education. https://nces.ed.gov/nationsreportcard/pdf/main2002/2003521.pdf

National Center for Educational Statistics. (2004). *National assessment of educational progress: The nation's report card: Reading 2004.* U.S. Department of Education. https://nces.ed.gov/nationsreportcard/pdf/main2009/2010458.pdf

National Center for Education Statistics. (2011). *National assessment of educational progress: The nation's report card: Reading 2011.* U.S. Department of Education. https://nces.ed.gov/nationsreportcard/pdf/main2011/2012457.pdf

National Center for Education Statistics. (2014). *National assessment of educational progress: The nation's report card: Reading 2014.* U.S. Department of Education.

National Center for Education Statistics. (2015). *National assessment of educational progress: The nation's report card: Reading 2015.* U.S. Department of Education. https://www.nationsreportcard.gov/reading_math_2015/files/2015_Results_Appendix_Reading.pdf

National Center for Education Statistics. (2019). *National assessment of educational progress: The nation's report card: Reading 2019.* U.S. Department of Education. https://www.nationsreportcard.gov/reading/states/groups/?grade=4

National Center for Youth Law. (2018, July 18). COPAA challenges secretary DeVos's decision to delay implementation of equity in IDEA regulations [Press release]. https://youthlaw.org/copaa-challenges-secretary-devoss-decision-to-delay-implementation-of-equity-in-idea-regulations/

National Center on Improving Literacy. (2021). Florida State Education (SEA) dyslexia legislation. https://improvingliteracy.org/state-of-dyslexia/florida

National Center on Intensive Intervention. (2018, July). Measures of academic progress (MAP) for primary grades. https://charts.intensiveintervention.org/chart/academic-screening

National Council of Teachers of English. (2002). Resolution on the reading first initiative. www.ncte.org/positions/statements/readingfirst

National Education Association. (2018). *Racial justice in education: Resource guide.* https://www.nea.org/professional-excellence/student-engagement/tools-tips/racial-justice-education-resource-guide

National Education Association. (2021). New business item 39 action: Adopted as modified. https://www.catholicleague.org/wp-content/uploads/2021/07/web.archive.org-New-Business-Item-39-ActionAdopted-as-Modified.pdf

National Equity Project. (2021). National equity project definition of educational equity. https://www.nationalequityproject.org/education-equity-definition

National Governors Association. (2012). NGA center for best practices. https://www.nga.org/bestpractices/

National Governors Association. (2022). Florida Governor, Jeb Bush. https://www.nga.org/governor/jeb-bush/

National Park Service. (2022). Sarah Paul. https://www.nps.gov/people/susan-paul.htm

National Reading Panel. (2000). *Teaching children to read: An evidence-based assessment of the scientific research literature on reading and its implications for reading instruction* (NIH Publication No. 00-4769). U.S. Government Printing Office.

National Research Council. (2001). Science, evidence, and inference in education: Report of a workshop. In L. Towne, R. J. Shavelson & M. J. Feuer (Eds.), *Committee on scientific principles in education research.* National Academy Press.

National Research Council. (2002). *Scientific research in education. Committee on scientific principles for education research.* National Academy Press.

Neal, D., & Schanzenbach, D. W. (2010). Left behind by design: Proficiency counts and test-based accountability. *Review of Economics and Statistics, 92,* 263–283.

New Hampshire State Senate. (2021). N.H. Rev. Stat. § 354-A:29). https://casetext.com/statute/new-hampshire-revised-statutes/title-31-trade-and-commerce/chapter-354-a-state-commission-for-human-rights/right-to-freedom-from-discrimination-in-public-workplaces-and-education/section-354-a29-right-to-freedom-from-discrimination-in-public-workplaces-and-education

New Worlds Reading Initiative Tax Credit. (2021). newworldsreading.coms

New Worlds Reading Initiative Tax Credit. (2022). https://floridarevenue.com/taxes/taxesfees/Pages/newworlds.aspx

Next Generation Sunshine State Standards. (2022). FL SB 1048.

Nieto, S., & Bode, P. (2017). School reform and student learning: A multicultural perspective. In J. A. Banks & C. A. Banks (Eds.), *Multicultural education: Issues and perspectives (9th ed.)* (pp. 258–274). Wiley.

No Child Left Behind Act Law and Legal Definition. (n.d.). https://definitions.uslegal.com/n/no-child-left-behind-act/

No Child Left Behind Act of 2001, Pub. L. Mo. 107-110, 115 Stat. 1425 (2002).

North Carolina Academic Transparency Bill. (2021a). Bill 755 https://www.ncleg.gov/BillLookup/2021/H755

North Carolina Senate Bill 387. (2021). Excellent public schools act. https://www.ncleg.gov/Sessions/2021/Bills/Senate/PDF/S387v0.pdf

O'Connor, C., & Fernandez, S. D. (2006). Race, class, and disproportionality: Reevaluating the relationship between poverty and special education placement. *Educational Researcher, 35*(6), 6–11.

Office for Civil Rights. (1968). Elementary and secondary schools Civil Rights Survey, 1968–1984, 1986, 1988 (M131V1) https://dataverse.harvard.edu/dataset.xhtml?persistentId=doi:10.7910/DVN/MOHJSP

Oregon Organic Laws (1843). https://www.oregon.gov/boppps/Documents/Statutes/1843.pdf

Orfield, G., & Ee, J. (2017). *Tough choices facing Florida's governments: Patterns of resegregation in Florida's schools.* A report for the LeRoy Collins Institute, Florida State University.

Palmer, B. C., & Hafner, L. E. (1979). Black students get an edge in reading. *Reading Horizons: A Journal of Literacy and Language Arts, 19*(4), 324–328.

Paludi, M., & Haley, S. (2014). Scientific racism. In T. Thomas (Ed.), *Encyclopedia of critical psychology* (pp. 1697–1700). John Wiley & Sons.

Parents Involved in Community Schools v. Seattle School District No. 1, et al.; Crystal D. Meredith, Custodial Parent and Next Friend of Joshua Ryan McDonald v. Jefferson County Board of Education, et al., 127 S. Ct. 2738 (2007).

Paris, D., & Alim, H. S. (Eds.). (2017). *Culturally sustaining pedagogies: Teaching and learning for justice in a changing world.* Teachers College Press.

Parker, N. D. (2020). Black codes and slave codes. DOI: 10.1093/obo/9780190280024-0083

Payne D. G. (2020, August 5). Standing with you against social injustice. https://www.linkedin.com/pulse/standing-you-against-social-injustice-david-g-payne

Peavy, L. (1993). Promoting liberation literacy: A grassroots solution. *Cultural keepers: Enlightening and empowering our communities. Proceedings of the First National Conference of African American Librarians* (pp. 212–215). Black Caucus of the American Library Association.

Peele-Eady, T. B., & Foster, M. L. (2018). The more things change, the more they stay the same: African American English, language policy, and African American learners. *International Journal of Qualitative Studies and Education, 31*(8), 652–666.

Peguero, A. A., Varela, K. S., Marchbanks, M. P., Blake, J., & Eason, J. M. (2021). School punishment and education: Racial/Ethnic disparities with grade retention and the role of urbanicity. *Urban Education, 56*(2), 228–260).

PEN AMERICA. (2022). Educational gag orders: Legislative restrictions on the freedom to read, learn, and teach. https://pen.org/report/educational-gag-orders/

Perea, J. (2016). Private: The proslavery constitution. https://www.acslaw.org/expertforum/the-proslavery-constitution/

Perry, I. (2018). *May we forever stand: A history of the Black national anthem.* University of North Carolina Press.

Perry, T. (2003). Freedom for literacy and literacy for freedom: The African-American philosophy of education. In T. Perry, C. Steele, & A. G. Hillard (Eds.), *Young, gifted, and black: Promoting high achievement among African-American students* (pp. 11–51). Beacon.

Peter P. v. Compton Unified School District. (2015–2021). https://casetext.com/case/pp-v-compton-unified-sch-dist-3

Peterson, C. L. (1995). *"Doers of the word": African-American women speakers & writers in the North (1830–1880)*. Oxford University Press.

Petrilli M. J. (2019). *Fewer children are left behind*. Thomas Fordham Institute.

Phelps, R. P. (2018). The Council of Chief State School Officers and National Governors Association: Whom do they serve? *Nonpartisan Education Review, 14*(4), 1–23.

Plessy v. Ferguson, 163 U.S. 537 (1896). *Proceedings and debates of the House of Representatives of the United States at the second session of the Second Congress, begun at the City of Philadelphia*, November 5, 1792, Annals of Congress, 2nd Congress, 2nd Session (November 5, 1792 to March 2, 1793), pp. 1414–1415. https://housedivided. dickinson.edu/ugrr/bill_fugitive1793.html

Plyler v. Doe, 457 U.S. 202 (1982).

Polanin, J. R., Caverly, S., & Pollard, E. (2021). A reintroduction to the What Works Clearinghouse. National Center for Education Evaluation at IES. https://files.eric. ed.gov/fulltext/ED610864.pdf

Pollack, M., Rogers, J., Kwako, A., Matschiner, A., Kendall, R., Bingener, C., Reece, E., Kennedy, B., & Howard, J. (2022). The conflict campaign report: Exploring local experiences of the campaign to ban "critical race theory" in public K–12 education in the U.S., 2020–2021. UCLA's Institute for Democracy, Education, and Access. https://idea.gseis.ucla.edu/publications/files/the-conflict-campaign-report

Pope, J. G. (2010). Contract, race, and freedom of labor in the constitutional law of "Involuntary Servitude." *The Yale Law Journal, 119*(7), 1474–1567.

Popkewitz, T. (1994). Paradigm and ideology in educational research: The social functions of the intellectual. Farmer.

Prendergast, C. (2003). *Literacy and racial justice: The politics of learning after Brown v. the Board of Education*. Southern Illinois University Press.

Presley, A. [Ayanna Pressley]. (2018, December 27). #Disparities & inequities don't just happen, they are created. They are created by discriminatory laws & predatory actions, & they are preserved by the complicit silence of many. [Tweet]. https://twitter.com/ ayannapressley/status/1078368202940473344

Price, J. (1934). Negro-White differences in general intelligence. *Journal of Negro Education, 3*, 424–452.

Public Broadcasting Service. (2004). *Beyond brown*. The Civil Rights Project at Harvard University; the National Center for Education Statistics. https://www.pbs.org/ beyondbrown/legacy/gifted_facts.html

Quarles, B. (1961). *The Negro in the American revolution*. University of North Carolina Press.

Quarles, B. (1969). *The Negro in the civil war*. Little, Brown.

Race to the Top, (2009). Race to the Top district. *CFDA, 84*, 416 https://www2. ed.gov/programs/racetothetop-district/index.html

Radhakrishnan, R. (2021, February 24). Landmark federal class action lawsuit results in innovative trauma programming. https://www.compton.k12.ca.us/news-release/ news/2021/class-action-lawsuit

Randall, D. (2020). *Disfigured history: How the College Board demolishes the past*. National Association of Scholars.

Range, P. (1995, March). MM interview: William J. Bennett. *Modern Maturity*, 26–30.

Reading Excellence Act. (1997–1998). https://www.congress.gov/105/crpt/srpt208/ CRPT-105srpt208.pdf

Reff, A. M. (2018). Network and third grade reading policy: Neoliberalism and new governance in the classroom. [Dissertation]. University of Arizona. http://hdl.handle. net/10150/631486

Renaissance's Star Early Literacy Assessment. (n.d.). https://www.renaissance.com/products/star-earlyliteracy/?utm_source=google&utm_medium=cpc&utm_campaign=Star_Assessment_Brand&gclid=CjwKCAjw682TBhATEiwA9crl3_41Ybd47oLVaa-IjDNnDito3bm3nYKjdtLs_9BX-Oiyszn_F0urNxoCkawQAvD_BwE

Reschly, A. L., & Christenson, S. (2013). Grade retention: Historical perspectives and new research. Introduction to featured articles. *Journal of School Psychology, 51*(3), 319–322.

Reschly, D. J. (1997). *Disproportionate minority representation in general and special education: Patterns, issues, and alternatives.* Mountain Plains Regional Resource Center.

Rhode Island Right To Read Act. (2019). http://webserver.rilin.state.ri.us/Statutes/TITLE16/16-11.4/16-11.4-6.HTM

Richardson, E. (2003). *African American literacies.* Routledge.

Richardson, J. M. (1969). Florida black codes. *The Florida Historical Quarterly, 47*(4), 365–379.

Richardson, T., & Johanningermeier, E. V. (1998). Intelligence testing: Legitimation of a meritocratic educational science. *International Journal of Educational Research, 27*(8), 699–714.

Rickford, J. R., & Rickford, J. R. (2000). *Spoken soul: The story of Black English.* John Wiley and Sons.

Robinson-Cimpian, J. (2015). *Review of the effects of test base retention on student outcomes overtime: Regression discontinuity evidence from Florida.* National Education Policy Center.

Roderick, M. (1994). Grade retention and school dropout: Investigating the association. *American Educational Research Journal, 31*(4), 729–759.

Roderick, M., & Nagaoka, J. (2005). Retention under Chicago's High Stakes testing program: Helpful, harmful, or harmless? *Educational Evaluation and Policy Analysis, 27*(4), 309–2340.

Rogoff, B. (2018). AERA factsheet: *Children from underserved minority backgrounds have strengths for learning.* American Education Research Association.

Rosa, J. (2019). *Looking like a language, sounding like a race: Raciolinguistic ideologies and the learning of Latinidad.* Oxford.

Rosa, J., & Flores, N. (2015). Undoing appropriateness.: Raciolinguistic ideologies and language diversity in education. *Harvard Educational Review, 85*(2), 149–171.

Rose, S., & Schimke, K. (2012). *Third grade literacy policies: Identification, intervention, retention.* Education Commission of the States. https://eric.ed.gov/?id=ED535949

Royer, D. J. (1994). The process of literacy as communal involvement in the narratives of Frederick Douglass. *African American Review, 28*(3), 363–374.

Rufo, C. (2021, June 28). The battle over critical race theory. *Wall Street Journal,* A 17.

Rury, J. (1988). Race, region, and education: An analysis of black and white scores on the 1917 Army Alpha Intelligence Tests. *The Journal of Negro Education, 57*(1), 51–65.

Rutherford, M. L. (1920). *A measuring rod to test textbooks, and reference books.* United Confederate Veterans.

Sailant, J. (2002). *Black Puritan, Black republican: The life and thought of Lemuel Haynes, 1753–1833.* Oxford University Press.

Samuelson, F. (1977). World War I intelligence testing and the development of psychology. *Journal of the History of Behavioral Sciences, 13*, 274–282.

Sandford, T. (1965). The compact for education. https://www.ecs.org/wp-content/uploads/Compact-for-Education-Dec1965.pdf

Schwartz, S. (2022, July 27). 5 Insights on getting the "Science of Reading" into classrooms. https://www.edweek.org/teaching-learning/5-insights-on-getting-the-science-of-reading-into-classrooms/2022/07

Schwerdt, G., West, M. R., & Winters, M. A. (2017). The effects of test-based retention on student outcomes over time: Regression discontinuity evidence from Florida. *Journal of Public Economics*, 152, 154–169.

Scott v. Sandford, 60 U.S. 19 How. 393 393 (1856).

Scott, M. P. (2021). Disparate impact: What is disparate impact? https://www.investopedia.com/disparate-impact-5114526

Seidenberg, M. (n.d.). Reading matters: Connecting the science of reading and educational practices: https://seidenbergreading.net/science-of-reading/

Seidenberg, M. S., & Borkenhagen, M. C. (2020). Reading science and educational practice: Some tenets for teachers. https://seidenbergreading.net/wp-content/uploads/2020/03/Reading-Science-and-Educational-Practice-Some-Tenets-for-Teachers.pdf

Selena of @ SelenaCarrion. (2022, January 18).

Sensoy, O., & DiAngelo, R. (2017). Understanding the structural nature of oppression through racism. In O. Sensoy & Di Angelo (Eds.), *Is everybody really equal? An introduction to key concepts in social justice education* (2nd ed., pp. 119–140). Teachers College Press.

Shannon, P. (1989). *Broken promises: Reading instruction in twentieth-century America*. Bergin & Garvey.

Shannon, P. (1990). *The struggle to continue: Progressive reading instruction in the United States*. Heinemann.

Shannon, P. (Ed.). (1992). *Becoming political: Readings and writings in the politics of literacy education*. Heinemann.

Shannon, P. (2007). *Reading against democracy: The broken promises of reading*. Heinemann.

Sheals, D. (2018). *Thirst for knowledge: Historic context for the 1872 Neosho Colored School*. Carver Birthplace Association and the National Park Service.

Shepard, L. A., & Smith, M. L. (1990). Synthesis of research on grade retention. *Educational Leadership*, 47(8), 84–88.

Shifrer, D., Mueller, C., & Callahan, R. (2011). Disproportionality and learning disabilities: Parsing apart race, socioeconomic status, and language. *Journal of Learning Disabilities*, 44(3), 246–257.

Silberglitt, B., Appleton, J. J., Burns, K. M., & Jimerson, S. R. (2006). Examining the effects of grade retention on student reading performance: A longitudinal study. *Journal of School Psychology*, 44(4), 255–270.

Simkin, J. (2014). *Slavery in the United States* (Kindle ed.). Spartacus Educational Publishers.

Skiba, R. J., Simmons, A. B., Ritter, A. C., Gibb, M. K., Rausch, J., Cuadrado, J., & Chung, C. C. (2008). Achieving equity in special education: History, status and current challenges. *Exceptional Children*, 74, 264–288.

Sledge, M. (2008). "A is an Abolitionist": The anti-slavery alphabet and the politics of literacy. In M. Elbert (Ed.), *Enterprising youth: Social values and acculturation in nineteenth-century American children's literature* (pp. 69–82). Routledge.

Sleeter, C. E. (2021). Challenging racism thought ethnic studies. In H. P. Baptiste & J. H. Writer (Eds.), *Visioning multicultural education: Past, present, future* (pp. 44–61). Routledge.

Sleeter, C. E., & Zavala, M. (2020). What the research says about ethnic studies. In *Transformative ethnic studies in schools: Curriculum, pedagogy, and research* (pp. 44–68). Teachers College Press.

Smith, C. (2021). *How the word is passed: A reckoning with the history of slavery across America*. Little, Brown.

Smith, J., & Spodak, C. (2021, April 25). Black or "Other"? Doctors may be relying on race to make decisions about your health. (https://www.cnn.com/2021/04/25/health/race-correction-in-medicine-history-refocused/index.html

Smith, N. B. (1986). *American reading instruction: It's development and its significance in gaining the perspective on current practices in reading.* International Reading Association (originally published in 1934).

Smith, T. L. (1972). Native Blacks and foreign Whites: Varying responses to educational opportunity in America, 1880 to 1950. *Perspectives in American History, 6,* 309–335.

Smith, V. (1789). *A narrative of the life and adventures of venture, a native of Africa, but resident above sixty years in the United States of America. Related by himself.* New London: (Reprinted 1835, and published by a Descendant of Venture. Revised and Republished with Traditions by H. M. Selden, Haddam, Conn., 1896). https://docsouth.unc.edu/neh/venture2/summary.html

Smitherman, G. (1981). "What go round come round": King in perspective. *Harvard Educational Review, 51*(1), 40–56.

Smitherman, G. (1998). Black English/Ebonics: What it be like? In T. Perry & L. Delpit (Eds.), *The real Ebonics debate: Power, language, and the education of African American children* (pp. 29–37). Beacon.

Smitherman, G., & Baugh, J. (2002). The shot heard from Ann Arbor: Language research and public policy in African America. *Howard Journal of Communication, 13*(1), 5–24.

Snow, C. E., Burns, M. S., & Griffin, P. (Eds.) (1998). *Preventing reading difficulties in young children.* National Academies Press.

Snyder, T. (2021, June 29). The war on history is a war on democracy. https://www.nytimes.com/2021/06/29/magazine/memory-laws.html

Sokal, M. (Ed.) (1978). *Psychological testing and American society, 1890–1930.* Rutgers University Press.

Solochek, J. S. (2021, November 4). Florida changed rules for special education students. Why many say it's wrong. https://www.tampabay.com/news/education/2021/11/04/florida-changed-rules-for-special-education-students-why-many-say-its-wrong/

Solochek, J. S. (2022, April 4). Florida charter schools mostly exempt from 2022 education laws. Here's why. *Tampa Bay Times.* https://www.tampabay.com/news/education/2022/04/04/florida-charter-schools-mostly-exempt-from-2022-education-bills-heres-why/

Sotero, M. M. (2006). A conceptual model of historical trauma: Implications for public health, practice and research. *Journal of Health Disparities Research and Practice, 1*(1), 93–108.

Spencer. (2010). A conversation with Margaret Beal Spencer. https://mag.uchicago.edu/law-policy-society/conversation-margaret-beale-spencer

Spring, J. (1972). Psychologists and the war: The meaning of intelligence in the Alpha and Beta tests. *History of Education Quarterly, 12*(1), 3–15.

Squires, J. (2015). CCELO/Retention in the early years. fast_fact_retention_final_web.pdf

Stanford, J. (2013, December 12). Bush's "Texas Miracle" debunked, Lone Star State sparks anti-testing revolution. www.msnbc.com/msnbc/bushs-texas-miracle-debunked-lone-star-s

Stanovich, K. E., & Siegel, L. S. (1994). Phenotypic performance profile of children with reading disabilities: A regression-based test of the phonological-core variable-difference model. *Journal of Educational Psychology, 86*(1), 24–53.

Stetson, G. R. (1897). Some memory tests of whites and blacks. *Psychological Review, 4*(3), 285–289.

Striving Readers Comprehensive Literacy Program. (2017). https://www2.ed.gov/programs/strivingreaders-literacy/index.html

Strum, P. (2010). *Mendez v. Westminster: School desegregation and Mexican-American* rights. University Press of Kansas.

Stump, S. (2020, March 4). High schools could lose AP classes if they ban "required topics" from being taught. https://www.today.com/parents/parents/high-schools-lose-ap-classes-banning-required-topics-rcna18813

Sturdivant, T. D. (2021). Racial awareness and the politics in play: Preschoolers and racially diverse dolls in a US classroom. *International Journal of Early Childhood, 53*, 139–157.

Sturdivant, T. D., & Alanis, I. (2020). "I'm gonna cook my baby in a pot:" Young Black girls racial preferences and play behavior. *Early Childhood Education Journal, 49*, 473–482.

Swann v. Charlotte-Mecklenburg Bd. of Education, 402 U.S. 1. (1971). https://www.oyez.org/cases/1970/281

Tavassolie, T., & Winsler, A. (2019). Predictors of mandatory 3rd grade retention from high-stakes test performance for low-income, ethnically diverse children. *Early Childhood Research Quarterly, 48*(3), 62–74.

Terman, L. (1916). *The measurement of intelligence.* Houghton Mifflin.

Terman, L. (1920). *National intelligence tests, with manual of directions.* World Book.

Texas Education Code. (1984). [TEC] §21.721, *Grade requirement for advancement or course credit. Texas school law bulletin.* West Publishing.

The Comprehensive Literacy State Development. (2020). https://www2.ed.gov/programs/clsd/index.html

The Intercultural Development Research Association. (2019). www.idra.org/wp-content/uploads/2018/05/eBook-Failing-In-Grade-Retention-IDRA-2018.pdf

The Making of the Modern U. S. (1896). Louisiana Separate Car Act (1890). https://theberkshireedge.com/connections-5/

The Oxford Review Encyclopaedia of Terms. (2022). Strategic silence.

Thompson, G. L. (2007). *Up where we belong: Helping African American and Latino students rise in school and rise in life.* Jossey-Bass.

Thompson, G. L., & Shamberger, C. T. (2015). The gift that can save lives: Teaching Black students to become good readers. *Journal of Research Initiatives, 1*(3), 1–10.

Thompson, J. C. (1992). Toward a more humane oppression: Florida's slave codes, 1821-1861. *Florida Historical Quarterly, 71*(3), 324–338.

Thorndike, E. (1918). The nature, purposes and general methods of measurements of educational products. In G. Whipple (Ed.), *The 17th yearbook of the national society for the study of education.* Part 2. The measure measurement of educational products (pp. 16–24). Public School Publishing.

Townsend, H., & Townsend, M. (1846). *Anti-slavery alphabet.* Merrihew & Thompson.

Transcontinental Treaty. (1821). https://history.state.gov/milestones/1801-1829/florida

Travers, R. (1983). *How research has changed American schools: A history from 1840 to the present.* Mythos.

Treaty of Adams-Onis. (1819). https://history.state.gov/milestones/1801-1829/florida

Trump, D. J. (2020). Executive order 13950, *Combatting race and sex stereotyping.* https://www.federalregister.gov/documents/2020/09/28/2020-21534/combating-race-and-sex-stereotyping

Tuck, E., & Yang, K. W. (2012). Decolonization is not a metaphor. *Decolonization: Indigeneity, Education & Policy 1*(1), 1–40.

Tucker, W. H. (2002). *The funding of scientific racism: Wickliffe Draper and the Pioneer Fund.* University of Illinois Press.

U.S. Department of Education. (2005). Justesen memorandum. Office of Special Education and Rehabilitative Services. https://www2.ed.gov/policy/speced/guid/idea/letters/2005-2/osep0509privsch2q2005.pdf

U.S. Department of Education. (2007, January). Questions and answers on response to intervention (RTI) and early intervening services (EIS). https://sites.ed.gov/idea/files/070021.RTI_.pdf

U.S. Department of Education. (2008a). Coordinated Early Intervening Services (CEIS) guidance [Memorandum]. https://www2.ed.gov/policy/speced/guid/idea/ceis_pg2.html

U.S. Department of Education. (2008b). Knudsen memorandum. Coordinated Early Intervening Service Guidance. https://www2.ed.gov/policy/speceguid/idea/ceis_pg2.html

U.S. Department of Education. (2011). Office of special education and rehabilitative services [Memorandum]. www.ed.gov

US Department of Education. Assistance to States for the Education of Children With Disabilities and Preschool Grants for Children With Disabilities; Final Rule, 71 Fed. Reg. 46539 (August 14, 2006) (to be codified at 34 C.F.R. pts. 300 & 301). https://www.govinfo.gov/content/pkg/FR-2006-08-14/html/06-6656.htm

US Department of Education Office of Educational Technology. (2015). *Grit, tenacity, and perseverance in 21st-century education: State of the art and future directions.*

US Department of Education. (2002). The facts: Reading achievement. No Child Left Behind. https://www2.ed.gov/nclb/overview/intro/factsheet.html

US Department of Education. (2004). Part A—English Language Acquisition, Language Enhancement, and Academic Achievement Act. Retrieved from https://www2.ed.gov/policy/elsec/leg/esea02/pg40.html

US Department of Education. (2006). Building the legacy: IDEA 2004. https://sites.ed.gov/idea/building-the-legacy-idea-2004/

US Department of Education. (2008a). Inspector General's reading impact study: Final Report. https://ies.ed.gov/ncee/pubs/20094038/summ_b.asp

US Department of Education. (2008b). Knudsen memorandum. Coordinated Early Intervening Service Guidance. https://www2.ed.gov/policy/speceguid/idea/ceis_pg2.html

US Department of Education. (2008c). Coordinated Early Intervening Services (CEIS) Guidance [Memorandum]. https://www2.ed.gov/policy/speced/guid/idea/ceis_pg2.html

US Department of Education. (2008d). New race and ethnicity guidance for the collection of federal education data. https://www2.ed.gov/policy/rschstat/guid/raceethnicity/index.html

US Department of Education. (2011). Office of special education and rehabilitative services [Memorandum]. www.ed.gov

US Department of Education Title I—Improving the academic achievement of the disadvantaged. 84 Fed. Reg. 31660 (2019, July 1). Title 34: CFR 200, 299. https://www2.ed.gov/policy/elsec/leg/esea02/pg1.html

US Justice Department. (2021, September 1). U.S. Department of Justice Guidance under Section 2 of the Voting Rights Act, 52 U.S.C. 10301, for redistricting and methods of electing government. https://www.justice.gov/opa/press-release/file/1429486/download

USDOE Assistance to States for the Education of Children with Disabilities, 83 Fed. Reg. 8396 July 3, 2018. 34 CFR 300. https://www.federalregister.gov/documents/2018/07/03/2018-14374/assistance-to-states-for-the-education-of-children-with-disabilities-preschool-grants-for-children

USDOE Assistance to States for the Education of Children with Disabilities, 81 Fed. Reg. 92376 (2016, December 19), 34 CFR 300. https://www.federalregister.gov/documents/2016/12/19/2016-30190/assistance-to-states-for-the-education-of-children-with-disabilities-preschool-grants-for-children

USDOE Coordinated Early Intervening Services (CEIS) Guidance. (2007). Updated Feb. 2018. https://cifr.wested.org/wp-content/uploads/2015/12/CIFR-CEIS-QRG.pdf

Van Alstyne, W. W. (1963). "The administration's anti-literacy test bill: Wholly constitutional but wholly inadequate" (1963). *Faculty Publications*, 772. https://scholarship.law.wm.edu/facpubs/772

Varghese, M. M. (2017). Language diversity and schooling. In J. A. Banks & C. A. Banks (Eds.), *Multicultural education: Issues and perspectives* (9th ed., pp. 188–210). Wiley.

Vinovskis, M. (1999). The road to Charlottesville: The Education Summit. The National Education Goals Panel. https://govinfo.library.unt.edu/negp/reports/negp30.pdf

Virginia Constitution. (1901). www.virginiaplaces.org/government/constitution1902.html

Voting Rights Act. (1965). https://www.archives.gov/milestone-documents/voting-rights-act

Voting Rights Act. (1965). https://www.ourdocuments.gov/doc.php?flash=false&doc=100

Voting Rights Act. (1970). https://www.justice.gov/crt/history-federal-voting-rights-laws

Voting Rights Act. (1982). https://www.congress.gov/bill/97th-congress/senate-bill/1992

Walker, A. (2012). Uncle Remus. No friend of mine. *The Georgia Review, 66*(3), 635–637.

Walker, D. (1829). *David Walker's appeal to the colored citizens of the world.* https://docsouth.unc.edu/nc/walker/walker.html

Walsh, C. (2021, April 5). "Taxpayer dollars": The origins of austerity's racist catchphrase: How the myth of the overburdened white taxpayer was made. https://www.motherjones.com/politics/2021/04/taxpayer-dollars-the-origins-of-austeritys-racist-catchphrase/?utm_source=twitter&utm_campaign=naytev&utm_medium=social

Wantabe, T. (2021, September 1). UC must immediately drop use of the SAT and ACT for admissions and scholarships, judge rules. https://www.latimes.com/california/story/2020-09-01/uc-may-not-use-the-sat-or-act-for-admissions-scholarship-decisions-for-now-judge-rules

Wanzek, J., Stevens, E. A., Williams, K. J., Scammacca, N., Vaughn, S., & Sargent, K. (2018). Current evidence on the effects of intensive early reading interventions. *Journal of Learning Disabilities, 51*(6) 612–624.

Warren, J. R., Hoffman, E., & Andrew, M. (2014). Patterns and trends in grade retention rates in the US, 1995–2010. *Educational Researcher, 43*(9), 433–443.

Waxman, O. (2022). Louisiana Gov. Pardons Homer Plessy, 125 years after SCOTUS "Separate but equal" ruling. https://time.com/6128436/homer-plessy-ferguson-pardon/?amp=true

Welner, K. G., & Carter, P. L. (2013). Achievement gaps arise from opportunity gaps. In P. L. Carter & K. G. Welner (Eds.), *Closing the opportunity gap* (pp. 1–10). Oxford University Press.

Weyer, M. (2018). A look at third-grade reading retention policies. Legis brief. National Conference of State Legislatures. https://www.ncsl.org/documents/legisbriefs/2018/june/LBJune2018_A_Look_at_Third_Grade_Reading_Retention_Policies_goID32459.pdf

Whitehead, C. (2019). *The Nickel boys: A novel*. Doubleday.

Wiederholt, J. L., & Bryant, B. R. (2012). *Gray oral reading tests—Fifth edition* (GORT-5). Pro-Ed.

Williams, H. A. (2005). *African American education in slavery and freedom: Self-taught*. University of North Carolina Press.

Williams, P. (1987). Spirit-murdering the messenger: The discourse of finger pointing as the law's response to racism. *University of Miami Law Review, 42*(1), 127–157.

Williams, S. O. (2007). *The mis-education of the Negro continues: The connection between the beginning reading instruction delivered to three high-performing Black girls and the instruction delivered within schools designed to colonize*. University of Illinois at Urbana-Champaign, ProQuest Dissertations Publishing.

Willis, A. I. (2002). Literacy at Calhoun Colored school, 1892–1943. *Reading Research Quarterly, 37*(1), 8–44.

Willis, A. I. (2007). James McKeen Cattell: His life and contributions to reading research. In S. Israel (Ed.), *Shaping the reading field: The impact of early reading pioneers* (pp. 35–60). International Reading Association.

Willis, A. I. (2008). *Reading comprehension research and testing in the US: Undercurrents of race, class, and power in the struggle for meaning*. Lawrence Erlbaum.

Willis, A. I. (2015). Literacy and race: Access, equity, and freedom. Literacy research association presidential address. *Literacy Research: Theory, Method, and Practice, 64*, 23–55.

Willis, A. I. (2018). Re-positioning race in English language arts research. In D. Lapp & D. Fisher (Eds.), *Handbook of research on teaching the English language arts research* (4th ed., pp. 30–56). Routledge.

Willis, A. I. (2019a). Race, response to intervention, and reading research. *Journal of Literacy Research, 50*(4), 1–26.

Willis, A. I. (2019b). Response to intervention: An illusion of equity. *Language Arts, 97*(2), 83–96.

Willis, A. I. (2022). Black literacy education in the United States. *Oxford research encyclopedia*.

Willis, A. I. (forthcoming). Literacy access, the law, and racism in the United States: A critique. *International encyclopedia of education*.

Willis, A. I., & Williams, S. O. (2001). Reading the reading reports: The implications for practice and research of 'preventing reading difficulties in young children'. A paper presented at the annual meeting of the National Council of Teachers of English, Baltimore, MD.

Willis, A. I., Thompson-McMillon, G., & Smith, P. (2022). *Affirming Black students' lives and literacies: Bearing witness*. Teachers College Press.

Wilmot, J. M., Migliarini, V., & Annamma, S. A. (2021). Policy as punishment and distraction: The double helix of racialized sexual harassment of Black girls. *Educational Policy, 35*(2), 347–367.

Winn, M. T., & Behizadeh, N. (2011). The right to be literate: Literacy, education, and the school-to-prison pipeline. *Review of Research in Education, 35*, 147–173.

Winters, M. A., & Greene, J. P. (2012). The medium-run effects of Florida's test-based promotion policy. *Education Finance and Policy, 7*, 305–330.

Wolfe, P. (2007). Settler colonialism and the elimination of the native. *Journal of Genocide Research, 8*(4), 387–409.

Woo, I. (2023). *Master slave husband wife: An epic journey from slavery to freedom*. Simon & Schuster.

Wood, F. B., Fenton, F., Flowers, L., & Naylor, C. (1991). Neurobehavioral definitions of dyslexia. In D. D. Duane, & D. B. Gray (Eds.), *The reading brain: The biological habits of dyslexia* (pp. 1–26). York Press.

Wood, P. (2015, September). *Drilling through the core: Why Common Core is bad for American education.* http://pioneerinstitute.org/drilling-through-the-core/

Woodson, A. (2017). "There ain't no white people here": Master narratives of the Civil Rights Movement in the stories of urban youth. *Urban Education, 52,* 316–342.

Woodson, C. G. (1933). *The mis-education of the Negro.* First Africa World Press.

Woodson, C. G. (1937a). Lemuel Haynes, the servant of all the people in New England. *Negro History Bulletin, 1*(3), 1–2.

Woodson, C. G. (1937b). The thrilling escape of William and Ellen Craft. *Negro History Bulletin, 1*(1), 4–5.

Workman, E. (2014). *Third-grade reading policies. Reading/literacy: Preschool to third grade.* https://files.eric.ed.gov/fulltext/ED560984.pdf

Wright, B. L., & Counsell, S. L. (2018). *The brilliance of black boys.* Teachers College Press.

Xia, N., & Kirby, S. N. (2009). *Retaining students in grade: A literature review of the effects of retention on students' academic and nonacademic outcomes* (Technical Report No. 678). www.rand.org/pubs/technical_reports/TR678/

Yamamoto, K., & Byrnes, D. A. (1987). Primary children's ratings of stressfulness of experiences. *Journal of Research in Childhood Education, 2*(2), 117–121.

Yatvin, J. (2000). Minority View. In National Reading Panel. (2000). *Teaching children to read: An evidence-based assessment of the scientific research literature on reading and its implications for reading instruction* (NIH Publication No. 00-4769) (pp. 1–6). U.S. Government Printing Office.

Young, P. (2019, October 17). Negro school burned by White men-Outrages of the KuKlux Klans Tennessee Feb. 1868. https://thereconstructionera.com/negro-school-burned-by-white-men-outrages-of-the-kukluxklan/

Zigler, E., & Styfco, S. J. (2010). *The hidden history of Head Start.* Oxford University Press.

INDEX

Page numbers in **bold** refer to tables, those in *italics* indicate figures.

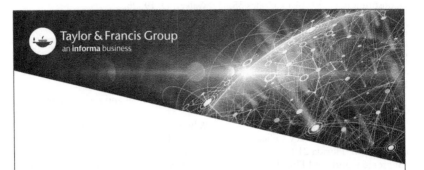

For Product Safety Concerns and Information please contact our EU
representative GPSR@taylorandfrancis.com Taylor & Francis Verlag GmbH,
Kaufingerstraße 24, 80331 München, Germany

Printed and bound by CPI Group (UK) Ltd, Croydon, CR0 4YY
08/06/2025
01896986-0005